Communism's Jewish Question

Europäisch-jüdische Studien Editionen
European-Jewish Studies Editions

Edited by the Moses Mendelssohn Center
for European-Jewish Studies, Potsdam,
in cooperation with the Center for Jewish Studies
Berlin-Brandenburg

Editorial Manager: Werner Treß

Volume 3

Communism's Jewish Question

―

Jewish Issues in Communist Archives

Edited and introduced by
András Kovács

ISBN 978-3-11-066067-8
e-ISBN (PDF) 978-3-11-041159-1
e-ISBN (EPUB) 978-3-11-041163-8

Library of Congress Cataloging-in-Publication Data
A CIP catalog record for this book has been applied for at the Library of Congress.

Bibliographic information published by the Deutsche Nationalbibliothek
The Deutsche Nationalbibliothek lists this publication in the Deutsche
Nationalbibliografie; detailed bibliographic data are available in the Internet
at http://dnb.dnb.de.

© 2019 Walter de Gruyter GmbH, Berlin/Boston
This volume is text- and page-identical with the hardback published in 2017.
Cover illustration: Presidium, Israelite National Assembly on February 20-21, 1950, Budapest
(pho-tographer unknown), Archive "Az Izraelita Országos Gyűlés fényképalbuma"
Typesetting: Michael Peschke, Berlin
Printing: CPI books GmbH, Leck

♾ Printed on acid-free paper
Printed in Germany

www.degruyter.com

Table of Contents

Abbreviations —— vii
Introduction: The "Jewish Issue" and the East-Central European
    Communist Systems —— 1
  Continuity of the "Jewish question" and antisemitic discourse after the
  Holocaust —— 2
  Post-war and Stalinist Communist policy and the continuity of the "Jewish
  question" —— 5
  Jewish policy of the Communist states in the post-Stalinist period —— 9
  About the collection —— 15

I Communist Policies and the Jewish State

Introduction —— 21
Documents —— 32
  1 On Emigration —— 32
  2 Meeting with Golda Meir —— 34
  3 Second Meeting with Golda Meir —— 37
  4 Negotiations on Compensation with Israel —— 39
  5 On the Israeli Legation in Budapest —— 41
  6 Negotiations on Compensation with Israel —— 42
  7 Negotiations on Compensation with Israel —— 44
  8 The Condition of Hungarian-Israeli Relations —— 51
  9 Current Issues of Hungarian-Israeli Relations —— 53
  10 Problems Concerning Relations with Israel —— 55
  11 Relations Between Israel and the Socialist Countries in 1966 —— 58
  12 Principles of the Relations with Israel —— 62
  13 Hungarian-Israeli Economic Relations —— 66
  14 Summary of Hungarian-Israeli Relations 1967 —— 69
  15 Trade Relations with Israel —— 72

II The Eichmann Affair

Introduction —— 77
Documents —— 84
  1 Minutes of the Political Committee of the Hungarian Socialist
     Workers' Party —— 84
  2 Tasks after the Decision of the Political Committee —— 87
  3 Tasks in Connection with the Eichmann Case —— 89

4   Consultation Issues in Respect of the Eichmann Case —— 92
5   Official Request of the Legation of Israel —— 95
6   Position of the Czechoslovak Socialist Republic of the Case of Eichmann —— 97
7   On Co-Operation with Israel —— 102
8   On Measures to be Taken in the Eichmann Case —— 106
9   On the Kasztner Issue —— 108
10 Letter of S. Mikunis, General Secretary of the Communist Party of Israel —— 110
11 B'nai B'rith Report on Media Coverage of the Eichmann Case in Communist Countries —— 112

III The Six-Day War and its Aftermath

Introduction —— 129
Documents —— 140

1   Telephone Conversation between János Kádár and Leonid Brezhnev —— 140
2   Soviet Ambassador's Meeting with János Kádár —— 141
3   Telephone Conversation between János Kádár and Leonid Brezhnev —— 142
4   Soviet Ambassador's Meeting with Zoltán Komócsin —— 144
5   Information from Leonid Brezhnev's Personal Secretary —— 145
6   Soviet Ambassador's Meeting with János Kádár —— 146
7   Message from Deputy Head of the Foreign-Affairs Department of the CPSU —— 148
8   On the Moscow Meeting —— 149
9   Telephone Conversation between János Kádár and Leonid Brezhnev —— 157
10 Minutes of the Meeting of the Political Committee —— 158
11 The Presidium of the CC CPČZ on the War in the Middle East —— 171
12 Message from Deputy Head of the Foreign Affairs Department of the CPSU —— 178
13 Information from the Soviet Embassy to János Kádár —— 179
14 Leonid Brezhnev's Telegram to János Kádár —— 180
15 Minutes of the Meeting of the Political Committee on 18 July 1967 —— 181
16 Report on the Opinion of Members of the Hungarian Jewish Congregation from an Anonymous Informer —— 186
17 Report on the Mood within the Hungarian Jewish Religious Denomination —— 190
18 The Political Committee's Resolution on Hungarian-Israeli Relations —— 193
19 Proposal on Hungarian-Israeli Relations —— 198
20 Appraisal of Draft CC Proposal on Restoring Hungarian-Israeli Diplomatic Relations —— 211

IV The International Jewish Organisations, the Jewish Community and the State

Introduction —— 219
Documents —— 229
1. Conversation with Meir Vilner, Member of the ICP CC —— 229
2. Proposal for the Exit of the Hungarian Jewish Denomination from the World Jewish Congress —— 233
3. The Aims of the World Jewish Congress with Regard to the Hungarian Jewish Denomination —— 235
4. On the Foreign Relations of the Hungarian Jewish Religious Denomination —— 238
5. On the Fifth Conference of the World Jewish Congress in Brussels —— 242
6. The Fifth Conference of the World Jewish Congress —— 246
7. The Foreign Relations of the Jewish Religious Denomination —— 249
8. On the Visit to Hungary of Dr Nahum Goldmann and his Colleagues —— 252
9. Conversation with Dr Philip Klutznick, President of the World Jewish Congress —— 255
10. Negotiations Held with the Leaders of the World Jewish Congress —— 258
11. On the Suggestion to Hold in Budapest the 1987 Annual Assembly of EJC —— 260
12. Comments of the Secretary-General of the WJC —— 262
13. The Meeting in Budapest of the Executive Committee of the WJC —— 264

V Mechanisms of Repression and the Jews

Introduction —— 269
Documents —— 285
1. The Current Situation of the Jewish Denomination —— 285
2. The Jewish Denomination —— 288
3. Operational Situation of the Jewish Denomination —— 292
4. Operational Work against the Zionist Movement —— 297
5. Conditions for the Indemnification of the Hungarian Jews —— 303
6. On Zionist Issues —— 305
7. On the Israeli Embassy —— 308
8. Campaign to Reduce the Influence of the Israeli Embassy —— 312
9. The Economic Situation of the National Representation of Hungarian Israelites and the Budapest Israelite Congregation —— 314
10. Chairmanship Elections at the National Representation of Hungarian Israelites and the Budapest Israelite Congregation —— 318

11 Policy Measures in the Field of the Jewish Religious Community —— 321
12 Reports on the World Federation of Hungarian Jews and the Meeting of the Former Pupils of the Jewish Grammar School —— 324
13 On the Activities of Domestic and Foreign Zioinsts —— 327
14 On the Operations in the Jewish Religious Community in 1977 —— 330
15 The Centenary of the National Rabbinical Seminary —— 338
16 The Jewish Clerical Reaction in the Past 3 Years —— 343
17 Appendix. Orientation for a Systematic Register of the People of Jewish Origin —— 350

Biographical Notes —— 354

Bibliography —— 361
  Archival sources —— 361
  Archival sources online —— 362
  Monographs and articles —— 362

Index of Persons —— 367

Abbreviations

ACNS	Administration of the Corps of National Security in Czechoslovakia (Sbor Národní Bezpečnosti)
ÁEH	State Office for Church Affairs (Állami Egyházügyi Hivatal)
APO	Agitation and Propaganda Department (Agitációs és Propaganda Osztály)
ARTEX	Art Export, Hungarian Foreign Trade Company
BIC	Budapest Israelite Congregation (Budapesti Izraelita Hitközség, BIH)
CC	Central Committee
CDU	Christian Democratic Union of Germany
CPC	Communist Party of China
CPCz	Communist Party of Czechoslovakia
CPSU	Communist Party of the Soviet Union
ČSSR	Czechoslovak Socialist Republic
CSU	Christian Social Union in Bavaria
EJC	European Jewish Congress
EXIMIS	Export-Import Bank of Israel
FIJET	World Federation of Travel Journalists and Writers (Fédération Internationale des Journalistes et Écrivains du Tourisme)
FRG	Federal Republic of Germany
GDR	German Democratic Republic
HPR	Hungarian People's Republic
HSWP	Hungarian Socialist Workers' Party (see also MSZMP)
IBUSZ	Tourism, Purchase, Travel and Transport Private Limited Company (Idegenforgalmi, Beszerzési, Utazási és Szállítási Zártkörűen Működő Részvénytársaság)
ICP	Israeli Communist Party
ICR	Institute for Cultural Relations
JOINT	American Jewish Joint Distribution Committee
JRC	Jewish Religious Community
KSZB	Central Social Committee (Központi Szociális Bizottság)
MAHART	Hungarian Shipping Company (Magyar Hajózási Részvénytársaság)
MALÉV	Hungarian Airlines (Magyar Légiközlekedési Vállalat)
MAPAI	Workers' Party of the Land of Israel (Mifleget Poalei Eretz Yisrael)
MFA	Ministry of Foreign Affairs (Külügyminisztérium)
MFT	Ministry of Foreign Trade
MIOI	National Bureau of Hungarian Israelites
MIOK	National Representation of Hungarian Israelites, NRHI (Magyarországi Izraeliták Országos Képviselete)
MSZMP	Hungarian Socialist Workers' Party, HSWP (Magyar Szocialista Munkáspárt)
NATO	North Atlantic Treaty Organization
NB[H]	National Bank [of Hungary]
NRHI	National Representation of Hungarian Israelites (see also MIOK)
PC	Political Committee
PLO	Palestine Liberation Organization
PPR	Polish People's Republic
PSR	Polish Socialist Republic
SABENA	Belgian Corporation for Air Navigation Services (Societé Anonyme Belge d'Exploitation de la Navigation Aérienne)
SC	Security Council

SSE	Société de Sécours et d'Entraide
SPD	Social Democratic Party of Germany
TASS	Telegraph Agency of the Soviet Union (Tyelyegrafnoye agyentstvo Sovyetskogo Soyuza)
TSKŻ	Social and Cultural Association of Jews in Poland (Towarzystwo Społeczno-Kulturalne Żydów w Polsce)
UAR	United Arab Republic
UN	United Nations
UNESCO	United Nations Educational, Scientific and Cultural Organization
USSR	Union of Soviet Socialist Republics
WFHJ	World Federation of Hungarian Jews
WJC	World Jewish Congress

Introduction: The "Jewish Issue" and the East-Central European Communist Systems

To the surprise of many, antisemitism resurfaced in East-Central Europe almost concurrently with the collapse of Communism. It was present not only in publications by minor political groups and in the texts of fringe politicians, many of whom were returning émigrés, but was also present, at least in Hungary, Poland and Slovakia, and with increasing frequency, in pronouncements made by public figures with close ties to the political centre. One frequent claim was that antisemitism was a tool for political and intellectual actors to rally support among social groups most affected by the transitional crisis. While this explanation is clearly a possibility, or even a likelihood, it fails to explain why such efforts were positively received by certain groups, or why a small but not insignificant minority in post-Communist countries proved receptive to the ideological message of political antisemitism.

Antisemitic politicians and ideologues were not acting in a vacuum. Sociological research conducted in the years immediately following the collapse of Communism showed that although the public expression of antisemitic views had been a punishable crime throughout the decades of Communism, and Communist regimes' official ideology had rejected and condemned antisemitism, a substantial part of society continued to harbour antisemitic prejudice. Indeed, surveys have shown that in the early 1990s, at least 10 per cent of the adult population in Poland, Czechoslovakia and Hungary could be regarded as strongly antisemitic.[1] This proportion is clearly greater than what might be explained by the presence and activities of antisemitic élite fringe groups, which were still rather insignificant at the time. We may conclude therefore that in the four decades after World War II, anti-Jewish prejudice had survived beneath the surface of society, despite the prosecution of public displays of antisemitism, and the state's official rejection of antisemitic ideology. Indeed, in view of the enduring nature of Communist regimes, whose "tenure" spanned several generations, it seems likely that antisemitism also received new impulses. This volume – the documents published and commented upon herein – supports the hypothesis formulated elsewhere that antisemitism:

> [...] did not simply emerge out of nothing after the fall of Communism. In their efforts to impose the fullest possible control over society, the Communist parties that seized power in East-Central Europe after World War II eliminated the political, religious, social and cultural institutions of surviving Jewry, or made them dependent on the state. However, despite their total control over Jewish institutions and Jewish community life, East-Central European Communist Parties continuously and systematically identified and regarded the conflicting historical memories about Jews, and the presence of Jews in Polish, Czechoslovak and Hungarian society, as a disturbing factor. They permanently kept the problem on the political agenda, and in this way they permanently

---

[1] See András Kovács, *The Stranger at Hand. Antisemitic Prejudices in Post-Communist Hungary* (Leiden and Boston, MA: Brill, 2011), 32–35.

(re)constructed their own "Jewish Questions", which, then, they were eager to "solve". [...] This mostly concealed, but restless preoccupation with the "Jewish Question" kept the whole issue alive in the decades of Communist rule, and it explains to a great extent its open re-emergence after 1990.²

Continuity of the "Jewish question" and antisemitic discourse after the Holocaust

Post-Holocaust continuity of the antisemitic worldview, language and prejudice can be observed in several forms, the three most important of which were: (1) discourses in the everyday sphere; (2) reactions to differing Jewish and non-Jewish perceptions of pre-war antisemitism, the Holocaust, and reintegration of Jews in post-war society; and (3) the policies of the Communist parties before and after seizing power.

A large amount of material gathered by the Hungarian political police points to the post-war survival of undisguised antisemitic views and a blunt antisemitic language in several radical anti-Communist circles. In her analysis of police surveillance and the ensuing court cases against right-wing youth groups in the 1960s, Éva Standeisky cites the following typical conversation between the leader of a monitored group and his friends:

> If this were truly a government or system chosen by the Hungarian people, then they would not seek to deny people their intellectual freedom. In this regard, the Jews are their most faithful supporters. They keep some professions as a privilege for themselves, not allowing others access. And so the press, theatre, TV and radio, and foreign trade are primarily in their hands. Since they are Jews, they neglect the interests of the Hungarian people, and for the sake of their own power they place the country in the service of the Soviet Union.³

A whole series of memoirs published after 1990 prove that post-war experiences and events in the aftermath of the Communist takeover reproduced pre-war narratives⁴

---

2 András Kovács, Antisemitic Elements in Communist Discourse. A Continuity Factor in Post-War Hungarian Antisemitism. In *Antisemitism in an Era of Transition: Continuities and Impact in Post-Communist Poland and Hungary*, eds. François Guesnet and Gwen Jones (Frankfurt am Main: Peter Lang, 2014), 137.
3 Éva Standeisky, Mélyrétegi metszet. Jobboldali fiatalok az 1960-as években [Deep Cross-Section. Right-wing youths in the 1960s]. In Éva Standeisky, *Antiszemitizmusok* [Antisemitisms] (Budapest: Argument, 2007), 96–130 (104). On everyday antisemitism in Poland, see Alina Cała, *The Image of the Jew in Polish Folk Culture* (Jerusalem: Magnes, 1995). On antisemitism in reporting on the post-1967 antisemitic campaign, see Bożena Szaynok, *Poland–Israel 1944–1968. In the Shadow of the Past and of the Soviet Union* (Warsaw: Institute of National Remembrance, 2012), 430–.
4 See Viktor Karády, Zsidóság és modernizáció a történelmi Magyarországon [Jewry and Modernization in Historical Hungary]. In Viktor Karády, *Zsidóság és társadalmi egyenlőtlenségek (1867–1945)* [Jewry and Social Inequalities (1867–1954)] (Budapest: Replika, 2000), 7–40; and Krisztián Ungváry, *A Horthy-rendszer mérlege* [The Balance-Sheet of the Horthy Regime] (Budapest and Pécs: Jelenkor and OSZK, 2012), 20–38.

that set and maintained boundaries between Jewish and non-Jewish sections of the middle class.[5] In these narratives, which appeared mostly in private communication, traditional anti-Jewish stereotypes and prejudices were continuously present. As the late historian Pál Engel recalled family discourse in his childhood in the early 1950s: "In addition to my 'Christian' middle-class upbringing, I began to realize gradually my place in society, that there were 'proles', 'petty bourgeois', and 'Jews'. We, however, were 'gentlefolk'."[6]

Even decades after the war, rival intellectual and middle-class groups interpreted confrontations in multiple areas as a conflict between Jews and non-Jews, and used narratives rooted in contradictory and opposing historical memories. In Hungary, which had the region's largest post-Holocaust Jewish population and where Jews were, throughout the Communist period, very much visible in prominent intellectual positions, such conflicts sometimes became so acute that they even attracted the attention of the political leadership. A Party functionary described the situation after an inquiry in 1967 at the Institute of History of the Hungarian Academy of Sciences as follows:

> [E]veryone is aware of the conflicts, they [*those who complain that Jews are dominating the profession* – AK] have precise statistics on Jewish and non-Jewish functionaries filling leading historian positions, as they would say, even with a lantern one cannot come across elements of popular [*that is, non-Jewish* – AK] ancestry in these positions. [...] [T]he question should be addressed in some form, because according to them, the statistics they reported on are the institutionalised reason for the increase of antisemitism.[7]

The surviving elements of pre-war discourses on the "Jewish Question" and the old antisemitism were not the only factors to sustain the language of prejudice and stereotyping. Additional impulses came from the perception of conflicts that arose between surviving Jews and non-Jews after the war. In the immediate aftermath of the war, significant tensions arose in Czechoslovakia, Hungary and Poland around such issues as: antisemitism in the interwar period; responsibility and legal accountability

---

5 István Bibó, A zsidókérdés Magyarországon 1944 után [The Jewish Question in Hungary after 1944]. In István Bibó *Válogatott tanulmányok* [Selected Studies], ed. Tibor Huszár (Budapest: Magvető, 1986), 621–798 (754–778); András Kovács, A zsidókérdés a mai magyar társadalomban [The Jewish Question in Hungarian Society Today]. In András Kovács, *A Másik szeme. Zsidók és antiszemiták a háború utáni Magyarországon* [The Eye of the Other. Jews and Antisemites in Post-War Hungary] (Budapest: Gondolat, 2008); Aleksander Smolar, Les Juifs dans la mémoire polonaise [Jews in Polish Memory], *Esprit*, June 1987, 1–31; Heda Margolius-Kovály, *Under a Cruel Star: A Life in Prague, 1941–1968* (Teaneck, NJ: Holmes and Meier, 1997), 45–47; Jan Láníček, *Czechs, Slovaks and the Jews, 1938–48. Beyond Idealization and Condemnation* (New York: Palgrave Macmillan, 2013), 188–190.
6 Pál Engel, Úrigyerekek tévúton [Young Ladies and Gentlemen on the Wrong Path], *Népszabadság*, 12 May 2001. On the perpetuation of antisemitic stereotypes in private intellectual discourses of the 1950s and 1960s, see Éva Standeisky, Értelmiségi antiszemitizmus a korai Kádár-korszakban [Intellectual antisemitism in the early Kádár era]. In Standeisky, *Antiszemitizmusok*, 79–95.
7 National Archives of Hungary, M-KS 288/36/5/1967, (30 October 1967) 48–56.

for the discrimination and persecution suffered by Jews; restitution of stolen or seized Jewish property; the fate of heirless Jewish assets; and reparations for Jewish victims.[8] In Hungary, additionally, an antisemitic discourse on "Jewish revenge" arose, which related to the role played by Jewish public prosecutors and judges in the prosecution of war criminals at the People's Tribunals. The non-Jewish perception of Jewish survivors' post-war status and social mobility further added to tensions. Due to the large proportion of Jews among Communist Party leaders, army officers and trade unionists in East-Central Europe, and in the post-war governments of the three countries, many segments of society perceived and rejected the new regime as an instance of "Jewish power." This perception was reinforced by the visible upward social mobility of Jewish survivors who tried to overcome handicaps caused by the former regime's antisemitic laws, which had prevented Jews from studying at university, or working in professions they were qualified for.[9]

The third factor that strongly contributed to the continuity of antisemitic discourses was Communist parties' policy. When Communist parties started to fight for domination in Czechoslovakia, Hungary and Poland, they had to face the presence of traditions and language of the old "Jewish Question", embedded antisemitism in society, and the conflicts of the post-Holocaust period. Even so, the policies of the respective Communist parties had a decisive influence on the extent to which such views and issues – and, in a general sense, the "Jewish Question" – remained on the agenda in the three countries in subsequent decades.

Post-war and Stalinist Communist policy and the continuity of the "Jewish question"

Many local factors influenced the "Jewish policy" of Communist parties and states: the historical background to the legal, economic and social status of Jews; local traditions of antisemitism; the country's role in World War II; events during the Holocaust; the number of Jewish survivors and the public positions they held; and the Commu-

---

[8] See Eugene Duschinsky, Peter Meyer, Bernard D. Weinryb, Nicolas Sylvain (eds). *The Jews in the Soviet Satellites* (Ithaca, NY: Syracuse University Press, 1953); Bibó, op. cit.; Jan T. Gross, *Fear. Antisemitism in Poland after Auschwitz: An Essay in Historical Interpretation* (Princeton, NJ: Princeton University Press, 2006); Lánicek, op. cit.

[9] See Viktor Karády, *Túlélők és újrakezdők* [Survivors and Re-beginners] (Budapest: Múlt és Jövő, 2002), 141–186; András Kovács, Hungarian Jewish Politics from the End of the Second World War until the Collapse of Communism. In *Jews and the State. Dangerous Alliances and the Perils of Privilege. Studies in Contemporary Jewry, XIX*, ed. Ezra Mendelsohn (Oxford: Oxford University Press, 2004), 124–156; Smolar, op. cit.; Stanislaw Krajewski, Jews, Communism, and the Jewish Communists. In *Jewish Studies at the CEU. Yearbook 1996–1999*, ed. András Kovács (Budapest: Central European University, 2000), 119–133; Jeff Schatz, *The Generation. The Rise and Fall of the Jewish Communists of Poland* (Berkeley, CA: University of California Press, 1991); Gross, op. cit., 226–243.

nist movement and the Party's "embeddedness" in post-war societies. Due to differences in these respects, "Jewish policy" varied from country to country. However, certain traits seem to be common in all East-Central European countries, and present throughout the Communist period, although their relative importance changed over time.

The first common trait concerns church policy, since "Jewish policy" was considered one aspect of general policy towards the churches. This viewed the churches as political adversaries, proclaimed the official ideology of atheism, and generally aimed at diminishing religiosity and the influence of religious denominations. Although Communist church policy swung between repression and tolerance depending on local factors, and varied from country to country, the characteristics outlined above remained constant.[10]

Second, Jewish survivors – many of whom were secular Jews with no ties to the religious community –also had to realize that the Communist states either completely rejected the institutional, ideological or cultural expression of national and minority identity, or tolerated it only under the strictest conditions. In those countries where Jewry was recognized exclusively as a religious denomination (Czechoslovakia, Hungary and the GDR), Jews who maintained and occasionally displayed any secular form of Jewish identity were subject to repression, manifested in various forms of the official "anti-Zionist policy."

The third factor that created striking similarities in East-Central European Communist countries' "Jewish policy" was their membership of the Soviet political and military bloc. They had little choice but to adjust their policies on this issue to the position of the Soviet Union, and the political expectations of the Soviet leadership. Such expectations had a decisive impact on local "Jewish policy". Throughout the entire Communist era, periodical changes in local "Jewish policies" reflected changes in Soviet policy, and the means by which they were realized. A number of sub-periods can be identified here: the years before the establishment of the total dictatorship (1945–49); the Stalinist era; the post-Stalinist "thaw"; the aftermath of the severance of diplomatic relations with Israel in 1967; and, finally, the second half of the 1980s, the years of the system's decline.

The Communist parties, which had enjoyed very little pre-war social support or influence (at least in Poland, Hungary and Slovakia), faced serious legitimacy problems, and so attempted to represent views and support decisions which they deemed in line with majority expectations. Communist parties were aware that antisemitic traditions were still very much alive in society, and that a large number of people had greatly benefited from anti-Jewish discrimination and persecution. On many important issues that emerged in the post-war years, Communist parties tried to adjust their

---

10 See Sabrina P. Ramet (ed.), *Religion and Nationalism in Soviet and East European Politics* (Durham, NC: Duke University Press, 1989); and Sabrina P. Ramet (ed.), *Catholicism and Politics in Communist Societies* (Durham, NC: Duke University Press, 1990).

rhetoric and policy to what they perceived as the majority position. Such was the case, for example, in conflicts over reparations, the restitution of stolen property, and postwar antisemitic civil disturbances and pogroms.[11] In these debates and decisions, Communist rhetoric and conduct had less in common with the positions of the Jewish organizations and community representatives than with those of other parties in the "anti-Fascist coalition", such as the social democrats. Communist parties were quite prepared to ignore the sufferings of the persecuted Jews, their rightful demands for compensation, and their expectation that justice be served. To further Party political interests, parties occasionally formed temporary or lasting alliances with known antisemites,[12] and also sought to exploit latent antisemitism, or, at the very least, to make concessions to antisemites in the hope of increased political support. Today, it is generally acknowledged that the Communist parties benefited from incitement and the political exploitation of antisemitism, and even, on occasion, played a role in the unleashing of pogroms and other forms of violence, for instance in Kunmadaras and Miskolc in Hungary, and in Kielce and several other places in Poland.[13]

The reason for this behaviour, however, is not to be sought merely in the opportunistic strategy of the Communists, but also in the way they regarded the surviving Jews in their country. Politicians of the various Communist parties – regardless of whether they were of Jewish descent or not – consistently took as their starting point the view that Jews represented a bounded group in society, whose collective interests not only conflicted with those of mainstream society, but also with the vision of the political system they wished to establish.

Evidently, the Communist parties could not, in view of their ideological traditions, anti-Fascist rhetoric, and role in the "anti-Fascist" coalitions, overtly use the language of antisemitism; nor could they openly support antisemitic policies. For this reason, they instead chose to simply neglect the rightful and legitimate demands of Jewish survivors, and to discount them when making political decisions.

This period also saw the development of a Party language that came to be used throughout subsequent decades when speaking about "Jewish affairs". In this language, old stereotypes and prejudices were often used in rather blunt fashion in non-public forums and in internal documents,[14] whereas in material destined for

---

11 See Duschinsky et. al. (eds), op. cit.
12 See, for example, Gross, op. cit., 222–226. In Hungary, the National Peasant Party was the closest political ally of the Communist Party from 1945 until 1949. Some of the main figures in the Party had belonged to antisemitic populist circles prior to 1945.
13 Much literature exists on the latent antisemitic policies of the Communist parties and post-Holocaust pogroms. The latter are described and analysed in Bożena Szaynok, The Kielce Pogrom (July 4, 1946), Accessed on 27 August 2016 at http://www.jewishvirtuallibrary.org/the-kielce-pogrom; Gross, op. cit.; and in János Pelle, Az utolsó vérvádak [The Last Blood Libels] (Budapest: Pelikán, 1995), 167–247. For events in Czechoslovakia, see Lánicek, op. cit., 165–. This general feature of Communist policy is covered in detail in Gross, op. cit.; and Standeisky, Antiszemitizmusok, 15–38, 131–173.
14 See Kovács, Antisemitic Elements in Communist Discourse.

public use, the word "Jewish" was replaced by code words such as "Zionist", "cosmopolitan", "urban bourgeois", and "unreliable petit bourgeois elements infiltrating the Party". Naturally, all this was done while formally maintaining the rejection of antisemitism. Such "double speak" emerged in the propaganda of the Communists and their allies in the immediate aftermath of the war.[15] It appeared in a much more explicit form in the first post-war trials against Zionists, which were a direct consequence of the outbreak of the Cold War,[16] and it was also present in the language used in the Rajk trial in Budapest, the first major Soviet type show trial after the war.[17] After the Communist takeover, and the subsequent Soviet policy turn against the newly-founded Jewish state of Israel, official propaganda began to employ the language of "anti-Zionism" far more consistently, both within the Party and during purges of Jewish officials from the army and state apparatus.[18] Anti-Zionist rhetoric with a barely concealed antisemitic message assumed its most developed form during a series of investigations and court cases in Czechoslovakia, Hungary and East Germany in 1952–1953, which were modelled on the antisemitic trials in the Soviet Union. East-Central European examples include the Slánský trial in Czechoslovakia, the arrest and detention of Hungary's Jewish religious leaders, and the Merker affair in East Germany.[19]

---

15 Erik Molnár, Zsidókérdés Magyarországon [The Jewish Question in Hungary], *Társadalmi Szemle* 5 (1946); József Darvas, Őszinte szót a zsidókérdésben! [An Honest Word on the Jewish Question!], *Szabad Nép*, 25 March 1945.
16 A case in point was the court case initiated in Hungary in May 1949 against Zionist leader Béla Dénes, who was then imprisoned for four years. See Béla Dénes, *Ávós világ Magyarországon. Egy cionista orvos emlékiratai* [The World of Secret Policemen in Hungary. Memoirs of a Zionist Doctor] (Budapest: Kossuth, 1991). On the prosecution of Zionist leaders in Hungary, see Ágnes Szalai, A magyarországi kommunista diktatúra zsidó áldozatai (1949–1954) [The Jewish Victims of the Communist Dictatorship in Hungary (1949–1954)]. In *Tanulmányok a holokausztról*, 4. kötet [Studies on the Holocaust, vol. 4], ed. Randolph L. Braham (Budapest: Presscon, 2006), 217–268.
17 At the trial, "anti-Zionism" was still treated merely as a side issue: the original Jewish-sounding names of the Jewish defendants and their participation in pre-war Communist-Zionist movements were listed in minute detail. See *Rajk László és társai a népbíróság előtt* [László Rajk and his Associates at the People's Tribunal] (Budapest: Szikra, 1949), 137.
18 See Kovács, Antisemitic Elements in Communist Discourse; Szaynok, *Poland–Israel 1944–1968*, 164–.
19 For the minutes of the Slánský case, see Ministerstvo spravedlnosti, *Proces s vedením protistátního spikleneckého centra v čele s Rudolfem Slánským* [Ministry of Justice, The Trial against the Leadership of the Conspiratorial Center of Traitors Headed by Rudolf Slánský] (Prague: Orbis, 1953). For an analysis of the court documents, see Jacob Ari Labendz, Lectures, Murder, and a Phony Terrorist: Managing "Jewish Power and Danger" in 1960s Communist Czechoslovakia, *East European Jewish Affairs* 44 (2014), 1, 84–108. For the Hungarian court cases, see Szalai, op. cit. On the Merker case, see Jeffrey Herf, East German Communists and the Jewish Question: The Case of Paul Merker, *Journal of Contemporary History* 29 (1994), 627–661; and Stefan Meining, *Kommunistische Judenpolitik. Die DRR, die Juden und Israel* (Münster, Hamburg, London: LIT Verlag, 2002), 159–176.

The anti-Zionist turn in Communist policy was a serious disappointment for Jews, both those who sympathized with Marxist ideology and the Communist parties, and also those who were not attracted to Communist policies or to Marxist-Leninist ideology, but who believed that Communist universalist and anti-antisemitic rhetoric would abolish the language of the "Jewish Question" forever. Instead, they had to realize that the new path to assimilation offered by the Communists would not lead to the disappearance of boundaries based on stereotypes or prejudice. Indeed, the coded language of Communist discourse used in connection with Jews, its tacit inferences and predispositions to the existence of an invisible anti-Communist Jewish network, contributed to the construction of this boundary anew, whereby the old stereotype of "dual loyalty" acquired new content. The image of the "anti-Christian" and "nation-destroying" Jew was replaced by one of the Zionist hostile to the working class and the Soviet Union, who marvelled at and secretly supported "Western imperialism", while pretending to be faithful to the socialist system and the Party.[20]

Political practices grounded in the conviction that Jews were fundamentally disloyal began long before the staging of the famous anti-Zionist trials. Immediately after the takeover of power, the Hungarian Communist Party leadership sought to limit the number of Jews within the government and Party apparatus by issuing internal directives. For party leaders of Jewish descent who issued such directives, or supported them inside the Party, the main motive for doing so was to refute the accusation of "Jewish power", but the directives themselves referred, in the spirit of class-war rhetoric, to the unreliability of the "petit bourgeois" Jewish cadres:

> Comrade Rákosi [...] has emphatically underlined that we should steer clear of "clever, petit bourgeois Jewish intellectuals". We might have just as many problems with them as with the intelligent workers that we are going to bring in, with the difference, however, that whereas several years of laborious and toilsome work will bring forth its own fruit in the case of the worker cadres, in the case of the former group, we may never know when they will become spies and when they will spoil our efforts under the pretext of enforcing the Party line.[21]

In the Stalinist anti-Zionist campaigns and trials of the early 1950s, such suspicions were transformed into grave accusations. They subsequently reappeared – with an unchanged structure but different content – in texts later used to criticize former Stalinist leaderships by several proponents of "Communism with a national face", stating that Stalinist policy was a consequence of the "rootlessness" of the Jewish Stalinist leaders in their respective countries. This argument was used not only by some members of the Natolin faction in Poland, the later leaders of the antisemitic campaign of 1967,[22] but even by the non-antisemitic Imre Nagy, who was Hungarian

---

20 On this see Labendz, op. cit., 86–89.
21 Losonczy Géza levele Révai Józsefnek, 1949. július 14-én [Géza Losonczy's Letter to József Révai, 14 July 1949], *Budapesti Negyed* 8 (1995), 209–227. Letter published by Éva Standeisky.
22 See Schatz, op. cit., 267.

prime minister at the time of the 1956 Hungarian revolution. Prior to his trial and execution, Imre Nagy wrote the following in his notes regarding the Stalinist Rákosi-style leadership policy:

> What explains such behaviour on the part of Rákosi's clique? A crucial factor was that as most of them were Jews – indeed, mostly Jews from Moscow[23] – consequently, broad sections of the Hungarian people had a hatred of them, turned against them, and were not willing to accept them as representatives of the Hungarian national interest, still less as their leaders. [...] Just as Stalin wanted to be more Russian than the Russians… so the Jewish Rákosi and his clique followed the same path, wanting to be more Hungarian than the Hungarians.[24]

Jewish policy of the Communist states in the post-Stalinist period

The post-Stalinist period of Communist policy brought changes in "Jewish policy." After Stalin's death, the anti-Zionist campaigns, with their thinly-veiled antisemitism, were halted for a time in the East-Central European countries. Indeed, from 1956 until 1967, a "thaw" could be observed in this area, too. This changed only after the 1967 war and the severance of diplomatic relations with Israel. At that time the antisemitic – "anti-Zionist" – campaigns re-emerged, particularly in Poland, but also in Czechoslovakia, after the suppression of the Prague Spring.[25]

The post-Stalinist period also saw a change in the methods used by Soviet policy-makers to control the states in the Soviet bloc. In the first half of the 1950s, the Soviet Union had directly managed key areas of politics and the economy in the countries comprising the bloc. For instance, Poland's Minister of Defence had been a Soviet general, Communist émigrés returning from the Soviet Union (some of whom were officers in the Soviet secret services) occupied key positions in the governments of the three countries, and in most government ministries, the resident Soviet "advisors" had the major say. After 1956, certain areas remained under close Soviet control, including military and security matters. In general, however, one can state that while dependence on the Soviet Union severely limited the scope for action of the Warsaw Pact and Comecon countries in the fields of foreign and defence policy, the situation was different concerning domestic, economic, and also religious policy. The various countries were more able to develop independent policies or, in the terminology of the time, policies that were "better suited to local conditions".

---

[23] Nagy meant that most members of the Rákosi group were Hungarian Communist emigrants who had lived in Moscow until 1945.
[24] Imre Nagy, *Snagovi jegyzetek. Gondolatok, emlékezések 1956–1957* [Snagov Notes: Thoughts and Recollections 1956–1957], ed. István Vida (Budapest: Gondolat, 2006), 93–94.
[25] See *The Jewish Situation in Czechoslovakia after Dubcek*. Background paper no. 13. London: Institute of Jewish Affairs in association with the World Jewish Congress 1969.

Communist governments and politicians considered their policies towards Israel and their policies towards their Jewish communities different parts of the same problem. Evidently, the first reason was that emigration to Israel was an alternative available in the life strategies of Eastern European Jews throughout the period, regardless of whether or not they accepted the ideal of Zionism. Israel's existence gave rise to a strong emotional identification even among those groups that were not seeking to migrate. The Jewish state was perceived as a direct result of the Holocaust, as a place where relatives, friends and old acquaintances had settled, and where refuge could be sought in the case of renewed persecution. Such perceptions of a special relationship were strengthened by the contemporary Israeli interpretation of political Zionism, which regarded the remaining European Jews as potential immigrants, and prioritized efforts to enable their emigration both at a political level and in practice. Unsurprisingly, the regulation of emigration, a factor that fundamentally influenced the life strategies of local Jewish populations, became the subject of both policy and political discourse related to Israel, and of policies towards the local Jewish communities. The documents in this volume illustrate this very well.

Discourses and policies relating to domestic Jews were greatly influenced by international politics. After 1948, Israel had increasingly close ties with the West and found itself in constant conflict with the Arab states, which, in turn, sought an alliance with the Soviet Union. With the exception of Romania after 1967, the Soviet Bloc countries gave their unconditional support to the Arabs in this conflict; still, unconditional support for Soviet policy was resisted not only by those Jews who were opposed to Communism; even many of those sympathetic to the Communist regime, and Jewish Party members or officials, were unable to fully identify with this policy. The Party leadership and Communist politics in general reacted to this phenomenon by making accusations of disloyalty and, in its extreme form, treason: Jews were accused of being the "fifth column of imperialism".[26] Even if policy on Jews and Jewish organizations differed from country to country, the loyalty of Jews and Jewish organizations to Party policy – and thus to the regime – was viewed as questionable everywhere. Evidently, policy on Israel and on the Middle East conflict had to accommodate the interests of the Soviet Union in its status as superpower. Consequently, the presumption of disloyalty of Jews and their organizations to this policy had a direct effect on

---

[26] For an analysis of the famous speech made by the Polish Party secretary, Władysław Gomułka, on 19 June 1967 in which he allegedly referred to Poland's Jews as a fifth column, see Szaynok, *Poland–Israel 1944–1968*, 412–415. The same kind of language was used by the Czechoslovak secret service when justifying the drawing up of a full list of Czechoslovak Jews; see the documents of the "Pavauk" (Spider) initiative in this volume, as well as Alena Heitlinger, *In the Shadow of the Holocaust and Communism. Czech and Slovak Jews since 1945* (New Jersey and London: Transaction, 2006), 34; Jacob Ari Labendz, Renegotiating Czechoslovakia. The State and the Jews in Communist Central Europe: The Czech Lands, 1945–1990. PhD thesis, Graduate School of Arts and Sciences of Washington University, 2014, 209, 486. See also in this volume the speech made by Hungarian party leader, János Kádár, on 13 June 1967 (Chapter 3, Document 10).

government policies towards the local Jewish communities. Whereas Soviet politics and policy-makers now had little interest in the various countries' policies towards their Jewish communities, suspicion of disloyalty required that appropriate political attention be given and responses sought.[27]

The policies of the Soviet Union and its allies towards Germany was a further special factor that contributed to the treatment of Jewish matters. When it became clear that efforts to establish a neutral and united Germany were illusory, and that West Germany was being drawn ever closer into the Western economic and defence community, Soviet policy switched to supporting the idea of "two Germanys", whereby the Federal Republic of Germany – viewed as "revanchist" and neo-Fascist – was treated as the manifestation of continuity with Hitler's Germany, while the German Democratic Republic (GDR, East Germany), as the incorporation of anti-Fascist traditions, became "the other Germany". Such rhetoric was weakened, however, by increasingly good relations between the Federal Republic and Israel. While West Germany was willing to pay substantial reparations to the Jewish victims of wartime persecution, and took steps to establish diplomatic relations with Israel, the GDR stubbornly refused to acknowledge any responsibility for Nazi crimes, a stance that led Israel to rule out diplomatic relations with the East German state.[28]

The East-Central European governments acted in line with the direction of Soviet policy. They sought to manipulate anti-Fascist sentiments, among them the emotions felt by Holocaust survivors, to organize protests against the FRG–Israeli rapprochement by re-heating the libel of Zionist-Nazi collaboration. Such efforts, reflected in the documents in this volume, became more intense during the discussions on reparations, during the Eichmann trial, and during the establishment of diplomatic relations between the FRG and Israel. On these issues, Jewish organizations found themselves under strong pressure to support the government's position, both domestically and on the international stage. This expectation had to be met even when it obviously ran counter to the fundamental interests of the local Jewish communities, such as on the issue of reparations.

Economic difficulties experienced by the East-Central European regimes also contributed to the intertwining of domestic Jewish policy with foreign policy. By establishing good relations with local Jewish communities, the leaders of the various countries which struggled with permanent foreign currency problems hoped to promote economic relations with both Israel and the United States. The aim was to create new opportunities in Western markets, and to facilitate favourable loans. Such hopes were expressly nurtured by the Israeli economic partners, who made no secret of their expectation that improved economic ties with the East-Central European regimes should be reciprocated by individual governments' gestures towards their domestic Jewish populations. These

---
27 On cooperation between the Soviet and Polish security organs, see Szaynok, *Poland–Israel 1944–1968*, 325, 383.
28 Meining, op. cit., 106–108, 353.

gestures were expected, first of all, in the field of facilitating emigration and easing contacts with international Jewish organizations. From the 1970s onwards, pressure on East-Central European governments steadily grew as American policy-makers regarded the situation of Soviet and other Eastern European Jews, their opportunities for emigration, and their unhindered contact with international Jewish organizations, as primary indicators of the state of human rights. Though in dire need for Western economic support, considering the political sensitivity of these issues, the Hungarian, Czechoslovak and Polish governments had to carefully weigh up how far they could go in improving economic relations and, in connection with this, in removing or mitigating restrictions on their local Jewish communities without annoying the Soviet Union or provoking economic retaliation from the Arab countries.

For these reasons, the foreign and domestic threads of "Jewish policy" became inextricably intertwined. As the documents published in this volume reveal, even if "Jewish policy" in the various Communist countries was not determined exclusively by direct instructions from the Soviet Union, "Jewish matters" were repeatedly to be found on the political agenda of Soviet bloc states' institutions even during those periods when "anti-Zionism" received less emphasis in Communist policy. The relevant government, Party and security organs would then discuss such matters among themselves or occasionally at international level, whereby the conceptual frame and language of the "Jewish Question" was kept alive throughout the period.

As was the case with other religious denominations, state control of Jewish organisations was established by integrating them into the nomenklatura system of the Party-state. In practical terms, this meant that the Jewish religious denomination was made fully dependent, both financially and in terms of staff, on state bodies overseeing religious and denominational affairs. Their budgets (which came mostly from the state budget) were set by the state, while decisions on personnel (for instance, on congregation leaders, rabbis etc.) were made subject to the prior approval of the state. Jewish organizations in Hungary and Czechoslovakia could only function legally as denominational (that is, religious) institutions. In Poland, due to different historical traditions, a secular Jewish social and cultural institution, the Social and Cultural Association of Jews in Poland (TSKŻ), was allowed to function under close state control. In all three countries, the state authorities were suspicious of, and acted sooner or later to prohibit, any attempts to create organizations or to pursue activities that were not strictly controlled by officially approved institutions. Individuals involved in such efforts were usually subjected to repressive measures.[29]

State authorities were particularly strict when it came to monitoring contacts with foreign and international Jewish organizations. There were political and ideological reasons for this, as international Jewish bodies were regarded as the representatives of hostile powers and, indeed, as cover organizations for foreign intelligence services.

---

[29] See, for further details, Heitlinger, op. cit., 105–142.; and Kovács, Hungarian Jewish Politics from the End of the Second World War, 124–156.

Another factor, however, was the state's desire to cut off or control any financial source that might grant Jewish organizations a degree of independence. As the documents in this volume show, while membership of the WJC (World Jewish Congress) was permitted or prohibited primarily in response to the WJC's momentarily positive or negative stance towards both Soviet Jewry and Soviet policy, the main factor influencing policy towards international Jewish welfare organizations (above all, the American Jewish Joint Distribution Committee and other related bodies) was economic, in particular, the hope of gaining access to Western currency reserves. Hence, in such cases, the aim was to strictly control contacts and to channel as much of the aid as possible to the state, which could then redistribute it from the centre.

State authorities naturally imposed strict controls on institutional and private relations with Israel. Emigration to Israel was strictly regulated, although regulations were changed from time to time. Economic relations were maintained throughout the period, but their intensity varied over time as interests changed. One enduring concern was that such relations receive the least possible publicity, in order to prevent sanctions from and loss of trade with the Arab countries which, in terms of volume, was more significant. Limited publicity also served to minimize the risk of Soviet annoyance. Meanwhile, cultural relations, which the Israeli side would have liked to expand, were severely limited until the very late 1980s, and were prevented almost completely at the institutional level. In each of the East-Central European countries, Israeli diplomatic representations, diplomats and private individuals (business people and tourists) were strictly monitored.[30]

In the Party-state regimes and the documents of their institutions, control and overt or covert influencing of domestic Jewish institutions and individuals, as well as relations with foreign Jewish organizations, were treated as intertwined affairs. The activities of Party, governmental and security organs were coordinated: from the late 1950s onwards, state organs maintained official relations with the Jewish institutions through the State Office for Church Affairs (Állami Egyházügyi Hivatal, ÁEH) in Hungary, and the State Office for Ecclesiastical Affairs (Státní úřad pro věci církevní) in Czechoslovakia, the latter being amalgamated by the Ministry of Culture and Education in 1956. These bodies passed on Party decrees and requirements on the basis of secret information provided by the Ministry of Interior. In this area too, however, there arose differences of opinion between various Party-state institutions: they often only supplied partial information to each other, and sought to realize their own institutional interests. In doing so, they even accepted minor conflicts with other institutions, as for instance, in Hungary in the mid-1960s, when the Ministry of Foreign

---

30 See Labendz, Renegotiating Czechoslovakia, 444–449; Szaynok, *Poland–Israel 1944–1968*, 328, 334; and the Hungarian documents published in this volume.

Trade, seeking to increase foreign trade, came up against opposition from foreign policy departments and Party organs.[31]

In Hungary, major Jewish matters were addressed by the Political Committee (the most important operational organ of the Hungarian Socialist Workers Party, HSWP) and by the Central Committee, the Party's principal decision-making body. Major Jewish matters included the Eichmann affair, the crisis in the aftermath of the Six-Day War, and even antisemitic statements made by high-ranking Party functionaries.[32] Such matters, as well as other less significant ones, are constantly addressed in Party apparatus documents produced by departments dealing with agitprop, cultural, religious and scientific affairs, foreign affairs, and security affairs. These departments were in constant contact with relevant governmental institutions and personnel. As far as religious and denominational issues were concerned, the monitoring bodies were the State Office for Church Affairs, the Ministry of Foreign Affairs, the Ministry of Culture and Education, and last but not least, the security organs. In many cases, the same documents – for instance, papers referring to relations with international Jewish organizations – can be found among the papers of three organizations – the State Office for Church Affairs, the Ministry of Foreign Affairs, and the foreign affairs department of the Party. Jewish organizations' officials and the rabbis were briefed by state bodies on a regular basis, and whenever extraordinary matters arose. However, as the documents show, the security organs influenced the activities of religious congregations not only by means of the state organizations that functioned as official points of contact, but also in an indirect way using agents, "social contacts", and via the officials they were required to consult on a regular basis.

The documents in this volume offer an insight into the mechanisms that produced similarities in certain features that characterized the "Jewish policy" of each Party-state and its institutions. For instance, when important policy decisions were being weighed up, the likely Soviet reaction was always a consideration in every country. In many instances it was, of course, difficult to know for certain how the Soviet Union would react to a particular decision. Consequently, representatives of the Eastern Bloc countries (members of the diplomatic corps accredited to Israel, staff at bodies dealing with religious denominations, ministry personnel and Party departments responsible for relations with the Middle East) regularly consulted each other about their respective stances and policies. On the one hand, they sought precedents for decisions they were preparing to take. Secondly, they wished to avoid the risk of one of the "allies" drawing Soviet policy-makers' attention to perceived deviations from the "common line". The documents dealing with Israel and international Jewish

---

31 On the conflict between the Ministry for Religious Affairs and the Ministry of Interior, see Labendz, Renegotiating Czechoslovakia, 383. On the conflict in Poland between the Ministry of Interior and foreign policy apparatus, see Szaynok, *Poland–Israel 1944–1968*, 375. On the conflicts between the political, economic and foreign affairs apparatuses in Hungary, see several documents published in this volume.
32 See Kovács, Antisemitic Elements in Communist Discourse.

organizations contain much information on this strategy. This meant that certain common features of "Jewish policy" in the East-Central European Communist Party-states were produced by processes of mutual accommodation, even in the absence of actual consultations on every concrete case between the various institutions, or clear signals from the Soviet leadership. Still, this political game, built on mutual suspicions but also a search for policy precedents, made it far easier for Soviet policy-makers to ensure – without directly intervening – that the countries in question pursued roughly the same policies towards the Middle East and towards their local Jewish communities. It should also be noted, however, that when it came to major political issues, such as the Eichmann affair and wars in the Middle East, the Party leaders were in direct contact with each other (see, for example, the papers on the Six-Day War in this volume). Moreover, on major issues, officials at each country's Ministry of Foreign Affairs consulted with one other on the stance to be taken at international forums. Similarly, religious affairs bodies and departments of the security organs held lengthy and regular negotiations with one another on religious denominations and measures against "international Zionism".

Another common feature of "Jewish policy" in the Communist countries of East-Central Europe was a desire to maintain the semblance of legality, even in cases of blatant interference by the political leadership in religious denomination's internal affairs. The documents published here, as well as similar documents produced by the Czechoslovak and Polish authorities, reveal the methods used by the religious affairs and security organs to manipulate religious congregations while taking care to avoid formal violations of the legal regulations.[33] In almost all of the countries, this was made possible because the political and security organs used a large proportion of denominational leaders and rabbis as instruments of state policy, in various ways. Those individuals able to defy the authorities' will were subjected to constant surveillance and pressure.

About the collection

This introduction and the book do not seek to offer a systematic analysis of the "Jewish policy" of the Communist countries of Central and Eastern Europe. Rather, the aim is utilize the materials stored in former top secret archives, and provide access to documents which reveal the many features of "Jewish policy".

The documents selected for and commented upon in this volume are from the period 1957–1989. The main reason for this choice was that this period – referred to as the post-Stalinist era – marked the consolidation of the Communist regimes, and was four times longer than the Stalinist era itself (1949–1956), which may, from

---

[33] See Labendz, Renegotiating Czechoslovakia, 395, 503; and the Hungarian documents in this volume.

this perspective, be regarded as an exceptional state of affairs. Documents from the post-Stalinist era provide deep insights into the institutional system, conceptual basis, ideology and language used by representatives of the Communist regime in relation to the Jewish population and the Jewish communities, and which aided the development of Communist policy in this field.

Most of the volume consists of papers from the Hungarian archives. Documents from the Czechoslovak archives were only included in the volume where there was a direct link with matters documented in the Hungarian papers. This selection principle was applied due in part to space limitations, and in part to considerations of content.

Research on "Jewish policy" in Communist Czechoslovakia and Poland is far ahead of that undertaken for Hungary. Whereas several collection of documents and monographs have been published on the two countries' post-war policies towards the Jewish community and Israel,[34] the studies published on Hungary have addressed only partial questions, and have usually covered the period 1945–1956. Yet among the three countries, Hungary had the highest share of Jewish Holocaust survivors, and during the period covered in the present volume – 1956–1989 – more Jews lived in Hungary than in the other two countries combined. Accordingly – and although most Jews in Hungary were secular – the number of Jewish congregations, their total membership, and the extent of their activities were far greater in Hungary than in Czechoslovakia or in Poland. Thus it was in Hungary that Communist "Jewish policy" had the greatest impact on the Jewish community in terms of the number of people and congregations affected.

After the post-Revolution repression, the post-1963 Communist regime in Hungary is usually portrayed as one of the most liberal and least repressive regimes. It also tends to be characterized as a regime that achieved substantial independence from Moscow. For this reason, we might regard the "Jewish policy" of the Hungarian leadership as the most liberal policy possible during the period in the region. Similarly, the situation of the Hungarian Jewish community and the conditions within which Jewish institutions operated may be viewed as the "maximum" achievable in a Party-state. The documents published below reveal the characteristics and boundaries of this "maximum".

We have organized the documents in the volume around important cases, events and affairs. These papers, edited according to subject-matter and presented (mostly) in

---

[34] Among the many publications, the following are some of the most comprehensive: Marie Bulínová (ed.), *Československo a Izrael v letech 1945–1956. Dokumenty, Ústav pro soudobé dejiny* [Czechoslovakia and Israel in the Years 1945–1956. Documents at the Institute for Contemporary History] (Prague: AV CR, 1993); Labendz, Renegotiating Czechoslovakia; Alina Cała, Helena Datner-Spivak (eds), *Dzieje Żydów w Polsce 1944–1968* [The History of Jews in Poland 1944–1968] (Warsaw: Teksty zdrółowe, 1997); Szyman Rudnicki, Marcos Silber (eds.), *Stosunki Polsko–Izraelskie (1945–1967). Wybór Dokumentów, Nczelna Dyrekcja Archiwów Panstwowych* [Polish–Israeli Relations (1945–1967). Selection of Documents, Head Office of State Archives] (Warsaw: Archiwum Panstwowe Izraela, 2009); Szaynok, *Poland–Israel 1944–1968*.

chronological order, do not document all Jewish-related matters in the entire period; nor do they cover all the details of the various matters. Our primary aim was to reveal in detail Hungarian policy in matters that were on the agenda in each of the East-Central European countries. In doing so, we also sought to provide insights into the operation of the Party-state system in the country with the region's largest Jewish community. The documents published in this volume were created by functionaries working for various institutions of the Party-state, and who used the Communist Party jargon characteristic of the era. This language cannot, in general, be reproduced in English translation. Still, the ambiguous or clumsy sentences in the English text reflect this stifled language. The published documents are texts that their authors dictated to typists. In consequence, they contain numerous typos, particularly with regard to foreign personal names, and the names of foreign institutions. We have not corrected such errors in the text but have marked them with [*sic!*]. Personal names are shown in their correct form in the list of names at the end of the volume. All documents in the volume were classified or marked as "top secret". We omitted this label from the document headings. Further omissions in the documents are indicated by [...]. All emphases in the documents were made by the authors of the document. Emphases and explanatory comments added by the editor appear in [*square brackets* – AK].

The first chapter in the volume contains documents on policies concerning conflicts surrounding emigration to Israel, and the regulation of economic and cultural relations with Israel until 1967. These documents clearly show the intertwining of foreign and domestic policy aspects discussed above.

The second chapter contains Hungarian documents relating to the Eichmann affair, as well as papers from the Czechoslovak archives that offer insights into differences of opinion between the two countries, and into the consultation mechanisms that arose.

The third chapter reveals, by way of Hungarian documents on the Six-Day War, and Soviet sources that were shared with the Hungarian leadership, the *modus operandi* of Eastern bloc leaders at a time of crisis, the means used by Soviet leaders to achieve their goals, and the on-going attempts to manage differences of opinion between the various countries. This chapter also contains documents that show the consequences of the crisis in the Middle East for Jewish policy in a "consolidated" country such as Hungary, where it did not lead to an antisemitic campaign (unlike in Poland), or to internal conflicts among the Communist leadership (unlike in Czechoslovakia). Also contained in this chapter are documents that show the path to the re-establishment of diplomatic relations with Israel in the late 1980s.

The documents in the fourth chapter reveal the policies of the official Hungarian state authority for religious affairs – the State Office for Church Affairs – towards Jewish organizations. Most of the documents relate to policy concerning international Jewish organizations. They clearly show the strategies employed by the major international Jewish organizations during the period, as well as the response of Hungarian Jewish institutions and the Hungarian state to such initiatives.

The fifth chapter contains mainly documents from the archives of the security services. These reveal which matters came under the radar of the security apparatus, the relative importance assigned to such matters, and the aims and means of the surveillance and intimidation of Jewish communities and individuals.

The documents in the collection originate from various periods and cover various matters and institutions. Viewed from today's perspective, however, they are closely related. Overall, they display the conceptual and discursive frames, and the vocabulary used to discuss "Jewish issues". This language – based on old but recontextualized historical stereotypes – was used to communicate on Jewish issues both internally and externally, and remained almost unchanged throughout the period in the region. It was even in Hungary, the most liberal Communist Party-state, a self-evident means of discussing and managing these issues. This was the soil that kept the "Jewish Question" alive during the decades of Communist rule until the very collapse of the system and which then enabled, after 1990, its new public reappearance.

***

Several institutions and persons played an important role in the creation of this volume. The source research, which spanned several years, and the compilation of a volume in English were made possible through generous grants from the Central European University Research Support Scheme, the Public Foundation for Hungarian Jewish Cultural Heritage (MAZSÖK), the Rothschild Foundation Europe and the Alexander von Humboldt Foundation. I am indebted to the Zentrum für Antisemitismusforschung at the Technical University of Berlin, in particular to Werner Bergmann and Stephanie Schüler-Springorum, for hosting me for the research period in Berlin.

For their collaboration in archival research, I am grateful to Kata Bohus, Vera Pécsi and Ágnes Szalai in Hungary, Marie Crhová, Eliška Pekárková and Luboš Studený in the Czech Republic, and Magda Adamovicz, Piotr Andrzejewski, Alexandra Kubica and Krzysztof Palos in Poland. I am also indebted to Michael L. Miller, János Tischler, Krisztián Ungváry and Sergio DellaPergola for their assistance and advice. I would like to express my thanks to Dr Julia Brauch and Dr Werner Treß for their support and patience. Thanks are due to Andrew Gane for translating the documents and to Tamás Fóti, Borbála Klacsmann and Ágnes Ruzsa for helping in the editorial work. The publication of this book would not have been possible without the professional editorial contribution of Dr Gwen Jones. I am very thankful to the Tett és Védelem Alapítvány (Action and Protection Foundation) in Budapest and to the Moses Mendelssohn Center for European-Jewish Studies at the University of Potsdam for supporting the editorial work.

Special thanks are due to Julius H. Schoeps, director of the Moses Mendelssohn Center for European-Jewish Studies at the University of Potsdam, for the support given from the book's conception to its realization.

I Communist Policies and the Jewish State

Introduction

A combination of factors determined relations between East-Central European Communist countries and Israel in the decades between the establishment of the Jewish state and the collapse of the Communist regimes. The role and relative significance of various political, economic and ideological factors changed over time, and the changing circumstances were reflected in these countries' relations with Israel.

During periods when Soviet power interests and an intensification of the Middle East conflict were the main determinants of the relationship, such as in the early 1950s, or after the 1967 war, these countries' policies converged more than they did between 1957 and 1967. Greater policy autonomy at the individual state level was later regained in the second half of the 1980s, when each country had more leeway to develop its own policy towards Israel in line with its particular interests.

These similarities and differences became manifest in several fields: emigration policy, which particularly affected local Jewish communities; economic and cultural relations; and positions taken at international forums. In this chapter we have selected documents that relate to the first two subject areas.

Despite significant differences in numerical estimates, experts agree that the post-1945 waves of emigration to Palestine/Israel from Czechoslovakia, Hungary and Poland rose and subsided concurrently.[1] Between 1945 and 1950, Palestine/Israel received around 20,000 Jewish migrants from Czechoslovakia, over 14,000 from Hungary, and about 100,000 from Poland. Over the next five years, the number of emigrants from these countries fell drastically for several reasons, including restrictions on emigration. In the following period however, the number of emigrants from Poland and Hungary increased once again: between 1956 and 1960, there were probably more than 40,000 Jewish emigrants from Poland (30,000 of them left the country in 1957),[2] and in 1956–1957, more than 4,000 legal emigrants from Hungary. This last figure could be increased by around one-third of the 10–15,000 Jewish emigrants who left Hungary illegally in the aftermath of the 1956 Revolution. By the early 1960s, there had also been an increase in the number of migrants to Israel from Czechoslovakia, a country that had been relatively hesitant to move on from the former Stalinist policies in the wake of 1956: between 1962 and 1966, more than 1,000 persons left the country for Israel.[3]

---

1 I am indebted to Professor Sergio DellaPergola at the Hebrew University of Jerusalem who shared the results of his research on *aliyah*, based on published and unpublished data of the Israel Central Bureau of Statistics. For a review of previous research on Jewish emigration from the various countries to Palestine/Israel, see Karády, *Túlélők és újrakezdők*, 125–133; for a comparative analysis of the data for Czechoslovakia, see Labendz, Renegotiating Czechoslovakia, 31, 104–105, 254–255; and for Poland, see Szaynok, *Poland–Israel 1944–1968*, 202, 297, 385.
2 Ewa Węgrzyn, L'émigration des Juifs de Pologne en Israël dans les années 1956–1959, *Bulletin du Centre de recherche français à Jérusalem* [En ligne], 22 | 2011, mis en ligne le 25 mars 2012, accessed on 24 November 2016 at http://bcrfj.revues.org/6531
3 See Labendz, op. cit., 104–105.

While the figures indicate certain similarities – a degree of liberalisation – in the policies of East-Central European Communist countries towards Jewish emigration at the beginning of the post-Stalinist era, significant differences came to the fore as the post-Stalinist regimes consolidated. It seems that at this time, the official policies of each country, as well as fluctuations in the number of emigrants, were influenced to a far greater degree by local crises which instrumentalised antisemitic sentiment, such as the antisemitic campaign that began in Poland in 1967, and the crushing of Czechoslovak reform attempts in 1968. After the initial waves of immediate post-crisis emigration, the number of emigrants to Israel soon plummeted, such as after 1957 in Hungary and Poland, and after 1968 in Czechoslovakia. During this period, local circumstances and considerations were important factors. The documents presented in this chapter should enable a deeper understanding of the policies pursued during the first post-Stalinist decades. These policies were generally designed to maintain a delicate balance between external factors and expectations on the one hand, and local circumstances and interests on the other.

After the Hungarian Revolution of 1956, the Israeli government was among the first to recognise Kádár's internationally isolated regime, and to establish relations with the Hungarian government at ambassadorial level.

Even before the outbreak of the revolution, the Hungarian government had sought talks with Israel on trade expansion. After the revolution, the Hungarian government moved quickly to reestablish ties broken in 1956. Clearly, it was of great importance to the newly-established Kádár regime to break out of its international isolation. Most of the documents found among the foreign-affairs materials which relate to Israel indicate that the Hungarian government greatly appreciated Israel's willingness to normalise diplomatic relations, and to develop bilateral economic relations. The documents help to explain why the Israeli authorities demonstrated flexibility towards Hungary's Communist government, which was otherwise completely isolated internationally. It appears the Israelis believed that such flexibility, and the rapid expansion of relations between the two countries, would facilitate the migration to Israel of Jews from what was one of Europe's largest Jewish communities. Discussions had commenced in 1956, and were resumed in early 1957. On 12 January 1957, the Hungarian chargé d'affaires in Tel Aviv wrote the following to his superiors in Budapest: "[It] would be of great significance in our economic relations [...] if the Hungarian government were to show a permissive attitude in the matter of Jewish emigration on a larger scale. With appropriate caution, the authorisation of Jewish emigration on a larger scale could be linked with some of our economic aims".[4] Hungarian policy-makers even outlined the first step towards what they hoped to achieve. As Deputy Foreign Trade Minister Jenő Baczoni wrote in an internal memo addressed to Deputy Foreign Minister Károly Szarka: "I suggest that the Ministry of Foreign Affairs should raise with the Israeli government the question of a loan to Hungary in freely convert-

---

4 National Archives of Hungary, XIX-J-1-j 9.d. 15/1957 (12 January 1957).

ible currency via some banking institution [...] the aim could be six to seven million dollars at an interest rate of 2.5–3 per cent, and repayable within five years".⁵

The view that Israel would be open to favourable economic deals in return for the liberalisation of emigration was not unrealistic. A note attached to the previous document, written on 30 July 1956 by a foreign-trade and banking expert negotiating in Paris, contains the following:

> During my most recent stay in Paris, Messrs Pachta and Ernest [*these names reappear in documents relating to subsequent developments – AK*], who own the Transcomin company, and who also have an interest in the Geneva-based Banque Suisse-Israël, raised the following matter: the Israelis would be very pleased if the Hungarian government authorised, within a certain period of time (roughly 12 months), the emigration of 10–12,000 Jews, those with relatives living in Israel. [...] If they were to receive a verbal promise from the Hungarian government, that this request would be considered, , the financial group with close links to the Israelis would be prepared – even without the two matters being visibly connected – to offer certain economic benefits. Indeed, they have offered five million dollars in a cash loan, which would be made available by either Banque Suisse-Israël or another European bank as indicated by them, for a period of several years and at the favourable interest rate of three per cent.

The message relayed by Pachta and Ernest formulated what was to serve as the foundation for discussions and deals in the ensuing years: Israel would offer economic advantages in return for a liberalisation of emigration, while the act of paying ransom for Jews – which neither side could publicly admit to – would never be made apparent, either in official documents, or to the public.

The Israeli authorities thought that after the experiences of the first half of the 1950s, and the suppression of the revolution, many of Hungary's 150,000 to 200,000 Jews would choose to make *aliyah*. Only rough estimates exist on the number of Jews who illegally left the country in the months following the revolution: the numbers fluctuate between 10,000 and 25,000. According to Israeli immigration statistics, about 8,000 of these Jewish emigrants went to Israel.⁶ The Israeli authorities calculated that if legal channels for emigration were opened, this trend would continue, and this assessment seemed to pay off in the first months after the revolution. Israeli Foreign Ministry data do indeed show an increase in legal migration: whereas just 223 persons officially migrated from Hungary to Israel between January and November 1956, the number of official migrants rose to 4,142 between December 1956 and the end of April 1957.⁷

---

5 National Archives of Hungary, XIX-J-1-j 9.d. 1-00109/1957 (15 February 1957).
6 Mark Tolts, Population and Migration. Migration since World War I, *The YIVO Encyclopedia of Jews in Eastern Europe*. Accessed on 28 September 2016 at http://www.yivoencyclopedia.org/article.aspx/Population_and_Migration/Migration_since_World_War_I#id0emxbi.
7 See National Archives of Hungary, XIX-J-1-j 1.d. 001632/1957 (20 May 1957). Citing an estimate of the Israeli legation in Budapest, the document indicates that between 14,000 and 15,000 "persons of Jewish religion" left the country illegally at the time of the revolution and thereafter.

Still, it was not long before this liberal migration policy came to an end. The main reason for this reversal was clearly the general political situation: the Kádár government, installed and imposed upon the country after the Soviet invasion, could not afford to challenge Soviet policies in the Middle East. After the Suez Crisis, relations between the Soviet Union and the Jewish state reached a low point. The principal aim of Soviet policy in the region was to improve and expand relations with the Arab countries in order to achieve greater Soviet influence. After 1956, Hungarian foreign policy could not ignore this fact, particularly because, as Foreign Ministry documents show, the Arab countries had already criticised the improvement in Hungarian–Israeli relations, exemplified by the enhancement of diplomatic relations and the dispatch of a legate to Israel in early 1957. Hungary's Communist government feared that the country's improving relations with Israel might exert a "negative influence" on its own Jewish population, and encourage the Jews to migrate, which was viewed as an undesirable development. The fundamental position of the Hungarian government is reflected in a letter dated 4 May 1957 sent by Péter Kós, head of the Political Department of the Ministry of Foreign Affairs, to the legate Iván Kálló, in response to the latter's report concerning the surprisingly warm welcome he had received on taking up his post:

> The demonstrative ovation on the part of the Israeli official bodies, made in response to the legate's arrival, is a positive phenomenon only in an apparent sense, since it is, at the same time, a dangerous one for us with undesirable effects [...]. An attempt is being made to overstate the cordiality of Hungarian–Israeli relations [...]. But we have no need for such large-scale demonstrations, because irrespective of the transmission of the letter of appointment of their legate during the most difficult period for us [*during the complete foreign-policy isolation of the Kádár government* – AK], to which we wished to respond by sending you, Comrade Legate, there, we still regard Israel as an aggressor [...]. [Israel] is an obedient instrument of the Western imperialist powers which actively cooperates with the Western powers in suppressing the independence ambitions of Arab countries in the Middle East.
>
> By consenting last year to the exchange of legates between the two countries, we did not wish to establish particularly close relations, or to expand relations. For us, the emphasis placed by the Israeli bodies on relations is also unwelcome [...], because this [...] is sincere only as long as we refrain from preventing emigration to Israel by certain sections of the Jewish population living in Hungary [...]. We wish to avoid, at all costs, our relationship with Israel giving rise to an undesirable and needless counter-effect among the Arab countries, of which there have been signs for some time. The General Secretariat of the Arab League has already addressed two diplomatic notes to us, once in connection with the emigration issue and, a second time, concerning the speech made by you, Comrade Legate, on the submission of the letter of appointment in Jerusalem. We ask you, Comrade Legate [...] not to be misled by the apparent affinity shown toward us by the official bodies. At the same time, however, you should continue to seek [...] to assist the expansion of our commercial trade by using your connections, in which field we are willing to expand our relations.[8]

---

8 National Archives of Hungary, XIX-J-1-j 1.d. 001459/2 (4 May 1957).

Against this background, an unexpected incident arose between the countries at just the right moment for the Hungarian authorities. The documents (2–7) below were created during this rather odd episode in Hungarian–Israeli relations, an episode which, however, well illustrates the political aspirations of both sides, and the political mechanisms they used.

In the spring of 1957, shortly after the Hungarian ambassador arrived in Tel Aviv, the Hungarian authorities learnt that a staff member at the Israeli legation in Budapest was regularly receiving cash sums and property from individuals seeking to migrate to Israel. These individuals had been promised that their property and money would be returned to them after arrival in Israel. This was the beginning of what was called the "smuggling affair".

The first suspicions arose when Hungarian authorities noticed that the Israeli legation in Budapest had hardly exchanged any foreign currency for Hungarian forints at the National Bank of Hungary; the sum was certainly not enough to cover its expenditures (Document 2). Then, on 8 April 1957, the head of the Hungarian trade mission in Tel Aviv forwarded a memorandum to his superiors containing a complaint from a recently arrived migrant, who claimed that he had been unable to reclaim his assets deposited at the Israeli legation in Budapest, whereas others arriving in Israel at the same time had been able to reclaim their property.[9] Based on such information, on 3 June 1957, the Hungarian authorities summoned the Israeli Ambassador Meir Tuval and, in a verbal note, they announced their decision to expel the Israeli commercial attaché, whom they considered responsible for these unlawful transactions. The Hungarian authorities also demanded substantial damages, and announced the suspension of all further migration until compensation had been paid.[10]

The government of Israel was embarrassed by the affair, as shown by Ambassador Iván Kálló's report on a meeting with Israel's Foreign Minister Golda Meir on 10 June (Document 2). However, as a memorandum on a second meeting with Meir indicates (Document 3), within a few weeks, the Israelis had established their position: the Israeli legation as an institution had played no part in the matter, but Israel was open to negotiations on compensation. This was music to the ears of the Hungarian authorities.

Hungarian policy-makers in foreign trade and finance (Document 6) first took a pragmatic approach. However, this was not supported by senior staff at the Hungarian Ministry of Foreign Affairs, who had direct and day-to-day contacts with Soviet foreign-policy actors, and with the Soviet legation in Budapest. According to the Hungarian Foreign Ministry, an expansion of and improvement in relations with Israel would elicit a negative reaction in Arab countries where the Soviet Union was seeking to increase its influence. Even prior to the eruption of the "smuggling affair", Péter Kós, head of the relevant department at the Ministry, and reacting to the above offer

---
9 National Archives of Hungary, XIX-J-1-j 1.d. 001632/3 (8 April 1957).
10 National Archives of Hungary, XIX-J-1-j 1.d. 78/Sz-1957 (3 June 1957).

transmitted by Deputy Minister Baczoni, had informed the Hungarian ambassador in Tel Aviv of the following:

> Subject: Conversation with Péter Veress, head of department at the Ministry of Foreign Trade, on Hungarian–Israeli trade problems. [...] Veress inquired whether we could draw advantage from the fact that recently, a larger number of individuals of the Jewish religion have been allowed to move to Israel. In this context, he mentioned that during the discussions in Geneva, certain Israeli individuals had made an offer of a financial loan of around two million dollars, subject to the Hungarian government showing greater understanding for the migration of Jews to Israel. We have not reacted to the offer [...]. We do not wish to make use of a more liberal position on emigration in order to obtain a loan. Moreover, under current political circumstances, we do not intend to request credit from Israel, as this would weaken our positions in the Arab states.[11]

The position of the Hungarian Ministry of Foreign Affairs did not change subsequently. Indeed, on 4 July 1957, having discovered the "smuggling affair", the head of the Fourth Political Department at the Ministry stated the following to the Ambassador:

> [When] the note in question was submitted, our concern was not so much the financial damages suffered in consequence of the irregular administration of emigration, but rather political considerations. In fact, the matter concerned putting a stop to steps taken by the Israeli government (in the aftermath of the exchange of diplomats) to improve relations in a manner that was not desired by us, and to return our relations to the level at which they had been a year previously. Thus, as far as we are concerned, forcing our demand for compensation is unnecessary, particularly because it is primarily in the interest of the Israeli government to settle the issue for its own sake. For them, a more important issue than fulfilling the damages demanded by us is that migration should proceed smoothly. If we were to urge the fulfillment of our claim for damages by the Israeli government, then we might give the appearance of having taken this step expressly because of the claim for damages [...] and that we want to utilise it to obtain dollars.[12]

Amid the unfavourable political and economic circumstances in the aftermath of post-1956 international isolation, and a dire lack of foreign currency, the hardliners did not prevail in the end. The Hungarian side was very keen to continue the talks on financial compensation, while the Israelis wanted the emigration process to resume. Consequently, both sides drove the talks noiselessly towards an agreement without loss of face for either side. Of course, the Israelis continued to insist that they had done nothing illegal, and thus did not owe any compensation. For their part, the Hungarians still claimed that they were not "selling" Jews, and had no intention of allowing Jews to migrate in return for economic favours. In actual fact, however, both sides were thinking the opposite, and both were clearly aware that this was rather obvious to their counterpart. The task was to find a mode of negotiation and compromise that would preserve the two fictions, while also achieving the desired result. Given the

---

11 National Archives of Hungary, XIX-J-1-j 10.d. 001488/1957 (5 March 1957).
12 National Archives of Hungary, XIX-J-1-j 1.d. 002149/2/1957 (4 July 1957).

likely reaction in Arab countries and the close Soviet control of foreign policy, discussions through diplomatic channels were not suitable for this purpose. It was at this point that talks began to be directed by János Fekete, head of the foreign-currency department at the National Bank of Hungary. Fekete was contacted by acquaintances in the banking world, among them Ernest and Pachta, and asked to mediate.

The course of negotiations was summarised by Fekete in his report of 25 June 1958 (Document 7). The bankers in Geneva wished to reach an agreement. Initially, they envisaged making a favourable loan to Hungary, with the Israelis having to make do with rather vague promises of a renewed authorisation of emigration. Shortly after the discussions in Geneva, on 3 September 1958, the Hungarian Ministry of Foreign Affairs submitted a draft motion to the Political Committee of the Party, requesting its approval. Signed by Minister of Foreign Affairs Endre Sík, the motion contains the following:

> If the Israeli side accepts [...] the economic conditions, we authorise Comrade Fekete to adhere to the following negotiating tactics and to finally establish the following agreement concerning the emigration issue. a./ Verbally inform the Israeli side that prior to the completion of negotiations, a senior staff member of the Hungarian Ministry of Foreign Affairs will inform the Israeli legate in Budapest that in the event of the successful conclusion of Hungarian–Israeli financial and economic talks, the competent Hungarian authorities will terminate the restriction on emigration to Israel that was announced in our note of 4 June 1957. If the Israeli side seeks further assurance, then they can be informed that the Hungarian authorities are willing to authorise, as a gesture, the commencement of emigration even before the agreement has been approved. (If the agreement were not to be approved for any reason, emigration could be halted once again.) b./ If the Israeli side does not consider the verbal information to be sufficient assurance, Comrade Fekete should propose the acceptance of the joint statement appearing as an appendix to this motion, in which the oral statements proposed in Point 2 are set down in writing. [*The motion envisages the making of a written guarantee in the form of an exchange of notes* – AK.][13]

An agreement was soon reached. On 22 September 1958, the two sides agreed that Israel would transfer to the National Bank of Hungary the sum of 1.5 million dollars in four instalments. In return, the Hungarian government would resume its authorisation of emigration to Israel. The rather lax definitions of the Hungarian obligations led to the next dispute. The Israelis immediately transferred the first instalment (500,000 dollars) of the agreed sum. This amount, as the documents show, was put together by the Jewish Agency for Israel. The second and third instalments, however, did not reach the National Bank of Hungary by the dates contained in the agreement (30 April and 31 August 1959), because the Israeli side believed that the Hungarians were failing to keep their promise concerning emigration. It would seem the Hungarian government sought to get around the part of the agreement relating to emigration by basing the number of permits on the small number of passports issued in the first six months of 1956, rather than on the number of authorisations in 1957. Thus, the

---
13 National Archives of Hungary, XIX-J-1-j 2.d. 605/SE/1958 (3 September 1958).

Hungarian authorities permitted the emigration of only eight to ten individuals each month.[14] Meanwhile, they cynically gave the impression of being surprised that a connection might be drawn between the two matters of "compensation" and emigration. They argued that:

> 1/ the financial agreement has nothing to do with the issue of emigration; 2/ we undertook to stop discriminating and to provide an opportunity that is generally made available to every Hungarian citizen with regard to emigrating to any point in the world [...]. Therefore, we have fulfilled everything that we undertook and, indeed, we have gone further than this in terms of family unification and humane purposes; for a matter in progress is that of five children seeking to emigrate, whose parents live in Israel.[15]

By the summer of 1959, the emigration of Hungarians had come to a complete halt, and so Golda Meir personally contacted the Hungarian Minister of Foreign Affairs with a view to "reviving" the matter of "compensation" and emigration. Thanks to her efforts, targeted financial talks were reopened between Fekete and Ernest in the autumn. After some haggling, a new agreement was reached by the end of the year: the Israelis agreed not only to the prompt transfer of the remaining instalments, but also to the payment of an additional sum equivalent to an annual rate of interest of five per cent for the duration of the delay. Thereafter, the authorisation of emigration gradually resumed, but the number of permits was far below the level envisaged by the Israelis. According to a memorandum of the Hungarian Ministry of Foreign Affairs, between 1 January and early May 1960, 165 individuals received emigration permits, of whom 55 per cent were between the ages of 20–60, 33 per cent were over 60 years of age and 12 per cent were between the ages of five and 20.[16] After further disputes and mutual reproaches, the Israelis finally transferred the last instalment on 6 January 1961. In the ensuing years, the Hungarian authorities favourably appraised a relatively large proportion of emigration requests, but the percentage began to fall once again from 1964.[17] However, even if Hungarian authorities had authorised all the emigration requests, the total number of migrants would still not have met Israeli expectations. Perhaps this partly explains why, in subsequent decades, the issue of emigration declined in significance as a factor determining relations between Hungary and Israel.

---

14 Between October 1958 and April 1959, the Hungarian authorities permitted the emigration of 60 persons, while around 160 applications were rejected. The Israelis were expecting 4–5,000 people to migrate to Israel. National Archives of Hungary, XIX-J-1-j 2.d. 51/Sz-1959 (16 April 1959).
15 National Archives of Hungary, XIX-J-1-j 2.d. (25 February 1959).
16 National Archives of Hungary, XIX-J-1-j 2.d. 00354, 2.d. (11 May 1960).
17 Authorized emigration from Hungary to Israel was as follows: 1962 – 202 permits from 275 applications; 1963 – 280 permits from 349 applications; 1964 – 201 permits from 396 applications; 1965 – 175 permits from 364 applications. National Archives of Hungary, XIX-J-1-j 2.d. 11/66 (14 January 1966). See Document 8.

After 1961, the waves of the "smuggling affair" gradually subsided, although relations developed mostly in line with the aforementioned guiding principles. The Israeli government, sensing that the Hungarian side had a great interest in the maintenance and possible expansion of economic relations, and in the maximum utilisation of the advantages stemming from such relations, repeatedly attempted to expand relations in the fields of culture, academia and sport. By multiplying and diversifying ties between the two countries, the Israeli side hoped that Hungarian Jews would become closer to the Jewish state, and that more Hungarian Jews would consider making *aliyah*. These attempts, however, were consistently warded off by the Hungarian side, especially whenever the possibility of a bilateral agreement arose. On the other hand, the Hungarians did everything to utilise economic opportunities proffered by Israel, while being very careful to ensure that this was not made public, or brought to the attention of Arab governments.

This situation appears to have changed in the mid-1960s. The documents indicate that some officials directing Hungarian foreign policy and foreign-trade policy believed that the time was right for an expansion of relations with Israel. Evidently, this development was not unrelated to the economic reform efforts that were under way at the time.

Documents (9–15) illustrate this change. They reveal the various factors that had to be considered by those seeking arguments legitimising an expansion of relations, as well as the importance of Hungarian policy not appearing out of step with other Communist governments. Policy-makers in favour of enhancing relations argued that as a consequence of the shift: "We can give assistance to the Israeli progressive forces and can, on occasion, influence the policy of the State of Israel" (Document 12, 15 February 1967). The documents contain detailed information on diplomatic, economic and cultural relations between "Socialist countries" and Israel, indicating to the officials involved how far Hungary could go without upsetting "friendly countries". Indeed, the papers include examples and precedents that Hungary's diplomats could cite in the event of a further improvement in relations with Israel. For those working in the field of foreign relations and trade who supported such a cautious improvement, a constant point of reference was the opinion of the Israeli Communist Party. Evidently, the latter benefitted whenever relations improved, for, as the documents show, the Israeli Communist Party's enterprises oversaw a significant share of Israel's cultural and trade relations with Hungary. In various legation reports and foreign-affairs documents, the presence of a large number of Hungarian native speakers among the Israeli population was also often cited as an argument for expanding relations. For the authors of the reports, this was a factor that the Hungarian government and even the entire "Socialist camp" could exploit to increase political influence. "Even the Soviet ambassador has noted the failure to make use of this opportunity, as have the leaders of the ICP [*Israeli Communist Party*]", stated a summary report dated 15 February 1967.

Yet the documents also show how this policy encountered significant resistance "at home", particularly among officials of the Ninth Department of the Ministry of Foreign Affairs, responsible for relations with Arab countries. Critics of an expansion of relations with Israel cited the likelihood of negative repercussions in Arab countries, and economic retaliatory measures. Supporters of improved relations with Israel countered such arguments by noting the lack of unity in the Arab world (see Document 10): "Within this Arab policy, a certain nuance has recently appeared, and today the position of Arab states (Tunisia, Lebanon and Jordan) is not a unified one". Additionally, the pro-Israeli wing felt itself strong enough to use a political argument: "It would not be correct to treat our policy concerning this relationship merely as a function of our policy towards Arab countries. Those present agreed that if it is rational and necessary, the political efforts of Arab countries should be taken into account, but that this should not be to the detriment of Hungarian sovereignty". At this point, the department responsible for relations with Israel went on the offensive: they suggested that if its proposed policy were to be rejected, the Israel desk should be given to members of staff responsible for relations with Arab countries.

Finally, in early 1967, an expansion of relations seems to have become a real possibility. The document issued on 19 February 1967 by the Sixth Department of the Ministry of Foreign Affairs (responsible for relations with Israel) proposes a relatively broad opening, listing tactical and conceptual arguments. The document, tacitly accepting the Israeli suggestions, proposed to the upper Party organs that relations with Israel should be developed at several levels, and in fields such as transportation, culture, communication, media and tourism.

The minutes of the meeting that relate to the document reveal, however, that this goal was rejected by some foreign policy-makers. In early 1967, opponents of the pro-Israeli wing seemed to be fighting an uphill battle, but the Six-Day War caused a reversal. After the severance of diplomatic relations with Israel, the Ninth Department launched a triumphal counter-offensive. In the document dated 3 November 1967, it took a clear position: "We consider it necessary to review once again Hungarian–Israeli economic relations, so that they are in line with our political position. Currently, these relations are noticeably overplayed, and in our opinion, a significant reduction would be possible without detrimentally affecting our national economy". Still, exploiting the political atmosphere that had emerged in the wake of Hungary's economic reforms, several officials at the Ministry of Foreign Trade sought to resist any drastic changes in economic relations. In a craftily-worded document issued on 17 September 1968, they stated: "We strive to ensure that our commercial trade with Israel should not exceed the level of commercial trade for 1966". (Foreign trade relations had peaked that year.) They then added: "In view of our foreign-exchange situation, the repayment of these items [*long-term debts* – AK] was not considered desirable by our financial authorities". The handwritten remark on the document, signed by Vencel Házi, the Deputy Minister of Foreign Affairs, leaves no doubt that, in this case, political considerations had overwritten economic rationality: "In political terms, our indebtedness is very unwelcome. I discussed [*the matter* – AK] with Comrade P. Veres at the MFT [Ministry of Foreign Trade] and with Comrade Fekete at the NB [National Bank]. We should endeavour to reduce significantly our debt to Israel".

Thereafter, relations between the two countries deteriorated further, and it was only in the 1980s that relations began to improve once more.

Documents

1 On Emigration

Tel Aviv, 8 February 1957

National Archives of Hungary, XIX-J-1-j-Izrael-1/a-00/210-1957 (1.d.)
Collection: Ministry of Foreign Affairs [Külügyminisztérium]

From: Legation of the Hungarian People's Republic in Israel
Subject: reorganisation of the legation's work

[....]

On the emigration issue

We would consider it appropriate for the government to make concessions in this area. This appears particularly justified if we consider the domestic housing shortage and the problems of unemployment. We are convinced that most of those wishing to emigrate are dispensable to our economy. Of course, we must also reckon on the departure of a few good experts. But such people, inasmuch as they wish to leave the country, would not like to work there anyway. It is certain that there would be an international response to this resolution.

On the other hand, we consider it essential to objectively inform those intending to emigrate, in order to prevent the unnecessary to-and-fro migration of people, and bitter disappointment on the part of the migrants. Administrative means can be used to achieve results (e.g. preventing the return [of migrants], etc.), but this will not resolve all the problems. (The Polish chargé d'affaires here, Comrade Slovikovski [sic! – AK], has said that police assistance had to be requested recently in order to deal with the crowds descending upon the legation with the intention of returning [to Poland]. The Poles do not permit the return of recent migrants.) We have to find a way of informing those wishing to emigrate about what awaits them in Israel. With a few individual exceptions (those with rich relatives here or some special connections – above all, a Zionist past), the masses face unemployment and a lack of housing, possibly as well as hard physical labour in the development zones. They have to understand that in Israel there is no need for officials, traders or academics without knowledge of Hebrew, etc. Here, people who work with their two hands are needed, especially cheap agricultural workers. We are of the view that such people are not so common among migrants – on the contrary. The need here is for young people, as soldiers. Unemployment in Israel is nearly catastrophic. Overt disturbances are an indication. The number of unemployed people is rising higher and higher, and this is made even worse by increased immigration. Most migrants face a humiliating life, subsisting on relief aid.

It is not because we disagree with the facilitation of the emigration process that we note all of this. Still, we would like to draw attention to the problems that are likely to arise later on, for which we have no need. Preventing emigration will not solve the problem. But by informing those who are still Hungarian citizens, we can reduce it. In our view, the work of informing people should be the task of the Israeli side, too. They are the ones who know best the difficulties they have with immigrants.

In addition to informing people, there is also a need for administrative measures. It should be made impossible for people to return within a short period of time (or possibly to return at all).

Concerning the effect of facilitating emigration upon relations between the two states, our opinion is as follows. A facilitation of emigration possibilities would clearly have a significant impact on relations between the two states. Doubtless, it would also have some kind of economic impact. But a principle change in these relations is not to be expected. The present ruling circles here are fundamentally opposed to anything that is Communist; thus, we should hardly expect a principal change in their position with regard to our government. Clearly, in terms of outward appearances, there will be signs from the Israeli side of an improvement in relations, but we are sure that as time passes, they will perceive the facilitation of emigration as a sign of the weakness of the Socialist system, rather than as a humanitarian measure on the part of the Hungarian government. It is also to be expected that they will use it as a means for a renewed attack on our system. For the Israeli government, in addition to the general significance, there is particular value in attracting migrants from Socialist countries. First, they hope in this way to obtain productive workers forced to work in Socialist countries. Secondly, by pointing out this emigration, they can assert the non-viability of Socialist countries.

As well as proposing the facilitation of emigration, to the greatest possible degree, we consider it desirable to take the above into account with regard to this issue.

Róbert Garai
Temporary chargé d'affaires

2 Meeting with Golda Meir

Tel Aviv, 10 June 1957

National Archives of Hungary, XIX-J-1-j-Izrael-4/a-02127/1-1957 (2.d.)
Collection: Ministry of Foreign Affairs [Külügyminisztérium]

From: Legation of the Hungarian People's Republic in Israel
Subject: an hour-long meeting with Golda Meir

Completed in 3 copies
2 copies to the Centre
1 copy for the Legation

To Comrade Imre Horváth, Minister of Foreign Affairs
Budapest

As I have already reported by other means, Golda Meir summoned me to a meeting at 3pm on the 7th. I guessed what she wanted to talk about, so I prepared myself to give appropriate answers to all her questions.

At first she assumed a prim and supercilious air, but then quickly retreated.

"I think," she said, "you know why I summoned you. We have here this grave difficulty and, in this connection, the sudden action on the part of the Hungarian government. They have expelled Mr Korem with 72 hours' notice. True, they have now extended it to a sixth day, but it is [punishment] for something that I do not believe happened and cannot even imagine. You know that the Israeli government has the right and opportunity to proceed in a similar manner".

"I know," I said, "but this will not solve the issue of emigration. It was Mr Korem who made the mistake, and that is the truth. I consider it impossible that something like this could have been done without the knowledge of the government and, above all, of the minister [of the legation – AK] or Mr Tuval".

"As a minister [of the legation – AK] I know how much [money – AK] is being transferred by our ministry via the National Bank, I always know how much of that amount is in the bank in Tel Aviv, and whether it is enough or not. Without my signature, no one can withdraw even a pruta. It is needed by the legation. It is impossible not to know about it, and even the government knows how we cover the costs of the legation. It would raise suspicions if we did not ask for money for several years."

She turned as red as paprika. Meir then said that perhaps their aim had been to help Jews that were emigrating. I stated: "The important thing is not why they did it, but that they did it". Once again she made excuses for Tuval and said that they were waiting for Korem and would hold him to account and punish him severely if it were shown that he really did these things.

"We know that it is true because people have come to the legation telling us that they gave 100,000 forints to Korem and received not even a tenth of this sum in Tel Aviv...." (We tried to get something in writing about this which we could send home but, unfortunately, we failed.)

Meir just stared at me and did not refute anything; rather, she said, "I am very sorry that you did not warn me about this, so that I might have stopped it immediately".

I replied that my task is, of course, to inform my own government of such things. "True," she said, "we would accept Mr Korem being sent home, but the fact that your government has simply stopped the emigration is a disaster for us. We think that this is all because the Arabs are exercising pressure on the Hungarians and that you were seeking to satisfy their wishes in this way".

I replied that the Hungarian government has good relations with the Arab countries, as it seeks to have with any other country, but that we are not in any manner dependent upon them and they cannot exert pressure on us, particularly in view of the fact that migrants are also from Arab states. She agreed this was true, but then asked, "Why do you and the Soviet Union prefer to be in a good relationship with the Arabs rather than with us, and yet this is our wish?" I replied that I did not have to explain this.

"Alright, but it is dreadful that your government, in addition to expelling one of our diplomats, is also saying that there will be no more aliya and is demanding 3.5 million dollars. You know that our entire budget is 12 million, and so it is impossible, it cannot be done."

I replied: "If Mr Korem had done harm to the country for just one or two months rather than for years, then the situation would be different".

"Yes," she said, "but 3.5 million – we do not spend such an amount on all the Israeli foreign missions..."

I said: "It is not just that you harmed our country by not making transfers for years, but also that you smuggled out the forints paid there".

Meir did not deny any of this, but then said: "Three and a half million dollars – if the Hungarian government had told us that it needed dollars and that the Israeli government should give it such and such an amount and then it would release so and so many Jews, then you could have understood it".

I rejected this: "Our public finances require dollars and other hard currency as much as other countries, even Israel. One can read and hear quite a lot about the many dollars that are coming here from America. The aim of the Hungarian government was not to make money out of emigration or to defraud the emigrants or Israel, but to provide an opportunity for family reunification. To enable emigration not only for Jews going to Israel, but also for emigration to other places – where such was justified. We did this with the knowledge that this is the correct course of action, and we thought that the Israeli government would also be pleased. What is the point of deflecting from Mr Korem's incorrect actions by making such a statement?"

She was silent for some minutes. "I shall wait," she said, "for Mr Korem [*to explain his actions* – AK] and then I shall ask you once more to meet with me. It is my wish that the good friendship we have should be continued and, of course, the emigration too. I ask also for your assistance. We are pleased to accept the Hungarian government's proposal not to make this matter public, and I hope that we can resolve all the difficulties that have arisen".

I said that in my view, the Israeli government should draw the necessary conclusions and pay damages.

Meir said: "That will be very difficult because it would be the same as acknowledging and admitting to the mistakes".

Meir thanked me for meeting with her again and asked me once again to assist in resolving the matter and to go in again the following week if she summoned me.

Concerning the above, I note that it was good that the Centre informed me of developments in time; it was right to inform Meir of the legation's other remarks concerning the issue.

In my opinion, they will pay the 3.5 million. We were right not to force the loan they had suggested, which was intended merely as a bluff. It is better that we do not even give the impression of wanting to make money out of the matter of emigration – unlike them.

It is possible, and this is what I was informed by way of the Polish chargé d'affaires and the deputy head of department, Sattath, that the Israeli government is planning, in recognition of Tuval's success in managing and promoting emigration in our country, to move him to a place where this is not the case at the moment: to Romania, Bulgaria or the Soviet Union.

A contributing factor is that now, in addition to Korem, he too is involved in the matter, and they will consider it better to remove him from Budapest.

I was met on my arrival by Sattath, who waited for me in the lobby while I spoke to Meir.

(Signature)
(Iván Kálló)
Minister of the legation

3 Second Meeting with Golda Meir

Tel Aviv, 3 July 1957

National Archives of Hungary, XIX-J-1-j-Izrael-4/a-02127/2-1957 (2.d.)
Collection: Ministry of Foreign Affairs [Külügyminisztérium]

From: Legation of the Hungarian People's Republic in Israel
Subject: another meeting with Golda Meir

Completed in 3 copies
2 copies to the Centre
1 copy for the Legation

To Comrade Imre Horváth, Minister of Foreign Affairs
Budapest

As Golda had indicated during our previous discussion, having received Korem's report, she again summoned me; that is, she came here to Tel Aviv. She received me in the presence of Head of Department Eshel.

Golda now seemed much more confident than last time. One could feel that they had been thoroughly deliberating the issue and, possibly, that they had asked for and received counsel. This was clearly why Eshel was taking part in the discussion. He spoke on several occasions. He sometimes interrupted me and, more than once, Golda, especially when she said something untoward. Eshel also wrote down every word.

Both of them confirmed once again that Tuval was a very busy man, who even often works at night (just so that emigration can proceed?) and has no time to deal with economic and financial problems. Thus, it is certain that just as the Israeli government had no knowledge of Korem's activities, so Tuval did not know about them either. They claimed that on several occasions, a large amount of pounds or dollars had been transferred for use by the legation, and that the many consular fees and visa fees had also been used. They emphasised that the one report and the few malicious people who had spoken about Korem did not constitute proof that Korem really had done these things.

Golda stated that she had instructed Tuval to stop these things, and it was certain that they would not be repeated.

I asked what had been stopped, if Korem had not done anything and the report and the words of indignant people were not proof.

As Tuval was in Budapest, and had received the report and resolution indicating that emigration would be possible only within limits and had been told why this was, in my view the best course of action was for the matter to be addressed there. Golda then said that in a day or two she would travel to Vienna, to the conference of the

Socialist International, and would then hold a conference with envoys serving in the surrounding countries. She would meet with Tuval and would give him appropriate instructions on the 7th or 8th.

[....]

[Signature]
(Iván Kálló)
Minister [of the legation]

4 Negotiations on Compensation with Israel

2 September 1957

National Archives of Hungary, XIX-J-1-j-Izrael-4/a-02127/3-1957 (2.d.)
Collection: Ministry of Foreign Affairs [Külügyminisztérium]

To Deputy Minister Jenő Baczoni
Ministry of Foreign Trade
Budapest

Completed in 2 copies

With reference to the inter-ministerial discussion held under the leadership of Comrade Baczoni, Deputy Minister at the Ministry of Foreign Trade on the 24th of the above month and concerning the above issue, the Ministry of Foreign Affairs considers it necessary to record its position in written form below on several issues connected with the upcoming Hungarian–Israeli compensation negotiations.

Our note on the subject of smuggling undertaken by the Israeli legation in Budapest in the course of emigration from Hungary to Israel clearly states that the activities of the Israeli official organs, representing a grave violation of international law and the laws of Hungary, caused damage to the Hungarian national economy to a value of 3.5 million US dollars. For this reason, the Hungarian government suspended emigration until the above amount is refunded by Israel. The Israeli government could not refute the findings made in the note and, as the resumption of emigration is an important Israeli interest, it requested through diplomatic channels that an Israeli economic expert should negotiate with Hungarian economic experts on the issue of damages. The Hungarian government consented, again by diplomatic channels, to negotiations, subject to the talks being limited to determining the means of compensating for the aforementioned amount of damages and would not deal in any manner with the issue of emigration.

Based on the above, the Ministry of Foreign Affairs agrees that the Hungarian negotiating delegation should comprise representatives of the Ministry of Foreign Trade and Finance under the leadership of Béla Szilágyi, head of department at said Ministry.

The direct participation of a representative of the Ministry of Foreign Affairs in the delegation would enable the Israeli side to raise the issue of emigration, and so this would not be expedient. At the same time, it is, of course, necessary that the negotiating delegation should maintain a continuous and close relationship with the Ministry of Foreign Affairs and discuss with it any issue that falls into its purview. If such an issue – for example, the extent of payable damages – is raised by the Israeli side, then the Hungarian delegation should state that it is not competent to discuss the matter and that, if they so wish, they should follow diplomatic channels.

For the Comrade Deputy Minister's information, I state that the Ministry of Foreign Affairs considers the resumption of emigration to be possible only after our claim to damages, amounting to the sum indicated, has been paid off in full by the Israeli side. We cannot grant any obligation with regard to the number of people who will be allowed to emigrate in the future, as this would give rise to accusations of "trading in people". For this reason, the Israeli negotiating side should be made aware that it is in their interests to choose the quickest method for paying the damages caused in hard currency or commodities, or in some other way that the Hungarian government has accepted as suitable.

Concerning this matter, I will inform the Comrade Deputy Minister of any information I receive through diplomatic channels.

(István Sebes)
Deputy Minister

5 On the Israeli Legation in Budapest

12 December 1957

National Archives of Hungary, XIX-J-1-j-Izrael-4/a-02127/6-1957 (2.d.)
Collection: Ministry of Foreign Affairs [Külügyminisztérium]

From: Ministry of Interior
Subject: the illegal financial aid payments of the Israeli legation

Report

The Israeli legation in Budapest has been involved for years in illegal financial aid payments. The people that they consider important receive regular monthly payments amounting to between 300 and 2,500 forints. Prior to the counter-revolution [*the Hungarian revolution of 1956* – AK], the number of recipients was as high as 150 to 200. This financial aid programme resumed after the counter-revolution and is currently under way.

[…]

The activity described above is damaging from the perspective of the Hungarian People's Republic. One should also consider the fact that this amount could only have got to the legation illegally because, as we mentioned in our previous memorandum and the official memorandum of the National Bank, the most recent exchange of forints took place on 2 September, a sum that clearly does not cover their expenditures.

[…]

We think the Hungarian Ministry of Foreign Affairs should remind the legation of the aforementioned problems as described in the memorandum that is being drafted, and should demand from it the immediate termination of such detrimental actions.

[Signature]
Colonel Jenő Hazai, police investigator
Head of Department

6 Negotiations on Compensation with Israel

31 March 1958

National Archives of Hungary, XIX-J-1-j-Izrael-4/a-00760/4-1958 (2.d.)
Collection: Ministry of Foreign Affairs [Külügyminisztérium]

From: Ministry of Foreign Trade

To Comrade Károly Szarka
Deputy Minister of Foreign Affairs
Budapest

With reference to file number RK 1143/1958 and by way of our legation in Tel Aviv, we wish to give the following answer to Comrade Szendrő, if the Ministry of Foreign Affairs agrees in principle with the answer:

As before, it is desirable to present our position in the form of a private opinion. It is important in principle to insist on the compensatory nature throughout. Later, we can be conciliatory in how this is expressed in a formal sense.

We may possibly accept the offer [*of credit* – AK] of seven million dollars. In case of such a concession, however, we cannot relinquish our demand that we should receive the sum in dollars and completely free of interest. To facilitate discussions, we may possibly request a third of the sum in US dollars, while the remaining amount could be indicated in the following commodities: rubber; fine wool; wool fibre; synthetic yarn and fibre; industrial diamonds; copper; copper sulphate; sheet metal, and pulpwood. We consider a solution to be possible where, in place of some of the indicated commodities, the Israeli side agrees to finance our purchases, for instance by way of a Swiss bank.

Regarding the means of repayment, the guiding principle could be that we would repay using commodities according to the export structure traded in the Hungarian–Israeli clearing system, but the composition of the commodities may, of course, change in the course of the next ten years. It is important, however, that the repayment be made within a period fixed on expiry of the ten-year period: for example, over two to three years.

The opinion should be made known that if they see a possible solution based on our concession in accordance with the above, then it would be desirable for representatives to meet in a third country, who would clarify the framework, that is, who would conduct negotiations of a non-diplomatic nature.

In the above, while maintaining our principles, we have sketched flexible possible solutions. Comrade Szendrő may make full use of these in accordance with our interests. In support of this private opinion, it is desirable that he avoid finalising a position with respect either to the amount or to the commodities. Rather, he should indicate that he considers it possible that we might agree on an amount that is less than ten million. He should also list the articles, but [*indicate that* – AK] he considers it possible that these could be supplemented with other articles of similar value; and he should indicate only approximate estimates with regard to the ratios.

(Signature)
Gyula Karádi

7 Negotiations on Compensation with Israel

4 July 1958

National Archives of Hungary, XIX-J-1-j-Izrael-4/a-00760/6-1958 (2.d.)
Collection: Ministry of Foreign Affairs [Külügyminisztérium]

From: Ministry of Finance

To Comrade Károly Szarka
Deputy Minister of Foreign Affairs
Budapest

I attach János Fekete's report on the compensation negotiations with Israel.

With comradely greetings,
István Antos

Attachments: One

25 June 1958

Comrade István Antos
Minister of Finance
Budapest

Subject: report on talks concerning the compensation claim against Israel

Based on instructions from Comrade Kardos, Deputy Finance Minister, my task was to contact the persons who, in February 1958 in Vienna, had contacted me with the purpose of channelling the diplomatic negotiations between Hungary and Israel towards economic issues. Concerning that meeting, I informed Comrade Minister Antos in a memorandum after my return home.

The persons with whom I held talks in February are: Monsieur Ernest, who was already known to me through previous banking business and who is the director of the Parisian bank Société Bancaire et Financière d'Orient; and an individual who introduced himself as Joshua Dan, and possesses an Israeli diplomatic passport. As a personal colleague of the Israeli Prime Minister, Mr Dan claimed to have received a special assignment to channel the compensation talks conducted by diplomatic channels towards economic issues.

Concerning Joshua Dan, Szendrő, our commercial counsellor in Israel, has in the meantime obtained information according to which Dan's claims are true. Based on the information supplied by Commercial Counsellor Szendrő, I have further determined that Tuval, the Israeli minister of the legation in Budapest, is also aware of these separate talks.

With regard to the Parisian bank, of which Mr Ernest is a director, I have determined that 50 per cent of its share capital is owned by a bank called Banque pour le Commerce Suisse Israelién, while the other 50 per cent [*is owned by* – AK] Mr Ernest and a Parisian businessman called Pachta, who is also known to me by way of previous commercial business.

For its part, the Suisse Israelién Bank is 50 per-cent owned by the State of Israel and 50 per-cent by private capital.

My assignment was to seek to make contact with the aforementioned persons while attending the general meeting of the Bank for International Settlements, held in Basel on 7–10 June 1958. Prior to travelling, among the several means of communication (telephone, telegram, letter – each addressed to the bank in Paris), it was agreed that an intention to negotiate would not be communicated in advance, but that I would seek to come into contact with the aforementioned in an inconspicuous manner during my stay in Switzerland.

I departed for Basel on 7 June, travelling by way of Vienna and Zürich, and accompanied by Comrade Dénes Szántó. At Zürich Airport, we were required to wait around two and a half hours for the plane to Basel. While waiting at Zürich Airport I met with Mr Pachta, who was flying to Paris with his wife and two children and who happened, like us, to be waiting for his plane. Pachta greeted me with joy and, having remarked on some deals in Brazil, asked me whether I would be willing to continue the talks I had begun by way of his partner Mr Ernest in February. I replied that there was no point in my negotiating with them in this matter, and that to my knowledge talks were under way in Tel Aviv. He stated that if I were prepared to resume talks with him, Mr Dan would arrive in Switzerland within days, and he asked me to inform him of my schedule in Switzerland. I replied that at the start of the following week I would be busy with the general meeting of the Bank for International Settlements and would have no time for them; but that on the following weekend, I would spend a few days in Geneva, where I would only have a number of shorter bank meetings. I said that I did not believe that there was much point in resuming the talks begun in February, because as a banker I could only concern myself with talks on specific economic issues. However, if, in their opinion, the Hungarian compensation claim could be solved through talks of a specific economic nature, I would be at their disposal. He [*Pachta* – AK] stated that he would phone me from Paris mid-week and tell me whether or not, under such circumstances, Dan saw any purpose in holding the talks – and, if he did, where and when we could meet.

On Thursday 12 June, Mr Ernest phoned me and, with reference to the conversation with Pachta, he stated that on Saturday he and Dan would contact me at the Richmond Hotel in Geneva.

[....]

At midday on Saturday, he contacted me at the Richmond Hotel in Geneva and, after making several Brazil switch proposals relating to commercial deals of little significance, he said that he believed the negotiations in Israel would be fruitless, but that various members of the Israeli government and certain Israeli political circles would be pleased to see an agreement made. In his opinion, an agreement could be reached, as long as the demands were realistic. He stated that Dan would arrive shortly and then we could begin talks.

Dan did indeed arrive a short time afterwards, and we held the first talks, attended by Dan, Ernest and myself. Dan asked whether, since our meeting in February, I had concerned myself with this matter and whether I had some kind of authorisation to negotiate. I replied that in February, after my return home, I had, of course, sought information about the matter and had concluded, based on concrete data, that after the counter-revolution, the Hungarian government had permitted, completely free of charge, the emigration of a significant number of Hungarian citizens, who had been allowed to take most of their belongings with them. In an abuse of the generosity of the Hungarian government and in violation of the law, the official Israeli bodies in Budapest had assisted the illegal smuggling of Hungarians' assets out of the country. According to the Hungarian authorities, a great number of gold coins and other valuables had thus been smuggled out. As a manager at the foreign-currency department of the National Bank of Hungary, I saw a substantial foreign currency loss in the fact that the emigrants, rather than offering their gold and foreign currency assets for purchase by the National Bank, had smuggled those assets out of the country concealed on their person. Thus, in my view, leaving aside the other damages, they had caused a significant foreign-currency loss to the Hungarian People's Republic. Having uncovered such illegal manipulations, the Hungarian government had suspended emigration to Israel and announced its claim to compensation for the damages caused. Negotiations were under way in Tel Aviv between representatives of the Hungarian and Israeli governments.

The Hungarian government had thus appointed its representative in the matter. However, as Mr Dan claimed that the Israeli government was not seeking an agreement at the negotiations in Tel Aviv, and wished to settle the matter through a representative of the National Bank of Hungary, I would be willing to negotiate with them and if, on the basis of the talks, I saw an opportunity to reach an agreement, I would make a proposal to the competent Hungarian bodies concerning a settlement in this manner. However, prior to the commencement of substantive negotiations, I wished to inform them of the principles according to which I would be prepared to negotiate:
1. The Hungarian government has a legitimate claim to damages in view of the losses to its national economy stemming from the unlawful activities of the Israeli bodies.

2. As a banker, I am only prepared to negotiate a damages claim settlement involving free-exchange payment, as I am not competent in commodity exchange.
3. In the event of an agreement, I do not promise anything other than that I will make a proposal for the termination of the discrimination with respect to emigration, which was introduced against them due to their own errors. That is, even in the event of an agreement, the emigrants to Israel would have no greater right than people seeking to migrate to any other country.

In his response, Dan stated, in connection with the first issue, that they were unwilling to acknowledge openly the damages claim, because, for them, this would set a grave precedent. They were willing to make some compensation but only in such a form that the compensatory nature [*of the payment* – AK] did not become apparent. And this, however, could be achieved only on a commercial basis rather than through diplomatic channels, for their position regarding the negotiations in Tel Aviv was that discussions would carry on for years without a result being reached.

Concerning the second issue, his opinion was that they had always envisaged the matter being resolved in commodities and would like to retain this position.

Concerning the third issue, his response was that they would like to receive a specific promise, in the event of an agreement, concerning emigration.

Finally, he noted that he did not consider his responses to be final, and he would think about them one more time, and then give an answer the following day as to whether he accepted the principles outlined by me as the basis for negotiations. He assured me that the negotiations would be completely confidential in nature: in Israel, only the Prime Minister, the Finance Minister and the competent persons at the Ministry of Foreign Affairs would know, and he asked that we too should treat the negotiations confidentially. I agreed with him about this, and we came to an agreement.

We agreed to resume the talks on Sunday morning.

On Sunday morning, I duly appeared once again and, returning to the debate of the previous day, Dan asked why I was insisting on a settlement in free exchange. I replied that I was not insisting on this, because in the course of talks in Tel Aviv there was discussion of payment in commodities, but inasmuch as they wish to resolve the issue by means of talks with the representative of the National Bank of Hungary, it was only natural that the agreement would primarily be one of free exchange. In any case, it was their wish that the matter be settled by the narrowest possible circle, and this would be almost impossible if various commodity deals were made involving a lot of companies. It is my feeling that this greatly aroused the attention of Dan, for he answered that they had not even considered how a settlement in commodities might come at the expense of confidentiality, and that for his part he accepted free-exchange payment as the basis for negotiations.

Concerning payment for damages, they still did not wish to acknowledge in writing that they were obliged to provide compensation and, in his view, some kind of compromise solution had to be found. For if the compensation were to be made in the form of loan, for which there would be a minimal rate of interest, then on the one hand the interest saved would represent the compensation, while on the other hand, given that we were talking about a loan, an open acknowledgment of compensation could be avoided. I replied that inasmuch as we were to choose a form of credit, we would have to receive the loan completely without interest, because an interest-free loan would amount to acknowledgement of the compensation claim, and this would be the case even if they did not write it down. For our part, we insist that the agreement would in some way make clear that we are not seeking to link the emigration of Hungarian citizens to some financial benefit, but that the Israeli side should, at least in part, provide compensation for the loss to our national economy. At this juncture, we agreed that if negotiations were continued, we would return to this point.

With regard to the resumption of emigration to Israel in the event of [*the signing of* – AK] an agreement, they acknowledged what I had told them, but Dan expressed hope that such an agreement would lead to a general improvement in Israeli–Hungarian relations.

In conclusion, Dan proposed that I should consent to the resumption of talks as soon as possible in some Western country. He had no authorisation to make a final agreement, as his task was to clarify the possibility of such an agreement. He was to return to Tel Aviv and he or others would seek to resume the negotiations, having received full authorisation to do so. I replied that I could not travel to and fro to continue the negotiations, as I was busy. If, however, I were to be informed by way of the Parisian Bank that they wished to continue negotiations on the basis of a serious offer, then I would propose to Budapest that I or another economic expert should continue the negotiations. I emphasised, however, that this would only be possible if they assured me that in the next negotiations, authorised persons would make a realistic offer because I considered the offers made known so far to be insubstantial. Dan promised that he would inform me by way of the Parisian bank, prior to 30 June, as to whether the Israeli side wished to continue negotiations under these conditions.

Dan departed on Sunday evening, and on Monday morning I met once more with Ernest, reminding him that if he attributed importance to banking commercial relations with Hungary, then with respect to the proposal for further talks which the Israeli side would make through him, he should first check the seriousness of the proposal, for if on the resumption of talks they were to present an insubstantial offer, I would hold him personally responsible. Ernest replied that it was clear to him that if his role in this were to appear incorrect to us, this would influence detrimentally his bank's business relations in Hungary.

Finally, I inquired as to his opinion concerning how far the Israeli side was prepared to go. I said that I considered the Israeli offers that had been made so far to be insubstantial and that I saw no guarantee that this route could lead to more fruitful negotiations.

Ernest, while emphasising on several occasions that what he was saying did not imply an obligation, said that in his view an interest-free loan of three to four million dollars for three to four years might be obtained. This, however, was only his private opinion. He promised that if he were to be asked by the Israeli side to make a proposal concerning the resumption of negotiations, then he would first inform himself about the nature of the Israeli offer. If I had any further suggestions, he asked me to call him in Paris. If I had no such suggestions, then we agreed that he would contact me before the end of June.

[…]

During the conversation I obtained a few bits of information. According to Ernest, the Israeli side is insisting on negotiations with the National Bank of Hungary because they think that we will keep the promises made by the Bank, even if these promises are not made in writing. They base this on the fact that, so far, the National Bank of Hungary has always kept to its written and oral agreements. According to Ernest, there are problems with emigration in Romania too – it is important to the Israeli government that emigration from Hungary should resume, as they hope this would revitalise emigration from Romania. Concerning the Hungarian–Israeli negotiations, there are two positions in Israel. Some people are opposed to an agreement and the negotiations in Tel Aviv are being conducted in line with such an attitude, while some Israeli and other, principally international forces (Jewish Agency), give great emphasis to a resumption of emigration and they are calling for an agreement to be reached.

Summary:

Based on the negotiations and the conversation with Comrade Szendrő, in my view there do exist in Israel forces seeking the completion of the negotiations. Dan, who is conducting the negotiations, belongs to Prime Minister Ben-Gurion's immediate circle. It is also evident that in the course of negotiations, they will try to avoid making a public acknowledgement of the damages claim, for they fear that the other People's Democracies might then make similar claims on that basis. It seems that in general they are experiencing difficulties in connection with emigration, and they have a serious interest in the commencement of emigration from Hungary. For them, emigration results in a financial benefit, for they receive a certain amount of support from the international Jewish organisations, and in part it is also militarily significant. They know that we have data about their dealings in Hungary and they do not want such data to be made public. Thus, if an agreement is made between us, for the sake of their own interests they will not make it public.

Concerning the potential amount of damages, I think that the Israelis wish to come to an agreement on a loan worth approximately five million dollars.

A realistic goal – in my opinion – is that the repayment of the loan be made in four or five years' time, in part by supplying Hungarian commodities in the Israeli clearing system, whereby a part of the commodities will be soft articles.

If, by the end of the month, the Israeli side returns to the matter and proposes a resumption of negotiations by way of the Parisian bank, then in my opinion the negotiations should be continued along this route, while at the same time, we should keep alive the negotiations being conducted through diplomatic channels, neither calling for them nor imposing obstacles.

8 The Condition of Hungarian–Israeli Relations

7 September 1960

National Archives of Hungary, XIX-J-1-j-Izrael-4/a-sz.n.-1960 (3.d.)
Collection: Ministry of Foreign Affairs [Külügyminisztérium]

From: Ministry of Foreign Affairs
Sixth Regional Department
Israeli desk

Completed in 5 copies
Minister Sík
Deputy Minister Szarka
Department (2)

Memorandum

Subject: the condition of Hungarian–Israeli relations

The condition of Hungarian-Israeli relations has not changed essentially in relation to the situation in 1959. The Israeli government continues to assign the problem of emigration a central place in relations between the two countries, and its efforts are directed at increasing the number of migrants and at accelerating the process where possible. To encourage people to emigrate, the Israeli government is constantly making initiatives in the cultural field, a majority of which we seek to avoid.

The issue of emigration from Hungary to Israel:

Based on the amended agreement (December 1959) on the issue of compensation, we gave permission for the resumption of emigration to Israel as of January 1960. By 1 May 1960, we had issued in total 165 emigration permits. The Israeli government met its obligation: it paid three instalments of the compensation claim at the end of January, March and June, amounting to 1,250,000 dollars.
    The Israeli government, however, was still not satisfied with this rate of emigration, and by way of its diplomatic representative here, it has kept the issue on the agenda and has used every occasion to call for people to be allowed to emigrate. In April 1960, the Israeli minister of the legation submitted a list to the ministry, containing the names of 372 persons that they consider important. The competent authorities had already rejected, on several occasions, the emigration applications of persons on the list.

Since the Israeli minister of the legation was unable to persuade the leaders of the ministry to increase significantly the number of people permitted to emigrate, on 5 May, Mr J. Dan, a representative of the Jewish Agency, travelled to Hungary, where he and the minister of the legation contacted Deputy Minister Szarka. The aim of their visit was to express their government's dissatisfaction with the rate of emigration and to request the liberalisation of emigration. They also made mention of the idea that we should make emigration to Israel subject to special considerations. Their proposal met with a negative response.

Thereafter, on 18 May 1960 Yaron, the Israeli minister of the legation, bearing a letter from Minister of Foreign Affairs Golda Meir, contacted Comrade Minister Sík. In her letter the Israeli Foreign Minister referred to a conversation held with Comrade Sík in New York on relations between the two countries, concluding that the rate of emigration (family unification) had caused them disappointment. We did not reply to the letter of Minister of Foreign Affairs Golda Meir. As the letter was being delivered, Comrade Sík told the Israeli minister of the legation that the number known to us (165 persons) was considerably higher than the number Golda Meir had indicated in her letter (70 persons), and it significantly exceeded the number featured in the memorandum cited by Yaron (130 persons). At the same time, Comrade Sík reminded the minister of the legation of the information given to Golda Meir, according to which they should not expect mass emigration from Hungary.

According to the information available to us, between 1 January and 31 July 1960, in total 203 persons received emigration permits for the purpose of emigration to Israel. From this figure, 75 persons feature on the list submitted by the Israeli minister of the legation in April. Concerning the month of August, we have no data for the number of emigration permits granted. (Payment of the final instalment of the compensation sum and the five per-cent interest on the 1,000,000 dollars must be made, according to the agreement, on 30 September.)

[...]

9 Current Issues of Hungarian–Israeli Relations

14 January 1966

National Archives of Hungary, XIX-J-1-j-Izrael-4/a-sz.n.-1966 (2.d.)
Collection: Ministry of Foreign Affairs [Külügyminisztérium]

From: Ministry of Foreign Affairs
Sixth Regional Department

Completed in 5 copies

Gábor Bebők
Secretary, Second Dept.
11/66

Memorandum

Subject: information on current issues of Hungarian–Israeli relations

[...]

The State of Israel was formed at the end of May 1948 based on the 1947 Resolution of the General Assembly of the United Nations. Hungary recognised the State of Israel in 1948, establishing diplomatic relations with Israel. We opened our first foreign mission in Tel Aviv in June 1950, and it was headed until the spring of 1957 by a permanent chargé d'affaires. Given that after the counter-revolution, Israel was the first to recognise the Revolutionary Worker-Peasant Government at the beginning of 1957, we exchanged – having regard for Hungarian foreign-policy interests – envoys, and our legation was headed by a minister of the legation from March 1957 until July 1958. There were two reasons why our minister was summoned home: first, an improvement in our relations with the Arab countries; and second, the questionable actions of Israel in Hungary, which were prejudicial to our interests: the Israeli legation in Budapest engaged in serious economic misconduct in connection with the emigration of Hungarian Jews; to increase emigration, the Israeli side made use of the World Jewish Congress and the World Federation of Hungarian Jews, thereby causing considerable confusion among the Jewish population in Hungary. Since then, our legation in Tel Aviv has been headed by a temporary chargé d'affaires.

Emigration figures in recent years:
Authorised emigration in:
1962: 202 permits from 275 applications
1963: 280 permits from 349 applications
1964: 201 permits from 396 applications
1965: 175 permits from 364 applications

In our appraisal of applications, we take the position that we also take with respect to other Western countries.

At present, Israel is almost continuously calling for an exchange of ministers and for the upgrading of diplomatic relations; it also seeks closer relations in the economic and cultural fields.

For political reasons, we are keeping relations between Hungary and Israel within a modest framework. Despite this, Arab concerns about Hungarian–Israeli relations have been raised by the UAR's ambassador to Budapest and – most recently – by Jordan's chargé d'affaires in Moscow.

[…]

10 Problems Concerning Relations with Israel

Not dated, probably July 1966

National Archives of Hungary, XIX-J-1-j-Izrael-Vietnam-1-sz.n.-1966 (62.d.)
Collection: Ministry of Foreign Affairs [Külügyminisztérium]

From: Ministry of Foreign Affairs
Handwritten note: It will be discussed with the participation of Comrades Szarka and Szilágyi

Sixth Regional Department	Completed in 5 copies
Gábor Bebők	1. Péter Mód
András Ilyés	2. Károly Erdélyi
	3. János Berecz
	4. N. János Lőrincz
	5. István Beck, Comrades
Received earlier:	János Péter
	Béla Szilágyi
	Károly Szarka
	Elek Tóth
	Tibor Zádor, Comrades,
	Tel Aviv

For the Deputy Ministerial Conference

Memorandum

Subject: discussion with Comrade Csécsei on problems concerning relations with Israel

On the 15th of the above month, during the vacation of the heads of the foreign representations, we held the normal discussion on relations [with Israel – AK] with Comrade Csécsei at Deputy Minister Szilágyi's office [...].

[....]

3.) Concerning Hungarian–Israeli relations, we concluded that our political and cultural relations are falling behind our economic relations, and are also falling behind the relations maintained by other Socialist countries with Israel. The time has not yet come for the upgrading sought by the Israeli side, but filling the legate's post does seem necessary, although the practical realisation of this must be delayed until a more suitable time. (Soviet Union and Poland maintain relations at ambassadorial level, while Romania and Yugoslavia do so at legate level.)

The conference agreed with the department's proposal that we should also pursue a principled policy with regard to Israel, and that it would not be correct to treat our policy concerning this relationship as merely a function of our policy towards the Arab countries. Those present agreed that, if it is rational and necessary, the political efforts of the Arab countries should be taken into account, but that this should not be to the detriment of Hungarian sovereignty. At present, in many cases, the Ninth Regional Department [*responsible for the contacts with the Arab countries* – AK] rather than the department responsible for relations [*with Israel* – AK] decides upon our measures and actions. Consequently, we are not utilising sufficiently the opportunities at hand, a fact often noted by the parties of the left there and both groups within the Communist Party.

If a change in this area is not possible, we consider it necessary to place relations with Israel under the direction of the Ninth Regional Department in the future.

In the development of our cultural relations we have, until now, held back to the extent that even the Soviet ambassador in Tel Aviv has noted the matter. The existence of a Hungarian-speaking population of about 200,000 justifies an improvement in our cultural relations. Comrade Szilágyi agreed with the proposal that we should keep Hungarian–Israeli relations in a suitable framework and under control. With this in view, we should expand our cultural relations based on a working plan that is to be implemented mainly on an impresario basis containing four to five events annually (soloists, smaller ensembles, etc.) but still controlled by us (ICR [*Institute for Cultural Relations*]) and is not to be regulated by any kind of signed document. In this way, we wish to achieve the monitoring of relations and a reduction in the number of "private trips", and this would also help to ensure that our cultural life is represented in Israel only by such Hungarian cultural figures that have been found suitable by the bodies responsible.

An improvement in our informative work also seems necessary. We agreed with Comrade Csécsei's proposal that one should permit the legation to hold at least two film presentations annually, and that the necessary films should be provided to it. In addition, an appropriate number of short and feature films should be made available to the legation for the purpose of presentation in Hungarian-speaking areas (Kibbutzim, factories, etc.).

It seems expedient to provide our legation in Tel Aviv with literature in Hungarian, so that it can, from time to time, donate books to libraries operating in Hungarian-inhabited kibbutzim and plants.

Relations with the Israeli press are, generally speaking, satisfactory; in Comrade Csécsei's opinion, there are occasional opportunities to place articles. However, the legate's relations with the Hungarian-language daily Új Kelet [*New East*] have recently undergone a general deterioration, especially because of the articles by the chief editor, Dezső Schőn [sic! – AK], on Comrade Kállai's trips to Egypt and Kuwait. (We have placed Dezső Schőn on the blacklist and have denied him permission to enter Hungary in spite of his request.) Our legation does, however, maintain relations with other members of staff at Új Kelet.

[.....]

The flight issue is an old problem. According to the verbal information received from MALÉV [*Hungarian Airlines*], the most advantageous solution would be a direct flight, which we would operate with charter planes in the tourist season and would not feature in the schedule. The idea that scheduled MALÉV planes should transport passengers between Budapest and Nicosia has already been realised. In connection, we shall ask for MALÉV's official written opinion. In addition, IBUSZ [*the Hungarian tourist agency*] has signed an agreement – currently, for 1967 only – with SABENA, under the terms of which SABENA will spend 5,000 dollars per year in Israel on the promotion of tourism to Hungary, and will transport the tourists to Belgrade, from where they will be brought in MALÉV planes to Budapest. (For MALÉV, however, it would be more advantageous to bring the tourists from as far away as possible, if possible from the place of departure and without a stopover, because this would increase its foreign-exchange revenue.)

As regards setting up a boat service, the commercial department of MAHART [*Hungarian Shipping Company*] stated at a meeting that it would be economic to put on two or three ships, which would call at Israeli ports. A sufficient amount of goods seems assured. If the Arab countries were to put the boats and their personnel on the blacklist, the boats on this route could still be utilised in an economic manner, because they could, without hindrance, undertake trade with respect to Turkish, Greek, and Yugoslav ports. We shall request written information concerning the possibilities from MAHART as well.

The opinion arose that if it is economically advantageous for MALÉV and MAHART to establish contact with Israel, this should not be prevented by the Ministry of Foreign Affairs.

11 Relations Between Israel and the Socialist Countries in 1966

Tel Aviv, 5 January 1967

National Archives of Hungary, XIX-J-1-j-Izrael-1/t.-00652-1967 (49.d.)
Collection: Ministry of Foreign Affairs [Külügyminisztérium]

From: Legation of the Hungarian People's Republic
Subject: development of relations between Israel and the Socialist countries in 1966

Completed: in 5 copies
4 for the Centre
1 for the Legation

In 1966, there was no essential change in cultural relations between Israel and the Eastern European Socialist countries. There was a certain amount of growth, relative to the previous year, in ensembles and solo artists performing in Israel. Experience shows that the domestic political situation in Israel and the border incidents between Israel and the neighbouring Arab countries influence only slightly the implementation of the cultural agenda with the Socialist countries.

The socialist countries with commercial relations with Israel are slowly increasing their trade from year to year. With the exception of Yugoslavia, the Socialist countries do not generally deliver capital investment goods to Israel, for they do not want to jeopardise their political and economic relations with the Arab countries.

Socialist countries export primarily agricultural products, foodstuffs and raw materials to Israel. In its exports to Socialist countries, Israel is pressing for an increase in the export of citrus fruits, textiles, and small industrial finished products, in return for which it wishes to import foodstuffs and raw materials.

Below we present the number of ensembles and solo artists from the Eastern European Socialist countries performing in Israel in 1966, as well as the development of commercial trade in recent years.

From Bulgaria, in 1966, a circus and a solo violinist guest performed in Israel. The circus was here for more than half a year.

Commercial trade between Israel and Bulgaria, in thousands of dollars

	1961	1962	1963	1964	1965	1966, first half-year
Exports to Israel	1,419	2,172	2,842	2,776	3,478	1,090
Imports from Israel	1,304	2,229	1,813	3,146	3,078	1,363
	+115	−57	+1,029	−370	+400	−273

Relations between Israel and Yugoslavia did not strengthen in 1966; indeed, they became cooler to a degree. This was largely because of President Tito's discussions with Nasser and Indira Gandhi, leading to a joint statement criticising Israel. In 1966, two Yugoslav football teams played in Israel.

Commercial trade between Israel and Yugoslavia, in thousands of dollars

	1961	1962	1963	1964	1965	1966, first half-year
Exports to Israel	7,974	6,280	8,627	7,688	6,665	3,659
Imports from Israel	5,721	8,769	6,337	8,739	8,867	6,138
	+2,253	−2,489	+2,290	−1,051	−2,202	−2,479

Yugoslavia has substantial relations with Israel in the field of shipping. The Israeli shipping companies run ten to 12 boats monthly, and the Yugoslavs six boats monthly, between the Yugoslav ports on the Adriatic and the Israeli ports.

From Poland, in 1966, a pianist, a 120-member folk group, and two football teams performed in Israel. Relations between the two countries may be said to be the best of all the Socialist countries.

Commercial trade between Israel and Poland, in thousands of dollars

	1961	1962	1963	1964	1965	1966, first half-year
Exports to Israel	1,069	3,007	5,867	6,116	5,541	2,950
Imports from Israel	795	980	2,525	3,151	5,296	2,856
	+274	+2,027	+3,342	+2,965	+245	+94

Relations between Romania and Israel improved in 1966. At the beginning of the year, Romania sent a legate to Israel; for many years the legation had been led by a temporary chargé d'affaires. In 1966, an 80-member folk group and a football team performed in Israel. In addition, the Romanian legation in Tel Aviv is very active in pursuing cultural activities by way of the Romanian–Israeli Friendship Society.

Commercial trade between Israel and Romania, in thousands of dollars

	1961	1962	1963	1964	1965	1966, first half-year
Exports to Israel	957	1,255	600	1,203	2,727	1,061
Imports from Israel	2,275	2,202	846	2,425	1,948	1,564
	−1,318	−947	−246	−1,222	+779	−505

It is Romania's goal that about 50–60 per cent of the value of the raw and basic materials going to Israel should not be paid for through the clearing system, but in foreign exchange. So far, Israel has not shown a willingness to come to such an agreement.

Relations between the Soviet Union and Israel deteriorated markedly in 1966. The deterioration was caused primarily by Israel's provocative conduct towards Syria. Owing to the Syrian problem, the Soviet Union cancelled the exchange of philharmonic orchestras that had been planned for the autumn of 1966. Despite this, the Soviet Union's cultural programme in Israel was quite varied. In the spring of 1966, the writer Simonov visited Israel, and the violinist David Oistrakh and his student performed there. The Soviet circus performed in Israel for several months. In late 1966, a Soviet cellist guest-performed in Israel.

Commercial trade between Israel and the Soviet Union, in thousands of dollars

	1961	1962	1963	1964	1965	1966, first half-year
Exports to Israel	263	163	277	76	358	74
Imports from Israel	406	337	609	506	590	1,165
	−143	−174	−332	−430	−232	−1,091

In 1956, the Soviet Union broke off its trading relations with Israel because of the Suez aggression. Currently, the Soviet Union exports primarily books, magazines, records, and films to Israel in return for free foreign exchange. It is the Soviet Union's goal to place greater amounts of cultural products in Israel; for this reason, it regularly participates in the International Book Exhibition in Jerusalem and holds book exhibitions for a similar purpose in Tel Aviv, Jerusalem, and Nazareth.

In 1964, an agreement was reached between the governments of the Soviet Union and Israel concerning the sale of various Soviet-owned properties in Israel. A part of the purchase price was paid by the Israeli government in free foreign exchange, and it also made deliveries of goods to the value of approx. two million dollars.

Israel's relations with Czechoslovakia were, as they had been in previous years, cool in 1966. There were no major political or cultural events. The only event was an appearance by a four-member folk group, organised by the Czechoslovak–Israeli Friendship Society.

Commercial trade between Israel and Czechoslovakia, in thousands of dollars

	1961	1962	1963	1964	1965	1966, first half-year
Exports to Israel	171	34	209	252	196	67
Imports from Israel	3	5	117	199	115	78
	+168	+29	+92	+53	+81	−11

In 1956, after the Suez aggression, Czechoslovakia severed direct trading relations with Israel. Since then, indirect trade has been made with the involvement of Austrian firms.

Commercial trade between Israel and the GDR, in thousands of dollars

	1961	1962	1963	1964	1965	1966, first half-year
Exports to Israel	–	–	8	4	19	–
Imports from Israel	70	310	128	46	395	322
	−70	−310	−120	−42	−376	−322

Since the formation of Israel, the GDR has had neither political nor trade relations with Israel, owing to the unsettled political relations. On occasion, with the involvement of Austrian or West-German companies, goods of Israeli origin – principally oranges – have turned up in the GDR. By means of the same channels, a smaller amount of office equipment from the GDR has gone to Israel.

Israel has neither diplomatic nor trade relations with the GDR and with the people's democracies in the Far East.

Kálmán Csécsei
Temporary chargé d'affaires

12 Principles of the Relations with Israel

15 February 1967

National Archives of Hungary, XIX-J-1-j-Izrael-14-00784-1967 (48.d.)
Collection: Ministry of Foreign Affairs [Külügyminisztérium]

From: Ministry of Foreign Affairs
Sixth Regional Department

Completed: in 12 copies
Recipients: Comrades János Péter
Péter Mód
Károly Szarka
Béla Szilágyi
Károly Erdélyi
János Bojti
János Berecz
Mrs István Tömpe
István Beck (two copies)
Elek Tóth (two copies)

For the Deputy Ministerial Conference:

Subject: proposal for a summarisation of the principled foundations of our relations with the State of Israel

Changes in the international situation and foreign policy of the State of Israel and in the policy of the Arab countries, as well an assessment of our own interests, render it necessary to summarise once more the conceptual foundations of our relations with the State of Israel.

[....]

III.
The interests of the Hungarian People's Republic in the relations maintained with the State of Israel

In the political arena, it is necessary to increase the weight and influence of the Hungarian People's Republic in the territory of the State of Israel. [...] With our political presence, we can give assistance to the Israeli progressive forces and we can, on occasion, influence the policy of the State of Israel. The maintenance of our political relations and a gradual improvement depending upon the circumstances, justify our efforts to improve our relations, without abandoning our principles, with all countries recognized by us.

In the economic field, despite the limited possibilities, there are favourable conditions for obtaining raw materials, and for the export of Hungarian goods. In recent years, our foreign trade flow has gradually increased; in 1966, it reached seven million dollars on both sides; and, at the joint committee discussions held in Budapest in November 1966, 8.5 million dollars was scheduled for both sides in 1967. Changes in Israel's economic situation are increasing the role of Socialist countries in Israeli export efforts. In this context, it should be noted that the rules of the Arab boycott office [*the Central Boycott Office established by the Arab League Council and based in Damascus* – AK] do not prohibit simple export-import deals with Israel.

From Israel we are importing irrigation equipment, poultry-farm equipment, electronic equipment, household refrigerators, copper cement, steel pipes, technical diamonds, office machinery, phosphate, other chemicals, raw cotton, tropical fruits etc.

The most important export items are: machine tools; mechanical equipment; electric engines and other electrical goods; tools; locks; steel goods; medicines and basic materials for medicines; confectionery, as well as meat and sugar.

A significant problem affecting our trade is the lack of direct transport by ship. At the moment, all our goods are delivered by rail and ship with reloading, but we utilise capacity on foreign ships. We could achieve a substantial saving by using our own ships. This, however, would entail an Arab boycott of the ships brought into service and their personnel, and placement on their blacklist. Such ships could no longer use Arab ports. For us, the use of capacity on foreign ships means an annual sum of 8.3 million foreign-exchange forints in delivery plus associated costs. We also miss out on Austrian, Italian and West-German delivery orders, for which the countries in question have shown an interest.

The introduction of direct flights represents a similar problem, although this could be resolved via Cyprus, using a MALÉV flight.

Economically, the willingness of the Israeli National Bank to place a large amount of dollars at the National Bank of Hungary is important, primarily in terms of mitigating our lack of hard currency. In part, this has already taken place.

In the cultural field, a favourable but as yet unused opportunity for us is the circumstance that 200,000 people in Israel speak Hungarian. Many of these people are interested in Hungarian culture. Our cultural propaganda is received favourably above all by such people but also among the non-Hungarian-speaking population. Even the Soviet ambassador has noted the failure to make use of this opportunity, as have also the leaders of the ICP. Propagating the cultural achievements of Socialist Hungary would also strengthen our prestige and would assist the progressive forces operating in the country; indeed, in an indirect manner, it would also assist the progressive Arab forces.

IV.
<u>Connections between the interests of the anti-imperialist struggle of the Arab nations and the HPR's relations with Israel</u>

At the present stage of social development, the nature and role of the State of Israel violates progressive interests. Israeli policy towards the Arabs living in its territory has added to these violations. In consequence of all this, the State of Israel has found itself in opposition to the entire Arab world, whose declared aim has become the armed destruction of a state that they never recognised. Within this Arab policy, a certain nuance has recently appeared, and today the position of the Arab states is not a unified one. On this issue, Tunis has taken a different position from the Arab states; several years ago, it saw an opportunity for a more realistic appraisal of Israel's situation. In recent years, Lebanon has pursued a tolerant policy in connection with Israel. Despite the border conflicts, Jordan's position also differs from that of the Arab countries pursuing progressive policies.

The Soviet Union and the UAR – in part for domestic political reasons – endeavour to persuade the extremely militant Syria to exercise moderation. Socialist countries – including our country – support the Arab countries waging an anti-imperialist policy. The political and economic consolidation of the Socialist countries themselves increases the efficacy of such support. Therefore, it is also in the interests of the progressive Arab countries, if the Socialist countries develop their relations with Israel in accordance with their own interests.

Having regard for Israel's foreign policy and international role, we cannot treat it equally with the Arab states; that is to say, we cannot raise our diplomatic relations with it to the same level as [*our relations* – AK] with the latter; in our economic relations, we can only take into consideration our own interests, while in our cultural relations we must also limit, above all, the State of Israel's cultural propaganda possibilities. This also requires that we keep our own cultural activities within certain limits, lest we provide an opportunity for the application of reciprocity. Still, our cultural propaganda – since it popularises the achievements of a Socialist country and provides support to progressive forces in Israel – does not infringe upon the interests of the anti-imperialist struggle of the Arab nations; rather, it assists them indirectly.

V.
<u>Our tasks in the field of the continued formation of Hungarian–Israeli relations</u>

1.) In order to increase our political weight and efficacy, we should, at a suitable point in time, fill the legate's post in Tel Aviv. To prepare for this, we suggest the posting, in the course of the year, of a temporary chargé d'affaires of legate rank. If the Israelis wish to fill the legate post in Budapest, we should not object to this. In fact, the latter would be the ideal solution for us. <u>This could be hinted</u> [*to them* – AK].

2.) Similarly to the practice in foreign trade, we must apply our own interests in other measures of an economic nature. Bearing in mind these interests, we do not object to the running of MALÉV charter services between Hungary and Israel. Similarly, we agree with the introduction of cargo-ship services, if the competent economic organs deem this to be in our interest.

3.) Our cultural activities should be pursued primarily on an impresario basis, but in order to keep them within appropriate limits and to ensure our control – having regard for the applicability of reciprocity – we should administer our cultural relations on the basis of a working plan containing four to five events annually and regulated either verbally or through the exchange of letters. With an agreement of such nature, we secure for ourselves the possibility of rejecting an Israeli role that exceeds the limits and we also ensure that the only Hungarian cultural figures able to represent our cultural life in Israel are those who are found suitable to do so by the bodies responsible.

4.) So that our conduct influences Israeli policy in the desired way, the competent leaders and staff of the Ministry of Foreign Affairs, as well as the leader and staff of our legation in Tel Aviv – when holding discussions with the Israeli official figures and whenever relations between the two countries are mentioned – should make known our position and should refer to the reasons which, from the part of Israel, determine our conduct. In order to counter Zionist efforts, we propose that our emigration policy be upheld.

5.) So that the application of our own interests is not made to the detriment of our relations with the progressive Arab countries but rather strengthens such relations, the head of the Ninth Regional Department, as well as the comrades in contact with the Arab diplomats, should make known our own interests – if such are mentioned – and the harmony of these with the interests of the anti-imperialist struggle in our policy towards Israel.

6.) It is necessary to appraise in advance the likely propaganda effect, from the Israeli side, of some of our – positive – measures. We have to examine whether and what steps we can take to prevent such.

13 Hungarian–Israeli Economic Relations

4 November 1967

National Archives of Hungary, XIX-J-1-j-Izrael-5/t-002999-1968 (49.d.)
Collection: Ministry of Foreign Affairs [Külügyminisztérium]

From: Ministry of Foreign Affairs
Ninth Regional Department
Imre Helli

Completed: in …… copies.
Recipients:

Memorandum

Subject: Hungarian–Israeli economic relations

On 24 August 1967, the accredited heads of missions in Damascus of the Socialist countries were called into the Syrian Foreign Ministry and, on behalf of the Syrian Government, and accompanied by a brief verbal information session, they were given a circular note to be forwarded to the governments of the Socialist countries.

The circular note briefly recalls the Israeli aggression of 5 June and consequences of such, which necessitate a review of the relationship with Israel. It expresses "profound gratitude and sincere thanks" to the Socialist countries on behalf of the Arab states for the resolutions passed at the Moscow and Budapest conferences, for the severance of diplomatic relations with Israel and for the efforts made towards the convening of an extraordinary session of the UN General Assembly, and it welcomes the Belgrade conference aimed at offering economic assistance to the Arab countries. At the same time, it also notes that, in addition to the direct economic assistance provided to the Arab states and to be provided to them, it would be of extraordinarily significance and indirect assistance if the Socialist countries would also break off their economic relations with Israel. Finally, the Syrian government expresses its hope that the present request would be "studied in a positive spirit" by the Socialist countries at the Belgrade conference.

At the Belgrade conference of European Socialist countries [*on economic aid to Middle-Eastern countries in August 1967* – AK], none of the delegations mentioned the request of the Syrian government, so it was not even discussed.

In connection with the reply to be given to the Syrian note, our embassy in Damascus informed that the Soviet Union was the only Socialist country involved to have replied to the note, which it did even before the Belgrade conference, stating that there had been no economic relations between the Soviet Union and Israel, and that the Soviet Union had no intention of establishing relations of that nature in the future. The unanimous opinion of the heads of mission in Damascus of the other Socialist countries is that the note was closely related to the Belgrade conference which had already taken place, and so the response had lost its timeliness. The Yugoslav ambassador in Damascus had officially informed the Syrian prime minister about the conference, who made no reference to the effect on the conference of the Syrian note or even to whether the issue had been addressed at the conference. In consideration of this, even our embassy does not recommend making a written response to the note.

At the beginning of October, the issue was raised once again and almost concurrently by the Syrians and the Iraqis; Syria's ambassador in Prague asked our ambassador there whether the Syrian government's request had been discussed at the Belgrade conference. In response to our ambassador's negative answer, the Syrian ambassador stated on behalf of the Syrian government that the Syrian government was repeating its request, in the hope that the Hungarian government would address it. He added that the Syrian ambassadors were, at the same time, approaching the governments of the other Socialist countries involved; the Iraqi Foreign Ministry verbally communicated to the temporary chargé d'affaires of our Baghdad embassy the request of the Iraqi government that Hungary should sever its economic relations with Israel.

Based on what has been said, we propose:

1.) We should not reply to the circular note of the Syrian Foreign Ministry.

2.) At the behest of the Syrian ambassador in Prague – if necessary in response to the verbal communication of the Iraqi Foreign Ministry – we should make a verbal reply. The essence of our response: our position with regard to the Israeli aggression determines the future development of Hungarian–Israeli economic relations.

3.) We consider it necessary to review once again Hungarian–Israeli economic relations, so that they are in line with our political position. Currently, these relations are noticeably overplayed, and in our opinion a significant reduction would be possible without detrimentally affecting our national economy. (e.g., reductions in crate and sawn-timber exports as well as orange imports).

In the appendix, we briefly summarise the development of economic relations between Israel and the European Socialist countries. It shows that the economic relations of the Soviet Union, Czechoslovakia and the GDR with Israel were already insignificant. Bulgaria wound down all its economic relations after the Israeli aggression and even sold its commercial branch office building. They will review once more the future development of economic relations after the consequences of the aggression have been wound up. Between 1 January and 1 September 1967, Poland exported goods worth 1.34 million dollars to Israel and imported goods from there worth 3.9 million dollars. After the aggression, commercial trade almost ceased or was suspended by the Polish side. For the time being, there are no concrete plans concerning the content of trade relations and their continuation. In the first eight months of 1967, Yugoslavia exported goods worth approx. five million dollars to Israel and it imported from there goods worth approx. eight million dollars. After the aggression, imports declined because the Yugoslavs ceased buying tropical fruit. Further steps towards a reduction in the trade flow:

a.) they are to convert from the clearing system to free foreign-exchange accounting;

b.) with reference to the unfavourable structure of trade, they will remove a series of goods from both exports and imports;

c.) based on the government's decision – as well as winding up passenger ships – they will cease all types of cargo transport to Israel.

Examining the economic relations of the European Socialist countries with Israel since the aggression of 5 June, one can state that on our part the proposals made in Point Three are necessary, and that there is a real basis for their realisation.

14 Summary of Hungarian–Israeli Relations 1967

Budapest, 19 March 1968

National Archives of Hungary, XIX-J-1-j-Izrael-1/t-00811-1968 (46.d.)
Collection: Ministry of Foreign Affairs [Külügyminisztérium]

From: Ministry of Foreign Affairs
Sixth Regional Department
János Zagyi, secretary III.

Completed in 5 copies
Att.: Comrade Szilágyi

[....]

III. Hungarian–Israeli relations

1.) Until 12 June 1967, Hungarian–Israeli relations had been essentially unchanged for years. A chargé d'affaires had been at the head of the Israeli legation in Budapest and a temporary chargé d'affaires at the head of the Hungarian legation in Tel Aviv. On several occasions, Israel had urged an upgrading in the exchange of legates, the development of economic and cultural relations, and a visit by Comrade Béla Szilágyi to Israel. We had evaded all of these, with reference to Israel's pro-imperialist and anti-Arab policies.

In the final phase of its activities before the severance of diplomatic relations, the Israeli legation in Budapest increased its propaganda activity in support of the FRG [*Federal Republic of Germany*], as a part of which it slandered a third country which has amicable relations with us and is allied to us [*the German Democratic Republic – AK*], and it popularised the demand made by the FRG to represent exclusively the German people.

2.) We can hardly speak of *Hungarian–Israeli cultural relations*. There have been just one or two isolated actions such as, for instance, performances by a Hungarian circus group and trips by several artists on an impresario basis. In the same way, there could be no official cultural relations on the part of Israel; the official Hungarian bodies responsible provided the possibility to appear before a small audience to several artists coming as tourists or as visitors.

For 1967, there were no guest performances planned for Hungarian artists in Israel. Before the outbreak of the conflict, preparatory discussions were under way concerning performances by three Israeli artists later on; no contracts were signed or performances undertaken.

[....]

Israel urged once again the initiation of technical and scientific co-operation. In economic terms, they made a very favourable offer. We would have been willing to make the offer the subject of an examination, but events prevented this from happening.

[....]

4.) *Hungarian–Israeli commercial* trade is governed by the agreement signed in 1956 and by the protocols signed in subsequent years. The agreement mutually provides for treatment according to the principle of most-favoured nation.

Payments are governed by the payments agreement of 1954. Payments are made by way of the clearing system. The overdraft is currently 1.5 million dollars. In addition, until August 1968, a low-interest credit of 1.5 million clearing dollars is available to Hungarian buyers for financing purposes.

Over the past several years, our commercial trade has increased relatively quickly. The reasons for this were favourable financing possibilities and the preferential treatment provided by the Israeli government with respect to several Hungarian export articles.

In view of the fact that Israeli economic activity has recently undergone a slowdown, exports are being given significant support by the state and they are not adverse to re-export; indeed, in many cases such initiatives are broached by them. Since the June war, they are even willing to make financial sacrifices in order to sustain trade with the Socialist countries.

When diplomatic relations were broken off, our commercial office in Tel Aviv was closed, but we did not apply changes in the composition and volume of our trade flow. We wish to pursue relations based on mutual advantages, but we shall refrain from supplying any export goods that might increase Israel's military potential.

The Israeli market is an important market for several Hungarian export goods. These are: wooden crates and crate parts; sawn wooden and rolled goods; beef; sugar, and cables and machinery. Hungarian imports include numerous goods of importance to us. These are: carbon black; pneumatics; copper cement; bromides; synthetic fibres, etc.

Value of trade in millions of foreign-exchange forints

	1965	1966	1967
Exports	57.3	83.1	64.4
Imports	69.3	75.2	87.9

IV. The number of Israelis entering the country

After the severance of diplomatic relations and following a joint resolution on the part of the Ministry of Foreign Affairs and the ministries affected, we introduced visa restrictions and set up a committee which will make a separate decision concerning each visa request. When making a decision, the committee will take into consideration the pertinent resolutions of the Party, the interests of the national economy, and, on occasion, humanitarian aspects. We have reduced to a minimum the issuing of visitor, tourist, and transit visas.

Between 20 June and 30 December 1967, the committee examined 184 cases, doing so on the basis of petitions arriving from foreign representation bodies and the Hungarian authorities. Of these, it authorised 78 entry visas. Most of those entering the country travelled here in order to attend business meetings, while others could enter for specific family reasons and for fixed periods of time.

15 Trade Relations with Israel

Budapest, 17 September 1968

National Archives of Hungary, XIX-J-1-j-Izrael-5/t-00437/1-1968 (46.d.)
Collection: Ministry of Foreign Affairs [Külügyminisztérium]

From: Ministry of Foreign Trade

Memorandum

Subject: the development of Hungarian–Israeli trade relations and our trade policy with Israel

I.
The main basic principles of our trade policy relating to Israel

Since the events of 1966 [sic! – AK] in the Middle East, we have been applying the following main basic principles in our trade with Israel:

We do not take steps to abrogate the trade treaty with Israel or cancel the agreement on the exchange of goods and payments. At the same time, we are unwilling to consider signing a new agreement on the exchange of goods and payments, and we avoid any contact with the Israeli official bodies.

We strive to ensure that our commercial trade with Israel should not exceed the level of commercial trade for 1966. For this reason, we have made both exports and imports subject to individual authorisation.

We fully consider the boycott regulations of the Arab countries. We have only made ordinary export-import and re-export and re-import transactions. We have suspended the previous discussions on co-operation. We also refrain from making highly visible export-import transactions.

In export and import, we are trading largely within the existing price structure. We give importance to selling goods in the Israeli market that could not be sold elsewhere or which could be sold only at a substantial price loss. At the same time, in our imports, we wish to obtain primarily goods that are of a raw material nature and which, if they could not be acquired in Israel, could only be obtained for free foreign exchange.

We continue our re-export and re-import transactions to the same order of magnitude as in previous years, because they are economic.

We have upheld our significant debtor position vis-à-vis Israel (approx. three million dollars) for the sake of our balance of payments.

We have given major assistance to the newly formed Israeli [*Communist Party* – AK] party enterprise, which is already playing a significant role in trade between the two countries.

II.
The development of Hungarian–Israeli commercial trade in the past several years

Our foreign trade relations with Israel have stagnated since 1966.

Value in millions of foreign-exchange forints

	1963	1966	1967	1968. I–VI.
Exports	64.5	83.1	64.4	28.9
Imports	51.9	75.2	87.9	41.3
Total	116.4	158.3	152.3	70.2

In 1968, our total trade with Israel is not expected to exceed the level of 1967; according to estimates, it will be of the order of magnitude of 150–160 million foreign-exchange forints.

[....]

III.
Our balance account situation

In Israel we have an interest-free overdraft of 1,500,000 dollars and a special bank credit of 1.5 million dollars; the latter incurs annual interest of six per cent (in 1967 and at the beginning of 1968 it was five per cent).

At present we are making full use of both the overdraft and the special bank credit.

In view of our foreign-exchange situation, the repayment of these items was not considered desirable by our financial authorities. We do not consider our indebtedness to be worrying in practical terms either.

We consider it unlikely that the Israeli authorities would abrogate our agreement on the exchange of goods and payments.

Recently, the special bank credit was extended for an additional year. The only change was the increase in the interest rate from five per cent to six per cent.

Our indebtedness corresponds to about half a year of our export trade. If the payments agreement were to be abrogated, there would be a loan repayment holiday of half a year.

We are also able to achieve a price bonification of 8–8.5 per cent in the Israeli clearing system if payment is made in free dollars. (Our exit losses amount to around four per cent.)

In our view, the growth in credit is to be judged exclusively in financial terms. It is not in our foreign-trade policy interest to increase our indebtedness vis-à-vis Israel.

[*Handwritten remark on the last page:*]

In political terms, our indebtedness is very unwelcome. I discussed [*the matter –* AK] with Comrade P. Veres at the MFT [Ministry of Foreign Trade] and with Comrade Fekete at the NB [National Bank of Hungary]. We should endeavour to reduce significantly our debt in Israel.

[signature: Házi]

II The Eichmann Affair

Introduction

The capture of Adolf Eichmann on 11 May 1960 in Argentina embarrassed the leaderships of the European Communist countries: Eichmann had committed his crimes mainly on the territory of Soviet-bloc countries. Immediately after his arrest, the Israeli authorities signalled that they were counting on the assistance and co-operation of the Soviet, Polish, Czechoslovak and Hungarian governments in the legal proceedings.

The main political decision-making bodies of the concerned parties discussed the various issues arising from Eichmann's capture, and consulted with each other and their Soviet superiors on several occasions. The documents below were drawn up in the course of these consultations and, much like a case study, they offer insights into the mechanisms that resulted in a uniform policy strategy towards Israel and Jewish-related issues, a strategy that was adapted to Soviet interests. Furthermore, the documents also reveal the extent and nature of policy differences between the various countries, the manner in which they sought to realise their own goals, and how far they were prepared to go in pursuit of such goals.

Eichmann's capture was first mentioned in the Soviet press in a brief report on 25 May 1960.[1] It was only a few days after the capture that reports began to appear in the Hungarian, Polish and Czechoslovak press. As the B'nai B'rith analysis in this volume (Document 11) shows, significant differences of emphasis existed. In the latter half of June, the UN Security Council – of which Poland was a member at the time, in addition to the Soviet Union – debated, following a request from Argentina, the breach of Argentinian sovereignty. During the debate, Soviet and Polish delegates, while strongly condemning the Western countries (above all, West-Germany) for giving refuge to war criminals, refrained from taking a clear position on the issue itself. Indeed, at the vote, representatives of both countries abstained, thus choosing not to condemn outright Israel's actions. In response, the Israeli legate in Warsaw expressed special gratitude to the Polish government at a subsequent meeting.[2]

Following preliminary discussions on 27 June 1960, the Israeli government officially requested the Soviet Union's co-operation in the investigations preceding the trial.[3] Similar requests were then made to the Czechoslovak, Hungarian, and Polish governments. Whereas the Soviet Union and Czechoslovakia chose not to respond to this request,[4] the Polish and Hungarian authorities did respond, albeit in a rather

---

[1] For a review of the material published in the Soviet press on the Eichmann case, see Nati Cantorovich, Soviet Reactions to the Eichmann Trial: A Preliminary Investigation 1960–1965, *Yad Vashem Studies* 35:2 (2007), 103–141. See also the summary report by B'nai B'rith in this chapter (Document 11).
[2] A note from the director of the 5th Department of MSZ, Z. Wolniak, on the conversation with envoy R. Amir on 24 June 1960. AMSZ z-12 w-38 t-936/314, in Rudnicki and Silber (eds), *Stosunki Polsko–Izraelskie (1945–1967)*, 541–542.
[3] See Cantorovich, op. cit., 123.
[4] Ibid, 123; and Document 6, dated 12 August 1960 in this volume.

sluggish fashion.⁵ Meanwhile, however, consultations were being held in rapid succession on what to do next. At a meeting on 19 July 1960, the foreign ministers of the European Communist countries discussed measures to be taken in connection with the Eichmann affair.⁶ The Communist Party leaders wished to avoid the accusation of non-co-operation in the prosecution of a major war criminal, nor did they want to compromise their general policies towards the Jewish state or, even more importantly, towards the Federal Republic of Germany by the co-operation the Israelis asked for.

In the second half of the 1950s, after the West's rejection of the proposal to establish a unified, neutral and demilitarised Germany, Soviet policy-makers reacted with growing alarm to West Germany's increasingly close relationship with the Western economic and defence alliance. The unease of the Soviet leadership was heightened by the associated spectacular improvement in West Germany's relations with Israel, an obvious sign of which was a meeting held in New York on 14 March 1960 between West-German Chancellor Konrad Adenauer and Israeli Prime Minister Ben-Gurion. In order to discredit the pro-Western West-German political leadership, Soviet propaganda characterised West Germany as a post-Nazi, revanchist state that was harbouring Nazi criminals in high positions. Propagandists in the other Communist countries readily repeated this line. The spectacular improvement in West-German relations with Israel seemed, however, to undermine the legitimacy of such rhetoric. It is no accident that barely five days after the initial report of Eichmann's capture, Albert Norden, a leading functionary in the East-German Communist Party, the Socialist Unity Party of Germany [Sozialistische Einheitspartei Deutschlands, SED], wrote in an internal memo addressed to Party leader Walter Ulbricht, that it was incumbent upon the Communist countries to exploit the affair as part of the campaign against West Germany.⁷

Concerning Israel, since the beginning of the 1950s, Soviet propaganda had adhered to a strongly anti-Zionist line that was dismissive of the Jewish state's right to represent Jews, or to intervene in Jewish matters outside its borders. The governments of the Soviet-bloc countries were required, therefore, to address Israeli demands for documents that would facilitate the conviction of Eichmann for crimes against Jews without compromising their anti-Fascist stance. Moreover, co-operation with Israel on this matter was not to give rise to the impression that there had been a change in the position on Israel. Four principal issues reflecting this dilemma are made manifest in the documents: how to avoid recognising the authority of the Israeli court;

---

5 See Rudnicki and Silber, op. cit., 18 July 1960, 542–543; and Document 317, dated 4 August 1960, 544.
6 The contents of East German documents on negotiations between the Communist countries concerning the Eichmann affair are summarized in Meining, *Kommunistische Judenpolitik*, 267; and Ruth Bettina Birn, Fifty Years after: A Critical Look at the Eichmann Trial, *Case Western Reserve Journal of International Law*, 22 March 2011. Accessed on 10 April 2015 at http://www.thefreelibrary.com/Fifty+years+after%3a+a+critical+look+at+the+Eichmann+trial.-a0296255592.
7 See Meining, op. cit., 267.

whether or not to participate at an institutional level in the legal proceedings; how to provide inculpatory evidence for the prosecution without institutional involvement in the proceedings; and, finally, how to instrumentalize the trial for the purpose of denouncing West-German "neo-Fascism" and "revanchism".

The Hungarian Party bodies began to address the case in early June 1960, and it was placed on the agenda of a meeting of the Political Committee on 28 June 1960. This took place before the meeting of the foreign ministers of the Communist countries, and prior to receipt of the official Israeli note requesting co-operation (21 July 1960). From the outset, the Hungarian leadership strove to play down the Jewish aspects of the case, and to stress the general anti-Fascist ones. As János Kádár, General Secretary of the Hungarian Socialist Workers' Party, put it very clearly at the meeting (see Document 1):

> It is not a good idea to turn these awful Fascist affairs into an exclusively Jewish matter. If we do act in this affair, the decisive thing should be that Eichmann murdered hundreds of thousands of Hungarian citizens. This is where the emphasis should be, rather than turning this affair into a Jewish question. Eichmann did not only murder Jews; others were there, too. This is not a Jewish question; this is a question of Fascism and anti-Fascism.

Consultations on the issue went on until late autumn. Concerning recognition of the legitimacy of the Israeli court, a Hungarian Foreign Ministry proposal drafted in preparation for the foreign ministers' meeting on 19 July indicates that the Hungarians took a rather conciliatory position and were looking for a diplomatically acceptable solution (Document 4). The documents stress that according to general principles, the prosecution and punishment of war criminals was viewed primarily as the prerogative of those states on whose territory and against whose citizens the crimes had been committed. Even so, the Hungarians were ready to accept the argument that the Israeli court had at least partial jurisdiction insofar as Eichmann's crimes had affected people who subsequently became Israeli citizens or their relatives. Such a stance, it was argued, might offer a solution for several dilemmas facing the Communist countries:

> If we accepted the partial jurisdiction of the Israeli court, we would retain legal grounds for requesting Eichmann's extradition; at the same time, there would still be the possibility of providing data concerning specific crimes committed against Israeli citizens. In such a case, we could not be subjected to the propaganda accusation that we are rendering proceedings against a war criminal more difficult.

It would seem that although the political line to be followed in the affair – the need to exploit the trial for a campaign against "West-German neo-Nazism", Zionism and the Vatican – was decided upon at the foreign ministers' meeting, there was no final decision on matters of detail. The Communist countries initially considered demanding the involvement of an international court, or the extradition of Eichmann. After the meeting, however, such ideas were dropped, anticipating objection from the Federal

Republic of Germany, and the likelihood of the latter making a "rival claim". Hungary's position concerning the legitimacy of the Israeli court also encountered opposition. As the Czechoslovak documents show (see Document 6), the Hungarian proposition was not acceptable to the Czechoslovak Party leadership, which immediately turned to Moscow for guidance on the Soviet position. Having received such, they laid out their position clearly, arguing that explicit recognition of the Israeli court's authority might be construed as acceptance of the idea – forcefully promoted by Israel – that the Jewish state had the right to act on behalf of all Jews regardless of their citizenship. After some hesitation, they rejected Hungary's proposal that documents on Eichmann's crimes should be made available to the Israeli court by semi-official organisations. Instead, they proposed the publication of the relevant material, which could then be used by the Israelis.

The Soviet response to the Czechoslovak request, which supported the position of the Czechoslovak hardliners, is mentioned in the Hungarian Political Committee decision of 29 September 1960 (Document 7):

> As a result of consultation, one can state that all were in agreement with our political goals, while opinions differed on two other questions, which were summed up by the Soviet comrades as follows:
>
> 1. They do not consider it expedient to request Eichmann's extradition from Israel, since the rejection of such a request would diminish the prestige of the Communist countries.
>
> 2. Avoiding the issue of the jurisdiction of the Israeli court, they favour the Czechoslovak position that documentary proof should be given to Israel by means of some civil organ. In practice, this would take place alongside the simultaneous publication of the submitted material, in order to prevent Israel from hushing up the material it had received.

In light of the Soviet reaction, the Hungarian political leadership immediately revised its earlier position, and annulled the previous resolution of the Political Committee. In the following period, functionaries focused on realising the main political aim of the propaganda campaign: to reveal links between Eichmann's case and the Federal Republic of Germany's alleged practice of concealing and supporting war criminals. One means to achieve this was to establish continuity between Zionist rescue operations of World War II (such as Rudolf Kasztner's activities, which aimed to save lives through attempted bribery of Nazi officials, including Eichmann and his closest associates), and contemporary Zionism and German "neo-Fascism". It is no accident that this issue was strongly emphasised by István Szirmai, the head of the agitation and propaganda apparatus of the Hungarian Party, who had been imprisoned in the early 1950s on the basis of accusations concerning his pre-war Zionist past. As the letter of S. Mikunis, the Secretary General of the Israeli Communist Party, to the Central Committee of the Hungarian Socialist Workers' Party demonstrates (Document 10), the

Israeli Communists also wished to highlight this issue, since they saw it as a useful political tool to reveal collaboration between Zionists and the murderers of Jews.[8]

By the autumn of 1960, the four countries whose co-operation the Israeli authorities had officially requested – the Soviet Union, Czechoslovakia, Poland and Hungary – had reached a consensus on denying the Israeli investigative bodies permission to gather data in their countries. The Soviet authorities did not even respond to official Israeli requests,[9] while the Czechoslovaks, instead of handing over the requested documents, held out the prospect of the publication of a volume of material relating to Eichmann's activities on their territory. For their part, the Poles and Hungarians chose a different strategy: if not by way of state organs, they did show a willingness to make documents on Eichmann and his accomplices available to the Israeli state bodies through civil organisations such as the National Committee of Persons Persecuted by Nazism in Hungary [Nácizmus Magyarországi Üldözötteinek Országos Bizottsága] and the Main Commission for the Investigation of Nazi Crimes [Glówna Komisja do Badania Zbrodni Hitlerowskich] in Poland.[10] At the same time, however, the Hungarian authorities attempted to compile the documents in such a way as to prove that the Zionists and Nazis had collaborated, and to demonstrate indirectly that a number of Zionists (e.g. Kasztner) had helped war criminals such as Kurt Becher evade justice, some of whom were able to live unpunished in West Germany. Having selected the documents in this tendentious fashion, they then published them in the form of a book under the pretext of preventing the suppression of the "truth" in the course of the trial. Entitled *Eichmann in Hungary*, the volume was compiled by Jenő Lévai, the best-known Hungarian historian of the Holocaust of the immediate post-war years. The book was published in English and German by a Hungarian publisher who had never published anything before or since.

Policy differences among the various Communist countries arose not only with regard to the publication of documents pertinent to the trial, but also in the field of press reports. The last document in this chapter, a comparative report by B'nai B'rith on media coverage of the Eichmann affair (sent as a manuscript by the Hungarian embassy to the Foreign Ministry in Budapest), reveals significant differences in the media's handling of the issue in the various Communist countries. These differences were already apparent in the run-up to the trial. The B'nai B'rith report judged Polish and the Hungarian media coverage to have been basically correct, while it viewed Soviet, Czechoslovak and Romanian coverage as highly biased. (The explanation for

---

[8] On a similar letter sent by the Israeli Communist Party to the Polish authorities and the Polish reaction to the letter, see Szaynok, *Poland–Israel 1944–1968*, 316–317.
[9] See Cantorovich, op. cit., 123.
[10] See Rudnicki and Silber, op. cit., Document 320, dated 28 October 1960, 547. The Czechoslovak leadership had initially planned to make the documents available to the Israeli investigative bodies by way of the Union of Anti-Fascist Fighters in Czechoslovakia, but subsequently changed their minds. See Document 6 in this volume.

such differences given by the report's author(s) seems to have been influenced, at least in part, by the political climate at the time. Indeed, it is highly unlikely that various perceptions of the danger of renewed German expansionism would have such a strong influence over how the media in the various countries addressed the case, as the author(s) of the report believed.)

Three Hungarian journalists received permission from the government to be present at the court in Jerusalem, while more than 20 others produced articles or reports. A content analysis of Hungarian media publications[11] located 137 articles that dealt with the Eichmann affair, from capture to execution. According to the analysis, 98 of the 137 published articles might be considered objective reports on Eichmann's activities and the trial. The picture formed in the Hungarian press differed from the common position promoted by the Soviet Union: a relatively small proportion of the Hungarian articles addressed the propaganda themes identified during the consultations, and the overwhelming majority of press reports refrained from obscuring the antisemitic nature of Eichmann's activities and general Jewish suffering during the Holocaust, despite Party leader János Kádár's guidance to the contrary.

In the end therefore, the common policy strategy formed under Soviet pressure and strongly supported by the Czechoslovak and East-German Parties was not carried out in full in the Hungarian and Polish press. In the late 1950s, Poland had begun a spectacular improvement in its relations with Israel. Evidently, it did not want the conflicts surrounding the Eichmann affair to hinder this process. Even while it supported the common line in its official statements, Poland adhered to a policy of detachment that was manifest both in its bilateral meetings with the Israeli side, and in its press coverage of the trial. Such efforts were not without result: in June 1961, the Director-General of the Foreign Ministry of Israel, Chaim Yahil, visited Poland, which caused a sensation at the time.[12]

In Hungary, other factors lay behind the reluctance to adhere entirely to the common course of action. At the time of the Eichmann trial, there were at least 150,000 Jews living in Hungary, a majority of whom were survivors of the persecution that had occurred barely 15 years earlier. Many held important posts in the press, state administration and Party institutions. Practically every Hungarian Jew was familiar with the name Eichmann, and knew of his activities in Hungary. In view of this societal background, and the government's efforts to maintain social cohesion and nip potential conflicts in the bud in the wake of 1956, it doubtless seemed impossible to meet Soviet expectations in full. Indeed, there was an understanding on the part of the Hungarian authorities that any official measure that improved Eichmann's chances

---

11 Kata Bohus, Jews, Israelites, Zionists. The Hungarian State's Policies on Jewish Issues in a Comparative Perspective (1956–1968). PhD thesis, Central European University, 2013, chapter 3. See also Kata Bohus, Not a Jewish Question? The Holocaust in Hungary in the Kádár Regime's Propaganda During Adolf Eichmann's Trial, *Hungarian Historical Review* 4:3 (2015), 737–772.

12 For Poland's evolving policy on these issues, see Szaynok, *Poland–Israel 1944–1968*, 314–317.

of defence and relativized his role in the persecution and murder of Hungary's Jews – even if dressed up in general anti-Fascist rhetoric – would be damaging for domestic politics. They were also aware that an overly vehement anti-Zionist campaign could exacerbate antisemitism in the country, a development they evidently feared, given the historical links between antisemitism and anti-Communism.[13] Thus, while they loyally adhered to the common position in their political statements and in the course of negotiations and communications with "friendly countries", on issues where they believed that a separate course of action would not provoke a Soviet reaction, they endeavoured to tailor their measures to local conditions.

---

[13] The journalist Tibor Pethő recollected that before he left for Jerusalem to report on the trial, István Szirmai, in a shift from his earlier position outlined at the Political Committee meeting on 28 June 1960, had instructed him and other journalists to take care not to provoke a serious conflict with West Germany, and to avoid inciting antisemitic sentiment among the Hungarian population. "The core of Szirmai's instructions was [...] that the issue is still a painful point in Hungary, since there were, and in a certain sense still are, many antisemites in the country. Consequently, we have to present case in such a way that it does not provoke antisemitic sentiments." Interview with Tibor Pethő, in *A "hatvanas évek" emlékezete* [The Memory of "the Sixties"], ed. Adrienne Molnár (Budapest: 1956-os Intézet, 2004), 147.

Documents

1 Minutes of the Political Committee of the Hungarian Socialist Workers' Party

28 June 1960

National Archives of Hungary, M-KS 288/5/204/ p. 15-18.
Collection: Hungarian Socialist Workers' Party (HSWP), Central Bodies, Political Committee [Magyar Szocialista Munkáspárt (MSZMP) Központi Szervei, Politikai Bizottság]

[...]

Comrade István Szirmai:

I should like to draw the attention of comrades to a circumstance that is not mentioned in the motion. In my view, the Israeli government has an interest in the capture and judgement of Eichmann in the sense that there are certain matters which severely compromise the Israeli government and the Zionist movement. Eichmann knows about these things, and the Israelis do not want them to come to light. Such factors also exist. There was the Kaszner [sic! – AK] affair, whom the Israeli government had shot in order to shut him up. This was also a disturbing matter, but the important thing is that even the head of the Israeli government has an interest in the matter, because he too had connections with the Gestapo. This is a very interesting matter. Eichmann was kidnapped from Argentina, and just three days after this fact was made public, the grand chamber, where such a public trial could be held, burnt down. This is not insignificant either.

I suggest the following: Our campaign should be directed not only at drawing benefit from the Eichmann case in order to expose the Fascists of the Federal Republic of Germany, but also at trying to ensure that the Israeli government is exposed too. So our campaign should have two directions. Our main demand – which must be voiced – should be that, internationally, the trial be given full publicity. I share the view that the realisation of the proposals must be begun and that all means should be used and tried out, and that international pressure should aim to ensure that we too participate in the trial.

Another logical matter has arisen, namely, that the Israelis want to blackmail the Federal Republic of Germany with this matter. This is possible, but I also suppose the reverse. There are, in the Federal Republic of Germany, a number of high-ranking former Nazis with trump cards for blackmail. The Israeli government captured Eichmann in order to shut him up.

Comrade János Kádár:

I would say the following: I agree with the whole idea, but I have some reservations. It's not a good idea to turn these awful Fascist affairs into an exclusively Jewish matter. If we do act in this affair, the decisive thing should be that Eichmann murdered hundreds of thousands of Hungarian citizens. This is where the emphasis should be, rather than turning this affair into a Jewish question. Eichmann did not only murder Jews; others were there, too. This is not a Jewish question; this is a question of Fascism and anti-Fascism. We recognise the right of the Israeli court in this matter. And that is as far it goes when it comes to the Jews. We must be careful about this. I would say the following: I would begin by saying that under the 1943 declaration of the Allied powers, all war criminals, etc.... this should be the point of departure. Second, a person should be pursued as a war criminal and, under the present circumstances, brought to justice where he committed the crime. The following may be said here: Eichmann is a war criminal, a Fascist; it has come to our knowledge that he is a prisoner of the Israeli government. Then there would be the matter of what we want to do. It would also be correct to point out, first of all, that the Israeli court should hold a public trial, and that a representative could take part in the trial as an observer, rather than as an accusing party. In my view it is not possible, in a legal sense, at the court of one state, for the representative of another state to take action as an accusing party, commissioned by Hungary. We are aware that the war criminal Eichmann is being held by the Israeli authorities. We demand that a representative of the Hungarian body responsible take part in the trial.

Comrade Imre Hollai:

Ben-Gurion has already acknowledged that the trial will be public...

Comrade János Kádár:

Ben-Gurion just said it, that's all. We just say that it has come to our knowledge that Eichmann is being held by the Israeli authorities and that they want to prosecute him. After that, we say, we demand, a public trial, at which – and we will have to name the person in question – the [*Hungarian* – AK] Public Prosecutor's representative can take part.

Our second demand: we demand that after the trial, Eichmann be surrendered to the Hungarian authorities. And we'll say that this is a legitimate demand, because Jewish people... etc. We should not say anything there. These are our two goals, our demands, but what we do to achieve them is another matter.

Let us negotiate with the friendly countries that have been named – this is appropriate. A second task is to collect together the appropriate documents, the publication of certain material. It will not be expedient for the first four pages of every paper to be full of this. That shouldn't be done. After that, there is the matter of what we should do with Argentina. This is a separate matter; it's not compatible with the Eichmann case. It is a matter for consideration. To consider whether it is expedient or not. It requires a lot of consideration because our current position with them is that they have decided to buy locomotives from us. And if we overly concern ourselves with this matter, then we won't get a war criminal from them, nor will they buy a locomotive from us.

[....]

Comrade János Péter:

The Poles will probably be the first to make the demand for extradition – officially too. He [Eichmann] committed most of his crimes there. The Allied powers made a statement after the winding-up of the Nuremberg court that if a war criminal were found, then he should be brought to justice where he committed the crimes. Comrade Sobolev supported this view in the Security Council debate, as against Argentina's proposal. We shall probably have to make a demand for extradition, too, because [otherwise] there will be two friendly countries, on whose territory he committed these crimes, making requests for extradition, but the third will remain silent. Besides, there will also be some propaganda benefit, because when publishing the material relating to him, it will be good to apply a gradual approach; material should initially be made public which refers exclusively to crimes he committed in Hungary, and then gradually move on to material that relates to American or West-German figures.

2 Tasks after the Decision of the Political Committee

28 June 1961

National Archives of Hungary, XIX-J-1-Izrael-30/c-00850-1960 (11.d.)
Collection: Ministry of Foreign Affairs [Külügyminisztérium]

At its meeting of 28 June 1960, the Political Committee of the Hungarian Socialist Workers' Party decided, in a resolution concerning the Eichmann case, that the motion of Foreign Affairs Department and the Ministry of Foreign Affairs should be revised, taking into account the comments made at the meeting.

Based on the motion and the comments made, the Political Committee consents to the following measures:

1./ We should issue notes to the Israeli government, in which:
a./ We express the demand that the Israeli government hold legal proceedings against Eichmann in a public trial and that it permit the representative of the Supreme State Prosecutor of the Hungarian People's Republic to take part in the trial as an observer;
b./ We state our demand that after the conclusion of the Eichmann case at the Israeli court, the Israeli authorities surrender Eichmann to the authorities of the Hungarian People's Republic, so that he may be brought to justice for crimes committed in Hungary.

2./ We base the aforementioned demands of the Hungarian People's Republic on the following:
a./ Under the 1943 Moscow Declaration of the Allied powers, all war criminals that are responsible for atrocities "shall be pursued to the furthest corners of the earth" so that they do not escape punishment. Under the same declaration, all war criminals that are not brought before an international court must be extradited to the countries where they committed their deeds, so that the liberated peoples may pass judgement over them on the basis of their own laws. This is what was stated by the participating powers at the conclusion of the Nuremberg international court's work, thereby concluding that war criminals that had not been brought to justice by the international court must be brought to justice in the country in which they committed their crimes.
b./ Since Eichmann committed a series of war crimes and crimes against the people in the territory of Hungary in 1944, the justice bodies of the Hungarian People's Republic are competent to pass judgement on Eichmann's crimes in Hungary.

3./ By means of the Ministry of Foreign Affairs, consultative negotiations must be held with the competent authorities of the People's Republic of Poland and the Czechoslovak Republic, concerning the measures to be taken with respect to the Israeli government in the Eichmann case.

4./ Regarding the crimes committed by Eichmann in Hungary, the Supreme State Prosecutor and the Ministry of Foreign Affairs will take charge of the collection and documentation of data, diplomatic measures and the processing of such, in a form that can be used in any legal proceedings.

5./ The Ministry of Foreign Affairs shall compile material suitable for publication.

6./ The press shall cover the Eichmann case in accordance with the aforementioned plans.

7./ When dealing with the Eichmann case, the following concepts must be applied: in view of neo-Fascist symptoms visible in the life of the Federal Republic of Germany and the Zionist nature of the Israeli government's foreign and domestic policy, [*the case* – AK] must be used to strengthen the anti-Fascist front against Fascist efforts. For this reason, when condemning the guilt of Eichmann and his accomplices, in addition to crimes against Jews, the other crimes of Fascism against various progressive movements and individuals must also be exposed.

3 Tasks in Connection with the Eichmann Case

8 July 1960

National Archives of Hungary, XIX-J-1-j-Izrael-30/c-00850-1960 (11.d.)
Collection: Ministry of Foreign Affairs [Külügyminisztérium]

From: 2nd Political Department

Lajos Kiss, Third Secretary
Sík, Minister Comrade
Péter, First Deputy Min.
Puja, Deputy Min.
Szarka, Deputy Min.
István Varga, Head of Dep.
Z. Széphelyi, Acting Head of Dep.

Memorandum

Subject: tasks in connection with the Eichmann case

Based on our motion, the Political Committee has adopted a resolution concerning the diplomatic measures to be taken in the Eichmann case, and it marked out the main policy governing our conduct in this matter. Thus the following measures have become necessary:

1./ Consultation with friendly countries with an interest in the matter
    The Political Committee has charged the Foreign Minister with consulting with the governments of friendly countries on the Eichmann case and with co-ordinating our measures. The consultation has become increasingly urgent, as the Israeli government has taken official steps, both here and – as far as we know – in Prague, to have us provide it with data on Eichmann and to permit its official representative to enter [*the country* – AK] for the purpose of gathering information and data. Thus:

a./ We should inform the Czechoslovak government, which has already made such an inquiry to us in this matter, that we are prepared to take part in consultative discussions, and that we suggest that other friendly countries with an interest in the matter also take part in such discussions (Soviet Union, GDR and Poland).
b./ During consultations, based on the Political Committee's resolution, we should say what our conduct is and announce our measures.
c./ The consultative discussions will be an opportunity for us to request, from the Czech and Polish governments, additional data that are essential to the task of collecting data. The Czech comrades are in possession of Wisliczeny's [*sic!* – AK] interro-

gation report, while the Polish comrades are in possession of the memoirs and memorandum of Höss, camp commander at Auschwitz. Both men took an active part at the side of Eichmann while he was operating in Hungary.

According to reports we have received, it is expected that the consultative discussions will raise the idea of an international-type court comprising representatives of those countries in which Eichmann committed his deeds. In this regard, our representatives at the discussions should prepare to take an appropriate position. We suggest that if our partners insist on a joint stand, then we should not oppose it. The idea is unlikely to be realised in practice, but it does provide us with a good opportunity in our propaganda to take joint action for the sake of anti-Fascism and to demonstrate that Western [governments] do not want to take joint action even against Fascist mass murderers such as Eichmann. We, on the other hand, are prepared to do so, as interested countries.

2./ Memorandum to the Argentine government

According to the policy line of the Political Committee, the circumstances of the Eichmann case must be used to strengthen the anti-Fascist front and, in addition to crimes against Jews, attention must also be given to other crimes of Fascism, while exposing its current supporters. For this reason, we suggest that we request the Argentine government in a note to extradite Fascists who are known by it to be residing in the country. For this purpose:

a./ Data must be collected about known Hungarian Fascists reported by the embassy in Buenos Aires and residing in Argentina. [...] The State Prosecutor should issue arrest warrants against them.

b./ Based on that data, we should request their extradition in a note, without referring to the Eichmann Case. As part of this measure, we suggest that we should not ask for persons under consideration for extradition in a summary note, but one by one, which may provide us with an opportunity to manoeuvre.

3./ Note to the Israeli government

This measure should take place in accordance with the tactical principle that is jointly accepted at the consultative discussions. In the note

a./ We should make our demand that Eichmann's case be held in public

b./ We should ask for permission for the Supreme State Prosecutor of the Hungarian People's Republic to take part in the trial as an observer

c./ We should serve notice that we are considering a demand that after his trial in Israel is over, Eichmann should be surrendered to the Hungarian People's Republic, so that he may be brought to justice for crimes committed in Hungary.

We base our demand on the following:

a./ The 1943 Moscow Declaration of the Allied powers, according to which those who committed atrocities will be pursued to the furthest corners of the earth, so that they may receive proper punishment – and further, the statement forming part of the declaration, according to which all war criminals who are not brought before an international court must be extradited to the countries where they committed their deeds, so that the liberated peoples may pass judgement over them.
b./ Since Eichmann committed some of his atrocities and war crimes in Hungary, the Hungarian People's Republic considers itself competent to pass judgement over him.

4 Consultation Issues in Respect of the Eichmann Case

19 July 1960

National Archives of Hungary, XIX-J-1-Izrael-30/c-00850-1960 (11.d.)
Collection: Ministry of Foreign Affairs [Külügyminisztérium]

Completed in 4 copies

Consultation issues in respect of the Eichmann case to the foreign ministries of the Soviet Union, Czechoslovakia, the German Democratic Republic and Romania

1./ The policy line issue
When publishing documents concerning Eichmann and his associates, the anti-Fascist front should be used to attack:

a./ West-German neo-Fascism
b./ Zionism
c./ The Vatican (Eichmann reached Argentina with the assistance of the Vatican)

For this reason, when exposing the crimes of Eichmann and his accomplices, attention should also be given – alongside crimes against Jews – to acts committed against various other progressive individuals, movements and patriots.
Since by far most of his crimes were committed in Poland against Polish citizens, it would seem right for Polish comrades to be at the forefront of our campaign.

2./ The problem of the jurisdiction of the Israeli court
In this regard, the following issues require clarification:

a./ If we recognise the jurisdiction of the Israeli court with regard to all aspects of Eichmann's crimes, then the following negative consequences may arise:

aa./ We might give the impression that we recognise the legitimacy of efforts on the part of the government of Israel to regard itself as the general representative of Jews.
ab./ We would come into conflict with the 1943 Declaration of the Allied and associated powers, according to which war criminals are responsible for their deeds where they committed them.
ac./ We would place ourselves in the position of being unable to refuse to supply data relating to Eichmann.
ad./ Thereby, we would assist the government of Israel in using the Eichmann case for its own political purposes.
ae./ Finally, we would jeopardise our right to request the extradition of Eichmann.

b./ If we refuse to recognise the authority of the Israeli court in any respect, then the following negative consequences arise:

We shall have to refuse the provision of data – in both its official and private forms – relating to Eichmann.

By doing so, we would provide an opportunity, on the one hand, for the Israeli court to narrow the scope of the crimes and, on the other, for them to state in their propaganda attacks that the Communist countries are not assisting in exposing the crimes of a Fascist war criminal. If this happens, we will find it difficult to criticise the proceedings of the Israeli court, which are likely to be conducted unfairly.

c./ The question arises: would it be possible to recognise the partial jurisdiction of the Israeli court. The grounds for such partial recognition could be as follows:

The 1943 Moscow Declaration of the Allied and associated powers stated that persons are responsible for their crimes where they committed them. But it said this on the theoretical ground that the people who suffered the crimes should make judgement.

Large numbers of people who used to live in the territories of the Soviet Union, Poland, Czechoslovakia, Romania and Hungary are now living in the – subsequently established – State of Israel, as its citizens. Most of these people are individuals against whom personally, or against whose relatives Eichmann committed crimes.

Partial jurisdiction would apply to crimes committed against such Israeli citizens.

If we accepted the partial jurisdiction of the Israeli court, we would retain legal grounds for requesting Eichmann's extradition; at the same time, there would still be the possibility of providing data concerning specific crimes committed against Israeli citizens. In such a case, we could not be subjected to the propaganda accusation that we are rendering proceedings against a war criminal more difficult.

3./ Possible extradition proceedings would probably have merely propaganda significance, for it is unlikely that the Israeli authorities would accept an extradition claim. By extraditing him, they would reduce their own possibilities of exploiting the Eichmann case politically and economically vis-à-vis both West Germany and the Arab countries. Moreover, extradition would result in Eichmann inevitably giving information about Zionism and his removal from Argentina to the authorities of the Communist countries, and this would not be desirable as far as the Israeli government is concerned.

Nevertheless, there are advantages to launching extradition proceedings. After a rejection of such a request, possibilities would arise for us to gradually publish Eichmann's crimes, thereby permitting criticism of the policies of the Israeli government, or indeed for the continuation of the trial without the accused – on the lines of the Oberländer case.

It would not, however, be right to make the extradition request now. The disadvantage of an early announcement would be to push Israeli preparations for the case in an unfavourable direction and to add to the Israeli government's opportunities for continuing the bartering with the West-German government in connection with the case.

Extradition should be requested just prior to, or during, the lawsuit, with the demand that – after the trial and the announcement of the judgement – Eichmann should first be surrendered to the People's Republic of Poland, subject to a pledge that after judgement has been served or implemented, we give Eichmann back to the Israeli authorities.

4./ Provision of data to the Israeli authorities

If the Israeli authorities approach individual citizens of our countries with requests for information and data, their response should be that they can only give information to the authorities of their own countries.

Where Israeli requests are made to our own authorities, we shall surrender the type and amount of material that can serve, by documenting crimes committed against a significant share of current Israeli citizens, as procedural enforceable evidence, with a view to implementing capital punishment.

5./ The problem of responding to previous Israeli requests

In Poland, Czechoslovakia and Hungary, the Israeli foreign representations have expressed an interest in whether or not the competent authorities can offer assistance to the Israeli state prosecutor in collecting documentary evidence. Having regard to the above, the following official response may be given to such requests, which have not yet been made official in the literal sense.

As far as Eichmann is concerned, the Declaration of the Allied and associated powers is valid, according to which war criminals are responsible for the crimes where they committed them. Since, however, there are many people currently living in Israel as Israeli citizens, against whom Eichmann directly or indirectly committed capital crimes, the partial jurisdiction of the Israeli justice bodies should be recognised for those of Eichmann's crimes that were committed, directly or indirectly, against current Israeli citizens. Thus, our justice authorities will be prepared to surrender documentary evidence pertaining to the jurisdiction, if they receive official requests in such a matter. Official requests must state the questions of the Israeli justice bodies, concerning which they wish to present an indictment. Knowing the specific questions, we shall provide the information and documentary evidence as we are able to and to the best of our knowledge. After this has been submitted and the indictment has been made, we shall ask that our justice bodies be informed of the bill of indictment so that, if necessary, we can provide further possible evidence. Meanwhile, we shall ask that the lawsuit be held in public, so that the state prosecutor's observer can be present at the trial.

6./ Agreement on our procedure

Once we have clarified the aforementioned basic issues and reached an agreement, we should draw up plans for diplomatic measures on the one hand and gradual propaganda activities on the other. We should then make these known to each other and, within a consultative framework that is to be established later, we should try to achieve full co-ordination.

5 Official Request of the Legation of Israel

21 July 1960

National Archives of Hungary, XIX-3-1-j-Izrael-30/c-005022-1960
Collection: Ministry of Foreign Affairs [Külügyminisztérium]
[*Original English-language document reproduced here without amendment* – AK.]

Legation d'Israel

4326/60

The Legation of Israel presents its compliments to the Ministry for Foreign Affairs of the Hungarian People's Republic and – upon the instructions received from its Government – has the honour to make application for the kind assistance and co-operation of the Hungarian authorities in the following matter:

The judicial authorities of the State of Israel are instituting criminal prosecution against the notorious war criminal Adolf EICHMANN, who is at present detained in custody in Israel. Adolf EICHMANN has been charged under the laws of the State of Israel and has been remanded by order of a Magistrate's Court, pending his trial under the provisions of the

Nazis and Nazi Collaborators (Punishment) Law of 5710 (1950).

A Special Bureau of the Israel Police Force has been established to investigate and prepare the case for trial. This Bureau is now engaged in gathering, recording, perusing, analysing and classifying all available and obtainable evidence, relevant to the charges brought.

The war criminal Adolf EICHMANN, over a period of several months during the war years 1944/45, conducted his activities, aimed at what was called the "Final Solution of the Jewish Problem" in Hungary. He was personally responsible for initiating, organising and carrying out the deportation of several hundreds of thousands of Jews from Hungary and for their subsequent brutal and bestial annihilation in the notorious "extermination camps". Hence, it must be presumed that a considerable amount of important direct and factual evidence – testimonies and documents – may be obtained in this country, evidence which would support the case against one of the greatest war criminals in history.

The Government of Israel is, therefore, most anxious to enlist the support and co-operation of the Hungarian authorities in its quest to secure all available information, testimonies of witnesses and material documentary evidence, such as: originals or authenticated copies of documents issued, at the time, by EICHMANN, his Special Department or his accomplices and representatives who acted on his orders; protocols, records and copies of judgments delivered by Hungarian Courts, which implicate EICHMANN or his accomplices; photographs, photostatic copies, documentary films and, generally, any such relevant material which could be gathered or recorded in Hungary.

With a view to advancing and facilitating the ramified process of investigation of this unique criminal case, it is also proposed that the head of the Special Bureau of the Israel Police Force, or his representative, should be permitted to come to Hungary, so as to enable him – with the co-operation and aid of the competent Hungarian authorities – to examine on the spot the available information and documents bearing on this case and decide on its value for use in evidence at the impending trial of EICHMANN.

The Government of Israel feels confident that the Revolutionary Workers' and Peasants' Government of the Hungarian People's Republic will accede to this request and that it will authorise the respective Hungarian authorities to place all the available information and evidence pertaining to the criminal case against Adolf EICHMANN at the disposal of the Police and judicial authorities of the State of Israel. The Government of Israel should, furthermore, deem it a favour if a representative of the Israel Police Force would be allowed to visit Hungary in connection with the investigations in progress, and if all possible facilities and co-operation in this matter would be extended to him.

The Legation of Israel seizes this opportunity to reiterate to the Ministry for Foreign Affairs of the Hungarian People's Republic the assurances of its highest consideration.

6 Position of the Czechoslovak Socialist Republic of the Case of Eichmann

12 August 1960

National Archives of the Czech Republic, Archive of the Central Committee of the Communist Party of Czechoslovakia (Národní Archiv, Ústřední Výbor Komunistické Strany Československa)
Collection: Antonín Novotný II, carton 109, Nr. 210–212

From: Ministry of Foreign Affairs

Minister of Foreign Affairs
to Antonín Novotný, first Secretary of the CPCz and the President of the ČSSR, annexe 1

Dear Comrade,

Lately the Ministry of Foreign Affairs has been intensively dealing with the case of the Nazi war criminal Adolf Eichmann who has been recently captured by the Israeli espionage in Argentina, where he hid from justice. The ČSSR is naturally interested that Eichmann did not escape punishment and that his case was an impetus for further actions against still unpunished war criminals. It is common knowledge that Eichmann also committed his crimes in the territory of Czechoslovakia and a great number of Czechoslovak citizens fell prey to his homicidal activity. Some of the allied countries where Eichmann administered mass extermination of Jews, e.g. the Polish People's Republic, Hungarian People's Republic, the Soviet Union, German Democratic Republic and Rumanian People's Republic, have a similar interest as the Czechoslovak Socialist Republic.

The Eichmann case has aroused a considerable response on the part of world public and brought forth the issue of pursuit of war criminals and fulfilment of the Alliance treaties about their punishment. According to the Alliance treaties from the Second World War, particularly in accordance with the Moscow Declaration of the three major Allied powers from 1st November 1943, Nazi war criminals should be "sent back to the countries in which they committed their outrageous acts to be judged and punished there according to the law of these liberated countries". It is evident that, according to the principles of punishment of war criminals, primarily the countries on whose territory and against whose citizens Eichmann committed his crimes have the right of criminal prosecution and punishment of this war criminal.

In this context, the Ministry of Foreign Affairs has been meticulously dealing with the question of what position the Czechoslovak Socialist Republic should take on the fact that Eichmann is actually in the hands of the Israeli organs and is to be tried by an Israeli court. From legal point of view, an Israeli court cannot be authorised to judge Eichmann's crimes. <u>An explicit recognition of Israeli court's authority on the part of the Czechoslovak Socialist Republic and other Socialist states might be considered as</u>

sanctioning the concept that Israel has been systematically exercising, i.e., that Israel as a Jewish state has the right to act in the name of all Jews regardless of their citizenship. [*Highlighted in the original by Novotný* – AK.]

The Ministry of Foreign Affairs works on the assumption that the basic political directive for the procedure of the ČSSR in the Eichmann case should be, on the one hand, the quest for consistent revelation of Eichmann's crimes and their punishment, as well as the revelation of links between the Eichmann case and the politics of hiding and support of war criminals exercised by the ruling circles of the German Federal Republic; on the other, the principle that the ČSSR should not take any action, which would mean our recognition of Israel's claim to try Eichmann for the crimes on European Jews. [*Highlighted in the original by Novotný* – AK.]

Working on this assumption, the Ministry of Foreign Affairs so far has not answered Israel's request that the chairman of the Israeli committee for investigation of Eichmann's crimes be sent to the ČSSR and that the Czechoslovak official places provide the Israeli organs with co-operation when collecting evidential material against this criminal. In a similar vein, as we know, the Hungarian People's Republic and the Polish People's Republic responded to the Israeli claim.

In order to ensure concordant procedure of the Socialist states in the Eichmann case, the Ministry of Foreign Affairs through the Czechoslovak Embassy in Moscow has inquired about the position of the Soviet organs on the possible actions that would be taken by the Socialist states. In this context we primarily pointed to two basic alternatives that present themselves in determining our position:

a) To work on the actual fact that Eichmann is in the effective possession of the Israeli organs and most probably will also be tried in Israel, and to avoid any kind of steps that would mean explicit recognition of Israel's right to judge him. At the same time, however, to allow that selected evidential documents about Eichmann's crimes, available in the ČSSR, reach the Israeli court through unofficial means, e.g. through the Union of Anti-Fascist Fighters. Thereby, we would give weight to accusations against Eichmann and by a simultaneous release of the documents, we would withstand possible attempts at their concealment, distortion and suppression at the trial.

b) To ask Israel for Eichmann's extradition to try him in the ČSSR or another Socialist country. It is, of course, necessary to reckon that Israel would not extradite Eichmann. Even if our claim would not be satisfied by Israel, we would thereby prove our determination to pursue war criminals from the period of the Second World War and consistently actualise the Allies' agreements about their punishment. This way would, however, bring certain danger and disadvantages. By our claim, we would, in fact, support Eichmann's defence, which will probably be based particularly on a plea to the Israeli jurisdiction, furthermore, we might provoke a similar claim from the German Federal Republic or another capitalist state and thus allow Israel to manoeuvre for the purpose of winning advantages. Besides, after rejection of our extradition claim, we would logically be obliged to take the position that Eichmann's condemnation is illegal, which would be completely inappropriate.

During the time when the Czechoslovak Embassy was sounding out the Soviet position, a number of bearings were not yet known and the Ministry of Foreign Affairs was inclined to the second alternative, i.e., to the claim of Eichmann's extradition. The Soviet comrades promised to promptly study our considerations and inform us of their opinion.

In the meantime, the MFA has been informed about the position of the governments of the Polish Socialist Republic and the Hungarian People's Republic on the Eichmann case.

According to the Polish comrades, the PPR does not intend to ask for Eichmann's extradition as there is not the slightest prospect of success, also because such a procedure would mean taking part in the conflict between Argentina and Israel – and because such a claim might currently stimulate a competitive claim by the German Federal Republic, which is undesirable. Nevertheless, the Polish Socialist Republic has been collecting documents on Eichmann and his crimes, especially his fellow workers nowadays active in the German Federal Republic. The PSR is, however, avoiding any steps in the Eichmann case that would be binding in the future. Later on, the PSR intends to hand the collected materials over to Israel, while publishing them simultaneously, and at the same time informing the Israeli government that the PPR stipulates to undertake every necessary step against Eichmann in relation to his crimes against Polish citizens.

Recently, the Ambassador of the Hungarian People's Republic in Prague informed us that the Hungarian organs have also been dealing with the question of what position to adopt on the fact that Eichmann is going to be tried in Israel. At the same time, he submitted a document, from which the considerations of the Hungarian comrades are evident (a translation is enclosed). The Hungarian comrades have been dealing with the question of a possible request for Eichmann's extradition. They see political advantages in the extradition request, although at present they do not consider submitting such a request to be appropriate. They think the extradition claim should not be submitted to Israel before examination of this criminal is finished. The Ministry of Foreign Affairs finds disadvantages in such a procedure, as it does not entirely appropriately solve the question of what position to take on the repeated Israeli requests for providing documents until the time when Eichmann would potentially be claimed. Similarly, the Hungarian comrades point to the impropriety of recognising the legitimacy of the Israeli court and, at the same time, they mention the danger that might arise from our negative position on Israeli requests for material on Eichmann. They find a way out of the situation in the concept of admitting the partial authority of the Israeli court as far as concerns Eichmann's crimes committed on people who became Israeli citizens, or on their relatives. As for providing the Israeli organs with documents, the Hungarian comrades do not have any objections to the Israeli court receiving from Hungary such evidential means that are necessary for proving the Eichmann's guilt for crimes against the present-day Israeli citizens. Therefore, they plan to answer the Israeli government's request for documents applying to Eichmann and the Allied conventions on judging war criminals. Here, a partial legitimacy of the Israeli court can be acknowledged and therefore the Hungarian organs are willing to deliver such material which does not fall out of the remit of this partial legitimacy. In return, the Hungarian organs are going to stipulate that the Israeli investigation bodies hand over to the Hungarian People's Republic the prosecution file against Eichmann and allow the presence of the Hungarian prosecutor's office observer during the trial.

The Hungarian concept of the partial legitimacy of the Israeli court does not have, according to the Ministry of Foreign Affairs opinion, a legal justification. Regardless of the legal side of the matter, this conception is running into difficulties in the sense that Eichmann's crimes are virtually impossible to divide along the citizenship of his victims, because Eichmann's major responsibility lies in his directive role =in the extermination of the European Jewish population as a whole. The MFA concludes that it is not so necessary to go into the negotiations with the Israeli government as far as the document of the HPR suggests, and that it is sufficient to unofficially deliver evidential material to the Israeli court without taking an explicit position on its legitimacy. This does not mean that in individual cases it is not possible to provide the ordinary co-operation of the state organs (e.g. courts when questioning the witnesses, authenticating various documents), although in principle it would be appropriate to stick to delivering material in an unofficial way, e.g. by the means of social organisations and the like.

Finally, the Hungarian comrades suggest that all steps of the Socialist countries in the Eichmann case should be coordinated with collective consultation.

The MFA agrees with the above objections, and with the HPR's proposals, and finds it particularly useful to actualise consultations with the Socialist countries, where all aspects of the matter would be considered and other possible solutions also taken into consideration; therefore the MFA is going to respond positively to the HPR's proposal to organise a joint session of the Socialist countries. At the session or at other bilateral consultations, the MFA intends to move the focus of its considerations to the alternative, which, for the time being, does not involve the request for Eichmann's extradition. This would allow for such a form of unofficial involvement of the ČSSR in Eichmann's trial in Israel that would not imply explicit recognition of the Israeli court's legitimacy on the part of the Czechoslovak government, but would unequivocally attest to our readiness to contribute in a due measure to the revelation of Eichmann's crimes and his appropriate punishment. Nevertheless, we do not exclude bestowal of evidential material and testimonies by request at the Czechoslovak courts and participation of an unofficial Czechoslovak observer at the Eichmann's trial. This position corresponds, according to the MFA's opinion, to the current state of affairs and probably to the future procedure of all Socialist countries as well. Therefore, the

MFA is going to employ this position at further consultations with befriended countries.

We kindly ask you, dear comrade, to express your approval of the proposed procedure.

With comradely regards,
Grygar

Comrade Dr Antonín Grygar, First Secretary of the Minister of Foreign Affairs

10.9.1960

Dear Comrade,

Regarding the proposed procedure in submitting evidential material on Eichmann that you mentioned in your letter of 7th September, I recommend to keep the original directive and, on principle, not to consider handing documents on Eichmann over to Israel, not even unofficially through the Union of Anti-Fascist Fighters.

However, it would be purposeful to prepare photocopies of the documents which would then be published at a press conference, so that they were available for press representatives as well as anyone else, hence possibly also for the Israeli organs if they show their interest.

With comradely regards,
Koucký

7 On Co-Operation with Israel

29 September 1960

National Archives of Hungary, XIX-J-1-Izrael-30/c-00850-1960 (11.d.)
Collection: Ministry of Foreign Affairs [Külügyminisztérium]

Completed in 24 copies
Copy no. 000001

From: HSWP CC Foreign Affairs Department and Ministry of Foreign Affairs

Motion

To the Political Committee of the HSWP CC
Subject: Eichmann Case

I

Based on the resolution of the Political Committee of the HSWP CC, adopted on 28 June 1960 and concerning the Eichmann case, we consulted with the friendly countries involved and requested clarification of the following matters:
1. Development of a uniform position on the jurisdiction of the Israeli court
2. Shall we accept the Israeli request that we should provide them with material for the lawsuit to be commenced against Eichmann?
3. In order to further our political goal – to attack from an anti-Fascist perspective West-German neo-Fascism, Zionism and the Vatican (since Eichmann reached Argentina with the latter's assistance) – we must consider whether we can achieve all this most effectively by requesting Eichmann's extradition and by taking a united stand.

The basic idea of our entire campaign is that when exposing the crimes of Eichmann and his accomplices, attention must also be given – alongside crimes against Jews – to crimes committed against the movement of progressive individuals and patriots, thereby ensuring the anti-Fascist basis of our campaign.

As a result of consultation, we can state that all were in agreement with our political goals, while opinions differed on two other questions, summed up by the Soviet comrades as follows:
1. They do not consider it expedient to request Eichmann's extradition from Israel, since its rejection of such a request would diminish the prestige of the Communist countries.

2. Avoiding the issue of the jurisdiction of the Israeli court, they favour the Czechoslovak position that documentary proof should be given to Israel by means of some social organ. In practice, this would take place alongside the simultaneous publication of the submitted material, in order to prevent Israel from hushing up the material it had received.

II

We have already begun collecting together the material. Based on what we have seen so far, the material at our disposal does not ensure, as is necessary, that our goals be reached; in terms of both quantity and quality, it is restricted in the main to the deportations of 1944. This circumstance gives rise to a further task, namely that we should look for additional means of ensuring that the material can be used.

III

After preliminary semi-official inquiries, the Israeli government has now diverted the whole issue to the official route, and has requested in a note the submission of documentary evidence for the lawsuit to be launched against Eichmann. They have requested permission for the representative of its special investigative body to enter the country, for support for its operations, as well as for permission to summon Hungarian witnesses and to have them appear at the trial.

IV

As a consequence of these new developments, we request that the Political Committee cancel its resolution of 28 June 1960 concerning the Eichmann case. Bearing in mind the new situation, we suggest the following:
1. We decline to request Eichmann's extradition, we should not mention this in any form.
2. We should not recognise the jurisdiction of the Israeli court; this should not be stated openly – we should avoid the issue. We should not acquiesce to the Israeli request that we permit the representative of its investigative body to enter the country, and we inform them that if they have any requests or questions, then our competent bodies will examine them.
3. If the Israelis urge us once again to submit the material, we shall inform them that as far as we know, a social body called the National Committee of the Hungarian Victims of Nazism is responsible for collecting the material and that they will receive the material from this body.

4. We should maintain on-going contacts with other friendly countries in the future and inform them of our various measures. We should obtain further information about several issues that still have to be clarified – relating to the quality and quantity of the material that is at our disposal and to be submitted.
5. In the field of press propaganda and taking into consideration the ideas of the friendly countries, the following must be done:
    a./ Prior to and during the lawsuit, we should ensure the appropriate publicity in the daily press;
    b./ The social organ mentioned above should organise a press conference for foreign and domestic press representatives;
    c./ We should publish a book under their publication, which should contain the material that has already been submitted;
    d./ [...] We should publish a brochure of documentary evidence, if possible in Israel, under the name of a publisher there;
    e./ Finally, in a publication of the Ministry of Foreign Affairs, we should publish documents exposing the above-mentioned connections [*of the case with FRG, Zionism and the Vatican* – AK], and this should also take the form of a book.
6. We should continue collecting material, in view of the one-sidedness of existing material. For this purpose
    a./ We should ask to view the material of friendly countries in our search for supplementary material relating to Hungary. The Polish comrades have already responded positively;
    b./ With the help of the Ministry of Interior, we should continue collecting material in respect of material incriminating Arrow Cross members and military exiles classed in the same group; this area would allow us to resolve the one-sidedness of the material, and we could thus get closer to our goal of exposing West-German neo-Fascism, in light of the close connections existing among the émigré population.
7. If our work aimed at resolving the one-sidedness of the material fails, then we shall revise our propaganda plan as follows:
    a./ We will not hold a press conference;
    b./ Articles appearing in the daily press should be limited in number;
    c./ We should not publish the planned documentation as a publication of the Ministry of Foreign Affairs;
    d./ We should still publish a book, with a social body as publisher and, if possible, we should also publish a brochure in Israel, thereby ensuring the publication of the documentary evidence.
8. Using the methods below we should exert our influence to ensure that the Israeli bodies do not hush up the documentary proof received in the course of the lawsuit and that, in possession of this material, they take a stand against the current German leadership.

a./ We should allow properly prepared witnesses to appear at the trial, who can influence the course of the trial though their statements and their questions.
b./ When the social organisation mentioned above submits the material demanded by the Israelis, it should ask to take part as an observer in the public trial to be held in the Eichmann case.

Draft resolution

The Political Committee of the HSWP CC revokes its resolution of 28 June 1960 concerning the Eichmann case.

The Political Committee of the HSWP CC approves the procedure planned in connection with the Eichmann case and described in the motion.

8 On Measures to be Taken in the Eichmann Case

8 February 1961

National Archives of Hungary, XIX-J-1-j-Izrael-30/c-0081/2-1961 (13.d.)
Collection: Ministry of Foreign Affairs [Külügyminisztérium]

From: 2nd Regional Department
Ferenc Esztergályos
Deputy Head of Department

To: Péter, First Deputy Min.
Puja, Deputy Minister
Várkonyi, Head of Department
Katona, Head of Department

Memorandum

On measures to be taken in the Eichmann Case

1./ To organise press conferences in the first half of March both here in Hungary and at our major embassies. We should organise the conference in Hungary by means of the National Committee of the Hungarian Victims of Nazism. We shall make material received from the Ministry of Interior available to the press department, as they are in charge of its preparation. [...]

2./ At the end of March, the book by Jenő Lévai will be published in three languages (German, English and French) on the Eichmann case. We are already examining how to distribute it, and the embassies have received instructions to this effect.

3./ If the Israelis should attack us in any way, e.g. that the Communist countries are making a political issue out of the Eichmann case or the German question, and are using it to discredit the FRG – since we can count on such attacks, if this does happen, then we shall make public the Kasztner material, which exposes the Zionist bargaining over human lives. Incidentally, we can use this for manipulation even during the lawsuit, depending on how the trial develops. Moreover, we have in our possession the original letter of the Israeli police, in which it asks the Israeli Foreign Ministry which material it should obtain from us, and it is full of requests concerning German material. We could, under certain circumstances, publish this letter, in order to prove that they were those who raised the understandable and logical German question.

4./ As a more distant perspective, at the end of the lawsuit, publication of a collection of documents which would contain all the important documents.

5./ An extremely urgent task is the selection, by the legation, of the person to travel out to the trial; due to the lack of time and space, the Israeli legation has once again urged the general secretary of the legation to address this tasks.

9 On the Kasztner Issue

10 February 1961

National Archives of Hungary, XIX-J-1-j-Izrael-30/c-0081/3-1961 (13.d.)
Collection: Ministry of Foreign Affairs [Külügyminisztérium]

From: Frigyes Puja, Deputy Minister of Foreign Affairs
To: Gyula Nyerki
Comrade Chargé d'affaires
Tel Aviv

Dear Comrade Nyerki,

Returning to the issues mentioned in your January letter, I wish to inform you that, for technical reasons and a consequent shortage of time, the planned book will not be published. There is, however, an important issue which arose during conversations with comrades there and which deserves serious attention in our view. The issue is the Kastner [sic! – AK] affair. In the course of the Eichmann lawsuit, this issue will arise in some form or other, and in our judgement this is the point where we will be able to address the contacts that existed between Eichmann – and the Nazis in general – and the Zionist leaders.

Some Western newspapers covering the case have recently questioned whether the district court in Jerusalem is in fact qualified to administer the trial. The president of the court is Dr Hahlevi, who has already been a judge in a case in which Eichmann was one of the accused. The case was a lawsuit between Dr Kasztner and a Jerusalem hotel owner by the name of Grünwald, during which much was said about contacts between Hungarian Jewish leaders and the Nazis, including Eichmann himself. At the time Dr Hahlevi expressed critical and morally disparaging opinions about the co-operation between the Jewish leaders and the Nazis, thereby causing quite a stir throughout Israel at the time.

These current news reports and a piece of information telling us that one of Dr Kasztner's closest colleagues in Hungary, Joel Brand, is to appear in the trial as a defence witness, compels us to supplement our material proving Kasztner's activities, so that we can react to the question in the right manner and at the right time.

We therefore ask you to promptly obtain important supplementary material; the comrades there will certainly be able to help you, since they mentioned this question in connection with the brochure, calling our attention to its importance. We require the following:

1./ The judgement brought in the aforementioned lawsuit, and possibly that somebody should view the documents for several important and characteristic details. Press articles and commentaries published in connection with the lawsuit.

(If possible, we are thinking of original newspaper issues in Hungarian or other languages; if this is not possible, then at least photocopies.)

2./ The press's reaction to, and its commentaries on, the attempt on Dr Kasztner's life. Our requirements here are similar to those indicated above. Of course, if we could receive reliable and publishable information about the background to the attempt on his life, this would increase its weight.

I request you, Comrade Chargé d'affaires, to proceed as soon as possible in this matter and, despite the circumstances but given the shortage of time, to send the material urgently.

10 Letter of S. Mikunis, General Secretary of the Communist Party of Israel

Tel Aviv, 24 April 1961

National Archives of Hungary, M-KS 288/32/1961/4
Collection: Hungarian Socialist Workers' Party (HSWP), Central Bodies, Foreign Affairs Department
[Magyar Szocialista Munkáspárt (MSZMP) Központi Szervei, Politikai Bizottság]

From: HSWP CC Foreign Affairs Department [*forwarded* – AK]
To: The Hungarian Socialist Workers' Party, Central Committee

Budapest

Dear Comrades,

Concerning the Eichmann lawsuit that is just getting under way in Jerusalem, we wish to make the following request:

Under the special law adopted by the Israeli parliament prior to the Eichmann lawsuit, civil claims cannot be enforced during the trial. As a consequence, the entire court proceedings and the questioning of Eichmann is in the hands of Servatius, the West-German pro-Nazi lawyer, on the one hand, and the state prosecutor of Ben-Gurion's government on the other, especially considering the Anglo-Saxon legal procedure, which restricts the court's influence over the trial.

Although it is possible that the use of this legal practice will not prevent some important political issues from coming to light, it does almost without doubt exclude the possibility that contacts maintained with the Nazis during World War II by the World Zionist Movement (which now clusters round Ben-Gurion's government), the Jewish Agency for Palestine and other Zionist bodies will be lambasted.

In the past, and especially in the course of the so-called Kastner [*sic!* – AK] trial, important facts came to light concerning the contacts maintained by Rudolf Kastner, head of the Budapest Zionist Relief Committee, with Eichmann, Becher and other Nazis during the final years of World War II, as well as with other criminal contacts.

There is now a possibility that a well known Israeli lawyer, who represented one of the participants in the Kastner trial, will succeed in achieving a renewal of the trial in order for Eichmann to be summoned for questioning as a witness. If this lawyer, incidentally a supporter of bourgeois ideology but nevertheless strongly against Ben-Gurion and Mapai, is able to question Eichmann as a witness in connection with the Kastner affair, this would be of great political significance for us, and could possibly be of historical significance.

The success of the request for a renewal of the trial depends on whether we are able to present further documents to the Supreme Court and we have determined, at the request of the lawyer, to try and help him in this respect.

We therefore ask for your fraternal assistance. As far as we know, important documents were left in Budapest after the defeat of the Nazis.

Material related to the following would be particularly interesting to us:

1./ The participation of Zionist and other reactionary Jewish organisations or persons in Nazi attempts to sign a separate peace with the Western powers.

2./ Negotiations held by Zionist and other reactionary Jewish organisations or persons with the Nazis concerning the rescue of Jewish individuals in return for money or automobiles that could only be used on the Eastern Front.

3./ Other relations of Zionist and other reactionary Jewish organisations or persons with Nazis working for Western spy agencies.

Dear Comrades, we are quite aware that the Institute does not usually send documents (or photocopies) that are still unpublished in your country to foreign countries, but the importance of the Eichmann case seems to be so great that an exceptional solution might be justified. We look forward to hearing from you soon.

With fraternal greetings:
S. Mikunis
General Secretary
On behalf of the Central Committee,
Communist Party of Israel

11 B'nai B'rith Report on Media Coverage of the Eichmann Case in Communist Countries

June 1961

National Archives of Hungary, XIX-J-1-j-Izrael-30/c-0081/3-1961 (13.d.)
Collection: Ministry of Foreign Affairs [Külügyminisztérium]
[Original English-language document reproduced here without amendment – AK.]

The Eichmann Case in the Mass Media of Communist Bloc Countries

The historic trial proceedings now unfolding in a Jerusalem courtroom have as their major purpose the demonstration to the world that prejudice towards Jews is "dangerous" for it can lead to the gas chambers and to genocide. Premier David Ben-Gurion described the object lesson of the Eichmann trial in the following way:

> "We want the nations of the world to know that there was an intention to exterminate a people. That intention had its roots in anti-Semitism. They should know that anti-Semitism is dangerous and they should be ashamed of it. I believe that through this trial all thinking people will come to realize that in our day the gas chamber and the soap factory are what anti-Semitism may lead to. And they will do what they can about it."

The largest segment of the trial proceedings focuses on the activities of the Nazi juggernaut in what are now the Communist countries of East Europe – on Poland, Czechoslovakia, Hungary, Bulgaria, Rumania and the Soviet Union. Is the Eichmann case being handled in these countries in the way Israelis hoped it would be handled? How much attention in the mass media is being given to the case in these countries? How much emphasis is being placed in the mass media on the ultimate effect of anti-Semitism – the martyrdom of Jews?

The most immediate impression reached by a study of the mass media treatment of the Eichmann case in Communist bloc countries is the great variation in the coverage. There is, to be sure, one parallel line followed in all these countries and which can be expressed in this way: Eichmann symbolizes not only the Hitler era but also many of the present leading elements in the Federal Republic of Germany. But, aside from this common approach, each Communist bloc country handles the Eichmann case quite differently with reference to both the extent and the character of its coverage. Indeed, the common line itself is considerably affected by the different approach used by each country.

The Soviet Union

The press treatment of the Eichmann case in the Soviet Union prior to the opening of the trial on April 11 was marked by 1) relative paucity; 2) an emphasis upon an alleged relationship between Eichmann's crimes and present-day rulers of West Germany; and 3) a general minimization of Eichmann's crimes against Jews as compared with his crimes against people generally. These features continued after the trial began.

On May 25, 1960, the Soviet journal SOVETSKAIA ROSSIIA – the day after the announcement of the capture of Eichmann – carried a brief news item of the event. Then for a period of an entire week, while the Eichmann case was the principal topic of discussion in the international press, Soviet newspapers maintained a black-out of news on the matter.

The silence was finally broken on June 1 by PRAVDA in a short news dispatch from Athens quoting sources in Bonn to the effect that the West German Government was worried that Israel's determination to try Eichmann would increase anti-German feelings and that Konrad Adenauer had written to Ben-Gurion requesting him not to give wide publicity to the case. The PRAVDA article established the official Soviet line on the Eichmann case.

Six days later, the Moscow evening newspaper, VECHERNAIA MOSKVA, published the first substantial Soviet account on Eichmann. A lengthy description of Eichmann as "one of the most blood-thirsty hangmen of fascist Germany" was accompanied by an accusation that Adenauer was sympathetic to Nazism and permitted "yesterday's assistants of Hitler, Himmler and Kaltenbrunner" to occupy leading posts in the Government, Army, and judiciary of West Germany.

On June 14, a long article in LITERATURNAIA GAZETA used the Eichmann case to attack West Germany as a place where "quite a number of war criminals are hiding" and where "the ruling circles of the Western Powers" were "encouraging" fascist political activity. The article charged that West Germany was fearful of the revelations that might flow from the Eichmann trial and that Adenauer had sought to obtain Eichmann's extradition both by appealing to Ben-Gurion and by seeking intervention in Washington.

In none of the above accounts was there more than passing reference to Eichmann's crimes against specifically Jews. In the lengthy VECHERNAIA MOSKVA article, for example, no mention was made of Jews. Instead it spoke of "six million shot, burned in gas chambers." The article did give Eichmann's official title as "Head of the Bureau for the Solution of the Jewish Question."

A brief spurt of press attention to the Eichmann case came in the latter part of June, 1960, during the course of the United Nations Security Council discussions of the Argentine complaint against Israel. PRAVDA on June 24 and TRUD on June 25 gave prominence to the speeches of both its Delegate to the Security Council and Golda Meir, Israel's Foreign Minister. The press made it clear that the Soviet Union was in favour of the right of Israel to try Eichmann and criticized Argentina for failing to arrest and extradite war criminals.

In August, 1960, one Soviet organ appeared to depart to some extent from the previous line insofar as references to Jews were concerned. NEW TIMES, a semi-official foreign affairs publication, carried a lengthy story on Eichmann describing in some detail his "butchery" of Jews. While genocide of Jews was the major object of description and criticism, and Israel's capture of Eichmann was sympathetically portrayed, the article also took the occasion to attack West Germany. It expressed the view that the trial "could bring disclosures that would compromise many big-wigs in Bonn" and, for that reason, West Germany's politicians were "very much perturbed by it."

NEW TIMES is, however, not a mass circulation journal and its article did not signal a new approach to the Eichmann case. Earlier issues of NEW TIMES had suggested that Israeli authorities, under the pressure of West Germany and the United States, were attempting "to go easy" and "to play down" the Eichmann trial. West Germany – it was argued – was fearful of incriminating evidence against some of its leading politicians; and the United States was fearful of the same thing, as well as concerned that revelations about Eichmann's passport would hurt the Vatican. After the summer of 1960, references to the Eichmann case did not appear in the Soviet press.

Two weeks prior to the opening of the Eichmann trial PRAVDA reported upon the publication in Russia of a new 7-volume edition of the Nuremberg Trials which the reviewer described as revealing the "ghastly, unheard-of, thoroughly planned and meticulously executed felonies aimed at the enslavement and extermination of peoples...." Those who may have regarded the publication of the massive work on Nuremberg as an indication of a fulsome press treatment of the Eichmann case were to be sadly disappointed. The political line of the Soviet Government to play down Jewish martyrdom and to play up current West German fascism was transcendent [sic! – transparent – AK]. In keeping with this objective, PRAVDA on April 8 – three days before the opening of the trial – used the Eichmann case as a peg for a wide-ranging attack upon West Germany's leaders and particularly the newly appointed Inspector-General of the Army, Friedrich Foertsch, whom PRAVDA called a "war criminal." From the point of view of the Communist organ, some Bonn leaders are "feeling a chill" because "maybe Eichmann will say too much." It went on:

> "After all, there is abundant evidence indicating a direct connection between Eichmann's past actions and the occupations of Hans Globke, the Federal Chancellor's present State Secretary ... Eichmann probably could tell something as well about other Nazis for whom Bonn has found comfortable jobs."

In the course of this lengthy article, not once did the word "Jew" appear. Eichmann is identified as the "killer of millions" or as one "who exterminated millions of men, women, and children in the furnaces of ...Hitlerite death camps."

The opening of the Eichmann trial in Jerusalem on April 11 was marked in the Soviet press by a black-out of news. Neither PRAVDA nor IZVESTIA on that day carried any reference to the historic occasion. (The day before, PRAVDA carried a short item from Tel-Aviv reporting that a group of "fighters against Fascism" in Israel had demanded that the "Eichmann trial must become a trial of Nazism" and that the group had carried placards reading: "Bring to trial the collaborators of Eichmann-Globke and Oberlaender.") On April 12, IZVESTIA had an item, almost completely buried, announcing that the trial had begun.

If the press was silent, Radio Moscow began developing a new line, the basic elements of which had but been only hinted at earlier. The line suggested that a conspiracy existed to prevent disclosure of the true facts about Nazism in new West Germany. In a broadcast on April 11, Radio Moscow noted the presence at the trial of a large West German press and observer delegation. It also noted that Eichmann's defense attorney is Robert Servatius, whose "political complexion" is shown by his zealous defense at Nuremberg of Fritz Sauckel, "the chief of Nazi concentration camps." The broadcast stated that Servatius and the Bonn delegation were in Jerusalem "to fulfil the assignment of the West German Government to prevent the Eichmann trial from turning into a trial of Nazism and to prevent the publication of testimony on the past of a number of Nazi criminals, such as Globke, who now hold high Government posts in the Bonn Republic." A radio commentator darkly hinted that there existed some kind of "secret understanding" between Bonn and Tel Aviv, the precise nature of which was not disclosed.

During the next two and one-half weeks, PRAVDA carried no reference to the Eichmann trial while IZVESTIA had one short item quoting an Italian newspaper reference to a "deal" between Bonn and Israel. No doubt Soviet leaders were waiting to see whether the Israeli prosecutors would provide the hoped-for disclosures of connections between Eichmann and Bonn leaders. When none appeared, the press was prepared to reveal the details of the "secret understanding." On April 28, PRAVDA charged that "the Israeli Government, to satisfy West Germany's ruling circles, have made a deal with the revanchist circles of the F.G.R. and is trying to protect other Hitlerite criminals from exposure." PRAVDA contended that as far back as July 1960, Ben-Gurion, after meeting with a representative of the Bonn Government in Brussels, "issued a directive to abridge the publication of the investigation materials in the Eichmann case and to acquaint the F.G.R. Government ahead of time with these materials." PRAVDA criticized Israel for making possible the appointment as Defense Attorney of Servatius, who is "virtually an official representative of numerous fascists" living in West Germany.

According to PRAVDA, Servatius is being used by "the ruling circles of Bonn ... to exert pressure simultaneously on Eichmann himself and on the court agencies of Israel ... to conceal instances of criminal activity by former Nazis." The Communist organ reproved the Israel prosecution for the "noticeable silence... about the past and present" of Eichmann's "partners in crime" – Oberlander, Schroeder (Minister of Interior in the Bonn Government), Foertsch, General Hans Speidel, and even Defense Minister F. Strauss. But if PRAVDA expressed "concern" about the "marked tendency on the part of Israel's ruling circles" to avoid a "genuine exposure of the bloody crimes of the Hitlerite butchers," the Party organ expressed the hope that the masses within and without Israel would compel the prosecution to make "a proper exposure of all those Nazi war criminals" so that the trial does not become "a simple farce in the interest of the dark forces of revanchism."

Following the PRAVDA blast, Soviet newspapers retreated to the black-out technique. Since April 28, not a single line about the trial has appeared in PRAVDA. (IZVESTIA has carried one brief story.) Radio Moscow has not been completely silent, however. On a few occasions, in early May, it reiterated the charge of collusion between Israel and Bonn to prevent revelations concerning other Nazi criminals. A significant departure came on May 3, when Radio Moscow carried a rather long passage from a France-Presse dispatch concerning accounts of witnesses describing Nazi atrocities in Poland.

During the third week in May, Radio Moscow shifted to a more favourable approach to the trial proceedings – a shift that may shortly be reflected in the press treatment. A commentator noted that "six million human lives are on the conscience of the former head of the Jewish Department of the Gestapo to Hitlerite Germany." More significantly, the commentator averred that while Bonn and Israel had initially arranged a "deal" to prevent exposure of "former Nazis now in power," this arrangement has proved to be "very difficult" to implement. The commentator noted that Israelis understand that Eichmann "could not operate alone" and that he needed such accomplices as Globke, "the interpreter of the notorious Nuremberg Laws ... the theoretical basis of the mass extermination of Jews." And if the "deal" was initially meant to shield Globke, reference to him had to be brought out and was, in fact, brought out in the trial proceedings.

Obviously delighted by the reference to Globke in the trial (on May 12, Globke's name was mentioned in one of the documents submitted by the Prosecution), the Radio Moscow commentator went on to say that "the crimes being revealed at the trial are arousing the wrath and indignation of the world public."

Radio Moscow also displayed a strong interest in the "revelations" of Dr Gregorio Topolevsky, former Argentine Ambassador to Israel. His "disclosures" about the hiding of Martin Bormann and Dr. Joseph Mengele in Latin American countries were carried on May 19 in a special half-hour telephone interview over Radio Moscow. Dr Topolevsky was also asked to come to Moscow next month to give his impressions of the Eichmann trial.

It is clear that the "intention" of the Israelis to have the trial of Eichmann become an object lesson demonstrating what the ultimate results of anti-Semitism can be, has been, for the time being, frustrated in the Soviet Union by limited treatment and by an emphasis placed upon Nazi "big shots" in high places. The one gratification that Israel may derive from the progress of the trial is that she now no longer is being charged with perpetrating a "deal" with Bonn to shield Nazis in high positions.

Poland

Press treatment of the Eichmann case in Poland stands in striking contrast to that in the USSR. In Poland, the trial and its preliminaries have received extensive documentary reporting. Eichmann's organization of the deportation and extermination of Jews was elaborated upon in considerable detail even though attention is also paid to the mass annihilation of non-Jewish Poles. While criticism of the current West German Government and its alleged links to Eichmann is to be found in press coverage, Jewish martyrdom is the dominant theme.

Immediately after the Eichmann capture, scores of articles and biographies of Eichmann as the murderer of millions of Jews appeared in the Polish press. TRYBUNA LUDU, the leading Party newspaper, called his capture "historic justice." KURIER POLSKI carried lengthy presentations which attempted to justify, from a legal point of view, Israel's right to prosecute Eichmann. The Catholic bi-weekly TYGODNIK POWSCHECHNE (*correctly: Powszechny – AK*) made this characteristic comment:

> "The young State of Israel has every right to appear in the name of the whole Jewish people throughout the world. It is right and proper that Eichmann, who was responsible for the greatest crime in history, the crime against the Jewish people, should stand trial before a court of law in Israel."

In December, 1960, and January, 1961, TRYBUNA LUDU carried five lengthy stories, based upon original historical documentation, of the crimes of Eichmann against Jews and Poles. Written by Zofia Krzyzanowska, the articles blinked no facts to place the full horrors of the "final solution" before the Polish people. A key section read:

> "Polish territories have a special place in the history of the extermination of Jews. The very first acts of extermination were committed on Polish Jews. In the first phase of the criminal plan the persecutions were directed against both the non-Jewish and Jewish population of Poland."

Aside from a passing reference in the articles to Globke as one who "provided the necessary legal grounds" for Hitler's extermination program, the overt political anti-Bonn elements were absent. In keeping with a general program to provide the Poles with object lessons of anti-Semitism, the TRYBUNA LUDU stories stress Jewish martyrdom.

A modification in the approach of Poland came two weeks prior to the opening of the Eichmann trial in two official Polish Communist Party organs. The modification took the form of a greater stress upon German fascism and revanchism accompanied by a growing criticism of Israel and its handling of the trial. The change brought the Polish attitude somewhat closer to the Soviet attitude (although significant differences still remained).

POLITYKA, the Party weekly, on April 1 carried a lengthy article entitled "Process or Alibi", which contended that the Eichmann trial "must be dealt with in ... broader aspects, which means ... [it] must be treated, above all, within social and political categories." The article argued that the crimes of Eichmann, like those of other war criminals, cannot be handled in the usual "courtroom" method because "no contemporary society has a law providing adequate sanctions against crimes of such magnitude as those committed by Eichmann."

The article then pointed to the Nuremberg Trials as an illustration of how the crimes of an Eichmann ought to be handled. At that trial, POLITYKA stated, not only were individual criminals tried, but a whole system – the Nazi Party, Hitlerite organizations, German militarism, the fascist ideology, German revanchism – was put on trial and then "condemned and sentenced."

What the Poles wanted to see placed on trial in the Eichmann case was then suggested:

> " ... the German Federal Republic where thousands of former Hitlerites today hold responsible positions in the State apparatus and Hitler's former Generals command the Bundeswehr. Such things as glorification of the SS, conventions of war veterans, anti-Semitic incidents, and armament indicate that the ruling circles of the German Federal Republic adopt the policy of militarism and revenge."

POLITYKA, after criticizing Israel for supporting "the political line of the Bonn Government" and for "its great sympathy for the German Federal Republic," went on to attack strongly the "sensationist" manner in which Israel and the Western press were treating the Eichmann case – e.g., "thriller" stories about the way Eichmann was captured, the bullet-proof cubicle in the court for Eichmann, the underground corridor through which Eichmann will be led from prison to the courtroom. POLITYKA speculated "whether the embellishments of such publicity are not intended to black out the fundamental social and political meaning of the Eichmann case" and whether Eichmann as a person was not "being used as a cover-screen for all those collaborators and accomplices of his who should be appearing with him in the prisoner's dock." The article concluded with the strongly expressed view that the trial should "not become an alibi for Adenauer, Globke and Company."

On April 2, the bi-weekly organ of the Polish Lawyers Association, PRAWO I ZYCIE, appeared, carrying an article accusing Israel of being a party to a secret agreement with Bonn, which had as its objective the twisting of the Eichmann trial from its initial purpose and course. The Polish Lawyers Association's organ first noted that "war criminals" occupied "high posts" in the Bonn Government and that "if the trial of the arch-criminal Eichmann were conducted according to its merits, it would lead to the incrimination of all that which now represents the more or less open continuation of that kind of fascism and militarism which gave birth to such monsters as Eichmann."

The article then went on to contend that Bonn circles were placing intense pressures upon Israel to prevent those "former followers of Hitler who now occupy high posts" from being "compromised." According to the organ of the Polish Lawyers Association, these pressures have been successful: "The Israeli authorities are preparing Eichmann's proceedings according to suggestions from Bonn. For instance ... it was decided ... to expose several second-rank war criminals and to leave in peace the criminals of higher calibre who occupy official posts in the German Federal Republic."

The new approach did not alter the earlier decision to give the Eichmann trial extensive public attention and to emphasize Jewish martyrdom. Once the trial began, unlike the Soviet press, the Polish press carried <u>almost daily</u> and frequently lengthy accounts of the proceedings. Moreover, in the main, these accounts have been <u>factual</u> summaries of the arguments and testimony. However, the factual summaries have been at times accompanied by an editorial commentary which incorporates part of the new emphasis developed by the Party organs in early April. For example, the opening day of the trial was given a full half-page in TRYBUNA LUDU with this editorial comment:

> "Eichmann's defender Servatius here assumes the added role of defender of the German Federal Republic. The intention of such is clear: at any cost whatsoever, Eichmann's trial must be prevented from becoming a trial of Hitlerism (and which Eichmann's defense tries to present as 'something which exists no more and has disappeared from the arena of history'); and the names of such Hitlerite criminals such as Globke, who occupy high positions in the Bonn Government, must not be mentioned in the courtroom ..... ."

Yet, specific criticism of Israel's handling of the trial has not been strongly apparent in the newspaper accounts. Indeed, on April 14, the Polish correspondent in Jerusalem reported the following:

> "In spite of various machinations of Bonn people, the Eichmann proceedings may reveal the names of criminals who still haven't been punished and who finally should be reached by the hand of justice."

Only on April 29 did open criticism appear. TRYBUNA LUDU, in addition to its regular factual summary, carried a brief item quoting the East German observer at the trial, Dr Friedrich Kaul, who criticized the "peculiar limitations" of the presentation that allegedly prevented the name of Globke from being mentioned. It also carried a short summary of the April 28 PRAVDA article that had blasted a so-called Bonn–Ben-Gurion "deal."

<u>Hungary</u>

Hungarian press and radio treatment of the Eichmann case has been as impressive as the Polish coverage. Frequent and lengthy stories on Jewish martyrdom are characteristic. As early as June 3 and June 5, 1960, the Communist newspaper NEPSZABADSAG carried long lead stories on Eichmann's activities in Budapest, and the trade union journal NEPSZAVA put out a series of articles on his role in exterminating Jews.

Beginning on January 11, 1961, and for a number of months thereafter, the Hungarian illustrated popular weekly magazine, ORSZAG-VILAG, ran a consecutive series of articles on Eichmann. Each article occupied an entire page and carried much data and numerous references to Eichmann's extermination of Jews. A similar series was carried over Radio Kossuth in Budapest. Beginning on March 29, the station broadcast a daily program entitled "His Name is Adolph Eichmann."

On March 25, the Hungarian historian, George Ranski [sic! – AK], presented to a press conference a detailed, comprehensive account of Eichmann's activities and illustrated his lecture with photographs of original documents. He asserted that Eichmann was responsible for the deportation of 550,000 Hungarian Jews, of whom 400,000 died in concentration camps. NEPSZABADSAG carried the details of the lecture the following day.

Hungarian press treatment of Eichmann also served the political function of presenting West Germany as a haven for Eichmann's accomplices. It played up the fear in West German circles that the Eichmann case may cast West Germany in an unfavourable light. More attention was, however, given to Austria, Hungary's historic enemy, as a hiding place of war criminals. For example, the Budapest daily MAGYAR NEMZET on February 21 published an article on Georg Wilhelm Hoettl, whose extradition from Austria had been asked for by Hungary. Hoettl, the article observed, had been an accomplice of Eichmann in the deportation of Hungarian Jews and is currently shielded by Austria. A special crack was directed against Allen Dulles:

> "While Dr Hoettl was described by Winkelmann as excessively ferocious in his dealings in Hungary, this did not prevent him from building up relations with Allen Dulles, the American espionage boss, then staying in Switzerland. This shows not only Hoettl's foresight but A. Dulles' flexibility."

Since the opening of the trial, NEPSZABADSAG has, like the Polish press, carried daily, often lengthy, factual accounts of the proceedings. Unlike the Polish press, the Hungarian Communist organ has engaged in objective reporting with virtually no editorializing. Reference to the alleged Bonn–Israeli "deal" to hush up supposed interconnections between Eichmann and some Bonn leaders has not appeared. Radio Budapest, on the other hand, during the opening days of the trial, carried on a continuous attack on West Germany, insisting that it harbored Eichmann's "comrades" in "important posts." One radio broadcast insisted that the Eichmann trial "was at the same time a trial against the Bonn Government…" Notwithstanding the attacks upon West Germany, it is clear that in Hungary, as in Poland, the purposes of Israel in holding the trial are, in large measure, being realized.

Czechoslovakia

Czechoslovak press coverage of the Eichmann case, while extensive and revealing (in the sense of providing additional documentation of Eichmann's crimes against both Jews and Czechs) has focused principally upon alleged interconnections between Eichmann and high West German officials. Also singled out for charges by the press are alleged connections between the Vatican and war criminals.

On May 28, 1960, the Czechoslovak Communist organ, RUDE PRAVO, reporting on Eichmann's arrest, charged that Bonn authorities had tried to suppress evidence of Eichmann's crimes as well as the crimes of other former Nazi leaders who allegedly occupy high positions in the Bonn Government. Three days later, the newspaper accused Eichmann of murdering five million German, Austrian, Polish, Czech, Slovak, and Hungarian Jews, and added that many leading Bonn officials will probably be involved in the Eichmann trial.

On June 3, 1960, RUDE PRAVO, taking note of the fact that Eichmann had obtained a Vatican passport before fleeing to Argentina, contended that the Catholic hierarchy had been influenced by "Adenauer's and Franco's regimes" and that it feared that Eichmann's revelations might "disclose the World War II collaboration between the Catholic clergy and anti-Jewish Nazi and Fascist authorities."

In November, the Communist newspaper described an exposition of documents on Eichmann's crimes in Czechoslovakia which attempted to show that he was personally responsible for the extermination of 360,000 Czechoslovak citizens, including 200,000 Jews. The February 1, 1961, issue published documentary evidence of the deportation by Eichmann of children from Lidice to Poland, and on February 20, it described, with photographs, the details of Eichmann's crimes against Jewish inmates of concentration camps. The latter article also took the occasion to note that "there are many Eichmanns, Globkes, and Oberlaenders in present-day West Germany" who deserve punishment.

One week before the trial opened, the Czech Party organ adopted the line toward Israel that the Polish Party organs had taken a little earlier. RUDE PRAVO on April 4 criticized Ben-Gurion's statement that Eichmann's trial would not impair Israeli–West German relations and concluded from it that "efforts aimed at preventing the unmasking of former Nazi criminals who occupy responsible posts in Adenauer's Government are now becoming more transparent." The Czech organ insisted that "Bonn's State apparatus is more than saturated with Nazis of Globke's kind."

On the day the trial opened, RUDE PRAVO returned to a violent attack on West Germany, and contended that Eichmann's trial must bring evidence "incriminating accomplices in Eichmann's crimes, many of whom ... occupy prominent posts in the German Federal Republic." An Israel–Bonn "deal" was hinted at: "But some facts indicate that another course has been set for the trial." The hint was not further developed in the later reporting of the trial.

The Czech Communist press, like the Polish and Hungarian press, gave the trial frequent and considerable coverage. However, unlike the press in the latter countries, both RUDE PRAVO and the organ of the Slovak Communist Party in Bratislava, PRAVDA, provided little factual reporting and, instead, carried on a running editorial campaign against Servatius as the "defender of Nazism," and against Globke and the West German Government. If anything, PRAVDA was even more violent in its castigations than RUDE PRAVO. Radio Prague and Radio Bratislava treated the trial in the same tendentious manner.

Bulgaria

The news media of Bulgaria have maintained an almost complete silence on the Eichmann case. Prior to the trial, two very brief references to Eichmann appeared in RABOTNICHESKO DELO, the Party organ. On February 3, a short dispatch from London reported that Eichmann would be tried in Israel for the mass killings of Jews in 21 European countries. The March 11 issue of the newspaper reported on the uneasiness felt by Adenauer concerning the possible negative effects of Eichmann's trial upon the attitude of world opinion towards Bonn.

Reportage of the trial itself by the Bulgarian Communist press has been inconsequential. On April 12, RABOTNICHESKO DELO carried a short factual report on the trial's opening. A second report came on April 24 which, while mainly factual, concluded with a complaint against the Israel press and not, significantly, against the Israeli Government. The Israeli press was accused of abstaining "from the slightest reference to a subject undoubtedly related to the trial, namely to the bonds connecting Adenauer's policy with that of his predecessor Hitler." Three days later, the Bulgarian organ carried a largely editorial attack upon West Germany for harboring former Nazi criminals in high positions.

Rumania

Like Bulgaria, Rumania has given the Eichmann case little attention. Whatever treatment she has given has been much more anti-German and anti-Israel than Bulgaria. Prior to the trial, the Rumanian News Service mentioned the Eichmann case but once, and this took the form of a violent attack upon the Israel Government. On March 22, Radio Bucharest broadcast a news item from Tel Aviv citing an Israeli newspaper as saying that "the Israeli Government has advised Chancellor Adenauer that it wants to prevent the trial of the war criminal Eichmann from influencing adversely relations between Israel and the German Federal Republic." The broadcast commented: "Covering up Hitlerite murderers who exterminated millions of Jews – that is what preoccupies the mind of influential circles in Israel and in the German Federal Republic."

The limited Rumania mass media treatment was continued after the trial an had begun. For the first few days of the trial, no stories on the proceedings appeared in the main Rumanian Communist organ, SCINTEIA. However, Radio Bucharest on April 11, did carry a short broadcast attacking West Germany and charged that Globke had made available a "special fund" to pay for the services of Servatius. Again on the 13th, it returned to an attack on West Germany, this time alleging that Servatius "acting under the influence of the Western German leading circles, has tried to convince Eichmann not to reveal his accomplices ... ." Lesser newspapers in the capital – MUNCA, the organ of the trade unions, and ROMINIA LIBERA, the organ of the People's Councils – carried similar comments.

SCINTEIA, on April 15, finally carried a short factual account of the trial and a week later carried another one – a strongly opinionated report emphasizing that Globke and "many other war criminals who occupy high posts in West Germany" should be tried with Eichmann.

The theme of a Bonn–Israel "deal" to suppress testimony on high German officials was played by ROMINIA LIBERA on April 16, and was the subject of broadcasts by Radio Bucharest on April 25 and May 2.

***

It is apparent that the objective which the Israel Government set for itself in placing Eichmann on trial is being achieved in only Poland and Hungary and, to a much lesser extent, in Czechoslovakia. In Rumania and Bulgaria, the Israeli objective is hardly being realized at all. The objective is but partly being realized in the USSR. Why? How are the differences in the mass media treatment of the Eichmann case by the Communist bloc countries to be explained?

Certainly, such internal factors as the size of the Jewish population in each country has no consequential effect upon the extent and character of the press coverage (as it probably does in the West). Poland has a relatively small Jewish population – approximately 30,000. Yet its mass media provides extensive coverage and highlights Jewish martyrdom. Rumania has a relatively large Jewish population – approximately 150,000. Its coverage is extremely limited and plays down Jewish martyrdom. The Soviet Union embraces some 3 million Jews and is the second largest Jewish community in the world. The extent of its coverage is much less than that of either Poland or Hungary or Czechoslovakia, but much greater than either Rumania or Bulgaria.

The particular attitude of the Government of each individual Communist bloc country toward its own Jewish community also does not appear to affect the extent and character of its coverage. Bulgaria, for example, practices a relatively high degree of tolerance toward its small Jewish minority of six thousand, permitting it 1) a centralized religious structure; 2) opportunities to use Yiddish as a medium of its culture; and 3) the right to emigrate to Israel. Yet, Bulgaria's treatment of the Eichmann case is minimal. The Soviet Union does not permit its Jewish minorities any of the above rights (and, in that respect, is unique in the European Communist world). However, its coverage of the Eichmann case is far greater than that of Bulgaria.

Analysis suggests that external considerations are controlling factors in the decision of each Communist bloc country in handling the Eichmann case.[14] One consideration that is immediately apparent is the degree of concern felt by each toward West Germany's potential expansionist objectives. Poland and Czechoslovakia are immediately and directly concerned with West German revanchism. Poland has fears of the pronounced aim of Bonn leaders to retake the former Prussian area east of the Oder-Neisse line and Czechoslovakia fears the ambitions of German emigré groups from Sudetenland. In their press coverage of the Eichmann case, both link evidences of the recrudescence of German Nazism with militarism and revanchism.

Hungary, too, must be concerned with the possibility of West German revanchism for future efforts to recoup former German territory in East Europe would directly affect the security of Hungarian Communist rule in Central Europe. At the same time, Hungarian Communist leaders look upon its old historic enemy, Austria, as a possible spearhead of a rejuvenated German expansionist program. Thus, unlike any of the other Communist bloc countries, Hungary in its mass media coverage attempts to link Eichmann to fascist elements living in Austria and "protected" by Austrian rulers.

The foreign policy of both Rumania and Bulgaria is, of course, much less concerned with the distant West German state, The orbit of their foreign policy concerns lies in southeast Europe. Thus, their interest in the Eichmann trial is much less.

The USSR is, of course, vitally concerned with the possibility of West German revanchism. There is the need to protect the former German territory of Koenigsberg, acquired after the war. More importantly, the entire structure of the satellite system built up so meticulously after the war as a security belt for the Soviet Union would come tumbling down if successful thrusts toward Polish or Czech territory were ever made by West Germany. Thus, the Soviet Union does deal with the Eichmann case to a far greater degree than either Bulgaria or Rumania. Yet, the extent of its treatment is much less than that provided by the mass media of Poland, Czechoslovakia and Hungary. Why?

The answer to that question is to be found in a second consideration which operates as a controlling factor in affecting the decision of Communist bloc countries on how to treat the Eichmann case. This consideration involves the degree of hostility (or, conversely, the degree of friendliness) to Israel on the part of each Communist bloc country. It is clear that any extensive treatment of the Eichmann case and, particularly, any treatment which stressed the martyrdom of Jews is apt to foster sympathy for the Israeli state.

---

14 The exception, perhaps, is one aspect of the Czech press treatment. The stress given in the Czech press to the „collusion" between Eichmann and the Vatican is principally a reflection of the internal war being waged by the Czech Communist rulers against the local Catholic hierarchy which they hope to separate from the Vatican.

How the consideration of the foreign policy attitude to Israel operates as a controlling factor is particularly apparent in examining the character of the mass media treatment of the satellite countries (excluding the USSR). Neither Poland nor Hungary are openly hostile to Israel. Indeed, to some extent, friendly relations between these two countries and Israel exist. Consequently, one finds emphasis in their press treatment on the martyrdom of Jews for neither are vigorously opposed to fostering a sympathetic attitude toward Israel. On the other hand, Czechoslovakia's attitude toward Israel is a negative one and the former, in part, reflects that attitude by playing down the martyrdom of Jews, emphasizing instead the racism, revanchism and militarism of the present West German regime. The mass media of Czechoslovakia also tends to give emphasis to the thesis of a secret "deal" between Bonn and Israel in order to "suppress" information on German fascism.

The above consideration is even apparent in the much more limited treatment of the Eichmann case by Bulgaria and Rumania. Rumania, far more hostile to Israel than is Bulgaria, minimizes to an even greater degree than does the latter the martyrdom of Jews and, instead, stresses to a much greater degree the so-called secret "deal" between Israel and Bonn.

The Soviet Union is the most militantly hostile of all the Communist countries to Israel. The provincial press and, to a lesser extent, the national press of the USSR have, for the past four years, been conducting an intense anti-Israeli, anti-Zionist campaign. This campaign is partly a consequence of the Kremlin's assumption of the role of champion of the Arab cause, an assumption which could hardly be attempted by the other Communist bloc countries. To give extensive treatment to the Eichmann trial and, particularly, to underscore Jewish martyrdom implicit in it would run counter to a basic line in its foreign policy. For that reason, Soviet mass media treatment of the Eichmann case is much less than that of Poland, Hungary or Czechoslovakia, and this treatment stresses much less than does Poland or Hungary the martyrdom of Jews.

On the other hand, the Soviet Union is obliged to weigh its anti-Israeli consideration against the consideration of West German revanchism. Because the latter consideration plays a more decisive role in its foreign policy determination than the former, some attention will be given to the Eichmann trial. Indeed, so vital is the West German question in the total structure of Soviet foreign policy that it is probable that the Soviet mass media would give the Eichmann trial more extensive coverage, including emphasis on Jewish martyrdom, if the disclosures of the trial were to provide the bases for an indictment of the present West German regime. A published report last fall of the comments made by TASS' chief correspondent in Israel to Jerusalem officials support this conclusion.

The representative of the official news-gathering agency of the USSR was reported to have told Israeli officials that Soviet coverage of the Eichmann trial was dependent upon the kind of headlines that would emerge from the trial. "Small headlines, small coverage; big headlines, big coverage," he was quoted as saying. He further explained – it was reported – that were the Israeli prosecution to stress the complicity of present-day officials of Adenauer's Government in Nazi genocide, it would be "big headline stuff" in the Soviet press.

Additional indirect substantiation of this thesis is provided by the manner in which the USSR press – both local and national organs – handled four trials last March of local Soviet citizens who had been Nazi collaborators. The singling out of Jews as the victims of the Nazi collaborators was high-lighted rather than suppressed. One trial was held in Tallinn, Estonia, where three defendants (one in absentia) were charged with the crime of killing Jews in Kalevy-Livy and Kaluga. LITERATURNAIA GAZETA commented on March 3 that the accused were responsible for the shooting of "men whose only guilt was to have been born Jews...."

A second trial was held in Latvia and involved a group of Latvian and Belorussian collaborators charged with killing Jews among others. SOVETSKAIA LATVIA commented on one of the charges: "Old men, women, infants were first driven into the local synagogue, then taken to the wood and bestially killed."

A third trial took place in Lithuania. According to a report in TRUD (March 1), the Lithuanian collaborators were charged with torture of Jews in Alituis and the extermination of 2,000 Jewish citizens. A fourth trial, that of a Nazi collaborator in Stavropol, was reported in SOVETSKAIA ROSSIIA on March 23.

It is perhaps less than coincidental that suddenly four separate trials of Nazi collaborators took place in the USSR but a few weeks before the curtain was raised on the Jerusalem courtroom. Was it only now, sixteen years after the War's end, that the otherwise efficient Soviet security police was able to uncover in its midst, former Nazi collaborators?

The answer to this curious anomaly perhaps lies in the fact that most of the March cases provided the USSR with an opportunity to attack the West for harboring "war criminals." In the Estonian case, the defendant in absentia was one, Mere, now residing in England. England was bitterly criticized in the Soviet press for refusing to extradite a "war criminal." In the Latvian case, the West was censured for giving asylum to two individuals identified in the trial as "war criminals" – Riblis and Ertsams. With reference to Lithuanian Nazi collaborators, the United States was singled out for condemnation because it protects one, Pashkavichius, now living in Chicago, charged by USSR as a "war criminal" responsible for the murder of Jews and others.

The handling of the four cases indicates that the Soviet press would not be unwilling to focus attention on specifically the Nazi murder of Jews if this could be exploited as part of the USSR's campaign against the West. The prosecution of the cases just a few weeks before the Eichmann trial facilitated the Soviet objective of charging the West, specifically West Germany, as a haven for war criminals.

Since the disclosure of Hans Globke's name in one of the documents submitted by the prosecution, Moscow Radio has begun to take a more favorable view of the trial proceedings. Were further disclosures to be made, the Soviet mass media handling of the Eichmann case may develop along lines not basically divergent from the objective which the Israeli Government set for itself in putting Adolph Eichmann in the dock.

III The Six-Day War and its Aftermath

Introduction

Based on the large number of publications on the 1967 Six-Day war, we now have a more or less accurate picture both of the war itself, and of the global political context in which it occurred. Archival sources published in recent decades document the central role of Soviet policy in the events leading up to the Six-Day War, its unfolding, and subsequent developments.[1] Since the opening of the Communist archives, however, few documents have been published on Eastern-European Soviet-bloc leaders' reactions to the war and the accompanying political crisis, the information the Soviet leadership shared with them during the crisis, their perceptions of the Arab world and Israel, and how events influenced their policies towards the Jews in their countries. Moreover, the great majority of the documents published to date were not created during the war or its immediate aftermath; rather, they stem from subsequent periods when there was no need for immediate reaction to daily events, when it was easier to make policy adjustments. Strikingly, however, Hungarian records are barely to be found even among such documents.[2]

Although the documents presented below provide some novel insights on Soviet Middle-Eastern policy, their primary purpose here is to facilitate an understanding of the issues mentioned above, particularly in the context of the Hungarian Socialist Workers' Party (HSWP). The documents reveal the immediate reactions of Communist politicians to events, how their stance evolved during the conflict, and how they

---

[1] See, for example, Galia Golan, The Soviet Union and the Six-Day War in Light of Archival Materials, *Journal of Cold War Studies* 8:1 (2005), 3–19; Yaacov Ro'i, Boris Morozov (eds), *The Soviet Union and the June 1967 Six-Day War*. (Stanford, CA: Woodrow Wilson Center Press, Stanford University Press, 2008). See also the relevant US State Department documents at Foreign Relations of the United States, 1964–1968, Volume XVIII, Arab–Israeli Dispute, 1964–67, *Office of the Historian*. Accessed on 27 September 2016 at https://history.state.gov/historicaldocuments/frus1964-68v18/comp1; and Lyndon Johnson Administration: State Department Documents from the 1967 War, *Jewish Virtual Library*. Accessed on 27 September 2016 at https://www.jewishvirtuallibrary.org/jsource/US-Israel/1967war7.html.

[2] One Bulgarian document and one Polish document are published in Ro'i and Morozov, op. cit., 294–301 and 336–339. For the contemporary Bulgarian policy, see Jordan Baev, Eastern Europe and the Six-Day War: The Case of Bulgaria. In ibid., 172–196. One important collection of documents from the former Warsaw Pact countries' archives does not contain material directly relating to the 1967 war: Vojtech Mastny, Malcolm Byrne (eds), *A Cardboard Castle? An Inside History of the Warsaw Pact, 1955–1991* (Budapest: Central European University Press, 2005). The documents online at the Woodrow Wilson International Center's Cold War International History Project only contain material from the period after 20 June 1967, some of which has already been published by Ro'i and Morozov. See also James G. Hershberg, The Soviet Bloc and the Aftermath of the 1967 War, *Cold War International History Project*, e-Dossier No. 13. Woodrow Wilson Center. Accessed on 26 September 2016 at https://www.wilsoncenter.org/publication/the-soviet-bloc-and-the-aftermath-the-june-1967-war; and Uri Bar-Noi. The Soviet Union and the Six-Day War: Revelations from the Polish Archives. *Cold War International History Project*, e-Dossier No. 8. Woodrow Wilson Center. Accessed on 28 September 2016 at https://www.wilsoncenter.org/publication/the-soviet-union-and-the-six-day-war-revelations-the-polish-archives.

sought to determine the scope for action in line with the interests of their own countries.

The most comprehensive published document on Soviet policy at the time of the Six-Day War is Soviet Party leader Brezhnev's account of events, given in a speech at the plenary session of the Central Committee of the CPSU on 20 June 1967.[3] In his speech, Brezhnev summarised and evaluated the Soviet view of events, and then explained Soviet policy on the Middle East. He also mentioned that during the crisis, he had kept in daily telephone contact with the Party leaders of the Soviet-bloc countries. Hungarian documents stemming from the file of collected papers of the Secretariat of János Kádár, the Hungarian Party leader, verify such contacts. The first group of documents presented here (Documents 1–7) is a selection of written records of Kádár's conversations with the Soviet Party leader, and with other Soviet officials in the days and immediate aftermath of the war.[4]

"Since six o'clock this morning, reports of combat operations in the Middle East have been reaching us." János Kádár, First Secretary of the Central Committee of the HSWP, wrote this laconic comment by hand at the top of the first in a series of documents that summarise a telephone conversation between Kádár and Brezhnev on the afternoon of 5 June 1967 (see Document 1). In the ensuing days and weeks, a large number of memoranda, reports and other papers followed: records of Brezhnev's daily telephone conversations with Kádár between 5 June and 12 June; and notes on the conversations with F. Y. Titov, Soviet Ambassador to Hungary, who also briefed Kádár daily in order to inform the Hungarian Party leadership of the latest military, diplomatic and political developments.

The Kádár documents essentially confirm what we already knew from other sources: the Soviet Union, despite having contributed to increased tension in the Middle East in order to expand its influence, had no wish for war between Arab countries and Israel, and had no knowledge of the unilateral Arab actions that had contributed to the outbreak of war, including the demand for the withdrawal of UN troops, and the closure of the Straits of Tiran. The Soviet Union advised Egyptian and Syrian leaders to avoid becoming embroiled in a war; Nasser pledged to heed this advice. Both before and after the war, the Soviet leadership opposed radical Arab propaganda calling for Israel's destruction. During the war, it gave no credence to the provocative reports issued by senior military circles in Egypt, which accused the United States of direct intervention. And throughout the period, the Soviet leadership kept the "hotline" to the American president open; indeed, it believed initially that, acting together, the Soviet Union and the United States might be able to persuade the Israelis to accept a cease-fire, and to withdraw to their antebellum positions. Brezhnev also informed Kádár of each diplomatic success. This included French President De Gaulle's acceptance of a

---

3 See Ro'i and Morozov, op. cit., 302–335.
4 For all the documents of Kádár's secretariat, see Kádár János Titkársága [János Kádár's Secretariat], National Archives of Hungary, M-KS 288/47.

Soviet ceasefire proposal that required a full Israeli withdrawal, Nasser's withdrawal of his resignation, and the apparently successful attempts to bolster Nasser's regime as a member of the Non-Aligned Movement rather than as a Soviet ally, a possibility raised by Nasser himself during Supreme Soviet President Nikolai Podgorny's visit to Egypt in the immediate aftermath of the war.[5] This last endeavour shows that the Soviet leadership was quick to recognise that despite its errors in the lead-up to the war, and a significant decline in its prestige as a result, the USSR could still benefit politically from Arab military defeat, which opened up new possibilities for increasing its influence and military presence in the Middle East.

The Kádár documents provide new information about the relationship between the Soviet Union and the dependent satellite states, the positions taken by various Warsaw-Pact countries, and the differences and tensions that arose among them. The first striking observation is that the Soviet leadership clearly decided to provide regular information to the satellite states' leaders, information that acknowledged political failures, as well as the risks entailed in various courses of action. Moreover, the Soviet leadership also asked for opinions from the other leaders on a host of issues. Thus, at the height of the crisis on 9 June, Communist Party and government leaders attended a summit in Moscow that had been convened at a day's notice. Subsequently, after the first wave of military strife and diplomatic friction, they met again at a conference in Budapest on 11–12 July. According to some analyses, the Soviet leadership's aim in holding such talks was to persuade the "fraternal countries" to shoulder a greater burden when it came to re-arming the Soviet Union's Arab allies, and offering them economic assistance.[6] This is a possibility, but the gesture may also have been indicative of Moscow's fear that a manifest weakening of Soviet superpower influence would strengthen those forces within the "fraternal Parties" that sought greater independence and autonomy in foreign-policy making, and perhaps other fields too.

Among the selected documents, the summary of the Moscow conference, urgently convened on 9 June, is most revealing of the reactions of the Warsaw-Pact countries to the new situation and to Soviet policy (Document 8). As the document shows, Gomułka, Novotný and Zhivkov (the Polish, Czechoslovak and Bulgarian Party leaders respectively) gave immediate support to the Soviet stance, and endorsed Brezhnev's proposal that a statement be issued condemning "Israeli aggression" and offering unreserved support to the Arab countries. A slightly different tone was struck by Walter Ulbricht, General Secretary of the Socialist Unity Party of Germany, who was one of the initiators of the meeting. Although Ulbricht favoured a joint declaration, he urged nevertheless for additional – presumably military – steps to "prevent

---

5 A Hungarian version of an account of Podgorny's visit to Egypt on June 21–24 is included among the Kádár papers. It has not been included in this selection because an almost identical document dispatched by the Soviet Foreign Ministry to ambassadors in the Soviet-bloc countries has already been published in English. See Ro'i and Morozov, op. cit., 340–347.
6 See Yaacov Ro'i and Dima P. Adamsky, Conclusions. In ibid, 271.

aggression," over and above diplomatic efforts. He also insinuated – in an implicit criticism of the Soviet leadership – that a lack of co-operation between the Socialist countries had contributed to the crisis. In his response, Brezhnev rejected such criticism. Ulbricht's radical stance in the conflict probably played a part in his subsequent fall from grace, and the loss of his position as Party Secretary in 1971.

Of the various speeches made in Moscow, it was the Romanian Party Leader Ceaușescu's contribution that provoked the greatest debate. Although Ceaușescu agreed in principle that the post-war situation needed to be achieved by peaceful means and to the benefit of the Arab states, nevertheless he did not think that Israel alone should be blamed for the outbreak of war. In his view, the Arab countries had set out to destroy Israel, and this had placed them in opposition to world public opinion, including that of Western Communist Parties and "the many branches of the progressive movement". For this reason, Romania could not support the Arab countries unconditionally. Ceaușescu also expressed opposition to the issuing of a joint declaration.

The Hungarian Party Leader, János Kádár, attempted to strike a balance between the various positions. In his record of the meeting, he wrote the following by hand next to Ceaușescu's words: "At present, the important thing is not the issuing of a declaration. It would be enough to publish a communiqué stating that a meeting was held between representatives of our Parties and countries on the situation in the Middle East". It is difficult to decide whether Kádár wrote this comment in order to have a more accurate record of the Romanian leader's words, or as an expression of his own thoughts. At any rate, in his speech he proposed a compromise solution, that a statement or communiqué be issued, rather than a joint declaration; such a statement would indicate that the meeting's aim had been to reconcile the various positions, and that the participants agreed on the major issues and wished to take joint action. As we know, this proposal was not accepted.

From today's perspective, the most important speech at the meeting was that of Josip Tito, President of Yugoslavia. Since the Yugoslav Communist leadership generally kept its distance from joint actions organised by the Soviet-dominated Warsaw Pact, Tito's participation in the meeting was, in itself, an important sign of change, a fact noted with satisfaction in internal memos on preparatory consultations for the meeting (Document 7). The speech reveals that Tito, who maintained close relations with Nasser, the other major leader of the Non-Aligned Movement, knew all those things of which the Soviet leadership, by its own admittance, was ignorant – such as Egypt's intention to close the Gulf of Aqaba – and supported such action. The most important part of Tito's speech was the general strategic conclusions he drew from the Six-Day War. In effect, the Yugoslav leader proposed that the Communist countries should review their strategy on local wars. In his opinion, nuclear weapons had substantially reduced the risk of local wars becoming global wars. If the Communist countries continued to eschew involvement in local wars in order to avoid a global nuclear conflict, then this erroneous evaluation of the situation would create favourable conditions for the "imperialists", who were extending their spheres of influence by means of a whole series of local wars.[7]

With this line of thought, Tito appears to have touched on a subject that may have divided the Soviet leadership itself. The documents on the Six-Day War show that Brezhnev and his colleagues took the view that the Chinese (and the Cubans) were encouraging Egyptian and Syrian leaderships to intensify the Middle-East conflict until a war broke out. Indeed, it is Chinese influence which may explain why the Arab leaders took such provocative steps without first discussing their actions with the Soviet Union. Apart from one section of the Egyptian and Syrian military leaderships, the main regional spokesman for the Chinese position was Houari Boumediène, President of Algeria, whom the Soviet leadership welcomed in Moscow only after some hesitation (see Documents 9 and 15) and who, even then, attempted to persuade the Soviet leadership that the war must be continued in the spirit of Che Guevara, and by creating a "second Vietnam".[8] Until the Six-Day War, the Soviet leadership had considered the Chinese strategy to be a provocation aimed at bringing about a war between the Soviet Union and the United States, enabling China, as the third power, to emerge as the winner. Now, however, Tito – who could not be accused of sympathising with the Chinese Party or with Chinese policy – was proposing the same thing as the Chinese, and was doing so in a context that might also have been discussed by the Soviet leadership: local wars had to be undertaken, since they could be won without risking a global conflict. Tito's stance may have enhanced the influence of those within the Soviet leadership who held similar views. At any rate, this is one of the possible conclusions that can be drawn from Brezhnev's speech at the plenary session of the Central Committee on 20 June, at which he said the following:

> We rightfully thought and continue to think that our main protagonist is the United States and also, of course, the FRG. Whenever we discuss questions of war and peace, this principally is what we have in mind, and therefore, the possibility of a "major" world war. But life has shown that there can also be small, so-called local, wars. [...] Consequently, we must have strategic military and tactical plans regarding wars that have a local character. Our political, diplomatic and military people have to study all sides of the question where such wars may arise, and prepare their positions for such an event (*Cries: Correct!*) [...] In a word, our military doctrines, our military plans and calculations, as well as our concrete actions in the sphere of military policy, have to bear in mind all these new factors, and to anticipate in good time the possible course of events, not only in direct relation to the defence of the Soviet Union, but also regarding questions pertaining to the support of friendly states.[9]

---

7 According to Tito, Greece (after the Generals' Coup in April 1967) and Italy were preparing for such a local war against Yugoslavia.
8 See Brezhnev's Speech of 20 June 1967, in Ro'i and Morozov, op. cit., 332–333, and Todor Zhivkov's Account at the Plenary Session of the Central Committee of the Bulgarian Communist Party on 14 June 1967. In ibid, 295. Strikingly, the parts of Brezhnev's speech relating to China's policies are absent from the text.
9 Ibid, 333.

It seems, therefore, that Tito contributed to the change in strategy, which resulted in the Soviet Union's involvement from the mid-1970s onwards in a series of conflicts with catastrophic consequences, including civil wars in Africa and Afghanistan.[10]

Neither the summary of the Moscow meeting on 9 June, nor the other documents, indicate whether the participating countries decided collectively to break off relations with Israel. In his speech at the plenary session of the Central Committee, Brezhnev stated the following: "We did not ask the other Socialist countries to sever diplomatic relations with Israel. But our common understanding of the situation [...] and the atmosphere of unity led to [...] severing relations with Israel".[11] On 10 June, the second day of the conference, the Soviet Union announced the severance of diplomatic relations, and a similar announcement was made by Czechoslovakia several hours later, by Bulgaria the next day, and finally by Hungary and Poland on 12 June. Kádár informed Brezhnev of Hungary's decision on the same day. According to the records, Brezhnev replied that: "This is in line with the common position elaborated in Moscow. He [*Brezhnev* – AK] is pleased that everything is in order here and we can take this step"[12] (see Document 9). All of this indicates that although the Soviet leadership expected the other countries to break off relations, it also left a loophole open: countries could delay or avoid taking this decision by citing serious political difficulties, including intra-Party conflicts or social tensions. Kádár decided against such a course.

Based on the Kádár papers and the other Hungarian documents, it is possible to reconstruct the goals of Hungarian policy at the time of the Six-Day War, and in its immediate aftermath. Kádár set the tone at a meeting of the Political Committee

---

10 These strategic ideas on local wars outlined by Tito and embraced by Brezhnev were strongly criticized in a March 1968 internal memo by Otakar Rytíř, Chief of General Staff of the Czechoslovak army, who argued that the Warsaw Pact's military doctrine against the Western Alliance should continue to be based on the nuclear deterrent, because if this were to be replaced by a strategy of local wars, then the Western countries would necessarily win, given that they had a better qualified workforce, more advanced technology, and a stronger economic base. See Mastny and Byrne, op. cit., Document 47, Remarks by the Czechoslovak Chief of Staff on the Theory of Local Wars, 13 March 1968, 257–260.
11 Ro'i and Morozov, op. cit., 321.
12 Concerning the meeting of the Presidium of the Central Committee of the Czechoslovak Communist Party on the very same day, see Document 11 in this chapter. The Political Committee of the PUWP met on 10 June, and on 12 June, the wider leadership of the Polish Party had a meeting mostly on the situation in the Middle East; see Szaynok, *Poland–Israel 1944–1968*, 406–407. According to Polish documents quoted and analyzed by Szaynok, the Political Committee decided at a meeting on 19 June that Poland would sever diplomatic relations with Israel, but this decision was suspended in the evening hours of the same day, as Israel seemed to have accepted the decision of the Security Council, and was ready to halt military actions. The Polish diplomats (and, based on the documents, the Bulgarian diplomats too) thought that the Soviet Union, as a superpower, could not revoke its decision to sever diplomatic relations, for it needed to keep up the pressure on Israel. Yet, under the new circumstances, the other Eastern European countries did not have to abide by the Soviet decision. See ibid, 403–405.

that took place the day after the outbreak of war. He told those in attendance that the Middle-East conflict needed to be treated first and foremost as a foreign-policy issue. He did not deviate from this basic position until his speech to the Political Committee a week later, on 13 June (Document 10). In the second part of his speech, and without uttering the word Jew, Kádár left no doubt that he regarded Jews as a covert, clannish and influential group within the Party. According to him, although they appeared otherwise to support Party policy, in the crisis they were behaving in an "unreliable" fashion:

> A small section of the Party membership – *and I hope I shall not be misunderstood* [emphasis added – AK] – but a section that exists and is rather influential in a certain area, behaved in a non-Communist manner. And I don't want to make a racial thing out of this, and I understand that it is not sufficiently clear to everyone who the aggressor, the attacker is; it is possible to understand a certain anxiety, but this does not mean permission to challenge the position of the Party. [...] I would not allow this to pass without a response. [...] And if we then have fewer Party members, this is the lesser evil than if they were to waver. We must not tolerate or allow that. [...] If these trends spread, we shall have to adopt new measures. Because to fatten up people in good jobs who then behave like this in critical situations, this cannot be permitted![13]

At that time, Kádár was obviously well aware that various groups in society and among the country's intellectuals, including Party members, opposed the pro-Arab policy, and sympathised with Israel. Two documents in this chapter (Document 16, compiled by an unknown informer, and Document 17, compiled by leaders of the State Office for Church Affairs) about the views and opinions of members of the Jewish community prove that the official position on the war was strongly opposed both by community officials and by Jewish Party members and activists. Therefore, having given an account of the Moscow conference, Kádár obviously decided to announce in a rather harsh tone the introduction of measures against those deviating from the Party line. Documents published below in Chapter Five indicate that, at this time, state and security organs intensified their activities within the Jewish community, with a view to preventing the emergence and spreading of any form of views opposing Hungarian policy (see Chapter 5, Documents 1–4).[14] Kádár's announcement may also explain the purges that took place subsequently, and which primarily affected officials of Jewish ancestry working at the Foreign and Interior ministries, and in the military apparatus.

In general, Kádár and the Hungarian Party leadership had two main objectives. The first was to meet Soviet expectations in full, but to interpret them flexibly, or at least to avoid being the first country to fulfill them. The second was to keep the consequences of the conflict out of domestic politics. As the various documents show,

---

13 Ibid., 276–277.
14 In the aftermath of the war and the severance of diplomatic relations, the authorities in Czechoslovakia and Poland intensified the pressure on the Jewish institutions. See Labendz, Renegotiating Czechoslovakia, 460, and Szaynok, *Poland–Israel 1944–1968*, 420–423.

Kádár had a profound disdain for the Arabs, and believed that their poor military performance was due to the backward nature of their civilisation and culture. (Other Communist leaders, such as the Bulgarians, gave similar explanations for the humiliating defeat of the Arab armies despite being equipped with modern Soviet weaponry.) At the same time, Kádár's speech also contains common stereotypes of Jews as exclusively urban and highly educated people. Listing the reasons for the catastrophic defeat of the Arab forces, he declared the following: "And another factor was the difference in quality of available personnel [...] to go back to the roots [...] people with primary education were set against university graduates, and this represented a decisive superiority in all respects" (see Document 10). Kádár mistrusted the Arab leaders, even those pursuing pro-Soviet and anti-Western policies. As the record of his conversation with Egyptian Ambassador Fouad shows (Document 10), he was convinced that power in the Arab countries actually lay in the hands of soldiers, and thus it was impossible to have confidence in the intentions or promises of politicians. On the other hand, he considered the military leadership as incalculable and unreliable, as experience had shown. Kádár also feared that radical Arab political leaders such as Boumediène, or extremist elements in the Syrian or Egyptian military leaderships, might provoke further conflicts, thereby dragging in the Soviet Union and its allies. He raised this issue in the context of economic and military aid to the Arab countries at the Budapest meeting of Party leaders in July:

> In our public opinion, and I think that in other countries it is similar, the question looks like this: we were giving to Ghana – it failed; we gave to Indonesia – it failed; we gave to the Arab countries – that failed too. Therefore, the question raises doubts. Of course, the Socialist countries cannot have the same attitude as capitalist countries toward assistance to other countries, but the Socialist countries should have a minimal guarantee that assistance rendered by them will not be wasted.

Since Brezhnev had also criticised the Arab radicals at the conference,[15] Kádár took the opportunity at the ensuing meeting of the Political Committee to urge those responsible within the Party for information and propaganda to inform the membership of such dangers. The same meeting saw a discussion of how Hungary might fulfill Arab requests for assistance (Document 14). The document clearly indicates that the Arab countries sent the same list of needs to all the Socialist countries. The words of Prime Minister Jenő Fock and First Secretary János Kádár show that the Hungarian political leadership sought to make the smallest possible number of commitments, and to ensure that any obligations undertaken would impose a minimal burden on the

---

[15] Polish Record of Meeting of Soviet-bloc leaders (and Tito) in Budapest (excerpts). 11 July 1967. History and Public Policy Program Digital Archive, KC PZPR, XI A/13, AAN, Warsaw; document obtained by James G. Hershberg and Wanda Jarzabek; translation for CWIHP by Jan Chowaniec. *Wilson Center Digital Archive*. Accessed on 28 September 2016 at http://digitalarchive.wilsoncenter.org/document/113622.

country's economy. They strove to minimise the amount of assistance, and to supply items that were either plentiful or in stock. They also attempted to make sure that goods requested by Egypt or Syria were subsequently supplied to these countries as part of a financial transaction.

The final group of documents in this Chapter (Documents 18–20) present the process leading to the restoration of diplomatic relations between Hungary and Israel. During the 26 years following the severance of diplomatic relations, relations between the two countries barely existed. The Swedish embassy represented Hungarian interests in Israel, and the Swiss embassy represented Israeli interests in Hungary. Trade between the two countries slumped. Indeed, trade worth more than 100 million dollars a year in the first half of the 1960s decreased to around ten million dollars by the early 1980s (Document 19, Annexe 1).

In the early 1980s, the Hungarian economy faced an increasingly severe crisis: in 1980, the country's debt to the West was ten times what it had been in 1970. Foreign-trade earnings were insufficient even to pay the interest on foreign loans. In 1982, the country evaded bankruptcy only by joining the International Monetary Fund and the World Bank. Under these circumstances, the political leadership was prepared to use all means to increase foreign-currency earnings. On 20 December 1983, the Political Committee adopted a resolution on the revitalisation of relations between Hungary and Israel in the hope that this would help to solve the debt crisis (Document 18). The text of the resolution reveals the anticipated economic benefits: "Recently, Israeli business people have proposed the mutually beneficial expansion of our economic relations and co-operation in third markets. According to the calculations of the Hungarian economic bodies, trade volumes could be doubled without endangering, in the first place, our economic and trade interests with the Arab countries". Hungarian Party leaders believed that if they managed to limit the improvement in relation to the economic sphere, then under the given circumstances – following the Israeli–Egyptian peace agreement, and during the Soviet Union's domestic political struggles after the death of Brezhnev – they might be able to adopt such measures without incurring major political risk. They also expected an improvement in relations to exert a positive impact on economic relations with the West, and this expectation indicates the extent to which the stereotype of "international Jewish economic power" pervaded Hungarian Communist circles: "We should seek the support of the Israeli partners towards accomplishing greater financial co-operation with our country in the United States and in the Western European countries".

In the ensuing years, trade relations between the two countries developed spectacularly, albeit at a far lower level than in the pre-1967 period. Moreover, the number of visitors to Hungary from Israel increased significantly. The Hungarian authorities failed, however, in their attempt to limit relations to the economic sphere. Indeed, it seems that in 1985, after Gorbachev came to power, there was a real breakthrough in relations in other fields. For instance, the 9th Department of the Ministry of Foreign Affairs which was still noticeably opposed to an improvement in relations with Israel on account of the perceived threat to relations with the Arab countries and the risk of economic blowback, drafted a negative report listing instances of Hungarians participating in cultural and sport events in Israel, without having first requested the Department's consent. Clearly, this kind of behaviour would not have occurred in earlier decades (Document 19, Annexe 3).

In the spring of 1987, Hungarian diplomacy began secret talks with the Israeli government on expanding relations, during which the possibility of restoring diplomatic relations was not ruled out, although the general view was that such a step would not be feasible until a later date. In Berne on 14 September 1987, the heads of delegation exchanged notes concerning the opening of interest representation offices in each other's country for the purpose of enhancing economic, trade, cultural and humanitarian relations. Meanwhile, Hungarian politicians were closely watching the reactions of the Soviet Union and the "fraternal countries". According to the recollections of János Görög, the Hungarian diplomat who led the negotiations and who later became the first Hungarian ambassador to Israel, the Hungarian political leadership requested the opinion of the Soviet leaders prior to the commencement of the negotiations in 1987. The Soviet leaders "acquiesced to our holding discussions, on condition that there should be no mention of the restoration of diplomatic relations, of consular relations or of an embassy. They did not want us to set a precedent in this regard".[16] Thereafter, according to Görög, the Hungarians chose not to request the Soviet position. Rather, they waited to see whether there would be any reaction to Hungary's measures, and also took care to ensure that they never went much further than, for instance, Poland, in their relations with Israel.

Supporters of the restoration of diplomatic relations, or at least of measures leading to such, were required to put forth arguments against their opponents in the Party and the government. Typically, such arguments centred on pragmatic and economic factors, including the stereotype concerning the influence of "international Jewish capital", a stereotype that the remarks of the Israeli negotiating partner tended to confirm: "The involvement of international Jewish capital has given rise to business opportunities, including the realisation of an investment programme worth 300 million dollars, in which – at the initiative of Shimon Peres – 20 American-Jewish businessmen are engaged" (Document 20). The supporters of renewed diplomatic relations averted fears over the likely reaction in the Arab countries – fears often cited by their opponents in the Party and government – by referring to the absence of unity among Arab states, and by repeating statements concerning the strictly pragmatic nature of the planned measures, and the consistent application of practical aspects. "For this reason, when the Central Committee decides on the proposal, it would be necessary to declare its wish that our competent economic-financial bodies should

---

[16] Titkos kiegyezés a padlásszobában. Interjú Görög János volt izraeli magyar nagykövettel [A Secret Compromise in the Attic Room: An Interview with János Görög, Former Hungarian Ambassador to Israel], *Hetek* 4:20 (13 May 2000), 2–3.

elaborate, in a specific and detailed fashion, the conditions whose fulfillment would justify Hungary taking this decision – the restoration of diplomatic relations – which is so crucial for Israel" (Document 20). Although trade with Israel and the Israeli-assisted import of capital to Hungary failed to meet expectations, the reactions of the Arab countries were not as dramatic as had been predicted by the functionaries responsible for relations with those states. According to the memoirs of János Görög, by 1989, Israeli–Hungarian trade had returned to the level seen in the first half of the 1960s, and there had been no decline in trade with the Arab countries:

> The most interesting thing was the reaction of the Arabs. The pessimists had said that the establishment of diplomatic relations [with Israel] would result in a decline of at least 50 per cent in trade with the Arab countries. In contrast, since the Arabs believed that the Jews had paid us off or induced us in some fashion, and that the way to win us back was to order another freight train and 250 extra buses; in the year following the opening [to Israel – AK], total trade with the Arab countries increased by 15 per cent.

Finally, on 14 September 1989, only a few months before the collapse of Communism, Hungary and Israel signed an agreement on the restoration of diplomatic relations.

Documents

1 Telephone Conversation between János Kádár and Leonid Brezhnev

5 June 1967

National Archives of Hungary, M-KS 288/47/740/1967/ p. 193.
Collection: Hungarian Socialist Workers' Party (HSWP), Central Bodies, János Kádár's Secretariat [Magyar Szocialista Munkáspárt (MSZMP) Központi Szervei, Kádár János Titkársága]

Completed in 1 copy

At 3 p.m. on 5 June 1967, Comrade Brezhnev telephoned Comrade Kádár to inform him of the situation in the Middle East.

Currently, even the CPSU does not know exactly how the conflict erupted; the most important thing now is to do everything to achieve the immediate cessation of combat operations. Therefore, the Soviet comrades have contacted Nasser to request information and advice about what they might do to restore peace. There is no answer as of yet.

Comrade Kosygin contacted President Johnson by means of the hotline. He responded that he had appealed to the governments in the region and was trying to exert all his influence to bring about a settlement.

Nasser told the Soviet ambassador this morning that they are asking for aircrafts to make up for those that have been lost. He said that British and American aircraft carriers were stationed near Israel, and that planes had taken off from these ships, but in Comrade Brezhnev's opinion, this was "dramatising the situation".

[...]

Comrade Brezhnev has promised that as soon as he has something more to say, he will contact us immediately, either in person or – if it is too late – by way of the ambassador.

2 Soviet Ambassador's Meeting with János Kádár

6 June 1967

National Archives of Hungary, M-KS 288/47/ p. 195.
Collection: Hungarian Socialist Workers' Party (HSWP), Central Bodies, János Kádár's Secretariat [Magyar Szocialista Munkáspárt (MSZMP) Központi Szervei, Kádár János Titkársága]

Translated from Russian
Completed in 3 copies
[...]

On 6 June 1967, Comrade F.Y. Titov, the Soviet ambassador, visited Comrade János Kádár, and on behalf of the CC [Central Committee] of the CPSU and informed him of the following:

The Soviet government has taken the following measures in connection with the acts of war commenced between Israel and the United Arab Republic:

1. The Soviet Union's representative at the UN has been instructed to consult with the representatives of the U.A.R. and Syria and to immediately raise the issue of an urgent convening of the Security Council with a view to achieving the cessation of the acts of war.
2. The Soviet ambassador in Cairo has been instructed to immediately visit President Nasser, or Amer, and ask for information about the state of affairs, with reference to the communiqués that have been made public concerning clashes between the armed forces of the U.A.R. and Israel. It is imperative that Nasser is told that our point of departure is that the U.A.R. must do its utmost to avoid giving the aggressor a reason for a devastating armed conflict.

    The Soviet ambassador in Damascus has received similar instructions.
3. The Soviet government has appealed to Johnson, the U.S. President. The appeal emphasises that it is the obligation of all the major powers to strive for the immediate cessation of the military conflict between Israel and the U.A.R. The Soviet government calls on the United States to exert the appropriate influence on the government of Israel, particularly because the American side has every opportunity to do so.

    A corresponding appeal has also been made to the Prime Minister of Great Britain.
4. The Soviet government has appealed to De Gaulle, the French president. The hope has been expressed that France – and the President personally – will assist in bringing an immediate end to the military conflict...

3 Telephone Conversation between János Kádár and Leonid Brezhnev

6 June 1967

National Archives of Hungary, M-KS 288/47/ p. 196-197.
Collection: Hungarian Socialist Workers' Party (HSWP), Central Bodies, János Kádár's Secretariat [Magyar Szocialista Munkáspárt (MSZMP) Központi Szervei, Kádár János Titkársága]

Completed in 4 copies

Memorandum

For Comrade János Kádár

At 4 p.m. on 6 June 1967, Comrade Brezhnev telephoned Comrade Kádár and stated the following:

Today the leading Soviet comrades listened to the heads of the intelligence services and the army, who established that the armed conflict came as a surprise to our Arab friends. Additionally, because discipline is poor in their army, they are suffering great losses even without a struggle. Most of the airfields and aircraft have been destroyed without a fight. It is still difficult to give a full evaluation, but it is already clear that the unexpectedness of events had not benefitted the Arab countries. There are big losses in land forces, as well as in territories.

In reply to yesterday's Soviet letter, Nasser stated that he has no advice at present concerning what the Soviet government could do to end the conflict. His sole request is that as many aircrafts as possible be sent. It was suggested that these planes be flown by way of Yugoslavia and the Mediterranean (because Nasser requested that they come by air), but this is dangerous. The Soviet comrades think that Algeria should provide the planes, and the Soviet Union will then send some by ship or on civilian aircraft – in a dismantled state. At any rate, the Soviet comrades are seeking opportunities to help for as long as the fight continues in the Security Council.

At the UN, as we know, two positions and two draft resolutions are in conflict with each other. With reference to Johnson's message of yesterday, the Soviet government has today contacted the American president once again. Since he stated yesterday that he would do everything to resolve the conflict, the Soviet government hopes that the Soviet draft resolution will be adopted.

Soviet comrades working at the UN have indicated that the Americans are inclined to make some changes to their draft, but it is not known what they will be.

Yesterday Comrade Brezhnev spoke again with Comrade Ceausescu, informing him that he had spoken to the first secretaries of the other fraternal Parties, who all agreed with the idea of a collective letter that would be addressed to the Chinese. Comrade Ceausescu replied that they had discussed the matter and had concluded that the sending of a collective letter was not the right approach; rather, each Party should write to the CPC; they too might write. Comrade Brezhnev said that in this area viewpoints differ, but our goals are the same; those that are in agreement will write the letter.

With this, the "Romanian" part of the matter was closed, and Comrade Brezhnev himself has today signed the letter.

[...]

4 Soviet Ambassador's Meeting with Zoltán Komócsin

7 June 1967

National Archives of Hungary, M-KS 288/47/ p. 207-208.
Collection: Hungarian Socialist Workers' Party (HSWP), Central Bodies, János Kádár's Secretariat [Magyar Szocialista Munkáspárt (MSZMP) Központi Szervei, Kádár János Titkársága]

Completed in 2 copies
[...]

On 7 June 1967, Comrade F.Y. Titov visited Comrade Komócsin and, on behalf of the CC [Central Committee] of the CPSU, gave the following information:

"As we already informed you on 5 June, the Soviet government sent a message to Johnson, De Gaulle and Wilson.
We received replies from Johnson and De Gaulle.
1. In his reply, Johnson expresses agreement with our statement that every major power is obliged to seek an end to the conflict between Israel and the U.A.R. Johnson is in favour of the Security Council taking firms steps in this direction. Johnson assures us that the United States will exert all its influence to achieve the cessation of the acts of war.
2. De Gaulle, in his response, states that the French government wants the four major powers, as permanent members of the Security Council, to attempt to achieve an end to hostilities, co-ordinating their efforts for this purpose. De Gaulle suggests that direct contact be maintained on this issue between the governments of France and the Soviet Union.

On June 6, the Soviet government sent further messages to President Johnson, President De Gaulle, and Prime Minister Wilson.
In these messages, the Soviet government expresses its conviction that its firm demand for an immediate ceasefire and the withdrawal of troops to behind the demarcation line accords with the interests of upholding peace. We expressed our hope that the government(s) of the United States (France, Great Britain) will support the aforementioned demand in the Security Council. The Soviet government supports this.
The message calls upon the governments to do their utmost to ensure the Security Council adopts a positive resolution on this issue today.
Furthermore, in the message sent to President De Gaulle, we expressed our satisfaction with the regular consultations between the French and Soviet governments, and with the fact that the Soviet and French representatives are actively cooperating in the Security Council".

5 Information from Leonid Brezhnev's Personal Secretary

7 June 1967

National Archives of Hungary, M-KS 288/47/ p. 209.
Collection: Hungarian Socialist Workers' Party (HSWP), Central Bodies, János Kádár's Secretariat [Magyar Szocialista Munkáspárt (MSZMP) Központi Szervei, Kádár János Titkársága]

Completed in 2 copies

Memorandum

For Comrade János Kádár

At 4 p.m. on 7 June 1967, Comrade A.M. Alexandrov, Comrade Brezhnev's personal secretary, gave by telephone and on behalf of Comrade Brezhnev, the following information on the situation in the Middle East:

1. The Soviet comrades have received various pieces of information that despite the Security Council's resolution, Israel is continuing the acts of war on many fronts. In this regard, the Soviet government has instructed its representative at the UN to demand the immediate convening of the Security Council to examine whether the resolution of the Security Council has not been fulfilled. The Soviet representative shall raise the idea that the hour of the beginning of the ceasefire has to be confirmed and Israel must be forced to implement the resolution.

    The Soviet government has informed Johnson, De Gaulle and Wilson of the measure by way of the direct lines.

2. The Soviet government has sent a message to the government of Israel warning it that if it continues the acts of war, the Soviet Union will implement the appropriate consequences: for instance, it will re-examine the issue of diplomatic relations between itself and Israel and will conceive other measures. The tone of the message is firm and sharp. As soon as the Soviet ambassador to Tel Aviv submitted the message, it was made public and published in the Soviet press and on the radio.

3. The Soviet leadership is sending a message to Nasser and the leaders of other Arab countries. The message is encouraging in nature, and the Soviet comrades call upon their Arab friends not to lose their presence of mind, to defend their interests using all means, and to make efforts toward the implementation of the ceasefire resolution.

6 Soviet Ambassador's Meeting with János Kádár

8 June 1967

National Archives of Hungary, M-KS 288/47/ p. 211-221.
Collection: Hungarian Socialist Workers' Party (HSWP), Central Bodies, János Kádár's Secretariat [Magyar Szocialista Munkáspárt (MSZMP) Központi Szervei, Kádár János Titkársága]

Translated from Russian
Completed in 4 copies
[...]

On 8 June 1967, Comrade F.Y. Titov visited Comrade János Kádár and gave the following information on behalf of the CC [Central Committee] of the CPSU:

Supplementing the information sent previously, we wish to inform you of further developments in the Middle East and about the measures that we have taken on 6 and 7 June.

As we have already informed you, on 6 June, acting on behalf of the Soviet government, we sent messages to Johnson, De Gaulle and Wilson, in which we expressed our conviction that a firm demand for an immediate ceasefire and the withdrawal of troops would serve to restore peace.

In his response, Johnson noted that the United States will agree to accept a resolution at the Security Council that calls on both warring parties to implement an immediate ceasefire and withdraw their armed personnel without delay to behind the ceasefire line; to implement other suitable measures with a view to separating the forces, to renouncing violent acts and to decreasing tension in the region.

In his reply, De Gaulle emphasised that the French government, like the Soviet government, is in favour of the Security Council giving its support to an immediate ceasefire. This resolution – in De Gaulle's view – should be accompanied by a resolution on the withdrawal of troops. Concerning the line behind which the troops need to be taken, the French are of the view that this should be a ceasefire line which should accord with the positions taken by the two sides since the beginning of the acts of war.

We have not yet received an answer to our second message from Wilson. In reply to the message of 5 June, Wilson stated that the British government will do its utmost to end the military conflict, and to this end will aim for the adoption of a consensus resolution in the Security Council, calling for a ceasefire.

Throughout the day on 6 June and the night of 7 June, we contacted Cairo several times in order to clarify the situation. They informed us that the situation at the front was grave and so serious that – as Amer had stated – it is necessary to achieve a ceasefire by 5 a.m. on 7 June. Amer explained that the Israeli Air Force is beginning combat operations against the land troops of the U.A.R. on the Sinai Peninsula. In his opinion, this will result in even greater sacrifices and great losses, and will make it more difficult to withdraw troops from the peninsula.

From these reports, it was evident that the leaders of the U.A.R., who originally demanded the ceasefire and the withdrawal of troops, feared that, in view of the changed situation and the worsening situation, urgent steps needed to be taken via the Security Council in order to achieve an immediate ceasefire.

Our representative in the Security Council received suitable instructions to accept immediately a suitable resolution.

As you know, at 2.10 a.m. (Moscow time) on 7 June, the Security Council adopted a unanimous resolution, calling upon the governments involved as a first step to take all measures towards an immediate ceasefire and a cessation of all acts of war in the region. The U.A.R.'s representative stated that the U.A.R. agreed with the resolution.

The Security Council adopted a resolution for a ceasefire without any conditions.

However, reports coming in suggest that Israel is not fulfilling the Security Council's resolution for an immediate ceasefire and the cessation of all acts of war, and is continuing to wage war against the Arab states.

In this connection, the Soviet Union's UN representative has been instructed to demand the immediate convening of the Security Council to hear from both sides about the implementation of the SC's resolution and to adopt a resolution concerning a cessation of acts of war by 4 p.m. (GMT) on 7 June.

In addition, on 7 June, A.N. Kosygin, Chairman of the Council of Ministers of the Soviet Union, sent a message to Johnson, Wilson and De Gaulle, reminding them that Israel is not complying with the Security Council's resolution and making our suggestion that the Security Council be convened immediately.

7 Message from Deputy Head of the Foreign-Affairs Department of the CPSU

8 June 1967

National Archives of Hungary, M-KS 288/47/ p. 217.
Collection: Hungarian Socialist Workers' Party (HSWP), Central Bodies, János Kádár's Secretariat [Magyar Szocialista Munkáspárt (MSZMP) Központi Szervei, Kádár János Titkársága]

Completed in 1 copy

Record

For Comrade János Kádár

At 3 p.m. on 8 June 1967, Comrade K.V. Rusakov, Deputy Head of the Foreign Affairs Department of the CPSU, telephoned from Moscow and stated the following on behalf of Comrade Brezhnev:

Comrade Brezhnev has spoken to all the comrades and everyone agrees that the first secretaries and the chairmen of the councils of ministers should meet in Moscow at 11 a.m. tomorrow. Comrade Ceausescu agrees, too, and is coming. On the advice of some comrades, a preliminary conversation was held with Comrade Tito, who replied that he will discuss the issue and may possibly come.

Comrade Brezhnev awaits Comrade Kádár's answer, concerning whether the arrangement is convenient (above all the time of the meeting).

8 On the Moscow Meeting

9 June 1967

National Archives of Hungary, M-KS 288/47/ p. 219-230.
Collection: Hungarian Socialist Workers' Party (HSWP), Central Bodies, János Kádár's Secretariat [Magyar Szocialista Munkáspárt (MSZMP) Központi Szervei, Kádár János Titkársága]

Memorandum

For Comrade János Kádár
From: Ministry of Foreign Affairs
[Compiled by] Károly Erdélyi

[...]

II. <u>The Moscow meeting:</u>

1. <u>List of known participants:</u>
   - 9 June, Friday afternoon, 3.30 until midnight
   - Atmosphere: meeting with news coming in again and again
     - Amer's report
     - Nasser's resignation
     - Effect of Nasser's speech
2. <u>Brezhnev's information:</u>
   - The purpose of the meeting:
     - to announce and analyse facts
     - to draw consequences and decide on action
   - Task: – to restore Arab positions
     – to prevent the conflict from spreading

<u>The course of events:</u>

In mid-May, based on the data of military intelligence, the Soviet side informed the leaders of the United Arab Republic and Syria that Israel was preparing to attack the progressive system in Syria. They replied that they also had such reports, but were calm because they were prepared [for such an attack].

The Soviet Union was then surprised by the steps taken by the United Arab Republic – the demand for the withdrawal of UN troops, the closure of the Gulf of Aqaba – steps which Nasser did not discuss in advance. The Arab leaders stated that their goal was not the outbreak of war, but to restore the situation that had prevailed prior to the Suez aggression in 1956. In order to strengthen their defence forces, on 25 May they again requested military supplies from the Soviet Union, which they then received. Although in the final days of May there were increasing signs of an intensification of Israeli war preparations (even one of the advisors at the U.S. embassy in Cairo spoke of the danger of an Israeli attack), Nasser kept emphasising that the military factor had lost its significance, and that a political solution had to be found. Such ideas halted attempts by officers of the Egyptian army to achieve a first strike against Israel.

All of this shows that Nasser and his staff did not recognise the extent of the danger, they misjudged their own and the enemy's military abilities, and they did not take the necessary military measures.

Discussions with Syrian leaders in May showed that they were even more optimistic in terms of their judgement of the situation and the military chances. They thought that conditions were right for the military destruction of Israel. The Soviet Union called on them to demonstrate sobriety, moderation and realism.

At the end of May and in early June, the Soviet Union warned Israel several times, underlining that a peaceful way out of the complicated situation had to be found. The Israelis also misled the Soviet Union when Prime Minister Eshkol assured the Soviet ambassador that they had no aggressive plans or aims.

Until the outbreak of the military conflict, the Soviet Union focused its strength on the UN deflecting the pressure on the United Arab Republic in connection with the closure of the Gulf of Aqaba, and on preventing a military demonstration by the imperialist countries.

From the first hour of the Israeli aggression on 5 June, a crisis arose. In the first hours of combat operations, the United Arab Republic lost most of its military forces (air force and tanks). Organised resistance was completely absent, and the army of the United Arab Republic disintegrated at the first strike. Although Nasser gave an optimistic statement even on the morning of 6 June, it was clear from the words of Marshal Amer, who had better knowledge of the military situation, that for the Soviet Union the most important tasks were to save what could be saved, to preserve Nasser's regime even at the cost of compromises and concessions, and to achieve the cessation of armed hostilities. At the same time, in order to assist the Egyptians, they began to supply 200 fighter planes and 200 tanks via an air bridge to Egypt. In the Security Council, Comrade Fedorenko first demanded the condemnation of the aggressor, the guaranteeing of a ceasefire, and the withdrawal of troops to their starting positions. However, owing to the constant deterioration in the military situation, from 7 June, at the request of the United Arab Republic, the main tasks became the guaranteeing of a ceasefire and the prevention by political means of a further advance of Israeli troops. At the same time, in order to halt the aggression, the Soviet Union held out the prospect of breaking off diplomatic relations with Israel.

Analysing the events that have occurred, one must see the reasons why the situation developed in this way. Israel is not an independent country, but a satellite and pawn of American imperialism. The war against Israel is being fought against imperialism. The balance of power is not favourable for those in the Arab world. Imperialism has prevailed there for decades, while Socialism arrived just two decades ago, and so our possibilities are limited. Until 5 June, Nasser had achieved political successes and, as a consequence, he overestimated his strength and underestimated the extent of the military threat.

In the current situation and in the coming period, the goals must be the preservation of the progressive Arab regimes, the cessation of armed hostilities and then, in a lengthy diplomatic struggle, the withdrawal of the Israeli aggressor's troops.

It would seem worth publishing a statement on our consultations.

3. Comrade Grechko's report:

Israel has been prepared for aggressive action for some time. Since April of this year, it has increased the number of its troops from 70,000 to 200,000.

Regarding the quantitative data, the military situation prior to 5 June showed that the Arab countries had superiority.

In recent years, the Soviet Union has supplied many weapons to the United Arab Republic, worth 1.6 billion roubles (Rb.) in total. These weapons include:

570 combat aircrafts

820 tanks

2000 artillery and guns

160 air defence missiles

The military assistance of similar composition given to Syria has a value of 700 million Rb. The Soviet Union has trained more than 6,000 Arab officers at Soviet military institutions. At the time of the outbreak of combat operations, almost 500 Soviet military advisors were residing in the United Arab Republic.

Prior to combat operations, with regard to infantry, the air force, tank units and artillery, the United Arab Republic had, in general, 1.5 times the strength of Israel. Examining this same data, the warring Arab countries had a superiority of 2.5 over Israel.

Owing to the poor preparedness, disorganisation and lack of discipline of the military forces of the United Arab Republic – as well as the unexpectedness of the attack on the very first morning of hostilities – 50 per cent of the Egyptian Air Force was destroyed, as were most of the tank units and artillery. By the end of the first day, the uniform leadership of the Egyptian Army had ceased, the units were dispersed and the enemy had seized the military equipment.

According to data from Soviet military intelligence, American units did not directly participate in combat operations.

4. Comrade Novotny's statement:

The Egyptian and Syrian leaders acted irresponsibly and overestimated their own power and Arab unity. They thought they could easily defeat Israel.

Czechoslovakia has already given a lot of assistance: it has offered major military assistance and has sent military advisors. After 5 June, the Political Committee voted to send further military aid.

Under the current circumstances, Nasser has to be kept in power by all means.

The publication of a consensual statement is the correct measure.

5. Comrade Tito's statement:

Yugoslavia has been in contact with Nasser from the outset, and has supported his political steps: the closure of the Gulf of Aqaba and the restoration of the pre-1956 situation. At that time, Nasser had stated that he would not give a reason for the aggression, but if attacked, [Egypt] would fulfil its obligation.

Nasser was wrong: he did not know that announcing the desire for the destruction of Israel meant confronting the united front of imperialism. If someone wants to destroy Israel, he finds himself confronted not only by NATO but also by the European social democrats.

Yugoslavia has already supplied weapons and 50,000 tons of grain, and it has allowed the transfer of Soviet weapons. In the current situation, the main need is for political assistance. Now we have to take a stand against those seeking to topple Nasser, because he is more than a statesman. In the same manner, anti-Soviet propaganda as well as hostile slander discrediting the Soviet Union, which is arising in several regions in the Arab world, has to be repelled.

At the same time, it appears that the reality of some of our publicly represented positions is being revised amid the present circumstances. We have been saying for years now that local wars have to be avoided, because they can grow into world wars. We still think this, but the imperialists are acting in the opposite way: they are provoking an increasing number of local conflicts and are slowly pushing us back. It seems that the accumulation of nuclear weapons is leading to a proportionate decrease in the danger of local wars becoming global conflicts, and so we must be more steadfast; we should not allow them to use local wars to their advantage.

The coup in Greece should also be examined from this perspective for this, too, is part of the general plan to gradually destroy progressive forces and systems. Greece is not the last in the series: in collaboration with the Italians, the Americans want to destroy Yugoslavia, too.

This complicated situation requires us to meet more often in order to improve our relations. The imperialists must be shown that we are prepared to do anything, and that we will even go as far as war if our interests and our allies are at stake.

The Italian, French, Belgian and Scandinavian Communists who blame, in addition to Israel, the Arabs for this conflict, are not right. On this issue, support has to be given to the Arabs, because they are fighting against the imperialists. It is right for us to adopt a joint declaration, in which we condemn the aggressor and assure Nasser and the Arab people of our solidarity.

6. Comrade Zhivkov's statement:

He greeted those attending the meeting. The Bulgarian Party had also thought about proposing such a meeting.

From the first moment of combat operations, it was clear that the Arab soldiers are not capable of standing up to the Israelis. The Israelis had studied how to use weapons. The Americans and the British know that Israel, which they have supplied and trained, will win in the war, and this is why they have employed clever political tricks to announce their neutrality.

The Soviet Union has proceeded wisely; it has prevented the broadening of the conflict. At the same time, it has to consider that after the ending of combat operations there will be some fundamental questions, and our strengths should be concentrated on these questions.

They are:
a. The withdrawal of the aggressor to the starting point. The Israelis will try to sabotage this, but we still have to achieve this with the international organisations by mobilising public opinion.
b. We have to confront agitation against the Soviet Union and against Socialism; events have to be portrayed in an accurate way.
c. Doubtless, further economic support must be given to the United Arab Republic and to Syria.

He agrees with Comrade Tito that we have to be tougher. If we do not hit back at the aggressor, then they will grow bolder, and this will also affect our political prestige.

He agrees with the publication of a joint statement.

7. Comrade Ceausescu's statement:

The situation is grave. The question now is not, "how did we get here?", although it would be worth talking about this in greater detail at some point.

It would have been better to hold this meeting prior to the onset of combat operations.

The Romanian Communist Party had analysed the situation on several occasions and concluded that everything had to be done to pre-empt war. They knew in advance that the war could not end with an Arab victory and so, on behalf of the government, they called for the two parties to avoid war.

The Arabs thought they could destroy Israel. Their appeal in this respect did not serve to mobilise world opinion. Romania could not have supported such a position. Several Communist Parties in Western countries also faced a similar situation, as did the many parts of the progressive movement. The disputes in the region have to be resolved on the basis of the acceptance of the very existence of Israel and the Arab countries.

It would be worth studying what happened to the Egyptian Army, so that the necessary lessons can be drawn. The Egyptians knew everything two weeks in advance; the army was well equipped, but did not fight. Doubtless there are internal and external factors, and identifying them would offer important insights for a better understanding of the picture.

He agrees with Tito that we do not have well elaborated ideas for dealing with imperialism's strategy of local wars.

In the Arab situation, there is at present no military solution that could change the situation. For this reason, strong political and diplomatic pressure must be commenced, so that we compel the Israelis to withdraw from the occupied territories. The balance of power must be altered using peaceful means in favour of the Arabs, so that Israel also survives.

Given that the Romanian Communist Party cannot give its approval to a statement that condemns Israel alone for the outbreak of war, Comrade Ceausescu opposed the publication of a statement.

8. Comrade Gomulka's statement:

If we had met two or three days earlier it would not have changed the picture.

Nasser's fundamental mistake was first that he did not consult with his friends and allies, and second that he and many of our comrades underestimated Israel's capabilities. Nasser's action pre-determined the outbreak of war.

Aqaba was not a reason but a pretext. Nasser wanted to push back Israeli positions, to increase his prestige and achieve Jordan and Saudi Arabia's rapprochement with the United Arab Republic. This led the United States and Britain to conclude that Nasser had to be dealt with and toppled, because otherwise the Arab world would soon be completely lost to the West.

The military outcome of the struggle was largely determined by the fact that modern military equipment was placed in the hands of unskilled, undisciplined and illiterate Egyptian soldiers, who were unable to make it function. In terms of education, the Israeli army is far ahead of the Arabs. By threatening Israel's destruction, Nasser assured the fluctuating solidarity of the countries of the Arab world, but he denied himself the support of global public opinion. This is why the Israelis did not need American intervention, but if things had gone badly, the Americans would have immediately launched the Sixth Fleet.

The task now is to save Nasser. To this end, measures are needed that strengthen his internal positions among the people, while also showing the historical responsibility of Israel and American imperialism for three outbreaks of aggression in two decades. At present, a ceasefire seems to be the next important step. Then preparations are needed for further diplomatic measures: for the withdrawal of the aggressor and the realisation of the rights of the Arabs.

He supports the publication of a joint statement.

9. Comrade Ulbricht's statement:

The events in the Middle East are due to the aggression not only of Israel, but also of NATO. According to NATO, first the balance of power has to be changed in this region, and then the German Democratic Republic can be liquidated.

Nasser's actions were correct. If we had taken a stance together and in an organised manner, and if we had used other instruments in addition to diplomatic channels, the aggression could have been prevented.

Nasser should have consulted with the Soviet Union, but the relationship was not of that kind – and not only the United Arab Republic was at fault. Unfortunately, even among ourselves, we cannot always agree even on economic issues.

The manner in which the Soviet Union has proceeded was right, because it prevented the spread of the conflict. At the same time, we have to confront the United States' global strategy with our own strategy; we cannot concede to their blackmail.

He agrees with the publication of a joint statement.

10. Comrade Kádár's statement:

- Greetings to the participants in the meeting.
- Thank you for the information, it had illuminated certain issues.
- Antecedent: Israel threatened Syria. The oil conflict.
- The dissatisfactory nature of Arab political and military measures against Israel.
- The Soviet Union and other Socialist countries had done what they needed to do.
- The situation that has arisen is a defeat for progressive Arabs, and thus for us, too.
- The task: to fight for and assist the retaking of Arab positions – both politically and militarily.
- Politically: in propaganda – against Israel, particularly at the UN.
- Public opinion: [*partly* – AK] correct, [*partly* – AK] disturbed, the ceasefire agreement, us!

– On the basic issues, the same stance – or a joint stand – should be taken, [*for example* – AK] these talks, public statement.

11. Comrade Brezhnev's closing words:

Thank you for attending. The ideas and analyses raised were beneficial.
Loss awaits us wherever nationalism raises its head and all other aspects are ignored.
The Soviet Union has done everything to rescue the United Arab Republic and its achievements. They have been, and are, in daily contact with all the Socialist countries.
The Soviet Union cautioned Nasser, but others influenced him as well, including the Chinese.
The picture shows that the struggle continues between progress and the forces of imperialism. Now, owing to political and economic factors, the United States has a strong advantage in the region.
Today's experiences also prove the necessity of meeting more often.
He recommends the drafting of a joint statement.

III. The adoption of a joint declaration:

The Romanians' position – only a factual communiqué.

IV. Events since Saturday afternoon:

a. The Soviet Union broke off diplomatic relations.
b. Afternoon – Czechoslovakia.
c. Consultation between Hungary, Poland and Bulgaria. Warning to the Israeli government.
d. Sunday – Bulgaria broke off relations.
e. Monday – in agreement with the Poles, we did too.
   – grave act of aggression;
   – repeated violation of the Security Council's ceasefire resolutions;
   – territorial claims made by leading Israeli politicians;
   – ignoring the [need for] withdrawal of troops.

9 Telephone Conversation between János Kádár and Leonid Brezhnev

12 June 1967

National Archives of Hungary, M-KS 288/47/ p. 218.
Collection: Hungarian Socialist Workers' Party (HSWP), Central Bodies, János Kádár's Secretariat [Magyar Szocialista Munkáspárt (MSZMP) Központi Szervei, Kádár János Titkársága]

Completed in 2 copies

Memorandum

On 12 June 1967, Comrade János Kádár telephoned Comrade Brezhnev, who gave him the latest news regarding the situation in the Middle East. There is quiet on all fronts, although Syria complained both today and yesterday that the Israelis were sneaking forward even without a struggle. But overall the situation has stabilised.

Comrade Kádár informed Comrade Brezhnev about our action that had been agreed upon with the Polish comrades – the severing of diplomatic relations with Israel. Comrade Brezhnev replied that this is in line with the common position elaborated in Moscow. He is pleased that everything is in order here, and that we can take this step. This also applies to Comrade Gomulka and his fellows.

In Moscow there is credible data that the ambassadors of the Arab countries are speaking indignantly of the Romanians' conduct, and according to reports, their countries are even pondering whether to break off diplomatic relations with Romania.

President Boumediène has just arrived in Moscow, and he unexpectedly stated this intent this morning. He is now coming with Comrade Kosygin and other Soviet leaders from the airport towards Moscow.

Today the Political Committee of the CPSU convened, and it elaborated on further measures. They are awaiting the discussion with Boumediène, and then in all likelihood they will decide to demand the immediate convening of the UN General Assembly.

Finally, Comrade Brezhnev has promised to inform Comrade Kádár about the talks with the Algerians, and will do so this evening if it is urgent.

P.S. Comrade Kádár suggested that our foreign ministers should consider which country should represent the interests of the Socialist countries in Israel: Romania, Yugoslavia, or Finland, perhaps? Comrade Brezhnev's preference was also for the latter solution. Comrade Kádár also stated that it should be suggested to the Algerians that they ask Romania for its opinion on diplomatic relations, given that five Socialist countries have already broken off relations. Comrade Brezhnev will consider this.

10 Minutes of the Meeting of the Political Committee

13 June 1967

National Archives of Hungary, M-KS 288/5/427/1967
Collection: Hungarian Socialist Workers' Party (HSWP), Central Bodies, János Kádár's Secretariat [Magyar Szocialista Munkáspárt (MSZMP) Központi Szervei, Kádár János Titkársága]

[....]

Comrade JÁNOS KÁDÁR:

I would like to add to what Comrade Komócsin has stated, in part by mentioning several issues arising at the international conference and in part by repeating things so that we understand the factors requiring our consideration in the course of the work ahead.

I would also begin by mentioning what we have done already. The four members of the group have co-operated with each other, sometimes meeting several times every day. In addition, we have also worked in close co-operation with the Foreign Affairs Department, the Ministry of Foreign Affairs, the agit-prop group – above all the press section, the Ministry of Interior, and the Ministry of Defence. We have also maintained contact at the international level, informing each other and co-ordinating measures. In fact, the conference in Moscow should be seen as an integral part of these international consultations and negotiations, because this was what it was. I should add that, concerning important measures, the group has always striven to consult with members of the Political Committee and even with members of the Council of Ministers. We ask that this should be acknowledged and approved.

Concerning the measures, I think the Political Committee can see that we were right – despite the reality of war – to organise, on the domestic front, merely a state of alert in the top positions, while generally instructing the Party, state and civil bodies to continue their work normally.

At the same time, diplomatic steps were being taken – as well as several military activities. Let us examine the diplomatic steps, because we shall need this later, when reviewing. First of all, the Hungarian government issued a statement. We then examined the note sent to us by the Israeli prime minister and responded to it. Then a statement was made at the Moscow conference in the form of a joint communiqué; then on Saturday, a kind of warning was made to the Israeli government, and finally diplomatic relations were broken off. Under the circumstances, these measures were correct.

On the military front, the Ministry of Defence undertook a number of observation functions. In addition, another measure was taken: namely, on behalf of Hungary, we consented to the establishment of an airlift, which was directed across Hungary for the duration of the war. The Political Committee should know this. The route of the airlift was: the Soviet Union, Hungary, and Yugoslavia; the other half ran above the Mediterranean Sea. This was in operation, and is still operating now. I mention this because, under certain rules, this is automatically possible, but in such cases it is a matter for negotiation. In this regard, Yugoslavia responded immediately and agreed with it. These are the major aspects of the measures requiring approval. These measures must be registered, and this policy must be continued in the future too.

Comrade Komócsin has described the events leading up to the conference in Moscow. It was certainly organised remarkably quickly. Consultations began at two o'clock and by four o'clock everyone's response had already arrived and the decision was taken to hold discussions. The discussions were actually proposed by the Political Committee of the GDR, but their proposal fell on sympathetic ears, because all parties were aware of the need for a meeting. We didn't ponder over it for long either: we decided at four o'clock to depart at eight o'clock.

We took part in the joint efforts there. When we decided at four o'clock to travel, we already knew that the Romanians and Tito were coming too – and it should be said that it was they who announced their participation.

The real work – I just mention this for other reasons – began on Friday at 3.30 p.m. Moscow time and ended at 2 a.m. under very poor working conditions that were a consequence of the situation. The Soviets held a kind of information session, then we consulted; all delegations voiced their opinions, and the "fruit" of our labours was a brief statement of five, six or eight sentences. But even this was extremely difficult to put together. On Friday afternoon and evening, the situation on the front became critical; information was constantly being brought in for discussion, and the situation was changing every half an hour, so that whatever we had been discussing just an hour before lost its significance. Moreover, it was the usual collective wording, which is not always a good thing.

Concerning the whole conference, I would like to say – with a view to the Political Committee approving our attendance at the conference, in the knowledge of these facts – that in our judgement it was necessary and extremely useful for a variety of reasons. First, we received answers to issues that were/are troubling us and our leadership; second, it was really just a consultative exchange of views, the statement made there was, under the given political circumstances, of significance to world politics, surprised the enemy, was drawn up immediately, a significant collective force emerged, and this had the right effect both on the Arabs and the enemy.

I would like to speak about several aspects of the consultative conference and then, at the end, I shall return to the joint agreement about what has to be done.

First of all, a few words about the issues that we received information about, which then helped us to understand some things. For us too, it was an important question, because we didn't understand what had happened on the front – had preparations been poor or had there been a lack of force? And also the issue of the UN Security Council resolution, which referred merely to a ceasefire – which had been immediately denounced by the Iraqi Foreign Minister, and a stand had also been taken by various other Arab countries. Perhaps comrades will remember that the Soviet Union's stance was met in the capitals of various Socialist countries with astonishment – frankly, we too were surprised – because the framework of information and consultation had always included the need to gain approval for a double resolution, that is, a ceasefire and a withdrawal of troops to behind the demarcation lines. This was the reason the Soviet Union was struggling against the Americans – in the end, it came as a surprise that such a resolution was formulated. We could find no explanation for this.

I will cover several important and major issues, although I don't want to repeat myself. We were given exact and detailed information there about political matters as well as military matters.

Regarding political matters, perhaps the most important aspect is that, concerning the two measures by Egypt – namely, the withdrawal of UN troops and the closure of the Gulf of Aqaba – the Arabs failed to consult with the Soviet comrades; thus, the Soviet comrades were met by a fait accompli. Regarding the ceasefire resolution, I would like to emphasise that the fact is that this happened at the request of the Arabs – of the Egyptians. On Thursday evening, a situation developed in which Amer – who, at the time, was legally and formally commander-in-chief of the armed forces – was in contact with the Soviet Union and, as such, negotiated with the Soviet comrades. On Thursday afternoon or evening, Amer stated that a resolution on a ceasefire was very much requested and hoped for, because such a situation had developed. And following this there was no time to confer with anyone, they simply voted on the ceasefire.

The military situation is a different matter, and generally concerns the military part of the issue. The Soviet data are more exact than are ours, but they are roughly the same as the ones that we received. The comrades demonstrated what had been the military situation in the period prior to the Israeli surprise attack. They described it and backed it up with data, facts and maps. This showed that the Arab armed forces had been numerically superior in terms of men as well as the major military technical means like military aircraft, tanks and artillery. Furthermore – and this is just as important – the Soviet Union had exact knowledge of the position of the Israeli armed forces even before the attack and informed the leadership of the Egyptian armed forces accordingly. This is almost as important as the proceeding issue. And the Soviet comrades then provided us with exact information, revealing that the great majority of this military technology was Soviet military technology, which had been given to the United Arab Republic and Syria in a proportionate manner for years – worth in total two and a half billion Roubles non-repayable. These were up-to-date modern armaments, aircraft, tanks etc. and even rockets. So this is the situation as far as armaments are concerned.

In reality, of course, when talking about the balance of power we shouldn't just refer to numbers. If I say that on the Arab side this was the extent of their forces, men, military technology, armed power etc., then one should also remember that we are talking about five or so Arab countries – although it is true that a whole series of

Arab countries placed their armed forces under Egyptian command, but people who are intricately involved with such things know what this means. It means that there is no unified command. And another factor was the difference in quality of available personnel and the difference in quality between the various armies. To go back to the roots, it is a known fact that 80 per cent of Egypt's population cannot read or write, while Israel has more highly qualified and skilled human resources. That is to say, people with primary education were set against university graduates, and this represented a decisive superiority in all respects. This means that the level of organisation and discipline of the units of the Arab army, the Egyptian and Syrian Armies, was extraordinarily low, which casts a revealing light on the story of this blitzkrieg. As we have just heard, by launching a surprise attack with a small number of military aircraft, the Israelis were able to destroy approx. 270 military aircraft in the first three hours of the war, 14 aircraft on the second day and 12 on the third day. This means that, of the 270 aircraft destroyed on the first day, just one was destroyed in the air – and Arab loss of life on the first two days was 12 men in two sorties. Incidentally, exactly the same thing happened to the tank divisions as well as air defence. Most of the Egyptian armed forces were destroyed without combat. As a result, the situation was such that there was really no organised resistance after the first day, and this is how the first day looked.

I would like to mention something from a propaganda point of view. Nasser and his group say that there was a heroic fight and this is subjectively and individually true of many thousands of Arabs. This is not mere propaganda. The truth is that the army and most of the leadership failed to stand the test. [I would say] just one thing, in this connection. Everyone knows what is order during military practice manoeuvres and what is order in war. At six o'clock on Monday morning, the pilots of the battle aircraft were asleep at home with their families. Nothing more need be said. At such times it is rule no. 1 that they should not be permitted to leave the garrison or the airfield. Of course, none of this may ever be talked about, but we can say a couple of words about this – just between ourselves, and we must consider amongst the reasons for the events what the Egyptian leadership really represents. For their base is a world Communist movement, or Socialist camp, the Soviet Union and in part Czechoslovakia, which also sends personnel there every year, but at the same time the matter is extremely complicated, because these people were Muslims, anti-Communists, and we cannot say what was left of this in the minds of the officer corps. It is a fact, however, that in recent years the Israelis could rely fully and 100 per cent on the great powers supporting them and on their specialists and experts – whereas in Egypt, this was not the case. This does not apply to Nasser individually, but it is a point to consider. Comrade Novotny, for example, stated at a joint conference that they, too, have people and experts there, but that they were always in an abnormal situation and could not do anything worthwhile. This was the situation that unfolded before us, and thus there was no surprise that events on the battlefield developed as they did. I am no expert in strategy, but it is worth noting that this was a war fought over a relatively small area, and given how things looked on the Arab side, a small area was simply not enough. There is a difference between Israel and the Arab countries in terms of degree of mobilisation. If events had turned into a drawn-out war, the balance of power might have been reversed in three to six weeks....

[I shall now mention] two statements made at the conference – and perhaps I shall mention our own one too, so that comrades might see how we view our own situation.

Comrade Tito's speech – of course, simply the fact that they came and took part – was, in our judgement, extremely positive in a whole manner of respects. There was even an element of self-criticism from Comrade Tito in this matter, which is significant. I have already mentioned that the Arabs did not consult with the Soviet Union about the withdrawal of UN troops and the closure of the Gulf of Aqaba, or about another very important issue, namely the restoration of the pre-1956 position. Comrade Tito said that they had consulted with them and that they had supported these measures. At least he did say that this had happened, and this was a positive thing, because he didn't have to say it. That they had consulted with them, and this is indeed understandable since they have an old and close relationship with Egypt, a relationship that is older and more permanent than the Soviet Union's relationship. Comrade Tito also told us that they too had helped Egypt, by donating substantial quantities of food and technical military aid. By way of conclusion, he mentioned that they had immediately consented to the establishment of the airlift.

Comrade Tito raised several very important issues – of course there was little analysis; generally, we spoke very briefly, discussing just several aspects of the situation. He too did this – but he also mentioned an issue of great significance, and it was particularly important that _he_ mentioned it – on behalf of the Yugoslav Party, the Yugoslav Communists and the Yugoslav regime. His first such remark was that we should meet more frequently, to discuss developments and our responses, and to agree upon measures, so that we should put forward the same position and, if necessary, might act together. This was an important statement and, by personally attending the conference, he showed that he thinks it is, too.

Another matter: he said that we have an old precept that we should review – that in the present era, with the degree of development of military technology and in the era of atomic weapons, there are no local wars, because all local wars can develop into world wars. Thus we are against all local wars, and consider our sole task to localise and stub out local wars. He said that in their opinion, this precept was incorrect and that experience had demonstrated otherwise. Experience had shown that the more atomic weapons were accumulated, the more this acted against world war and against local wars developing into world wars, but that the imperialists were organising a whole series of local wars and attacks against us and other progressive forces, and that for this reason we should view local wars in a different light, and that we must formulate plans and concepts in this respect.

The third thing is partly related to this. He said that we the Socialist countries should have a concept and a plan against the imperialist concepts and the NATO plans. He referred to the Greek coup and said that, at present, they think the imperialists are seriously considering a plan to topple the Yugoslav regime by forging together the Greek and Italian bodies. In this connection, he said that we should meet several times, and given these developments we should have plans and concepts to bring an end to this process. In this regard, he even said that we should show the imperialists that we are prepared to do anything and that we would even go to war if our vital interests were at stake. This is a necessity in their opinion. These are matters worth thinking about.

[I shall mention] briefly, the Romanian statement. The Romanian speech was extremely generalised and was more concerned with assessing the situation rather than asking questions. That is to say, there was no word about what we should do then and there – on Friday afternoon or evening. Instead, their whole speech urged analysis. They pointed out that we had still not analysed what the Brazilian Party and the Indonesian Party had done what and when. That is, they called for analysis, and said that we should meet again and that we should have already met. Comrade Ceausescu said that if we had met around 20 May, we could have prevented the war. Several people reacted to this. Moreover, in addition to the statement that if we had met around 20–26 May we could have prevented war, he also seemed to infer that if – instead of the Soviet Union and the United Arab Republic – we and perhaps Romania had together taken the matter in hand, we could have prevented events unfolding; whereas, the fact that war took place showed the weakness or ineptitude of the Soviet Union and the Arab Republic. None of this was openly expressed, but this was somehow the meaning of what he said – at least this was what I made of his words.

He then criticised those Arabs – who really are to be criticised – who had said that they would destroy Israel. And he said that such statements had not served to mobilise the world's progressive forces etc. He then suggested we should study what had happened to the Egyptian Army, because this would provide us with valuable and important experience. And – let us not forget that this was stated on Friday evening – it was stated that, in the current situation, there was no military solution; instead there was a need for a political war.

Finally, [I should like to say] a few words about the communiqué. What happened was that there was a draft declaration, which was handed out to everyone. The Romanians stood up and said that they did not agree with the draft and that they suggested we should simply issue a factual communiqué stating that we had come together and had discussed the Middle-Eastern issue. The conference was being led at that stage by Comrade Brezhnev who said, in his reasons, that during the break the Romanians had told him they would not sign a communiqué calling Israel an aggressor. And that they had said they could not sign it, because all Parties and countries had their own opinions on this issue. At that point, the Romanians became irritated and interrupted him, saying that was not the point but that they did have a proposal and that Comrade Brezhnev should talk about that.

The Romanian proposal was received in a very interesting manner at the conference. Afterwards Comrade Tito asked to speak and he said that the sentence on the fourth page should be reworded in such and such a manner etc. Then everyone started to correct the text – the Romanians just sat there. Then Comrade Tito said that here in the text it reads Israel and the imperialist powers behind Israel, America... and let us write Britain too. Then he said, and let us also state that Israel is an aggressor, because, unless we do, I won't be able to go home, for we have told the whole of Yugoslavia who the aggressor is.

At the end of that debate, the Romanians again asked to speak, suggesting that there should be two communiqués, because if they didn't sign the disputed communiqué, it might seem as if they had not even been there. This is how the two communiqués came about. And they even suggested that the first communiqué should refer to the fact that some parties were issuing a statement while others were not. This suggestion was rejected, since it was going to be apparent anyway, because the two communiqués were to be made public side by side.

And concerning our impressions. The impression of those of us who were there was that the Romanian comrades wanted to come and to take part in the discussion, but that they had come with a determination not to call Israel an aggressor and to take a stand against this being done. Of course, we do not know what they were thinking, but perhaps they thought they could win over Yugoslavia to their position – although this is not certain. What could be felt much more strongly was that they wanted to be there and to take a stand, but that they would not accept any declaration calling Israel an aggressor.

Moreover, it also seemed to us that they really could not be bothered to explain their position. One could feel their commitment, but they did not mention a single reason for a neutral position.

In the end the view arose that the Romanians had somehow committed themselves somewhere. I don't want to go any further than this, because I do not mean that they had decided to sell out the Socialist Republic of Romania, but the kind of behaviour we had experienced at the time of their establishing diplomatic relations with the FRG re-emerged – but now under the graver circumstances of war.

I must also mention our own response. I will tell all of this so that you see and understand our position. Generally, most of the contributions were very short, just a sentence or so about the issues. Prior to this, however, I should like to return to what went before, and we spoke of such things there.

The affair began when Israel threatened Syria that it would topple the regime. However, one should also mention the oil conflict, which took place there some time ago – for this is also a starting point. We said that the Arab statements made against Israel were wrong. Then the Soviet Union and other Socialist countries – above all the Czechs, because of their armaments, and others, who collaborated in a specific manner, had done what they could. It had to be seen that the Soviet Union and other Socialist countries had done what they could in terms of military supplies and other assistance and at the level of diplomacy. It had to be stated that the situation that had arisen was a failure and a defeat for the Arabs, for the anti-imperialist and progressive Arab regimes – and for us too in a direct manner. This must also be accounted for. In this situation, for us the task is to fight and to assist the Arabs in winning back their positions on a political level, and, where there is war, at a military level too. Politically in the United Nations Organisation and in domestic and international propaganda, which is of great significance now. At that point I mentioned – because several speakers had mentioned the disquiet amongst fellow Parties in Western Europe – that there was disquiet in the Socialist countries too, but that public opinion had basically taken the right course and had correctly assessed the matter and was against the imperialists, but that in certain parts of public opinion, and even within the Party membership, there was disquiet. There was disquiet concerning the issue of aggressor and also concerning the issue of the judgement of the Arabs and other major issues. For this reason we support negotiated joint action and support such a continuation of the war, and we shall play our part in the political and every other respect, where necessary.

The whole conference – one can say this because even the Romanians did not protest (who sat there until two in the morning because the conference had not been wound up, even though it was clear by then that they would not sign the communiqué) – agreed that the battle to win back and keep Arab positions must be continued, that we should fight to maintain the progressive Arab regimes, because this was extraordinarily important, and thus, accordingly, some measures had been taken even in the meantime. We agreed with this.

I mention this because it is important that there was no mention, at the joint conference or within the framework of a separate discussion, of who should break off diplomatic relations, nor when and with whom – all were to decide that themselves. At that time, only the preliminary Soviet statement was known. I think this was the right way to proceed. That's all I have to say about the conference.

I must say something more about the whole matter. First of all, [I'd like to say] something about preliminary events. I would like to go over this again, and this is important because we will be dealing with these issues a lot in the future.

The official point of departure is that Israel threatened Syria on about 20th May that it would attack the country and topple the regime. The next development was that the United Arab Republic stated immediately that it would not allow this to happen. I think this Arab position is the right one. The next step – and this is very important and I should like to draw attention to it – was that on 26 May the United Arab Republic informed the Soviet Union that it was determined to restore, by any means, the pre-1956 position, and that nothing would deter it. This meant the Gulf of Aqaba and Lord knows what. Thus, here are the three essential issues upon which they failed to consult the Soviet Union or us, although they did tell the Yugoslavs. They did consult with us on their standing up for the Syrians, and we supported them in doing so. But they did not consult with us, in any manner whatsoever, upon restoring the pre-1956 position, and thus – in part as a consequence of this – they did not consult with us upon the withdrawal of UN troops or the closure of the Gulf of Aqaba. Moreover, they were also resolved to closing the Suez Canal. And they didn't consult upon that either. This, too, is of significance, of political significance, because all countries of the world involved in trade use the Suez Canal. To close the canal would amount to a measure against all countries involved in commercial shipping. Immediately 75 Soviet ships carrying vital supplies would be stuck there. This is also part of the course of events.

Another point: the Soviet Union opposed the four-power conference because the Arabs told them that they were against it.

Something more about Nasser, his resignation or his staying in power. These were dramatic hours then at the time, and just a few bits can be made known. And, by the way, Nasser did not consult with the Soviet Union about this either – or with anyone else. What happened was that at the right time Amer asked to see the Soviet ambassador and told him that they – that is, he and Nasser – were about to make their last announcement, then resign, hand over power to someone else, and be done with it. He didn't say anything else. Comrade Tito was pleased about the successor, because it roughly meant the continuation of the regime, but then it transpired that this was not the case, for the man in question had fought against Nasser, then co-operated with him, and then fought against him again. And again this happened, by the way, just as Comrade Gomulka had been expressing his thoughts for a half an hour on the need to save Nasser – and then came news of his resignation. Thereafter there was an on-the-record and off-the-record discussion of what could now be done. I said that whatever happens an effort must be made to place Nasser and Amer in safety – this is the first step! Tito immediately told Nasser to revoke his resignation – and this did have some effect upon him. Reading Nasser's speech after the events, we should dispense with one hypothesis. I have heard voices coming from a multitude of directions saying that Nasser wanted to blackmail the Soviet Union, and that his resignation was a clever tactical ploy. However, as I recall the situation, this was neither blackmail nor a tactical move, but rather an act that was to be expected. What he said in his speech, was, by the way, a right and proper matter. I think he was right to raise the issue of his own responsibility. I think what happened was that Comrade Tito sent a message and then probably the Soviet comrades sent a message too, and he then said he would delay his resignation until the next day, and then the mood of the public developed in the way that we already know about. And it is just as well that it did so, because as long as he is there, they won't go right.

Another aspect is that the Algerians are extremely irritated and dissatisfied with everyone, with Nasser and with the Soviet Union, because they are permeated with Arab nationalism. It has to be said that theirs is the only army capable of something, an army built on trained cadres that has fought tough wars over many years. They are full of rage and are saying that unfortunately they have no border with Israel, but that they will show how they can fight in a different way. My impression is that the Syrians too have slightly more earnest military procedures: the daily norm for armoured troops, particularly under such circumstances, is not an advance of 20 kilometres – that is, there was combat and resistance. Syria's society is more stable too; it has a workers' movement, industry, a working class, and even if the government is as weak as dew, it is still more stable.

I apologise for going over these things, but it is extraordinarily important to run through them, because the upcoming tasks will not be easy. I am saying this for our own benefit. Many things may not be said outwardly: for instance, we cannot say that 80 per cent of the Arab army is illiterate.

Regarding combat in the future, they have not directly requested us for anything. They did request military machinery even during combat from the Czechs, but in such a manner that it was impossible for them to say yes, because they asked for manned air units, which would have resulted in Czech units becoming involved in the war. They said they would provide weapons; furthermore, political assistance must be given at all levels, wherever possible.

Currently, an important event is the extraordinary general meeting of the UN, the exposure of the aggressor, its condemnation as such, and the exposure of the powers behind it. We have sent word to Moscow that if they do convene the UN general assembly, then the delegations to the assembly should be led by the foreign ministers. Moreover, it is very important that we deal with the issues in an appropriate manner in domestic propaganda and in the press etc. And, in my view, we also face a task within the Party itself, and I should like to draw attention to this.

Generalised propaganda must, of course, go to the roots of the matter and form a clear picture. What is at stake is nothing less than approx. 60 per cent of total oil trade commercially in the world. This oil plays an enormous role in the supply of oil to Western Europe and – as Nasser has said – the Sixth Fleet also operates on Arab oil. So we have to go back to the roots. The imperialists have been on the rampage in these areas for centuries, and now the region is falling out of their hands, and they will not accept this, and are fighting to retain it. For centuries they have been there, have left their marks there, have had means of influencing there, and these countries have had their own difficulties since independence. The Socialist countries have been present in the region for roughly just ten years or even more recently, and thus have not yet acquired any real influence, the world's two main political camps have been competing on unequal terms. And although we won't probably write it in the newspapers, nevertheless it must be stated clearly in Party debates that the Socialist countries have never supported the Arab propaganda formulation that Israel must be destroyed. This would contravene the principles of our foreign policy; we do not support it, and it would weaken our anti-imperialist struggle, if we were now to debate using such formulations. We must, however, be clear on the aggressor issue.

By the way, another aspect of the affair is that Western governments have acted in a much smarter manner than they did in 1956. At that time, two great imperialist powers – Britain and France – entered the war quite openly, and this permitted a quite different response from the Socialist countries, for it was far clearer who was the aggressor, and there was nothing like Israel with its population of three million beating an Arab force of 80 million. Moreover, the United States did not intervene in the battles and nor did anyone else. By the way, we received further information, which the Council of Ministers and we should know about. The Soviet fleet followed this Sixth Fleet visually at a distance of one kilometre – the aim was to ensure that they could see that the Soviets were following them. They passed alongside each other time and again. By the way, another aspect of this was that both fleets were armed with atomic weapons. So they were running alongside each other and a plane took off from the Sixth Fleet mother ship on one occasion for a trial flight and on another occasion to see how a torpedo had hit the American warship. There were no other sorties. This is the truth! This does not diminish their villainy, and there may be something in the Israeli bragging that they probably did have more tanks than we are aware of. This is possible, too.

By the way, everybody was operating there. Most Israeli airpower is French, and although the French government was neutral, it continued supplying spare parts. That is to say, they also participated in preparations, although they had no part in the combat itself – probably they thought that if the strike failed and Israel's very existence was threatened, they could intervene immediately, and would do so from a very favourable position, given that they were physically there. These things must be known, and the public must be told whatever it needs to know, while we shall respond to whatever is not for public consumption at an internal conference.

Probably many people in Hungary will ask why the Romanians didn't sign the communiqué. There are more people asking themselves this than there are people noting the presence of the Yugoslavs. And I don't want to draw any far-reaching conclusions from this one-off case, but I think the two things are not of equal weight. The fact that the Yugoslavs accepted the communiqué is far more important than the fact that the Romanians were there but failed to accept it. Moreover, the whole basic position is very interesting in the current situation. We shouldn't go in zigzags, because if calmer waters approach we may find that the position of the Yugoslavs differs from ours, but this was how it was manifested at this point. It is possible that the Yugoslav position on these issues may further improve and may become even closer to our own, because the situation that has arisen may be considered from very many aspects. And the Romanians will continue having to explain their behaviour for some time to come, unless they are no longer interested in anything but Western opinion. Of course, this is certainly not the case! Look at their statement. They left out the bit about Israel being the aggressor, but said all sorts of other things – they could have done nothing else. And, in connection with the Yugoslavs, there is another aspect worth examining. Apart from the great assembly of 1957, this was the first time they took part in discussions since 1948. And I would have liked to turn to Comrade Ceausescu and ask: why don't you look another five metres? The Yugoslavs went off for a while, but here they are now, with us once more.

Lastly, I would like to say something about what can be done inside the Party. I cannot say anything about this, but I do recommend firmness and consistency, and I ask that the PMO, the Agit-Prop Department or the Secretariat deal with the situation that has developed within the Party. I do not want anybody to panic, but we shouldn't close our eyes to what is happening. This is a matter like the Berlin or Caribbean Sea crisis, or the shock that accompanied Khrushchev's dismissal, and such things are always a lesson for the Party in general and particularly for the Party leadership. It is right here in front of our eyes that people's real nature is revealed. Generally speaking, such things are not manifest in day-to-day life. I am convinced that we are not talking about a mass and vast phenomenon, because the conduct of 500,000 Communist Party members and several hundreds of thousands of young Communists in the country is basically in order. A smaller part of the Party membership, and I hope nobody will misunderstand me here, a part with considerable influence in certain areas, has behaved in a non-Communist manner. And I don't want to draw some kind of conclusion based on race, and I understand that it is not clear to everyone who is the aggressor and attacker. A certain amount of anxiety is understandable, but this does not permit them to debate the position of the Party and the government on such a decisive issue as that of whom we should support and against whom we should fight. I cannot ignore this. This is a vital question for our system that the Party should be intact and stable. And if, as a result, Party membership were to decline, the danger would be a lesser one than a fluctuating membership. This may not be tolerated or permitted. Just think of the various relationships Party members and Hungarian citizens have beyond the borders – just as many as they do here at home. And does this mean we should divide up the Party into an Israeli section, an Upper Hungary section, a Transylvanian section, and the Soviet Union left just with the men who have married Russian college girls?

And there is another aspect. I recommend clear and consistent leadership in all areas rather than a fluster, but if such tendencies were to spread, then rules would have to be drawn up. Because to fatten people up in good jobs, who then take such positions in critical situations – this kind of thing cannot be permitted! So we must think about these things and do something too.

And I am thinking of minor matters as well. The agit-prop group did a good job in keeping things under control, but I didn't like the fact that they didn't give us anything from Comrade Szirmai's speech on what he said about the situation in the Middle East. And yet, in his speech, Comrade Szirmai certainly said something else and not merely that the 'central' question was that students should criticise more courageously. And then the radio informs people that this and that happened during the week, and then the news is over and someone starts singing in English or whatever. I am sure that if the United States were to issue a statement on the Cuban issue, they would not then broadcast on the radio a Cuban jambo record. The various positions taken by us must be better synchronised. Last week there was a war, and the fact that we were not involved in it is thanks to the good political stance taken. And if I meet any people who feel sorry for Israel, I will give them a sound beating! I hear that Illyés has said that he will go as a volunteer!

Today I saw an Izvestiya article explaining that people should not take positions based on whether they are Russian, Chinese, Arab or Jewish. This is a fundamental issue of contemporary world politics, and an appropriate position must be taken.

Comrade BÉLA BISZKU:

I recommend that the Political Committee should accept and acknowledge the information received and the measures taken.

I have spoken with Comrade Pullai about how we should deal with these issues in the coming days in the course of political action, in part to expound and explain our position within the Party. Comrade Pullai is to make a proposal concerning this. A primary task is to inform the county Party committees; moreover, consideration should also be given to the fact that Party meetings are being held on international issues, and that these should be used to orient the Party membership correctly. The speakers are even now relying on the joint statement.

I suggest that, under the circumstances, a minimum state of alert should be maintained, because this matter will continue to drag on; there will be long diplomatic battles, and there may also be other types of clashes.

11 The Presidium of the CC CPČZ on the War in the Middle East

13 June and 20 June 1967

National Archives of the Czech Republic, Prague, Archive of the Central Committee of the Communist Party, Presidium, *File*: 37, Nr. 37/28

Minutes of 36th session or the Presidium of the Central Committee, 13 June 1967

[....]

Comrade David (Minister of Foreign Affairs): [...] Pointed to various phenomena in our propaganda before and in the course of the Israeli–Arab conflict. He alerted to the preparations of celebration of the millennial existence of the Prague Jewish community and to the activity developed in relation to it. Also he informed about the measures taken by the Ministry of Foreign Affairs in this connection, and asked paying more attention to this issue. Further he asked drawing relevant conclusions against the radio and television, where the situation is not good and apparently there are people, who are trying to produce at least ambiguities around Israel. This is indicated, on the one hand, the course of comrade Pudlák's press conference, and on the other the character of information and journalist programmes in the radio and television during the Israeli aggression.

Also he pointed to anonymous letters supporting Israel, which the Ministry of Foreign Affairs has been receiving.

Comrade Novotný: [...] We have to instruct the Ministry of the Interior to act far more strictly against the elements which use the situation for anti-state and anti-Party demonstrations. Also in this respect it is necessary to take these measures.

As far as the cadre measures are concerned, particularly in connection with the press conference of comrade Pudlák, we will draw conclusions, because this is extremely incorrect movement.

The information shows that there are no pro-Israeli sentiments in our country, except for a few individuals. Our people soberly consider development of the situation. The worse thing is that there are antisemitic moods. This is not right. It is necessary that our newspapers, our propaganda, acted, in this respect, far more sharply and harshly, although reasonably. From the Ostrava region and Slovakia very serious warnings of chauvinistic sentiments are coming. This is extremely wrong. If we would concede this, we would get to the other extreme. Also racist sentiments, which we must combat, remained here.

Once again I point out that in press we should come back to Vilner's declaration, this is a fundamental and class position. This way we will give orientation to the sentiments, which has arisen here.

Resolution drafted at the 37th Session of the Presidium of the CC CPČz, 20 June 1967.

Reasons Account

Based on the discussion and conclusions of the CC CPČz's Presidium session on 13th June 1967 about consultation of the First Secretaries of the Communist and Workers' Parties, and prime ministers of European Socialist countries in Moscow, the committee established by the Presidium submits assessment of the situation resulting from Israel's aggression against the United Arab Republic and other Arab countries, with the aim <u>to draw some basic findings and definitely confirm conclusions for our own and joint procedure with other Socialist countries</u> in the immediate future. Another aim of the proposals is to give an impulse to a fundamental study and elaboration of the momentous questions of anti-imperialistic, anti-colonial and national-liberation movement and its attitude to the Socialist system and workers' revolutionary movement in capitalist countries. The material (without passages of purely internal character) would be <u>delivered to the Central Committee of the CPSU with a request for opinion and comment on the situation assessment</u> and a request for considering appropriate forms of how to secure a joint procedure of the Socialist countries in important questions – in this case how to coordinate actions of political and material help to the United Arab Republic, Syria and possibly also Algeria.

[....]

Basic instruction from the aggression and proposals for further procedure

The armed combat at the Near and Middle East has shown that world imperialism, in the lead with the USA, is making use of all opportunities, wherever these turn up in the world, to attempt to stop the progression of nations' fight for freedom and independence, and to reinforce its position. It utilises the fact that the countries of the Socialist system exercise politics of peaceful coexistence spend enormous efforts to keep peace in the world and liquidate centres of war danger. Imperialism is trying, by means of subversion and coups, to debilitate and discredit them in the eyes of the non-Communist progressive world public and especially the developing countries, which hesitate before decision which way their further development will turn.

The Socialist countries, hobbled in their possibilities by the subversive activity of the Chinese leadership, which is extremely harmful to the international Communist and workers' movement, have found themselves, facing the imperialistic powers' policy, on certain defensive, which reflects primarily the fact that they, including the ČSSR, do not have an elaborate and thus effective conception that would prevent the imperialistic states' policy from obstruction of progressive development in the world. It is necessary to consider the Arab countries' failure to oppose the Israeli aggression a failure of the world powers of progress, the Socialist countries including. It is therefore indispensable to draw appropriate conclusions from the experience and in the next phase of this fight to strive for limitation of negative impact of the military failure, and create prerequisites for gradual abrogation of successes, which Israel achieved by means of armed power. The ground on which it is possible to build is the fact that imperialism did not succeed to subvert the progressive regimes in the UAR and Syria by this attack, and, on the contrary, in the UAR, in case the reaction is successfully prevented from seizing the power, can reach faster development considering that the UAR leadership, as the first information show, learned from the military failure, and counter-revolutionary forces have been removed from responsible places and replaced by more progressive ones.

The situation that has arisen places us under necessity to strive for reduction of the impacts of the Israeli military success to minimum. It assumes fight for withdrawal of its army from the occupied territories and comeback to the status quo before aggression, i.e. behind ceasefire line of 4 June 1967.

The basis for reconciliation of the situation must be a gradual and long-lasting solution of the overall situation at the Near and Middle East on equitable basis, which would secure the rights of the Palestinian refugees and solution of the disputed territorial problems in accord with the Charter and resolutions of the General Assembly of the UNO.

At the same time it is necessary to affect the Arab countries so that these exercised responsible and realistic politics, especially in the spheres of economic and social development, and abandoned the slogans about Israel's liquidation, which give a strong weapon in the hands of Israel's protectors and confuse the world public opinion, and that they took into consideration the real situation and recognised Israel's existence after the agreement about compensation of damage, which the Israeli aggression caused, is reached.

[...]

The current state of affairs requires a resolute procedure of the Socialist countries on the international field in support of the Arab claims. With the interest to settle the situation in the Near and Middle East the Czechoslovak government expressed its approval of the Soviet initiative for convening special session of the General Assembly of the UNO and supports it completely. At the convention the Czechoslovak delegation will proceed co-coordinately with Socialist countries and other states in order to enforce condemnation of Israel as an aggressor and so that terms of Israel's withdrawal to the ceasefire line were prepared, while realisation of the second claim does not require unconditional realisation of the first one. Also it will be necessary to claim Israel's guarantees that it would cease being the center of turbulence and aggression in this part of the world.

Support for the Arab countries will also be expressed at the bilateral contacts between the ČSSR and countries of the third world, and some European and Asian capitalist states, especially within the framework of the UNO and other international governmental and non-governmental organisations.

As the first political measure it is suggested to sent, in the immediate days, a personal plenipotentiary of the president of the ČSSR to President Nasir. This plan will be materialised in case the negotiations of Nasir's plenipotentiary Ahmed Fuad, who is to come to Prague these days, vindicate its purposefulness.

The task of the plenipotentiary of the President of the ČSSR is:

To elicit Nasir's intentions in solving the conflict with Israel, internal political and economic problems of the country and its international relations.

To express our position on the situation and its solution. To emphasise that according to our opinion Israel must not be allowed to stay on the territories, which it conquered by aggression. For enforcing this claim the UAR and Arab countries can expect our full support. At the same time (we have) to explain why we have never agreed and would not agree to some Arabic countries' demands of liquidation of the State of Israel.

We are willing to extend our help in the interest of sustaining progressive development of the country. However, we need to have guarantees of its effective utilisation. Therefore we require an open statement on how would Nasir and his colleagues counter anti-Soviet and anti-Socialist sentiments and whether they restrict the influence of and remove reactionary officials from important places of the economic and political life, and the army.

During the negotiations with Nasir to emphasise the necessity of a most serious consideration and learning lesson from the past faults, necessity of a consistent adopting of realistic positions on the solution of the major questions and the importance of consultations with the befriended countries before he undertakes any important actions, above all those in the field of international politics.

To emphasise the importance of unity of the revolutionary powers in the country, and anti-imperialistic unity of the Arab countries, and to ask what steps is the UAR going to take in this respect in the immediate and more distant future, on the basis of the lesson learned from the course of the war conflict with Israel.

After discussing the political issues, basic questions connected to our help, and economic and business relations of both countries would be debated.

[...]

In the interest of preserving the centres of progressive development in the Arab world it is necessary to provide primarily the UAR and Syria with comprehensive help. While providing the help it is necessary to consistently monitor guarantees of its maximal effectiveness.

As a result of the destruction of a great deal of military technique of the Arab states and as a result of the Western states' position, above all the USA and England, in the military sphere, a situation has arisen, which is creates favourable conditions for supplies of military technique from the Socialist countries to the Arab world.

When keeping effective procedure, Czechoslovakia could use this situation for at least partial compensation of the losses and unfavourable impacts, which must be reckoned with. In order to achieve this goal it is suitable to keep the following principles:

1. To target our help primarily to accelerating supplies of the already contracted materials and to try to secure accelerated restoration of effectiveness of the technology, which has left in the Arab states, by supplies of spare parts, munitions, and possible assistance in repairs.
2. To convey to the UAR and Syria the fundamental willingness of the ČSSR to keep helping in building the economy and defence, however, the Czechoslovak possibilities of supplies of the special material, based on the requirements of the UAR and Syria, will be communicated after consideration of requirements of all Arab countries in accord with possibilities of the Czechoslovak national economy.
3. The questions of gratuitous or only partially paid help, whether it be by supplies of military technology or sending out experts, will be consistently considered in accord with the economic possibilities of the Czechoslovak national economy and attendant expenses, which arise with such a help, will be taken into account.
4. The prospective gratuitous help will be limited only to the UAR, possibly to Syria on smaller scale, while with the other states regular terms of payment will be asserted.
5. To utilise the fact that the Western Powers lent their help to Israel and sought to place supplies of special technology also in the Arab countries, which had so far been in a special sector the sole domain of the Western counties.
6. To consider the possibilities of direct negotiations with some Arab countries (Kuwait and Libya) about possibilities of settlement of the special technology supplies to the Arab countries, which are in a bad economic and financial situation.

[...]

The task of out economic organs is to explore and materialise the possibilities of our active utilisation of the newly emerged situation in the Middle East for the benefit of our economic interests; among others for example to negotiate with the Arab countries about the possibility to deposit part of the foreign currency drawn from the Western banks in the Czechoslovak State Bank.

In the organs of the Council of Mutual Economic Help to actively support proposals for a thorough and instant co-ordination of economic help to the Arab countries.

The Israeli aggression against the progressive Arab countries and the complex situation, into which their progressive powers and European Socialist countries got, the impact of this conflict on the position of the Communist Parties on capitalist countries and on the situation in the international Communist movement, once again underlined the urgency of a world consultation of the Communist and Workers' Parties representatives.

Consultation of the issue of developing countries and national liberation movement in relation to the International Communist movement should be one of the major questions of the next international consultation, which should consider the international situation and its development over the last years, and draw conclusions that would be abided by the whole movement in the questions of fight against imperialism, liquidation of all forms of colonialism, sustaining progressive development in the world against the imperialistic strategy of export of counter-revolution by local wars and other means (reactionary putsches) and obstruction of our support to the progressive powers by the threat of nuclear war.

In this respect it will be necessary to discuss also the joint procedure of the Communist and Workers' Parties towards the national democratic parties in power, and other progressive parties and organisations.

During negotiations with Comradely Parties' representatives about the urgency of consultation and its programme, we will emphasise the importance of discussion of the above-mentioned questions and exchange opinion on their solution.

We are primarily concerned about the basic question of how to confront the imperialistic attacks against the emerging centres of progressive development in various parts of the world. Within this framework it is necessary to elaborate a number of important questions, as e.g. the concept of reinforcing of the alliance of the Socialist system and national liberation movement, the concept of the political, military and scientific-technical help to the developing countries, etc.

The material covering positions and proposals of our side would then serve as a basis for elaboration of a joint assessment and procedure of at least those comradely parties and Socialist countries, which signed the Moscow declaration of 9 June 1967.

It is recommended to assign the International Department (of the CC CPČz) to immediately start elaboration on these questions in co-operation with relevant departments and institutions, and submit them for discussion by 15 September 1967.

Considering our relatively rich contacts with the progressive Arab countries (Party political, diplomatic, economic and technical relations) we had a relatively good picture of the situation in the countries and their weak points and flaws in various sectors. However, our co-operation lacked the aspect of an intensive, active effort to eliminate defective opinions and practice.

Only rarely we respond to incorrect tendencies and damaging opinions, for which we account by the principle of non-involvement in the internal affairs of other countries and Parties.

In the interest of supporting the progressive powers it will be necessary in our contacts to oppose, in a suitable way, incorrect opinions as well as practice, which would debilitate efficiency of our help, and actively intervene in discussion especially in questions dealing with relations of the Socialist camp and the Third World as well as with the liberation movements.

The course of events in the territory of the Arab East, which developed into the Israeli aggression, revealed defects and weak points in the activity of some authorities and insufficient political as well as moral preparedness of part of our workers abroad.

It is also necessary to mention that the crises at the Near and Middle East have shown certain imperfections primarily in the intelligence work of all departments of the representative organs in the territory of the Near and Middle East. Also certain imprudence and unwariness has turned up in taking necessary emergency measures.

It is recommended that the Ministry of Foreign Affairs, Ministry of Foreign Trade, Ministry of National Trade and the Interior Ministry made analysis of the causes of these defects and weak points and took measures, which would preclude their recurrence both in the Arab and other countries.

Reflection of the events in the near East in our country has also revealed some of our weak points in influencing the public opinion. While some magazines (Literární Listy) systematically propagated the state of Israel as a peaceful, economically successful, democratic and progressive, our public was not sufficiently informed about developments in the UAR and Syria. Similarly, in the beginning of the Israeli aggression, under the veil of "objectivity" and necessity to oppose the Western propaganda, information appeared in primarily the radio and television, which raised doubts about our assessment of the conflict's character as an Israeli aggression. This fact is, in some measure, related to the cadre situation in the media of mass propaganda.

It is recommended to assign the Ideological Department of the CC CPČz with analysis of these flaws and suggest necessary measures.

Nowadays the content of our propaganda must be targetted primarily at strengthening of the ideas of proletarian internationalism and international solidarity of the progressive powers. Explain the core of the conflict in the Near East, reveal the real nature of the State of Israel by concrete facts. Oppose the Zionist propaganda, but at the same time antisemitism. For this purpose use the analysis of positions of both groups of the Communist Party of Israel. Oppose the danger of defeatism and feelings of helplessness among the progressive citizens and contempt for the developing countries and their importance in the anti-imperialistic fight.

In the intra-Party life consistently pay attention that the reports at the members' meetings of the CPČz cells expressed solely opinions, which are in accord with the position of the CC CPČz to all questions discussed. For this purpose the organizational-political department of the CC CPČz will see that in the cells of the CPČz only the referees sent by higher Party organs are presented.

12 Message from Deputy Head of the Foreign Affairs Department of the CPSU

19 June 1967

National Archives of Hungary, M-KS 288/47/ p. 231.
Collection: Hungarian Socialist Workers' Party (HSWP), Central Bodies, János Kádár's Secretariat [Magyar Szocialista Munkáspárt (MSZMP) Központi Szervei, Kádár János Titkársága]

Completed in 2 copies

Record

For Comrade János Kádár

At noon today, Comrade K.V. Rusakov telephoned from Moscow and, on behalf of Comrade Brezhnev, stated the following:

The Political Committee of the CPSU is now in session, and so Comrade Brezhnev apologizes to Comrade Kádár for not contacting him in person. However, the following information is urgent.

Tomorrow the Central Committee of the CPSU will hold a meeting at which Comrade Brezhnev will report on the situation in the Middle East. The resolution adopted at the meeting will be published, but not the speech.

Nasser has strongly requested that the Soviet comrades send a senior Soviet leader – either Brezhnev or Kosygin or Podgorny – to Cairo in the days ahead on an unofficial visit. The aim of the visit would be exchanging views on important issues. As Comrade Brezhnev is holding a plenary meeting and giving a speech there, and Comrade Kosygin is in New York, the Political Committee has decided that Comrade Podgorny will travel to Cairo.

Comrade Podgorny will depart tomorrow morning shortly after the plenary session has begun (probably after the speech). He will fly via Belgrade, where there will be a technical stopover during which Comrade Podgorny will probably meet with Tito. During the conversation with Tito – if, indeed, such a conversation takes place – they will not think about agreeing on issues.

The Comrades will inform us regularly about Comrade Podgorny's discussions in Cairo. For the time being, the press will not report anything about the visit; the above information is for Comrade Kádár and a narrow group of leaders. The same information is being received by our fraternal Parties in the other Socialist countries, apart from Romania.

Comrade Rusakov has requested that we tell him whether Comrade Kádár has any questions in this respect or has something to say.

13 Information from the Soviet Embassy to János Kádár

20 June 1967

National Archives of Hungary, M-KS 288/47/ p. 233.
Collection: Hungarian Socialist Workers' Party (HSWP), Central Bodies, János Kádár's Secretariat [Magyar Szocialista Munkáspárt (MSZMP) Központi Szervei, Kádár János Titkársága]

Completed in 1 copy

Record

For Comrade János Kádár

At noon today, N.N. Sikachev, counsellor at the Soviet Embassy, at the behest of Comrade Kudryashov, informed Comrade Kádár of the following:

> "Yesterday Comrade Kádár was told in a message from Comrade Brezhnev of Comrade Podgorny's trip to Cairo, and of the secret nature of the trip. Today Comrade Podgorny travelled to Cairo.
> Immediately prior to his departure, Nasser let it be known that – apparently for some reason beneficial to him – he is to make public Comrade Podgorny's visit and hold a major reception for him. Thus, we are making the visit public."

14 Leonid Brezhnev's Telegram to János Kádár

17 July 1967

National Archives of Hungary, M-KS 288/47/ p. 244.
Collection: Hungarian Socialist Workers' Party (HSWP), Central Bodies, János Kádár's Secretariat [Magyar Szocialista Munkáspárt (MSZMP) Központi Szervei, Kádár János Titkársága]

Translated from Russian
Completed in 2 copies
Translated by Mrs Barta

On 17 July 1967, Comrade F.Y. Titov, the Soviet Ambassador, brought in a telegram transmitted by the secret channel, which Comrade Brezhnev sent to Comrade Kádár. The text of the telegram is as follows:

To Comrade János Kádár
Budapest

Dear Comrade Kádár,

We wish to inform you that early this morning we received the following "oral message from all those attending the conference of Arab heads of state in Cairo" from our ambassador in Cairo:

> "The Arab heads of state, who have come to the conference in Cairo, decided at their closing session on the evening of 16 July that at 10 a.m. on 17 July Presidents Boumediène and Aref shall travel to Moscow. The presidents will inform the Soviet leaders of the results of the conference and will consult with them about the situation in the Middle East.
> Boumediène and Aref will travel on a special Algerian plane."

The Arabs did not confer with us about this decision in advance. We shall not refuse to receive them. We shall negotiate.
We shall inform you of further developments.

With comradely greetings,
L. Brezhnev

15 Minutes of the Meeting of the Political Committee on 18 July 1967

18 July 1967

National Archives of Hungary, M-KS 288/5/430/1967
Collection: Hungarian Socialist Workers' Party (HSWP), Central Bodies, János Kádár's Secretariat
[Magyar Szocialista Munkáspárt (MSZMP) Központi Szervei, Kádár János Titkársága]

Completed in 2 copies

1. Report

On the Budapest conference of Party and government leaders of the Socialist countries

Comrade JÁNOS KÁDÁR:

The essence can be gathered from the written report, which – from the aspect of experience – I wish to supplement with several things that are worth mentioning.

[...]

Regarding the situation in the Middle East, I wish to mention that the Soviet Union is supplying a significant amount of arms after the war, primarily to Egypt. The supplies are so large that they have replaced all the combat aircraft that were lost – indeed, a somewhat greater number than what Egypt lost have been supplied. Of course, in terms of combat value, this is not the same amount because Egypt does not have the necessary number of qualified personnel – and it is worth thinking about this in two ways.

The manner in which the debate arose at the UN is known to everyone from the reports. I mention here that, according to the CPSU's assessment, a two-thirds majority could not be reached for two reasons. First, due to the great pressure of the U.S., which was exerted on various Latin American and other countries. This was also a factor in the case of African countries that were formerly under French influence, which now, under pressure from the United States, did not adhere to the French position, but adopted the position taken by Latin-American countries. The other reason, according to the – I think, correct – evaluation of the Soviet Comrades, was the excessive inflexibility of the Arab position, which rendered it impossible to establish some kind of sensible and measured compromise.

Concerning the Arab leaders, they seem to have been divided since the end of the war. We generally keep a record of progressive Arab countries with whom we must work, such as Egypt, Syria, Algeria, and Iraq – but there are also other Arab countries. Even among the progressive countries, a typical feature is the lack of a uniform position. Thus, a distinct and sharply different position is taken by the Algerian leaders, who are almost in agreement with the Syrian leaders. These leaders take a combative position; they argue for a continuation of the war and that the resolution of the issue must be sought by military means. Their position is so extreme on the need to continue the war that it does not matter [to them] if Cairo or Damascus falls. On the other side, Nasser takes an obviously different and somewhat more realistic position, and the Iraqi stance is not as extreme as the Algerian one.

I shall repeat the important findings of the conference, because they are decisive. At our conference, we took the view that under the present circumstances the only realistic and correct path to a resolution of the Middle-East issue is a struggle for a political solution. And this is contrary to the Algerian and Syrian position, which rejects this and emphasises a military solution.

Another important finding of the conference concerned the nature of assistance. Theoretically, we really have to help the three countries directly affected by the war: Egypt, Syria and Jordan. The conference concluded that Jordan can be left out of direct assistance, for it did not even request such help. Thus we have to concentrate on Egypt and Syria – and primarily on Egypt. There are two means through which their powers of defence have to be strengthened: 1. the supply of military technology; 2. the provision of military advisors. One can see that Nasser intends to reorganise the armed forces, and for this process he wishes to make use of advisors, primarily Soviet advisors.

One should mention here that Nasser even wishes to partially abandon his non-aligned stance and sign a treaty with the Soviet Union, or with another Socialist country. He further wishes that the Soviet Union or the Socialist countries would take control of Egyptian air defences. The Soviet Union does not consider this to be the right course of action, and the conference uniformly took the position that this could not be done, because this would lead to a very undesirable situation.

Regarding economic assistance, a major point of emphasis at the conference was that, in addition to prompt assistance – which is necessary, in view of the war losses and the situation with consumer goods – great emphasis should be laid on assistance. The assistance should specifically be aimed at restoring industrial and agricultural production, because this is very significant to society within the given country, and especially for the workers. If there is no production then there is no basic livelihood for workers, which can have extremely detrimental political consequences.

A resolution was also adopted on informing the Arabs – by internal means – of the positions taken at this conference. There were various suggestions. We proposed that the CPSU be asked to complete this task. They accepted. The next day the Soviet Comrades suggested that instead, the HSWP – as the host of the conference – should inform the Arabs. We did not agree with this, but subsequently, and as a substitute, we voted in favour of the Arabs being informed by two parties: the CPSU and the HSWP.

The information was compiled, with everyone's agreement, and on Sunday evening this internal information was submitted in writing in Cairo, without a signature, and in the form of a verbal note, or whatever it is called.

This information sheet highlights elements where we support a political solution, they receive combat technology and advisors, and as far as economic assistance is concerned, the goal is restoring production.

Here, one should note that the conference of Arab leaders was now under way, and that Malik, Soviet Deputy Foreign Minister, stayed there until the end. The experiences there show that Boumediène and the Syrian leader stated that they supported a military solution. They could not accept the formula that we offered, which is to accept a UN resolution that would declare the end of the state of war, because that would mean less than the granting of recognition to Israel – although indirectly it would mean this, as well. Boumediène stated that they could not accept this.

Yesterday morning we were informed by the Soviet Comrades that they had been unilaterally told that Boumediène and the Iraqi president were to travel to Moscow, and that they would receive them. They arrived there in the late evening. We shall receive information from the Soviet Comrades.

Thus, at present, things are not looking too good. It is difficult to fight in this way, because our position and the Arab position do not coincide. At our conference we said that if we managed to establish a resolution – by adding to the existing ones – in which we established a cessation of the state of war, the restoration of shipping freedom to the level of 4 June and the opening of Suez – but Israeli ships were not allowed to go there even prior to this – that is, if some such action is achieved (regardless of whether a two-thirds majority can be assured, at least the political initiative would be in the Arabs' hands), it would then be easier to fight at the political level within the UN and in terms of propaganda too. This was our proposition, but it did not gain favour with the Arabs.

2. <u>Report on the assistance (material and technical) to be offered to the Arab countries</u>

Comrade JENŐ FOCK

[...] Originally, the Comrades expected to deal with military aid – and such a specific request has been received. In the meantime there was the Budapest conference, where in accordance with the conference the emphasis shifted to the need to ensure the continuance of production, and such assistance must be given.

[...]

I suggest that the Political Committee accept a sum of 200 million forints for military defence assistance. Within this framework, there should be an effort made in the upcoming days to list articles in this that do not have to be replaced in domestic defence. During the consultation this must be carefully addressed, and if others can give such things then we should not give them. If the Political Committee accepts this allocation, we can then negotiate on this matter and on the basis of such an amount.

I think it would be of tangible assistance to Egypt for us to confirm that we consider the credit of 15 million Egyptian pounds to be valid. And let us negotiate on the extent to which they want to make use of this.

Perhaps authorisation would also be needed for transforming the five to seven-year credit into a seven to ten-year credit. And if the issue of a moratorium arises, we could provide this. Finally, the issue of skilled workers could possibly be formulated in such a manner that not only do we undertake to train 100–150 experts for a year, but for an equivalent amount, we could send technicians and engineers in order to guarantee production. Finally, I suggest that we include medicines in the food products worth three million forints.

We have a normal barter agreement for this year and for next year. Egypt may ask to cancel some important things in view of the current situation. Instead, a long-term credit should be given, but we must insist on delivery.

The matter of further assistance should be viewed in terms of the extent to which Egypt, Syria, Iraq and perhaps Algeria, show a real eagerness to divert some of their trade to the Socialist countries, including Hungary. So far, only baseless statements have been made, but no real action has been taken. We can provide assistance to the extent that they divert their trade. Just now we heard about some banking measures. So far little concrete action has been taken. We have arranged with the National Bank of Hungary that if they find that attempts are being made to place major sums here, we can offer as much interest – or even more interest – than the Bank of England.

To sum up: we cannot decide about everything now, and so a general authorisation needs to be given to the Government.

Comrade JÁNOS KÁDÁR

I support Comrade Fock's proposal, but I wish to make some comments.

The first, and this must be taken into account when giving assistance, is that in such a situation the problems and difficulties experienced by the countries affected stem from the fact that they are unable to assess precisely their technical and other needs. This explains the "circular" request, in which they send a list of items to the various countries, and not knowing the situation, they ask everything from everyone. One cannot see how this will become effective assistance. At the conference I suggested that we should primarily assist in enabling them to assess their needs in an exact manner, and if they are incapable of doing this, then perhaps the Soviet Union should help them. They alone can better see what they need.

Another observation of mine: I always recommend – based on certain experience – that we should never exhaust our possibilities completely. Firstly, in the case of the countries under discussion there is a likelihood that in a month's time, when they can better assess what they need, that they will come up with a new list. For this reason, we need to keep a reserve of the material and financial means to be used. Especially since if there will be fights against the imperialists in other places we will have to assist there as well. Thus, we need to assess our realistic possibilities, that is, assess what we can release without upsetting the material state of the country, thereby endangering the normal functioning of our own countries – and we should not exhaust [our resources] completely. Giving less than what they expect now is better than saying later on that we agree with their request but cannot fulfil it.

Concerning the implementation, I have the following comment: I do not know whether they are urging us to respond now, but I would say that if they are doing so and are seeking an answer, then we should respond. However, if there are things that are not urgent, then we should wait. At any rate, I would wait before providing military equipment support.

16 Report on the Opinion of Members of the Hungarian Jewish Congregation from an Anonymous Informer

21 June 1967

National Archives of Hungary, M-KS 288/22/9/1967
Collection: Hungarian Socialist Workers' Party (HSWP), Central Bodies, Agitation and Propaganda Department [Magyar Szocialista Munkáspárt (MSZMP) Központi Szervei, Agitációs és Propaganda Osztály]

From: Agitation and Propaganda Department

Memorandum

I report as follows on the frame of mind of Hungarian Jewry concerning the Middle-Eastern conflict:

As regards the general frame of mind, it may be stated that although the Middle-Eastern question concerns issues of significance to the fate of the Israeli people, generally speaking the loyalty of Hungarian Jewry to our Socialist country has not been undermined. Understandably, many of them nurture sentimentalist feelings towards the Israeli people. Many of them have relatives in Israel with whom they correspond constantly. Although most of them emphasise that they believe in the Socialist social order and do not desire a capitalist system or support for imperialism, nevertheless with respect to that part of the Middle-Eastern conflict that concerns Israel, many of them do not agree with the position of the Soviet Union – particularly with regard to Israel's being an aggressor. In their opinion, Israel took defensive action.

As regards the various personal conversations, I briefly note them as follows:

Dr M. M.: The Jews are frightened; they fear antisemitism. Unidentified individuals have thrown dirt at the windows of the grammar school. Jews have feelings of community with the Israeli people.

J. S.: I have spoken to people outside Budapest, too. They are afraid of antisemitism; this is a big problem. One should be quiet and cautious, because, in their hearts, Jews support Israel.

Dr V. L.: This is a very difficult and complicated issue. We are Hungarian citizens, and the policy of the Hungarian government should be continued; still, we are unable to feel animosity towards the Israeli people. We are a religious organisation; politics is not our concern.

Dr L. S.: It is time to keep quiet and be smart. For Israel is very close to our hearts. By sticking up for the Arabs, the Soviet Union has suffered severe damage to its prestige. And this has harmed us as well. Here in Hungary, the number of tourists has sunk. The rooms are empty at Lake Balaton, whereas all the tourist accommodation is full in Romania.

J. H.: Jewish and non-Jewish people all support Israel. They do not accept that Israel was the aggressor. It took defensive action. Hungarian Jewish Communists also support Israel, even though they continue to regard themselves as good Communists. In their judgement, truth is on the side of Israel rather than of the Arabs. Hungarian Jews are frightened; they fear antisemitism, and they do not feel themselves secure, because many non-Jews identify Israel with Jews. People regard Arabs as well-known as antisemites.

A Party secretary at a tailors' co-operative: As Communists of Jewish descent, we do not agree with the Soviet Union on this issue, because the Arabs have always been antisemites and anti-Communists. One cannot believe that they have changed and that they now have progressive ideas. The Israeli people are far more progressive, because three Communist Parties are operating there. Communists have never been persecuted in Israel, as they have been in Syria and Egypt, for instance. As people that otherwise support the Soviet Union, we fear for the prestige of the Soviet Union on this issue.

F. R.: Radio Free Europe stated that Hungarian Jewry was not supportive of Israel. The Polish Jewish newspaper, Volkstymme, has spoken in support of Israel.

J. Á.: The people to whom I have spoken are generally supportive of Israel – even high-ranking Party members. I am extremely anxious, because everyone is afraid of antisemitism. A Jewish person cannot say that he is a friend of Nasser, the antisemitic leader, or an enemy of the long-suffering Israeli people. This is a very odd situation.

Dr I. B.: The situation is difficult, because we cannot say the Arabs are our brothers and the Israeli people our enemy.

S. Á.: Israel was not an aggressor. Why don't people talk about Nasser's aggression in closing off the Gulf of Aqaba and by concentrating troops along the border? The UN troops were withdrawn, and a united Arab force of over 100 million men faced Israel. Nasser wanted to annihilate Israel, and Israel acted out of self-defence. The Soviet Union equipped the Arabs with arms and armoured vehicles, and its officers even trained Arab soldiers. A foreign broadcaster stated that the Soviet officers were unable to train the Arabs, because most of them could not even read or write. What would have happened if an Arab mass of over 100 million men had actually destroyed little Israel? What would they have said then? Israel's sin is to have defended its territory out of self-defence, and that it failed to give Nasser advance warning of where and when it would attack.

Népszabadság [daily newspaper – AK] did not report Komócsin's television address faithfully, for in his speech Komócsin also spoke of the 'Jewish question' – but this was absent from Népszabadság's account. People in Hungary have not talked about the Jewish question ever since Hitler. J. Á. asked who would have thought that 23 years after the Liberation, the Jewish question would again be talked about in Hungary.

B. P.: Jews fear antisemitism. The Arabs are incredibly antisemitic. Nasser's hatred of Jews and Communists is well known. And Bumedian drove out 300,000 Jews from Algeria. For some years, letters have been arriving from Israel describing the aggression of Syria and Egypt that has been going on for decades, as well as the effect on Israel of a whole series of border incidents. People can only work on the land in Israel if they have a weapon at their side. They are forced to defend themselves from the Syrians and the Egyptians, and all Jewish people with relatives in Israel know this.

Mr F. (Dohány Street Synagogue leader): I am an old person, and the Nazis incinerated my children. I can no longer find much joy in life. I am over 85 years old, and yet I still fret for Israel, because U Thant withdrew the defence troops, thereby providing the Arab masses with an opportunity to destroy Israel. Nasser is just like Hitler. May God grant that Israel will not be harmed.

Mr B. (Dohány Street Synagogue leader): Israel took defensive action. At the start of hostilities, it seemed that the large Arab mass would sweep Israel aside. It was a divine miracle that little Israel did not want to conquer territory, but wants borders that ensure its defence, so that people won't have to go to work bearing arms, nor fear attacks along the border.

Mr S. (Dohány Street Synagogue leader): Israel was not an aggressor, but merely acted to defend itself. This was the aim of the Palestinian Liberation Front – as Hungarian news also reported – when, on the Jordanian front and with the aim of liberating Palestine, the troops set off to destroy Israel.

K. H.: I have many very good Communist friends and acquaintances. All of them are saying just how disappointed they are. The Arabs cannot be more progressive than the Israelis. They think that the issue of Soviet antisemitism is in part behind the anti-Israeli position. Antisemites will be encouraged here in Hungary, too. These Communist friends of mine fear for the ideals of Communism. They have sunk into themselves as a result of events. All of them see – said K. H. – that the facts and propaganda of hostility towards Israel are not aimed at exposing the real facts and that Israel is the subject of a baseless campaign of slander.

Rabbi E. D.: Israel's success in combat was a divine miracle. It is to be feared that there will be antisemitism in the country, because the propaganda is anti-Jewish.

Dr P. H., a Budapest lawyer: He criticised the article by János Nemes published in the Népszabadság, which dealt with the Izvestiya article. He thought the article might incite antisemitism, owing to its content and the use of the word 'Jew'. He sarcastically remarked that 'we have received orders to worship Nasser, the second Hitler'. Dr P. H. said he also found it interesting that Hungary had broken off diplomatic relations with Israel because Israel was an aggressor. Whereas America really had been perpetrating aggression against Vietnam for many years now, and yet neither the Soviet Union nor Hungary had broken off diplomatic relations with America. This also shows that the Soviet Union was driven by antisemitism when it broke off diplomatic relations with Israel – but not with America despite years of American aggression in Vietnam – and that they were just fixing the blame on Israel.

M. S.: Yesterday I was with four top-level ministerial staff members. All of them are old and trustworthy Communists – some Jews, some non-Jews. They were filled with despair at the harm the affair has done to the Soviet Union and the cause of Communism. They said it really did seem as if there were a strong antisemitic tendency in the Soviet Union and that what the foreign newspapers have been writing about the Soviet Union with regard to antisemitism may not be fiction after all. M. S. said that these people were devastated by events.

Dr P. B.: Today I got a letter from my relatives in Israel. Israel is not an aggressor. People here are very afraid of antisemitism; Komócsin's speech did a lot of harm. Hungarian Jews are afraid that if Soviet policy continues to be marked by the lack of success, this could also strike hard against Jews living outside of Israel.

Dr M. B.: I received a telegram from my brother in Israel, saying that he's fine. It's awful what is happening around Israel. I have always been left-wing and I shall always remain so. My brother in Israel is an old Communist Party member. I don't think, however, that Israel is an aggressor; most people in this country don't think it is.

Dr Gy. F. (lawyer): In two of its editions in late May, Magyar Nemzet [*daily newspaper* – AK], writing about the Middle-Eastern crisis, published Nasser's speech on the closure of the Gulf of Aqaba, in which he said that he would destroy the whole of Israel if Israel took action over this or behaved like an aggressor. The second edition referred to Syria's repeated acts of terror against Israel, mentioning the acts of terror committed in May against Israel by a Syrian organisation called Hurricane. He asked: under such circumstances how can Israel be an aggressor? He then remarked sarcastically: 'Long Live Brother Nasser'.

Mr B. (museum employee): He also disputed that Israel was an aggressor and spoke, in connection with this, of Magyar Nemzet's reports of late May. He said that these reports clearly showed that Nasser, rather than Israel, had begun the aggression.

There were many people who did not comment on the events.

17 Report on the Mood within the Hungarian Jewish Religious Denomination

23 August 1967

National Archives of Hungary, XIX-A-21-d (39.d.)
Collection: State Office for Religious Affairs [Állami Egyházügyi Hivatal, ÁEH]

Completed in 5 copies
0020-2/a/67.
Recipients:
No. 1: HSWP CC, Comrade Á. Pulai
No. 2: Ministry of Foreign Affairs, Comrade J. Péter
No. 3: Ministerial Council, Comrade Pál Ilku
No. 4: HSWP CC, Comrade I. Balló
No. 5: State Office for Church Affairs,

Copy No. 2

Memorandum

on the mood observable within the Hungarian Jewish Religious Denomination regarding the situation in the Middle East

----

I.

The mood among the leaders and members of the denomination concerning the situation in the Middle East is today – after the initial panic – characterised by a more moderate judgment and a more realistic evaluation of the situation.

At the time of the Arab–Israeli wars, the great majority of Hungarian religious Jews sided emotionally with Israel. This emotional outpouring was motivated – and strengthened for many – by various familial, religious traditional relations and the feeling of community, based on a shared fate. This resulted in a situation where even the denominational leaders found it difficult – doing so only some time later – to distinguish between the Israeli people, the land of Israel, and the interests of the imperialist Israeli government.

Alongside the sympathy felt by various groups for the "rapid victory" of the Israeli troops, it caused concern among a majority of believers, for they feared that it could elicit a wave of antisemitism.

In the opinion of the leaders and priests of the religious denomination, Hungarian religious Jews cannot accept Israel being branded an aggressor, and they assert that the reason for the outbreak of armed conflict were the Arab threats and specifically the closure of the Gulf of Aqaba.

On the issue of aggression, even those denominational leaders that are closest to us were not completely clear; they were uncertain about supporting such a position of our government.

At the same time, they sought, to a greater extent than before, to prevent their emotional stance relating to Israel from influencing their loyalty and adherence to the Hungarian homeland and to Socialism. Rabbi Dr Hochberger expressed this as follows: "Hungarian Jewry will never forget that it was this system that removed the yellow stars and returned their freedom".

Those who are emotionally close to Israel and who sympathised with Zionism earlier on, seek openly to defend Israel.

For instance, Dr Sándor Scheiber, director of the rabbinical seminary, asked "why is Egypt [considered] a more democratic regime than Israel when in Egypt Communists are still being held in prisons, whereas in Israel they have their own political party and even now can go to Moscow to hold talks, and can make statements against the government, etc. Production co-operatives existed in Israel even before they were formed in Hungary," said Scheiber. Regarding the sympathy of religious Jews towards Israel, Sándor Scheiber asks for understanding from the state. He said "Jewry had been subjected to such suffering and persecution in the course of history that Jews need to know of a land, a country which would receive them at any time, if anywhere in the world new Auschwitzes were to arise. Even so, a Jewish person can be a very good Hungarian, Englishman, Frenchman or Russian – as indeed they are."

According to Dr Géza Seifert, chairman of the denomination, the emergence of the Arab–Israeli situation had impacted negatively, among religious Jews who are close to our state, on their relationship with the Soviet Union. They speak of a loss of prestige for the Soviet Union and draw a comparison between the result of American support for Israel and that of Soviet support for the Arabs.

In terms of resolving the conflict, various circles are hoping that differences of view among the Arab countries may lead to the break-up of Arab unity against Israel, which might result in the fixing of the present situation.

The more sensible and politically realistic majority are, however, convinced that Israel must return the Arab territories and commence peaceful negotiations with the Arabs.

In this regard, Deputy Chief Rabbi Dr Imre Benoschofsky stated the following:

> "Israel's territorial conquests have led to very mixed feelings among my congregation. They are saying that the situation is now even more alarming than it was on the outbreak of the conflict. It is impossible that Israel wants to retain the occupied part of Jerusalem or the Sinai territory, for it is quite a lot bigger than the country itself.
>
> Israel is currently reluctant to return the occupied territories because it wants to negotiate from an advantageous position."

Even the director Sándor Scheiber himself stated that it cannot be envisaged, from a political, economic or military perspective, that Israel should retain the occupied territories. At the same time, he considers it just that Jerusalem should remain fully in Israeli hands.

For religious Jewish circles, it has been extremely sobering that, under the influence of Israeli "successes", persons formerly known as reactionary and antisemitic have become, overnight, "philosemites" and have rooted for an Israeli victory.

In the unanimous opinion of the leaders and rabbis of the denomination, the supreme desire of members of the Hungarian Jewish Religious Denomination is that the Arab–Israeli conflict be settled through peaceful negotiations.

II.

The Board of the National Representation of Hungarian Israelites published an editorial article in this year's 1 August issue of the denominational publication Új Élet [*New Life, weekly newspaper of the NRHI* – AK] which was entitled "Our National Assembly and the Matter of Peace" and deals, among other things, extensively with the Middle-Eastern conflict.

In the course of prior negotiations concerning the article, we purposely did not make maximalist demands on the leadership of the denomination. We did not push them to use the expression "aggression", and we sought to ensure that the article – with its progressive content – would be acceptable, having regard for the real mood of Hungarian religious Jews, to them, while also influencing public opinion in the right direction.

The leading article firmly condemns Israeli government circles, which are acting with the support of the Western imperialists. Together with the entire Hungarian people, it approves the position taken by our government and our parliament.

It states that the use of violence will not resolve the Arab–Israeli situation and expresses the desire that the conflict will be settled by way of peaceful negotiations.

Based on the experience of the leaders of the Religious Denomination, as well as our own experiences, it may be stated that religious Jews received the article favourably and consider it to be realistic in its content and appropriate in tone.

According to our intelligence, the foreign press also received the article favourably and judged it to be moderate in terms of both content and tone.

We attach the report of Dr Géza Seifert, chairman of the National Representation of Hungarian Israelites, which reflects the opinion of various leaders of the Religious Denomination with regard to the published article.

18 The Political Committee's Resolution on Hungarian–Israeli Relations

20 December 1983

National Archives of Hungary, XIX-J-1-j-Izrael-14-002223/6-1986 (73.d.)
Collection: Ministry of Foreign Affairs [Külügyminisztérium]

Ministry of Foreign Affairs
Secretariat of the Ministry
00221/1/VP/1983.

The Political Committee's resolution of 20 December 1983 on the state of Hungarian–Israeli relations and timely tasks:

After Israel's aggression against its Arab neighbours of 5 June 1967, the government of the People's Republic of Hungary, proceeding in a manner that was agreed upon in close co-operation with the Socialist countries, severed diplomatic relations with the State of Israel on 12 June 1967. No position was taken by the body on relations of a different character, while the resolutions of the Political Committee adopted on 26 September 1967 and thereafter concerned various specific issues pertaining to the relationship.

In addition to breaking off official relations, we also reduced our contacts in the fields of economics, trade, culture and sport, and we severely restricted the opportunities for Hungarian citizens to travel to Israel and for Israelis to come to Hungary. We stopped inviting Israeli personalities to Hungarian events but we did allow them to participate in international meetings held in Hungary.

During the 18 years since the severance of diplomatic relations, we have, at various points in time and for different reasons, alleviated some of the restrictions, but a comprehensive review of relations and an evaluation of the possibilities of, and limits to, their enhancement, has not taken place to date. Developments in recent years, Israel's overt and covert attempts to expand relations, which have been made with increasing frequency and are mostly of a political and economic nature, as well as their proposals relating to the alleviation or lifting of our restrictions, have rendered it necessary to define in more concrete terms our conduct and our tasks. In this process, the fact that Israeli measures are primarily driven by political interests must be taken into consideration.

I.

Political relations between our country and Israel have been suspended since 1967. Since that time, Sweden has represented the interests of our country in Israel, while Switzerland has represented Israel's interests in Hungary. We have warded off Israeli initiatives aimed at establishing official political contacts. At the same time, our social organisations have maintained – and do maintain – relations with the progressive left-wing organisations. Recently, further organisations and persons opposed to the policy of aggression have sought contacts with organisations and persons in Hungary, above all by way of the peace movement.

Co-operation between the HSWP and the Israeli Communist Party is close.

Our trade has been administered since 1973 in free currency exchange and on the basis of an agreement that was signed in 1956 and is extended annually. The level of trade is low: USD 7.2 million in 1980; USD 9.5 million in 1981; and USD 12 million in 1982. Major Hungarian exports are: steel and rolled products, illuminants, photographic products, and seeds; our main imports are: synthetic yarn, organic basic chemicals, oranges and other citrus fruits. Israeli Communist Party enterprises account for 15–20 per cent of total trade.

Recently, Israeli business people have proposed the mutually beneficial expansion of our economic relations and co-operation in third markets. According to the calculations of the Hungarian economic bodies, trade volumes could be doubled without endangering, in the first place, our economic and trade interests with the Arab countries.

Banking relations between the National Bank of Hungary and the Bank of Israel have been vitalised. An agreement was made on mutual assurances for a USD 15 million + 15 million trade development credit framework. So far Israeli banks have provided a short-term credit of USD 18 million and have placed a USD 15 million short-term deposit at the National Bank of Hungary.

Representatives of the Israeli banks see an opportunity for offering trade credits promoting the financing of Hungarian imports. They show an interest in opportunities to supply goods for Hungarian investment projects financed from World Bank loans. They have signalled that Israeli banks are ready to proceed, with regard to their clients, in such a way as to develop financial co-operation with Hungary.

In 1981, at the behest of the Israeli Communist Party and with the participation of its enterprise, Israeli tourism to our country began. We gave our approval to the admission into Hungary of 2,000 persons per year in group tours. We did not authorise tourist travel from Hungary either for groups or individuals. The demand from Israel exceeded the quota. In 1983, with our consent, 3,000 tourists are anticipated to arrive in our country. Tourism from Israel is a good business for us; this year the foreign-exchange revenue will be one million dollars. In view of the demand, other Israeli and foreign – Austrian, West-German and Yugoslav – travel agencies have also sought to get involved in organising travel for Israeli tourists.

There is growing demand for the facilitation of individual visits by relatives. At present, we deal with such issues on an individual basis.

The practice of the Socialist countries with regard to authorising the admission of Israeli citizens differs. The Soviet Union generally refrains from issuing entry permits, or does so only in exceptional cases and for international conferences. Czechoslovakia only authorises visits to relatives, while Bulgaria and the German Democratic Republic make no distinction between Israeli citizens and those of other capitalist countries; thus, the general practice regarding visas applies to Israeli citizens too.

The World Federation of Hungarians has contacts with the organisations of Jews with Hungarian roots, including the World Federation of Hungarian Jews, the Public Life Committee, and the Association for the Development of Israeli-Hungarian Relations, which was established several months ago. There is an opportunity for the World Federation of Hungarians to establish relations with Israeli institutions and for the promotion of the Hungarian language and culture. The number of Jews with Hungarian roots living in Israel is estimated to be 200,000.

Relations in the academic, cultural and sport fields are sporadic. Based on individual assessments, we send experts and academic researchers to events in Israel and cultural forums. It is a problem that most of these are held in Jerusalem. In recent years, we have, on occasion, invited Israeli personalities to Hungarian events. There appears to be a mutual interest in enhancing academic relations – primarily in the fields of natural science and history – relations in the field of health care, and cultural exchanges on a commercial basis. Sport relations are limited to programmes arising from international sport obligations.

We must also take into consideration the fact that the Arab countries react sensitively to even the slightest change in Hungarian–Israeli relations. Owing to the strategies of the Arab countries, their political significance, their international economic and financial weight, and their geographical proximity, we give particular attention to developing multi-faceted co-operation with them. Our economic co-operation with the Arab countries is wide-ranging. In 1982, our exports to the region amounted to USD 729.8 million, of which the foreign-exchange revenue was USD 689.2 million.

Favourable and potentially promising credit and banking relations have been established with the oil-producing countries. In 1982, 5,128 Hungarian experts were working in Arab countries. They evaluate positively our position on the Middle-East crisis, on the basis of which they expect us not to have relations with Israel. This also justifies our proceeding in a careful and considered fashion when transforming our relations with Israel in the future, too.

II.

The Political Committee – as an internal document – accepts the submission on the state of Hungarian–Israeli relations and on the timely tasks, and it draws attention to the following:
1. Our position on a settlement of the Middle-East Crisis is unchanged; in the future too, we should stick to the line agreed upon with the Socialist countries which are working in close co-operation. Our political and economic interests continue to justify the further development of co-operation with the Arab countries in every

possible way. At the same time, we should avoid unfounded demands, made in regard to our policy towards Israel. Let us not rule out relations that serve our interests when such relations do not negatively affect our co-operation with the Arab countries.

2. With a view to exploiting the economic advantages, our trade relations with Israel can be vitalised. This activity should be undertaken at a business and enterprise level, avoiding the involvement of Israeli State bodies. Care should be taken that this activity does not negatively impact on our commercial and trade interests with other countries, above all the Arab countries. For this reason, co-operation in third markets as proposed by the Israeli side should take place only through neutral companies. We should strive to exploit the relations between the chambers of commerce in a non-official form. Financial, banking and credit relations at the expert level are also possible. We should seek the support of the Israeli partners towards accomplishing greater financial co-operation with our country in the United States and in the Western European countries. If justified by our economic, scientific-technical, cultural and sport interests, we should make it possible for our citizens to travel to Israel for such purposes. We should take care to ensure that their participation is not portrayed as support for Israeli policies (recognition of Jerusalem as the capital city). Having regard for our interests, we should invite to Hungarian events Israeli personalities who may contribute to the enhancement of our scientific and technical accomplishments.

3. While avoiding the establishment of relations at state level, tourism can be developed, especially group tourism. With this in mind, let us abandon the quotas for organised Israeli tourism targetting Hungary. We should continue to provide for the participation in tourism of the enterprise of our fraternal Party in Israel. The Interior Ministry should elaborate the economic and organisational conditions for the expansion, including tourism via third countries. Without announcing this, in the future we should handle the visa requests of Israeli individual travellers and those visiting relatives according to our general rules, and the technical conditions for the visa should be approximated to our general practice. In 1984–85, in connection with the remembrance events for the deportations and the commemoration of the 40th anniversary of our liberation, the appraisal of visa applications should be performed in this way. We should continue to restrict tourist travel from Hungary to Israel. In justified cases, we should appraise in a humane fashion petitions for travel for the purpose of visiting relatives and family.

4. Social organisations should continue to be in contact with their progressive partners and should react positively to initiatives of new organisations and personalities that serve our political interests. At the same time, we should be circumspect in ensuring that the endeavours of the State of Israel in the field of social relations are not given ground.

5. Avoiding spectacular actions, the World Federation of Hungarians should maintain contact with the World Federation of Hungarian Jews or with other Hungar-

ian Jewish organisations which can be used to promote Hungarian identity and Hungarian language and culture. Working in co-operation with the Hungarian League of Resistance Fighters and Anti-Fascists and the National Centre of Hungarian Jews, it should take part in organising the major historical anniversaries of Jews in Hungary, in accordance with action plans that have been elaborated and approved in an ad-hoc fashion.
6. The political co-ordination of the work of the Hungarian institutions, organisations and enterprises that are in contact with Israeli partners will be undertaken by the Ministry of Foreign Affairs in co-operation with the Ministry of Trade or with the competent supervisory bodies.

Our press and propaganda organs should not alter their tone with respect to Israel and should avoid reporting on Hungarian–Israeli relations.

Resolution to be received by:
- members of the Political Committee and the Secretariat, Chairman of the Central Control Commission
- Deputy Chairmen of the Council of Ministers
- heads of department of the Central Committee
- Interior Minister
- Minister for Internal Trade
- Minister of Foreign Affairs
- Minister for Foreign Trade
- Finance Minister

19 Proposal on Hungarian–Israeli Relations

26 August 1986

National Archives of Hungary, XIX-J-1-j-Izrael-14-002223/6-1986 (73.d.)
Collection: Ministry of Foreign Affairs [Külügyminisztérium]

9th Regional Department

Completed in 15 copies
1./	<u>Comrade Várkonyi</u>
2./	Horn
3./	Nagy
4./	Kővári
5./	Bényi
6./	Barity
7./	Kovács
8./	Varga
9./	Demus
10-11./	Kincses
12-15./	Own copies

<u>Proposal</u>

for the Ministerial Meeting

<u>Subject</u>: experiences made in implementing the PC's resolution on the situation and timely tasks of Hungarian–Israeli relations, proposals for action

On 20 December 1983, the Political Committee adopted – as an internal document – a proposal on the situation of Hungarian–Israeli relations and on timely tasks. Under the resolution, the Ministry of Foreign Affairs conducts the political co-ordination of the institutions, organisations and enterprises that have contacts with Israeli partners, doing so in co-operation with the Ministry for Foreign Trade and with the competent supervisory bodies.

In what follows – juxtaposing with the various points contained in the Political Committee's proposal – we summarise the development of Hungarian–Israeli relations in the period since the adoption of the resolution, having special regard for the execution of the political coordination tasks of the Ministry of Foreign Affairs.

1./ <u>International relations, political relations</u>

Both in bilateral talks and at international forums we have regularly and consistently stated our position on a settlement of the Middle-East crisis. At a press conference held in London last year, Comrade János Kádár stated our position on the restoration of Hungarian–Israeli diplomatic relations as follows:

> "... there is no theoretical obstacle to the restoration of diplomatic relations and the issue may become the subject of consideration if Israel conducts itself in accordance with the accepted norms of international life, that is to say, if the reasons that led to the severance of diplomatic relations cease to apply".

In September 1985, at the UN General Assembly, Comrade Péter Várkonyi met, at the behest of the Israeli side, with Yitzhak Shamir, the Israeli Foreign Minister, and explained directly our position on the restoration of diplomatic relations.

In recent years, the Israeli government has consistently sought an improvement in relations between the two states, making use of diplomatic, social and mass organisational, commercial and cultural channels. The main directions of Israeli attempts at building relations are:

a./ Initiating demonstrative political relations: inviting official Hungarian delegations to the celebrations held in Jerusalem to mark the 40th anniversary of the "Victory over Fascist Germany" under the patronage of the President of Israel, initiating a meeting between Losonczi and Peres at the jubilee meeting of the UN General Assembly in 1985.

b./ Although, having been made aware of our position, the Israeli government is not calling directly for the restoration of diplomatic relations, it is proposing some minor steps in this direction:
- It is urging the establishment of lower-level representations and the exchange of covert diplomatic representatives (Polish solution). Such a proposal was made at the Stockholm Conference, in a message forwarded by the Swiss Minister of Foreign Affairs Aubert to Comrade Várkonyi on 19 January 1984.
- On 19 February 1986, the counsellor of the Israeli Embassy in Washington, under central instructions, sought out a member of staff of our embassy and proposed the commencement of a regular political dialogue on the development of our bilateral relations, the situation in the Middle East and other international issues. He suggested the dispatch of unofficial commercial representatives to each other's capitals.

We have, in each case, dodged the proposals for, and initiatives towards, establishing official political and economic relations at the level of the state, but we have not excluded listening to such proposals. At the same time, concurrent with their [*Israel's* – AK] initiatives, there regularly arise, in the international press and often from Israeli sources, rumours that the two countries are on the verge of settling their diplomatic relations and that low-level representations are to be established.

c./ The Israeli side has endeavoured to form wide-ranging cultural, scientific, economic, sport and tourist relations, as if to prove that the two countries are in contact in many important areas, despite the absence of diplomatic relations and de jure state relations.

The diplomacy and press of the Arab countries have been attentively following the development of Hungarian–Israeli relations, the rumours about a settlement of diplomatic relations, and they sometimes voice their concerns at the Ministry of Foreign Affairs or, on occasion, they demand an explanation from our ambassadors in various Arab countries.

2./ Economic, financial, scientific-technical, cultural and sporting relations

a./ Economic and trade relations have developed to a modest degree in the past two years, but in terms of foreign-trade volumes they are at the level of preceding years. (For data on trade volumes, see Appendix I.)

When the Political Committee took the decision, the economic bodies considered a doubling of volumes to be possible. This did not take place; indeed, despite an increase in commercial trips to Israel and more frequent visits to Hungary by Israeli businessmen last year, our foreign-trade volume decreased.

[...]

In the judgement of the Ministry for Foreign Trade, in the foreign trade between the two countries, there are potential opportunities above all in the fields of agriculture and electronics, and in the recent past there have been trial orders. Overall, however, the real possibilities contained in the Israeli proposals are often far less modest than they appear at first sight. For example, the issue of kosher beef cuts would be resolvable, but we cannot compete with the South American countries.

[...]

b./ Financial, interbank and credit relations
Relative to the revival of two years ago, our relations in this area have declined. The financial difficulties of Israel and of Israeli banks are the main reason for this. The USD 15–15 million credit line for trade development has been used reciprocally since 1983. The National Bank of Hungary will not take on further loans from Israel, because the conditions of such are currently far more disadvantageous than those of banks in the capitalist world.

[...]

c./ Scientific-technical, cultural and sporting relations

During the period under examination and particularly since 1985, our relations in this area have expanded to the greatest extent. As part of this, the most spectacular development has occurred in the field of cultural contacts.

During the past two years, a significant number of Hungarian actors, singers and musicians have made guest appearances in Israel on a commercial impresario basis. Hungarian films have been shown regularly in Israel (between 1981 and 1985, 18 feature films were shown in commercial distribution and won great popularity). On occasion, the film directors and main actors are invited to the premieres. There have been advances in the field of book publication too (e.g. two books by Ephraim Kishont, who lives in Israel and has Hungarian ancestry, have been published by a Hungarian publisher).

In the future, there will be greater demand – both from the Israeli side and from Hungarian artists – for expanded cultural and artistic relations. Concerning the latter, alongside the friend/relative relations and Israel's cultural historical attraction, another factor is that the financial conditions for performances by Hungarian artists are very favourable. A problem is that the Israeli bodies seek, increasingly often, the staging of spectacular cultural events (e.g. a performance by the Hungarian State Opera company in Jerusalem). From the Israeli side, demands for reciprocity have also grown (e.g. performances in Hungary by the National Theatre, Tel Aviv, and the display of Israeli artistic works in our country).

Our scientific and technical relations are limited to mutual participation in international conferences and visits to scientific institutions. Under the terms of the circular letter no. 001031/1981 issued by the State Secretary, Hungarian participants are not permitted to attend international conferences held in Israel if they are to be held on territories illegally occupied by Israel (e.g. Jerusalem). In the past two years, the relevant part of the State Secretary's circular letter has not been implemented, and in line with a more nuanced notion of the Political Committee's resolution, we gave permission for 37 experts to travel to Jerusalem.

[...]

Strict adherence to the rules contained in the circular letter would have been deleterious to our scientific interests. At the same time, we sought to gain the support of the professional bodies for visits to Israel where such visits are justified (e.g. leading officials of a given non-government organisation, international authorities giving lectures and presentations, etc.).

Our sport relations are limited basically to fulfillment of the international obligations. There is a more active relationship between the football associations.

[...]

3./ Tourism relations

The appraisal of visa applications for Israeli individual tourists and for relative visits is today identical to general practice; the quotas on organised tourism have been lifted. As a consequence, the number of visitors from Israel has grown significantly (see Annexe 4).

[...]

Israel views as possible the opening of offices in Israel by all of the Hungarian tourism enterprises (e.g. IBUSZ, MALÉV). They have inquired whether Hungarian diplomats might work too in such offices. They even mentioned that, in the event of the restoration of diplomatic relations, tourism might increase, for it would significantly reduce the obligatory exit tax payable by Israeli citizens.

In connection with tourism growth, the Israeli side has urged the launching of a direct flight from Budapest to Tel Aviv, and there have spread reports on talks being held by representatives of the two airlines. To date we have refuted this initiative for political and security reasons and in view of the absence of an agreement between the two countries. For economic-financial considerations, MALÉV would, in fact, have an interest in the launching of a route, with two flights per week.

4–5./ Social and mass organisation relations, émigré political and church relations

a./ There are regular and high-level contacts between the HSWP and the Israeli Communist Party (ICP). A Party delegation took part in the 20th Congress of the ICP, held on 4–7 December 1985. From 15–21 May 1986, a Party worker delegation visited Israel headed by Comrade József Györke, Deputy Head of the International Affairs Department of the Central Committee. Recently, an ICP delegation led by Meir Vilner visited our country.

On several occasions the leaders of the ICP have raised with concern the issue of the restoration of Hungarian–Israeli diplomatic relations, although they have also indicated that statements by Comrades Kádár and Szűrös have helped to put aside misunderstandings. They have also expressed concern over the fact that, in their view, the development of Hungarian–Israeli cultural relations is being monopolised by a right-wing group operating with the covert control of the government (led by Moshe Sanbar, András Rónai, Ottó Rappaport, Yehuda Lahav). They consider it incomprehensible that Hungarian artists visiting Israel mostly take part in events staged by the right-wing organisations of Jewish-inhabited towns.

The trade volume of the Party enterprise (EXIMIS) with Hungary has fallen from a level of several million dollars in earlier years to 600,000 dollars in 1985, because, after the lifting of Hungarian measures restricting Hungarian–Israeli relations, the enterprise lost its privileged status in several areas (e.g. tourism).

[...]

h./ In the field of church relations there is a conflict of interest because, in Hungary, the organisation representing Jewry – the National Representation of Hungarian Jews (MIOK) – functions as a national religious denomination (religious organisation), whereas its Israeli partners are basically secular organisations (and Zionist in terms of their ideology). Further, the work of the organisations in Israel is directed in no small part at establishing in Israel the centre of the intellectual and material values of Hungarian Jewry. In its relations, MIOK tends to place the emphasis on upholding and preserving Jewish values in Hungary (memorials, cemeteries, etc.).

[...]

Political Co-ordination

We have undertaken the political co-ordination in accordance with the directives in the Political Committee's proposal and we have sought to apply the following considerations:
- We have warded off Israeli initiatives aimed at establishing political and economic relations between the two states.
- We have supported travel stemming from our international obligations in the scientific, cultural and sports fields and that promotes a strengthening of our international relations.
- We have supported travel aimed at forging trading links, contacts at the level of the enterprises, and contacts between scientists and various experts. At the same time, we have sought to avoid the establishment of institutional and official relations between scientific institutions, universities, theatres and other cultural institutions.
- We have not supported relations that are spectacular and high-profile, that can be used against us in propaganda, and that could be used to demonstrate the state level [of contacts] (e.g. the Losonczi–Peres meeting, an official Hungarian delegation at Israeli state celebrations, etc.).
- In accordance with the Political Committee's resolution, we are seeking to ensure that Hungarian–Israeli relations do not receive greater publicity in the Hungarian mass media than the desirable level.

- We are monitoring the official and press reaction of Arab countries, giving them information about the true situation; we have criticised information and value judgements that do not accord with the facts.
- Since the outrage at Vienna Airport [*attack of Arab terrorists on 27 December 1985* – AK] we have emphatically reminded travellers to Israel about the security considerations to be followed.
- We attempted to schedule the travel of people to Israel in such a fashion that a large number of Hungarian artists and scientists were not in Israel at the same time.
- Real co-ordination is realised primarily with respect to the partner bodies and authorities that request the opinion of the Ministry of Foreign Affairs. Enforcing the co-ordination requirement has run into numerous practical difficulties.

Journeys [to Israel] with a commercial aim fall under the jurisdiction of the Ministry for Foreign Trade, with whom we have regular working relations. It does happen, however, that the Ministry learns of some action only after it has taken place. They are informed of an event related to Hungarian–Israeli relations only retrospectively or from the press.

[...]

The Regional Department co-operates closely and consults regularly with the Department of International Affairs of the Central Committee of the HSWP. In particularly controversial or marginal issues, it submits its decision-making proposals to the heads of the Ministry.

II.
Conclusions

In summary it may be concluded that Hungarian–Israeli relations have developed fundamentally in line with the Political Committee's resolution of 20 December 1983. Contacts between Hungary and Israel in the non-state sector have been vitalised, above all relations in such fields as culture, science and sport, as well as tourism. Our relations with the population in Israel with a Hungarian background have strengthened. Commercial and economic and scientific and technical relations have not expanded to the extent considered possible in the resolution.

The recovery in Hungarian–Israeli relations is a consequence primarily of action by Israel. Thus, Israel has a greater possibility of moulding these relations in accordance with its interests and of making sure that its political, propaganda and economic interests are served. The Israeli government seeks to utilise the facilitation of travel for the purpose of restoring inter-state relations; meanwhile the propaganda organs, often exaggerating what is going on in terms of relations, seek to create the impression that a restoration of diplomatic relations is imminent.

Overall, the recovery of non-official Hungarian–Israeli relations did not cause a detectible disturbance in our relations with the Arab countries. At the same time, the tendentious Israeli propaganda did, on occasion, lead to a detectible lack of trust in Arab government circles with regard to our intentions concerning diplomatic relations.

Based on the experience of the nearly three years since the adoption of the Political Committee's resolution, it can be stated that the guidelines relating to Hungarian–Israeli relations are adequate, although in the future their uniform interpretation must be ensured, as must also their most consistent implementation and possible advance in, primarily, the economic and consular fields.

The Ministry of Foreign Affairs conducts its co-ordination tasks in line with the resolution of the Political Committee. The task is made more difficult by the fact that, in matters concerning Hungarian–Israeli relations, decisions are often taken outside the ministry – this is natural, but they are not always known to us in time – and we don't have sufficient resources to enforce the co-ordination and information requirements. With a view to the development of Hungarian–Israeli relations and the application of our interests, more efforts are needed to make complete the co-ordinating work of the Ministry of Foreign Affairs.

III.
Proposals

1./
Bearing in mind our position on the Middle-East crisis, which was elaborated with other members of the Warsaw Treaty, and the broad-based relations with the majority of the Arab states, there must be an attempt in the future to ensure that the recovery in Hungarian–Israeli relations should not harm co-operation with the Arab states or our foreign policy and foreign-trade interest. At the same time, we shall reject any unfounded demands made on our policies with regard to Israel.

We should continue to ward off Israeli initiatives aimed at a restoration of diplomatic relations.

For the sake of diplomatic contacts with the Israeli government, we should make use of the foreign representations covering our interest representation [*in other countries* – AK] and the UN missions, as well as occasional meetings.

Our other foreign representations should listen to the proposals and initiatives of the Israeli diplomats, but they should seek central approval before holding serious meetings with them. They should continue to refrain from inviting Israeli diplomats to Hungarian receptions and they should not attend events held by Israeli foreign representations.

2./
The Consular Department should elaborate a proposal for the establishment of direct consular relations, with the setting-up of a consular representation (consulate or consulate-general based in Tel Aviv), which would undertake tasks connected with the defence of the interests of Hungarian citizens and the development of economic, trade, cultural, scientific, technical and tourism relations between the two countries, also having regard for the 200,000–250,000 Israeli citizens who speak Hungarian.

3./
The Israeli relations of Hungarian social and mass organisations and those of the interest-representation organs have developed in line with the Political Committee's resolution of 20 December 1983. These relations – now under formation – make it possible for a dialogue between the two countries to be maintained or commenced in the political, economic and cultural fields, even in the absence of diplomatic relations. By way of social relations, a possibility arises for the exchange of accurate information. Meanwhile, the development of economic, cultural and tourism relations – strengthening the ties of Jews with a Hungarian background – may enhance trust between the two countries, which, in turn, may create favourable conditions for the bilateral and international search for compromises. Based on all of this, we consider it justified, in the spirit of the Political Committee's resolution, to further broaden Hungarian–Israeli social relations.

4./
We continue to support the development of economic and scientific-technical relations at the level of enterprises serving our interests. Israeli firms should not attend our major trade fairs, but we should not rule out organised, closed presentations of products to a professional audience. Similarly, we should permit Hungarian enterprises to hold product presentations in Israel, as long as this does not infringe on our interests in another field. Such events should not be of a character that implies an official Hungarian presence, and so we should avoid the holding of product presentations by several companies at one time, etc.

We suggest to the competent economic organs that, where there is a demonstrable Hungarian interest, they should permit the foundation of representative offices in Budapest by companies with origins in Israel that are registered in a third country. It is expedient to wait with regard to the granting of permission for the establishment of representative offices in Budapest by firms based in Israel.

Although the Ministry for Foreign Trade does not consider it to be necessary at present to establish in Israel a Hungarian enterprise representative office, if several Hungarian enterprises have an interest and the funding is available, we suggest a review of the issue on its merits, with a view to expanding our trade and economic relations and to increasing Hungarian exports.

We should avoid higher-level forms of economic co-operation (e.g. joint ventures, the import of Israeli capital, etc.).

We suggest that the Ministry for Foreign Trade and the tourism bodies should take steps to promote the activities in Hungary of the Israeli Communist Party's enterprise (Eximis).

Through its work, the Hungarian Chamber of Commerce should promote the development of relations at company level; it should give orientation to its members as they make deals by acquiring useful information.

5./
We should support the fostering and strengthening of cultural relations in line with the criteria elaborated by the Ministry of Culture (see Annexe 5). We must endeavour, while satisfying in unaltered fashion the needs of Hungarian speakers, to present to a greater extent in Israel the high-standard representative values of Socialist Hungarian culture, doing so on a business impresario basis. Cultural initiatives at the level of the state, however, must be avoided.

6./
An amendment should be made to circular letter no. 001031/81, issued by the State Secretary at the Ministry of Foreign Affairs and prohibiting Hungarian participation in scientific-technical conferences held in Jerusalem by non-governmental organisations.

We should permit – on an individual basis – Hungarian artists and artistic groups to make appearances in Jerusalem as long as this happens at non-official Israeli festivals.

7./
In view of the security issues, it is not the right time, in our view, to launch direct flights between the two countries.

8./
In order to improve co-ordination between state organs, we should make better use of the state secretaries' co-ordination conference, and the ministries affected should be kept informed about the condition of Hungarian–Israeli relations by way of an information booklet that is soon to be published by the Ministry of Foreign Affairs or, if necessary, by way of circular letters.

9./
The World Federation of Hungarians should continue to keep in contact with the World Federation of Hungarian Jews and give particular attention to such Israeli-Hungarian organisations, or Hungarian-Jewish organisations operating in addition to the

latter, which can be used to promote the preservation of Hungarian identity and the fostering of the Hungarian language and culture.

10./
Senior staff in the mass media should receive information and guidance about our policy relating to Israel and the foreign-policy criteria concerning the mass media.

11./
The Press Department, in co-operation with the 9th Department and the APO [*Agitation and Propaganda Department*] should evaluate, on a regular basis, the approach of the Israeli mass media towards our country.

12./
All of our foreign representations should receive information on our policy relating to Israel, on the tasks at hand, and the demeanour to be shown towards Israeli diplomats.

Annexe no. 1

Hungarian–Israeli foreign trade volumes (M USD)

	1964	1980	1983	1984	1985	Jan-July 1986
Exports	57.3	3.7	6.3	8.0	7.1	4.05
Imports	69.3	3.4	9.2	10.8	5.8	6.82
Total	126.8	7.1	15.5	18.8	12.9	10.87

[...]

Hungary's foreign trade with the Arab countries (M USD)

	1985	Jan-July 1986
Exports	569.2	273.0
Imports	72.2	28.3
Total	641.4	301.3

[...]

Annexe no. 3

In 1985, the number of trips to Israel agreed by the 9th Regional Department

	Cultural	Sport	Scientific	Total
Israel	29	28	16	73
Jerusalem	15	1	22	38
Total	44	29	38	111

[...]

Matters not granted authorisation (1985):

- Establishment of contacts between the Habima National Theatre in Tel Aviv and the Thália Theatre.
- The showing in Hungary of the "official" Israeli art exhibition material in Europe.
- Official exhibition exchange of the Israel Museum in Jerusalem with the exchange of ethnographic and/or archeological material. [...].
- Participation of State Puppet Theatre in the Jerusalem Festival in July 1986
- Exhibition exchange between the Israeli Artistic League and ARTEX [*Hungarian foreign-trade company dealing in works of art* – AK]. (Israeli material in Hungary and an exhibition in the foyer of the National Theatre in Tel Aviv and in the Shalon department store.)
- Guest appearance in Israel of the national football team.

Annexe no. 4

Tourism, no. of departures to and arrivals from Israel

[...]

2.) Total number of Hungarian visitors to Israel:

1980	1981	1982	1983	1984	1985
307	359	368	318	699	900

3.) Total number of Israeli visitors to Hungary:

1980	1981	1982	1983	1984	1985
1,079	1,564	2,726	3,902	11,177	13,200

Of the 13,200 persons in 1985, 12,200 came for the purpose of tourism. Last year the average length of stay of the Israeli tourists was 7.4 days (by way of comparison: tourists from West Germany: 9.1 days, and from France: 8.3 days).

In 1985, 37,000 citizens from Arab countries travelled to Hungary.

Annexe no. 5

Recommendations and proposals accepted by the Department of International Relations of the Ministry of Culture and Education for the shaping of Hungarian–Israeli cultural relations
1.) We should continue to avoid a situation in which our cultural relations receive an official bilateral tone.

[…]

6.) In the case of a series of Hungarian artistic, literary, etc. events to be held in Israel, there must be greater co-ordination to prevent an excessive number of events being held simultaneously […].

[…]

8.) Attempts by the Israeli side aimed at reciprocity must be stalled, especially in the case of actions of a more spectacular nature.
9.) The Ministry of Culture and Education requests the Ministry of Foreign Affairs to monitor the reception in the domestic press of Hungarian–Israeli cultural relations and ensure that it is the most modest possible.
10.) The department of the Ministry of Culture and Education responsible for international relations, and its other departments should assist the Ministry of Foreign Affairs in vetting planned journeys to Israel by providing more well-founded information than it has done to date.

Our position:

The above proposals are in accordance with the ordinances of the Political Committee and will enable the development of Hungarian–Israeli cultural relations in a direction and to an extent that is in our interests, while they also formulate the limits to such relations.

20 Appraisal of Draft CC Proposal on Restoring Hungarian–Israeli Diplomatic Relations

2 November 1988

National Archives of Hungary, XIX-J-1-j-Izrael-113-004390-1988 (50.d.)
Collection: Ministry of Foreign Affairs [Külügyminisztérium]

MINISTRY OF FOREIGN AFFAIRS
7th Regional Department
9th Regional Department

Completed: in 1 copy
Validity: until revoked

Memorandum

Subject: appraisal of draft CC [*Central Committee*] proposal on restoring Hungarian–Israeli diplomatic relations

Comrade Dr József Györke, Deputy Head of the Department of International Affairs of the HSWP CC, forwarded to the Ministry of Foreign Affairs the material on the restoration of Hungarian–Israeli diplomatic relations that is to be submitted to the Central Committee, and requested the 7th and 9th Regional Departments appraise the material. The Department of International Affairs considers the attached material to represent merely preliminary ideas; it wishes to submit its finalised proposal at the meeting of the Central Committee on 22 November.

The 7th and 9th Regional Departments are of the opinion that the ideas, which are truly preliminary ones, need to be made more specific and precise, and could be supplemented with arguments that strengthen the topicality of the proposal.

Given that the significance of the proposal – if it were to be adopted – goes beyond the subject-matter of Hungarian–Israeli relations and that the realisation of the resolution would also impose substantial tasks on the Ministry of Foreign Affairs in the future, we suggest that the Ministry of Foreign Affairs should assist the work of the Department for International Affairs in this area by drafting its own proposal.

We attach the proposal of the 7th and 9th Regional Departments. In the event of agreement, we shall send it to the Department for International Affairs of the HSWP CC.

Proposal

For the draft submission on restoring Hungarian–Israeli diplomatic relations

On 12 June 1967, the government of the People's Republic of Hungary – in agreement with several European Socialist countries – broke off diplomatic relations with the State of Israel. Our response to Israel's aggression against the Arab countries, a response that was an expression of solidarity with the countries that had been attacked and with the Palestinian people, was received favourably by the Arab countries. At the same time, it did not impact on the policies of the Israeli government; the measure did not enable us to exert the kind of pressure on Israel that would have resulted in an evacuation of the occupied territories. Meanwhile, the severance of diplomatic relations precluded any possibility of exerting a direct influence.

Since the Arab–Israeli war of 1967, there have been major changes in the Middle East. With Sadat's visit to Jerusalem and then the signing of the Camp David agreements, the United States and Israel succeeded in undermining the unity of the frontline Arab countries. In 1980, Egypt established diplomatic relations with Israel. Since then, the views and actions of the Arab countries with regard to a resolution of the crisis in the Middle East have become more polarised, and there has been a strengthening of acceptance of, and support for, the necessity of a settlement within an international framework.

Changes in the Middle East and our interest in utilising developments in Hungarian–Israeli relations and the opportunities arising therefrom, have made it necessary for the Political Committee of the HSWP to concern itself with the issue of Hungarian–Israeli relations and to consent to the lifting of some of the restrictions.

On 10 March 1987, the Political Committee, giving consideration to the development of Hungarian–Israeli relations, decided that we should initiate negotiations with Israel on the reciprocal establishment of interest representation offices in Tel Aviv and Budapest. The resolution drew attention to the importance of ensuring that the results of Hungarian–Israeli relations should not impact negatively on co-operation with the Arab countries.

Since the commencement of negotiations on the creation of interest-representation offices, we have sought consistently to achieve an understanding in the Arab countries for the reasons for our initiative and for our aims in developing Hungarian–Israeli relations, as well as reduce the chance of counter-measures on their part. However, our endeavours in this regard have been only partially successful.

The overall moderate reaction of the Arab countries conceals a different stance at the level of individual countries. Those Arab countries that are particularly sensitive to Israel and to Zionist ideology (Algeria, Libya, Syria and the PLO) reacted vehemently to the creation of the interest-representation offices, to developments in Hungarian–Israeli relations, in some cases voicing their reservations on multiple occasions. This was manifested in such demonstrative measures as the cancellation of the visit to Algeria of the Chairman of the Presidential Council [*of Hungary* – AK] and of Arafat's visit to Budapest, a refusal to receive Hungarian delegations or to arrange visits to Hungary (e.g. the visit to the Emirates of Comrade Zoltán Juhár, the visit to Libya of the Deputy Minister of Foreign Affairs and the submission of a message at the highest level, the cancellation of a visit by the Secretary General of the Arab League, and a statement on behalf of the Arab League condemning and criticising our policy).

In addition to the detrimental effects on our political relations, our economic losses (due to the failure of contracts under negotiation) are estimated to be USD 30–40 million. The planned visit of Palestinian businessmen has not taken place, and a delegation headed by Comrade Tamás Beck of the Chamber of Commerce did not receive entry visas to several of the Gulf States. However, of even greater significance than these losses are the foregone business opportunities, with potential Hungarian partners not even being invited to negotiate [such deals].

The overall poor reception in the Arab countries of the development of Hungarian–Israeli relations is linked with the fact that they suspect that Hungarian – and, prior to this, Polish – measures signify a change in the Middle-Eastern policies of the Soviet Union and the Socialist countries, and that they seek, by implementing measures against us, to put a brake on this process and discourage other Socialist countries.

The creation of interest-representation offices, the development of Hungarian–Israeli relations and the establishment of unofficial contacts at a high level have been unanimously welcomed by government and business/financial circles in our major Western partners. The economic benefits of this, however, are difficult to calculate. Its significance is to be seen primarily in a more favourable judgment of our country and an increased willingness to co-operate on the part of these partners. Several ideas were raised about new business opportunities by the involvement of international Jewish capital, including the realisation of an investment programme worth USD 300 million, in which – at the initiative of Shimon Peres – 20 American-Jewish businessmen were supposed to be engaged. According to Israeli figures, Hungarian exports to Israel amounted to USD 27 million in the first eight months of 1988.

The improvement in relations between the Soviet Union and the United States has made it possible for them to carry on a regular dialogue on the means of addressing regional crisis points, including the Middle-East crisis. As the consultations have become more worthwhile, one can also observe how both superpowers are endeavouring to improve relations with the affected parties. Within this framework, the Soviet Union is also seeking ways of gradually mending Soviet–Israeli relations. The Soviet Union – on account of its more complicated situation – has chosen another form of building relations; through the exchange of consular delegations, it has viewed the establishment of consular relations of a temporary nature as of benefit.

Reacting in no small measure to the creation of Polish and Hungarian interest-representation offices, to the swift development of Hungarian–Israeli relations and to the Soviet measures, Czechoslovakia and Bulgaria are also considering the creation of interest-representation offices, while the GDR is examining opportunities for enhancing relations with international Jewry.

Hungary's intent to assist in the resolution of the Middle-East crisis, as well as our endeavours to establish the external conditions necessary for developing the economy, require an examination of how, while retaining and deepening Hungarian–Arab political and economic relations and co-operation, we can utilise the opportunities inherent in the development of Hungarian–Israeli relations and in the international sphere of interests that is linked with Israel for the expansion of our international political, economic and financial relations. For this reason, it is justified to place the restoration of diplomatic relations between the People's Republic of Hungary and the State of Israel on the agenda.

Official Soviet statements indicate that the convening of an international conference on the Middle East is a condition for the restoration of diplomatic relations between the Soviet Union and Israel. Thus, if Hungary were to be the first Socialist country – among the countries that agreed to break off relations in 1967 – to renew diplomatic relations with Israel, then one must count on even greater retaliation from those Arab countries that oppose relations with Israel, including measures that they will not take against the Soviet Union in view of its superpower status and role.

Another consideration is that the restoration of diplomatic relations would take place at a time when – based on the election results – it is likely that a government will be formed led by the Likud party, which demand a harder and more forceful stand against the Palestinians. Restoration of diplomatic relations would translate into huge political capital for Likud; it would mitigate Israel's tight spot, and exert pressure on the other Socialist countries to swiftly improve their relations with Israel.

We must also bear in mind that our total exports to Israel – even despite the improvement seen since the creation of the interest-representation offices – do not make up for our calculable losses on the Arab market.

Based on the above, we consider it necessary, prior to the restoration of Hungarian-Israeli diplomatic relations, that decisions be taken in Israel or via Israel that strengthen the positions of our country in the international money markets, facilitate the import of working capital and advanced technology and/or result in the placement of greater deposits at the National Bank of Hungary. For this reason, when the Central Committee decides on the proposal, it would be necessary to declare its wish that our competent economic-financial bodies should elaborate, in a specific and detailed fashion, the conditions whose fulfilment would justify Hungary taking this decision – the restoration of diplomatic relations – which is so crucial for Israel.

The protection of our interests with regard to maintaining and developing co-operation with the Arab countries, and a reduction in the harmful consequences of the decision, require that, alongside the oral arguments made until now, which will be fully inadequate in the case of the restoration of diplomatic relations, we should also launch goodwill missions at a higher level. Our competent bodies should provide the funding necessary for concrete steps, whether such steps are delegation visits or other measures, e.g. events of a cultural nature.

After the Central Committee has given its approval, we should resume Hungarian–Israeli contacts. Depending on how such contacts proceed and how Israeli domestic politics and the situation in the region develop, it would be worth deciding on when to commence talks on the restoration of diplomatic relations.

It would seem necessary for us to concur and agree in advance with the Soviet Union on this decision, so that it does not stand in the way of the Soviet Union's endeavours in the Soviet–U.S. talks pertaining to the region.

IV The International Jewish Organisations, the Jewish Community and the State

Introduction

The documents selected for this chapter show the development of relations between the Jewish community in Hungary and the international Jewish organisations in the period 1956–1989. Contacts between the two sides were subject to the scrutiny of the Party State leadership throughout the period, and so the development of relations tended to reflect Party decisions and their implementation by the responsible state institutions. The "advice" received from the Soviet Union and the stances taken by "fraternal countries" were additional influential factors. These documents reveal the policies pursued by the Hungarian Communist Party State towards the World Jewish Congress (WJC), the largest international Jewish political organisation, and towards the American Jewish Joint Distribution Committee ("the Joint"), the world's leading Jewish relief organisation.[1]

The first signs of a softening of "Jewish policy" came in the immediate aftermath of the 1956 Revolution (see Chapter 1), when the National Representation of Hungarian Israelites (NRHI) was granted permission to join the WJC. In Zürich on 26 April 1957, the deputy chairman of the NRHI informed representatives of the WJC that the NRHI was in a position to restore relations, having received the approval of the Hungarian government for such a move.[2] Several months later, on 25 August, the NRHI officially announced its membership of the WJC. The Hungarian Jewish body delegated one member and one associate member to the Executive Committee of the WJC.[3]

The Hungarian government's decision to approve the NRHI's membership of the WJC, a measure aimed at mitigating Hungary's international isolation after the suppression of the 1956 Revolution, came under immediate pressure. In February 1958, the Hungarian legate in Tel Aviv announced that: "The diplomats of the fraternal countries' embassies in Tel Aviv have asked the Embassy's chargé d'affaires on several occasions whether the Hungarian government had consented to the NRHI's joining the World Jewish Council, or whether the NRHI's action should be viewed as having been taken independently".[4] Evidently, action by the Israeli Communist Party may have been, at least in part, behind such interest, as Document 1 suggests.

---

[1] On the policies of the World Jewish Congress between 1945 and 1953 in Hungary see Kinga Frojimovics. The role of the World Jewish Congress in the reestablishment of Jewish communal life in Hungary after the Holocaust (1945/1953). In *The Holocaust in Hungary. A European Perspective,* ed. Judit Molnár (Budapest: Balassi, 2015), 300–315.
[2] National Archives of Hungary, XIX-A-21-a 9.d. 170-11/1957 (16 May 1957).
[3] The text of the agreement and the consent of the State Office for Church Affairs see National Archives of Hungary, XIX-A-21-a 9.d. 170-19/1957, 170-20/1957/ (25 August 1957). For a chronology of the history of relations with the WJC, see National Archives of Hungary, XIX-A-21-c 87.d. 520/5 (2 April 1980).
[4] Letter of Péter Kós, Head of the Fourth Political Department of the Ministry of Foreign Affairs to János Horváth of the Ministry of Culture and Education], National Archives of Hungary, XIX-J-1-j 3.d. 0011/1958 (17 February 1958).

According to the legate's report of October 1958, Meir Vilner, one of the ICP leaders, had contacted the Hungarian embassy – and clearly the diplomatic representations of the other Communist countries too – to express the ICP's displeasure at the NRHI's decision to join an international organisation that was "under Zionist direction". Vilner had also implied that the "fraternal countries" disagreed with this decision. At the time, Hungary's Ministry of Foreign Affairs continued to express support for the decision, citing arguments that focused on the political factors, and which would be made repeatedly in subsequent documents. The Ministry argued, for instance, that as a full member of the organisation, the NRHI would find it easier to influence the policies of the WJC, and in particular, its policies towards the Soviet Union's Jewish communities. Furthermore, WJC membership would enable the NRHI to keep the topic of Israel's neutrality – a prospect raised by Soviet diplomacy at intervals in the aftermath of the Suez Crisis as a means of bringing an end to the Middle-East Crisis – on the agenda.

In the following year, however, Hungarian policy underwent a shift. This noticeable change was not only due to a cooling of relations with Israel (see Chapter 1). Rather, it reflected the fact that the WJC, along with other international Jewish organisations, had become increasingly vociferous in its defence of Soviet Jewry. In the summer of 1959, when the NRHI was still a member of the WJC, the State Office for Church Affairs prohibited Hungarian delegates from attending the WJC's conference in Stockholm. Then, in July 1960, following a proposal made by the State Office for Church Affairs, the Political Committee of the HSWP decreed that the NRHI should cancel its membership of the WJC. In its proposal, the State Office cited a resolution adopted at the Stockholm conference on Soviet Jewry, and the expression of gratitude made at the same conference to the West-German government in response to the latter's decision to offer compensation, as reasons for the NRHI's exit from the WJC. The NRHI announced that it was leaving the WJC on 24 July 1960.

In subsequent years, the WJC leadership, and in particular its European director, Siegfried (Stephen) Roth, who had Hungarian ancestry and who would become WJC director in 1966, made multiple attempts to improve relations with Hungary and Jewish organisations in Hungary. During these years, the main political objectives of the WJC continued to be an improvement in the situation of Soviet Jews, and the facilitation of their emigration. The WJC leadership believed that the situation of Soviet Jewry could be improved by disrupting the unity of the Soviet bloc, and by establishing bilateral relations of varying intensity with the Soviet Union's European allies and their Jewish communities. To this end, in its messages to Jewish and government leaders in Hungary, and in the course of personal meetings, the WJC leadership not only emphasised the shared interest in seeking out and bringing to justice war criminals, it also showed a willingness to consider Soviet foreign-policy interests, and to promote the economic interests of the Communist countries in the West (e.g. in resolving the matter of German reparations). A document dated 27 July 1962 and signed by a leading official of the political police working in the department responsible for church affairs (Document 3) reveals one such attempt. At the time, the response[5] of the Hungarian Ministry of Foreign Affairs was to reject, although it expressed a willingness to co-operate in the matter of Nazi war criminals. From the mid-1960s, however, the Ministry's tone modified somewhat, which seems to have reflected an improvement in relations with Israel (see Chapter 1). The contents of the document dated 16 May 1966 (Document 4) are symptomatic of this easing: the NRHI received authorisation to send an observer to the Brussels Conference of the WJC, and the decision was taken not to rule out the re-involvement of the NRHI in the work of the WJC during discussions with representatives of international Jewish organisations. A further step forward came in the summer of the same year, when authorisation was given for Hungarian delegates to actually participate in the Brussels Conference. The reports on conference proceedings, as well as a summary sent to Party and government officials (Documents 5, 6 and 7), reveal that Jewish leaders in Hungary were intensely lobbying for renewed membership of the organisation. The authors of these documents did not oppose this lobbying either, albeit only after "consultations" with the religious affairs organs in the Soviet Union and other "fraternal countries".

A rapprochement with the WJC is reflected in a decision taken in early 1967 by staff at the State Office for Church Affairs and the Ministry of Foreign Affairs, which gave consent to a visit to Hungary by Nahum Goldmann, President of the WJC. Correspondence between József Prantner, Head of the State Office for Church Affairs, and Deputy Foreign Minister Béla Szilágyi, reveals that Goldmann had expressed a desire to travel to Hungary on multiple occasions in earlier years, but the Hungarian side had not responded to his requests. Now, however, as Prantner wrote to Szilágyi, "it would be difficult to find any grounds" to reject a visit by Goldmann, since the Hungarian Jewish Religious Denomination had already established relations with the WJC. The Ministry of Foreign Affairs opted not to reject outright Goldmann's visit. Nevertheless, it appeared to link any final decision to the stance taken by allied countries: if they decided to admit Goldmann, then Hungary would not be in a position to reject him. "[W]e request clarification from the fraternal organs concerning the extent to which the media are dealing with the visit of Goldmann. In our opinion, his visit to Hungary should not get excessive publicity; neither, however, does it warrant concealment".[6]

Goldmann's visit to Hungary finally took place in the spring of 1967. Evidently, authorisation for the visit reflected the fact that he had been permitted to visit Czechoslovakia in 1966.[7] Document 8 contains an account of Goldmann's visit to Hungary. In the hope of receiving economic benefits, Hungary's political leaders had evidently become less dismissive of relations with the WJC. Their position contrasts with that of the Czechoslovak leadership, which in late 1966 had refused even to give its consent

---

5 National Archives of Hungary, XIX-A-21-d 17.d. 044-3/1962 (19 June 1962).
6 National Archives of Hungary, XIX-A-21-d 37.d. 005-2/1967 (31 January 1967).
7 Labendz, Renegotiating Czechoslovakia, 416.

to official observer status.⁸ Reflecting the Hungarian government's position, Jewish denomination leaders from Hungary attended the Milan conference of the European branch of the WJC as observers.

The gradual improvement in relations came to a swift end in 1967 with the severance of diplomatic relations after the Six-Day War. A memo of the State Office for Church Affairs dated 27 August 1967 records this change: "We have authorised the visit of Nahum Goldmann, but in the light of the situation that has arisen following the Israeli aggression the various factors surrounding the visit must be reappraised".⁹ In subsequent years, the WJC made repeated attempts to persuade the Hungarian authorities to reauthorise the NRHI's participation in the various events staged by the WJC. During this period, WJC officials visited Hungary in a private capacity. Thus, for instance, Armand Kaplan, Deputy Head of the International Department of the WJC, met with the heads of the NRHI and the State Office for Church Affairs in Budapest in both 1968 and 1969.¹⁰ During the discussions, emphasis was laid on the economic benefits of closer relations with the WJC, while the WJC leaders carefully avoided representing Zionist positions, and there was only muted criticism of the Soviet Union. WJC leaders also cited examples – often non-existent ones – in their relations with other Communist countries, which could serve as "inspiration". (Among other things, this demonstrates the extent to which the WJC leadership underestimated political co-ordination among Eastern-bloc countries. Furthermore, in some cases, the WJC's information was entirely false: for instance, the organisation had a very positive view of Tito's role in the aftermath of the 1967 war, whereas in reality – as the documents published in this volume show – Tito was encouraging his fellow Communist leaders to take a radically pro-Arab stance in the Middle-East conflict.) The WJC evidently overestimated its ability to mislead officials working at the State Office for Church Affairs, who noted the following in the conclusion of a report submitted to the Party and to the Ministry of Foreign Affairs:

> In connection with the visit of Armand Kaplan and in view of the fact that the State Office for Church Affairs is acquainted with his person and his political stance, there should be strong reservations about the views and opinions expressed in the aforementioned. Taking all these things into consideration, one can state that Kaplan's primary aim in visiting Hungary was to persuade the NRHI to co-operate more closely with the WJC and to call for open relations. In our opinion, this explains not only the promise of financial aid but also the positive assessment of the Soviet Union.¹¹

---

8 Ibid, 512.
9 National Archives of Hungary, XIX-A-21-d 39.d. 0020-3/b/1967 (27 August 1967).
10 National Archives of Hungary, XIX-A-21-d 43.d. 0020-1/1968 (28 March 1968) and 48.d. 0020-4/1969 (20 April 1969).
11 National Archives of Hungary, XIX-A-21-d 43.d. 0020-1/1968 (28 March 1968).

A change in the relationship with the WJC came only in the mid-1970s. In May 1975, the official in charge of Jewish matters at the State Office for Church Affairs still opposed the participation of a Hungarian delegate at a meeting of the European Branch of the WJC. Yet, at the top of the document, we find a comment by István Balló, Deputy Head of the State Office for Church Affairs: "I believe the issue requires consideration. In my view, a complete reassessment [*of the earlier position* – AK] is not required if someone attends the meeting of the European Branch. In the Middle-East region, the trend now is for détente. Why should we be the inflexible ones?"[12] In a development that was not unrelated to the process of détente and the signing of the Helsinki Accords, in the summer of 1975, the State Office for Church Affairs finally gave consent for Géza Seifert, Head of the NRHI, to attend a meeting of the European Branch – for the first time since 1967. The document approving Seifert's attendance at the meeting also reveals that the decision had been taken after prior consultations with the Soviet Union's Council for Religious Affairs, and the Hungarian Ministry of Foreign Affairs.[13] After further consultations, delegates from the Jewish religious communities in Czechoslovakia, Poland and East Germany were subsequently permitted to attend the WJC's December 1976 Madrid conference as observers. The political "tasks" of the Hungarian delegates, and those of delegates from the other Communist countries, were determined in advance by the authorities responsible for religious affairs: they were to prevent the adoption of decrees and positions relating to Soviet Jewry, and to Eastern bloc's Middle-East policy.

The policy tactics of the WJC did not change significantly in subsequent years. In their statements and over the course of their visits, WJC leaders pledged economic benefits in return for renewed membership. In the late 1970s, it was increasingly suggested that "most favoured nation" status should or could be one of these benefits. While no specific offer was made, the possibility of such an offer was hinted at during negotiations with the Hungarian side (Document 9), and with Czechoslovak officials.[14]

After lengthy preliminary negotiations, renewed Hungarian membership of the WJC was officially announced in 1981. The WJC leadership regarded this event as a major success, an important means towards achieving an improvement in the situation of Soviet Jews, and the facilitation of their emigration. All this is revealed in a rather aloof memorandum drafted in the summer of 1982 by Imre Miklós, Head of the State Office for Church Affairs. The memo contained details of a conversation between Miklós and Edgar M. Bronfman, President of the WJC, who had been invited to Budapest by the NRHI:

---

12 National Archives of Hungary, XIX-A-21-d 84.d. 0020-2/1975 (29 May 1975).
13 National Archives of Hungary, XIX-A-21-d 84.d. 0020-2/1975 (17 June 1975).
14 Labendz, op. cit., 518.

President Bronfman [...] mentioned the situation and operational difficulties of the Jewish communities in the Soviet Union. In his assessment, notwithstanding previous efforts, the issue is one of the hot spots at a time of increased tensions between the Soviet Union and the United States [...]. President Bronfman emphasised his conviction that the Hungarian State's good relations with the Hungarian Jewish community and with the WJC could be beneficial in terms of exerting a positive influence on the stance of the competent Soviet organs [...]. He asked for my assistance in arranging for talks to be held with the competent Soviet state organs as soon as possible [...]. In my response I stated that I am not competent to deal with this issue [...]. It might be beneficial to broaden the WJC's scope for action by making sure that relations between the Soviet Union and the United States are once again characterised by dialogue rather than by problems eliciting tensions [...][15]

For the WJC, a major political breakthrough came in late 1986 when the Hungarian authorities approved the holding a meeting of the enlarged WJC executive in Budapest the following year. In the end, the event was attended by delegates from 26 countries; it was the first time the meeting had been held in a Communist country. The negotiations that led to the meeting are revealed in the Documents 10 and 11. The contents of these documents show that Hungary's political leaders were well aware of the importance of the event for the WJC, and that almost any condition set by the Hungarian side would be accepted. Indeed, WJC leaders not only pledged to refrain from mentioning the re-emergence of antisemitism in Hungary (Document 12); they also agreed to seek the prior consent of Hungarian political leaders in advance of publication of the final communiqué. The WJC seems to have viewed such pledges as part of an acceptable compromise that would ultimately facilitate a change in Soviet policy on emigration, and the establishment of diplomatic relations between Israel and (at least some of) the Communist countries. The latter issue was the main topic of a July 1987 meeting between János Kádár, the Hungarian Party leader, and Edgar M. Bronfman. The meeting took place two months after the Budapest conference, and following a visit by Bronfman to the Soviet Union.[16]

Relations between the Communist countries and the American Jewish Joint Distribution Committee ("the Joint") – arguably the most influential Jewish relief organisation operating in the Central- and Eastern-European region – underwent similar periodic changes. As in the case of the WJC, the Joint's relations with government authorities in the various countries passed through various phases from the initial rupture in the immediate aftermath of the Communist seizure of power, to the formal restoration of diplomatic ties around the turn of the 1980s. On closer inspection, however, we find significant differences between the experiences of the two organisations. As an international non-political relief organisation, the Joint had already established robust and diverse relations with organisations and governments in Central and Eastern Europe in the immediate aftermath of World War II. The relief and assistance provided by the organisation after 1945 had proved crucial not only for Jewish survivors, but also for the governments of the

---

15 National Archives of Hungary, XIX-A-21-d 122.d. 0020-2/1982 (24 May 1982).
16 National Archives of Hungary, XIX-A-21-d 151.d. 0018/12-1/1987 (15 July 1987).

war-torn countries. In May 1947, a Hungarian Communist functionary of the Ministry of Welfare wrote in a confidential letter to one of the principal leaders of the Party:

> At present, our aim is to dig as deep as possible into the affairs of the Joint; we shall prevent their [*monthly* – AK] ten million forints [*worth about 700,000 dollars* – AK] from serving to support reactionary aims, and we shall defeat the Zionist line [...]. The question arises: Is it necessary that the Joint continue operating in Hungary? In the current situation it is absolutely necessary, because it means advantages from the economic and social point of view, but in terms of politics it must be brought under control.[17]

In the period 1945–1952, the Joint spent 342 million dollars on assisting victims of the Holocaust, with 52 million dollars being spent in Hungary.[18]

As a consequence of the "anti-Zionist" campaigns and trials of the early 1950s, formal relations between the Joint and governments in the various countries were severed. Thereafter, the organisation was often portrayed by Communist propagandists as one of the "espionage organisations of imperialism". Even so, the Joint always managed to find, even in the most difficult periods, the means to offer assistance to Holocaust survivors in Communist countries.[19] During the period of détente that followed Stalin's death, and together with the help of other organisations, the Joint sought to indirectly provide social support to Jews living in Communist countries. In Poland, the Joint was granted official permission to recommence its activities in the late 1950s; it was banned again in 1967. Meanwhile, in Hungary and in Czechoslovakia, the Joint could provide assistance via the Swiss-based Société de Secours et d'Entraide (SSE), an organisation founded by the Joint in 1953. Often such assistance was provided through informal channels, sometimes with the knowledge and tacit consent of the authorities in the two countries.[20] A document issued by the Hungarian Ministry of Foreign Affairs in 1960 clearly informs the leaders of the State Office for Church Affairs that: "the Ministry of Foreign Affairs does not object in foreign-policy terms to the Joint offering Hungarian Jewish organisations in the country far more financial support than before. This applies, however, only if the funds spent on this purpose do not arise from collections made for the assistance of Hungarian Jews".[21] According to a document from August

---

[17] Letter of Miklós Ajtai to Mihály Farkas, in László Svéd, Dokumentumok. A magyar zsidóság és a hatalom 1945–1955 [Documents. Hungarian Jewry and the Authorities, 1945–1955], *Múltunk* 2–3 (1993), 248–298 (260–264).
[18] Michael Beizer, American Joint Distribution Committee. *The YIVO Encyclopedia of Jews in Eastern Europe*. Accessed on 27 September 2016 at http://www.yivoencyclopedia.org/article.aspx/American_Jewish_Joint_Distribution_Committee#id0evlag.
[19] See Martin Šmok, "Every Jew is a Zionist, and Every Zionist is a Spy!" The Story of Jewish Social Assistance Networks in Communist Czechoslovakia. *East European Jewish Affairs* 44 (2014), 70–83; and Michael Beizer, "I Don't Know Whom to Thank": The American Jewish Joint Distribution Committee's Secret Aid to Soviet Jewry. *Jewish Social Studies: History, Culture, Society* 15 (2009), 111–136.
[20] See Labendz, op. cit., 516.
[21] National Archives of Hungary, XIX-A-21-d 7.d. 005-14/1960 (18 May 1960).

1967: "Since 1955, by means of the Swiss relief agency SSE and with the involvement of the State Office for Church Affairs and the Finance Ministry, financial aid worth nine million dollars has been sent to Hungary, as well as aid for the purchase of goods (medicines, food, clothing, vehicles, etc.), and for social purposes worth around 1.5 million".[22] In 1972, Imre Miklós, Head of the State Office for Church Affairs, gave the following summary of developments in the field of aid and relief:

> In 1955 an agreement was reached, which was signed by Dr Erwin Haymann [correctly: Hayman – AK] on behalf of the Swiss-based Societé de Secours et d'Entr'Aide [Société de Secours et d'Entraide – AK] and by János Horváth, who was Head of the State Office for Church Affairs at the time. Under the terms of the agreement, the Swiss relief organisation provided 300,000 dollars for social support. Subsequently, aid received from this relief organisation rose to as much as 774,000 dollars per annum, and the current annual sum stands at about 600,000 dollars. The provision of aid was tied to specific individuals, and the amount was determined on the basis of need. The sum steadily declined as the beneficiaries passed away. Our relations with the Swiss relief organisation have been smooth to date. We have ensured that the aid and relief is not tied to political conditions. The distribution of aid is undertaken centrally by the MIOK KSZB [National Representation of Hungarian Israelites, Central Social Committee]. The utilisation of the aid is verified annually with our consent by the Swiss aid organisation.[23]

According to the documents, in addition to the aid received for social support, in 1967, the sum of aid spent on culture (stemming mainly from the Claims Conference) amounted to approximately 200,000 dollars over a ten-year period.[24]

Whereas an improvement or deterioration in relations with the WJC depended exclusively on political factors, with regard to the SSE, the Hungarian authorities, who were struggling with a lack of foreign currency at the time, evidently had no interest in squeezing the agency out of the country. Rather, they sought to control the aid and relief arriving in the country, just as they had done with respect to the Joint between 1945 and 1952. Since the authorities did not have some of the required information about the exact amount and beneficiaries of foreign aid, the political police utilised secret informers for obtaining such information. This is revealed in a document stemming from January 1962. The document was placed in a file on Mihály Borsa, Head of the Central Social Committee, the Hungarian organisation charged with distributing SSE aid and relief:

> According to our information, in late January 1962 the Geneva attorney Dr Erwin Haymann [Hayman – AK], one of the leaders of the international Jewish relief bodies, will come to Budapest for a few days [...]. [O]ur experiences to date show that he will call on many people as negotiating partners. We also have reports indicating that [...] he will bring in illegally certain amounts of money.[25]

---

22 National Archives of Hungary, XIX-A-21-d 39.d. 0020-3/b/1967 (27 August 1967).
23 National Archives of Hungary, XIX-A-21-d 67.d. 0020-1/1972 (30 March 1972).
24 National Archives of Hungary, XIX-A-21-d 39.d. 0020-3/b/1967 (27 August 1967).
25 Historical Archives of the Hungarian State Security 3.1.5. O-13558/1, BM III/II. 4.a., Personal folder: "Milliomos" [Millionaire], Nr.: Sz-7088 (15 January 1962).

Still, the state organs responsible for checking on the Jewish denomination were even unable to take full control of the distribution of aid brought into the country officially. Mihály Borsa and Sándor Scheiber, Head of the Rabbinical Seminary, who oversaw the distribution of aid allocated for cultural purposes resisted – more or less successfully – the attempts of the National Representation of Hungarian Israelites, in collaboration with the state authorities, to take control of their organisations (Chapter 5 contains several documents that refer to these conflicts).

Between 1967 and 1975, the leaders of the Joint tried on several occasions to establish direct contacts with Hungary's Jewish organisations, with a view to dispatching various forms of assistance and support to the country, without Hungarian state interference. With this goal in mind, they reiterated their earlier offers to increase the amount of aid and relief. These attempts were averted by the Hungarian political leadership. For instance, in 1972, Imre Miklós, Head of the State Office for Church Affairs, reported to the competent state and Party officials the following:

> For years the Joint has been seeking for ways to send once again the aid and relief directly to the Hungarian Jewish Denomination. Recently, Luis Horovitz [sic! – AK], CEO of the Joint in Romania, specifically mentioned to Dr Géza Seifert, Head of the National Representation of Hungarian Israelites, the possibility of establishing direct relations. Dr Seifert [...] is of the view that the Joint would give far more aid than it does at present if it could transfer the sums directly. The giving of aid will not be made subject to political or other conditions. The Joint chairman also stated that the organisation had already been involved in the provision of aid to Hungarian Jewry by way of the Societé de Secours et d'Entraide. In the future they wish to be able to support the Hungarian Jewish Denomination directly. With this in mind, their representatives seek to visit Hungary to get acquainted with the work of the Central Social Committee and assess the specific needs for aid and relief. They stated that they themselves were able to accept the present administrative mode and control of aid-giving. Suggestion: we should give our approval to a visit to Hungary by representatives of the Joint. The State Office for Church Affairs should contact them for informative purposes only and listen to their ideas on aid-giving; during the talks, the State Office should not make any kind of commitment to the Joint's representatives or any reference thereto.[26]

From the second half of the 1970s, there was a shift in the basic position that had rejected direct contacts with the Joint. After the Soviet religious affairs authorities gave their consent to the restoration of relations with the WJC, and the Jewish organisations in the allied countries took such a step, WJC leaders raised the possibility of direct contacts with the Joint during their talks. These took place after the ceremonious return to Hungary of the Hungarian royal crown, which had been taken to the United States in the aftermath of World War II. The return of the royal crown marked a spectacular improvement in Hungarian-U.S. relations. As the contents of a document dated 25 January 1978 (Document 9) reveal, the Hungarian side had found out from a secret service source that during the talks in Budapest, Philip Klutznick, President of the WJC, had wanted to link the issue of relations with Jewish organisations with the

---

26 National Archives of Hungary, XIX-A-21-d 67.d. 0020-1/1972 (30 March 1972).

negotiations being between the Hungarian government and the United States on the granting of most-favoured nation status. At the time, those negotiations were in their final stages, but the U.S. ambassador to Hungary advised Klutznick not to link the two issues. (Hungary was then granted the most-favoured nation status in the course of 1978.) Despite these developments, and as revealed in a memorandum authored by Imre Miklós, the Hungarian authorities were convinced that not linking these issues was merely a tactic, and that both the WJC and the Joint were simply tools of the U.S. government for promoting U.S. interests, which thus set the guidelines for negotiations with the two organisations. As it turns out from the memorandum, in the negotiations with Klutznick, Miklós hinted clearly that the scope for action of Jewish organisations in Hungary was actually determined by Hungarian political authorities, and that under certain circumstances, the Hungarian government was open to the possibility allowing Hungarian Jewish organisations greater scope for action in their relations with both the Joint and the WJC. Then, in September 1978, the Hungarian Ministry of Foreign Affairs signalled to the State Office for Church Affairs that the U.S. Embassy was emphatically requesting that the Joint's leaders be invited to Hungary. In his response, Miklós sought to prevaricate:

> [...] The request of the U.S. Embassy in this matter is part of an intentional tactical approach that has been pursued for some years. In my judgement, the Joint needs the State Office for Church Affairs to issue the letter of invitation in order to give the impression that it is our initiative. We have never sought direct relations with the Joint; rather the Joint has sought direct relations with us, and our interests are best served by continuing to refrain from initiating anything in this matter.[27]

This stance, however, could not be maintained for long. In a memo dated 5 March 1979, Miklós reported that in a meeting with Donald M. Robinson and Ralph I. Goldman, the Chairman and Executive Deputy Chairman of the Joint Executive Committee respectively, an agreement had been made on direct and increased aid for Hungarian Jews. He then added, as if by way of an apology for his earlier position, the following: "[I]t was not because of us that the provision of aid was earlier subordinated to Hungarian–U.S. bilateral relations".[28] Similar steps were taken in Czechoslovakia and Poland only in 1981.

The 1980s saw relations between the Hungarian Jewish bodies on the one side, and the Joint and the WJC on the other, develop in a similar manner. As the final act in the story, following the resignation of Imre Miklós and, only a month before its abolition, the State Office for Church Affairs proposed to Miklós Németh, Hungary's last Communist prime minister, that the Joint be granted permission to open a permanent office in Budapest.[29]

---

27 National Archives of Hungary, XIX-A-21-d 101.d. 0020-5/1978 (14 September 1978).
28 National Archives of Hungary, XIX-A-21-d 107.d. 0020-1/a/1979 (5 March 1979).
29 National Archives of Hungary, XIX-A-21-d 164.d. 0017/6-1/1989 (5 June 1989).

Documents

1 Conversation with Meir Vilner, Member of the ICP CC

19 October 1958

National Archives of Hungary, XIX-A-21-d (2.d.)
Collection: State Office for Religious Affairs [Állami Egyházügyi Hivatal, ÁEH]

Report of the Embassy in Tel Aviv

Subject: Conversation with Comrade Vilner, member of the ICP CC

[...]

d./ [*Vilner said that* – AK] The International Jewish organisations are under the direction of the Zionists and they serve the policy of the Israeli government. This also applies to the World Jewish Congress. He [*Vilner* – AK] wants, in particular, to mention this "in view of its Hungarian aspects". The entry of Hungarian Jewry into the World Congress came as a surprise. In his opinion this happened because at the time, the Hungarian Party was under pressure. Clearly, some internal tactical issues play a role here, and he does not want to deal with this, as in his opinion, the Hungarian Party knows best which internal tactics to employ concerning the Jews, for instance. Entry into the World Congress, however, is not only a domestic but also an international problem, and so, in his view, co-ordination between the various parties would have been necessary. The situation today is that only the Hungarian Jews are in the Congress, which causes a problem for many. (He mentioned, for instance, that recently a Party meeting had been held in south Tel Aviv, where questions had been put to him: Why are only the Hungarians in the Congress, and why don't the Poles and the others join. If the Jewish organisation in the People's Republic of Hungary can join the World Congress, then why can't the Jews who belong to the ICP become members of the World Congress, etc.) Comrade Vilner had replied that it was entirely an internal matter of the Hungarian Party as to how it decides on this issue.

I noted how signals in the media suggest that the Poles and Romanians will also join soon.

According to Comrade Vilner, based on the World Congress's current political platform, neither the Poles nor the Romanians will join. If, however, the World Congress accepts the conditions of the Poles (which, he believes, the Romanians have adopted too), then their membership is a possibility. The Polish Party had sent its conditions to the Israeli Party for the purpose of appraisal, before talks begin between the Polish Jews and the World Congress on membership. The conditions demand, among other things, that the World Congress should give its support to the: struggle for world peace and for the prohibition of atomic and hydrogen weapons, against West-German rearmament, etc. (Unfortunately, I do not remember exactly the other points – G.) The ICP found these conditions to be the correct ones. If the World Congress gives them its support, then membership will be the right step. He does not consider it likely, however, that the reactionary and Zionist leaders of the World Congress will accept the conditions, even though the conditions are not Communist but merely the minimum democratic demands. If, however, they do not accept them, then the Poles will not join; the Polish Party is strong and capable of preventing this. He thinks that what has been said also applies to the Romanians.

Róbert Garai, manu propria
Temporary chargé d'affaires

Attachment

0004-13/1958/Eln.
Ref. no.: 001242/3/1958.

Ministry of Foreign Affairs
Budapest

With reference to the transcript with the above reference number, I inform of the following:

I.

I agree with what Comrade Garai writes about the appraisal, the objective, activities and tactics of the World Jewish Congress. It is clear that they are making great efforts to involve all the Jewish denominations of all countries, which can only be done if they conceal their Zionist aims or cleverly disguise them, setting forth a programme that is generally acceptable to the Jewish denominations of all countries. The recent conduct of Dr Nahum Goldmann proves that one cannot accomplish the participation in the World Jewish Congress of all the Jewish denominations by voicing extremist Zionist views and interests.

Evidently, they are not endeavouring to involve the Jewish denominations in the Socialist countries with a view to strengthening Socialism. Nor can one ignore, however, the fact that there are disagreements within the World Jewish Congress on the issue of relations with the Soviet Union and the other Socialist countries, but even from the perspective of national and capitalist interests one cannot call the World Jewish Congress a Zionist organisation that is united on every issue.

II.

On the basis of which considerations does the Hungarian Jewish denomination take part in the meetings of the World Jewish Congress?

The World Congress seeks to accomplish the participation of the Jewish denominations of the Socialist countries by offering international protection from antisemitism, by upholding religious life in our country through the financial and moral support granted to Jewish culture, by obtaining financial compensation for the family members of the victims of Hitlerism.

In our view, Hungarian Jews should take part in the organisation of the World Jewish Congress, because

1./ An attempt must be made for the peace policy of the Socialist countries to be voiced in the international religious organisation, let there be someone there from our country, who struggles against and uncovers the agents of imperialism dressed in religious clothing, someone who refutes and prevents the defamation of the Soviet Union and the Socialist countries. A specific task will be, in this forum too, to take a clear stand – vital for all of Jewry – against neo-Fascism and the arming of West Germany and the neo-Fascists.

2./ We wanted to ensure that the Congress take a stand in favour of Israel's neutrality, because this was a real possibility. [...]

3./ An attempt must be made to break into, to struggle against and disrupt the unity of the reaction.

4./ The conditions are there for the Hungarian Jewish denomination to represent itself at the Congress with delegates who fully support our cause and fight consistently for it.

III.

The Hungarian Jewish denomination has been in contact with the World Jewish Congress since 1957. In November 1957, Endre Sós, Chairman of the National Representation of Hungarian Israelites, and Dr Imre Benesovszky [sic! – AK], leading chief rabbi of Budapest, took part in the Paris meeting of the European Executive Committee of the World Jewish Congress.

In March 1958, the meeting of the European Executive Committee of the World Jewish Congress was held in Amsterdam, at which the Hungarian delegate (Endre Sós) rejected the accusations which had been made by various Western Jewish circles against the Soviet Union's policy on religion and the statements on the denial of cultural rights to Soviet Jewry.

In consequence of these comments the meeting did not proceed with the planned discussion of the pre-prepared anti-Soviet draft resolution. This is not only the result of Nachum Goldmann pursuing more cautious tactics against the Soviet Union but also a consequence of the Hungarian delegates' efforts, for the draft had already been elaborated and if the Hungarian delegation had remained silent, then a resolution would have been passed, as the example of the Rome conference also shows.

In the summer of 1958, the International Executive Committee of the World Jewish Congress convened in Geneva. Prior to the meeting the Hungarian delegation submitted a peace decree [*plan* – AK] which supported, in terms of its main principles, the resolution of the Stockholm congress of the World Peace Council. On this basis, the World Jewish Congress condemned, in a resolution, experiments with weapons of mass destruction and demanded that they be ended. The American delegation in particular fought against the resolution.

The Hungarian Jewish delegation propagandised in favour of neutrality for Israel, which received strong backing, with several Western Jewish delegations giving their support.

At the Geneva meeting, Nachum Goldmann approved the position of the Hungarian Jewish delegation. He pledged to end the anti-Soviet propaganda in the bodies of the World Congress. At the same time, he requested the Hungarian delegates seek to build a bridge between Soviet Jewry and the World Jewish Congress.

The events clearly show that the World Jewish Congress is playing tactics; it wants to use the Hungarian Jewish delegation to win over the Jewish organisations of the other Socialist countries. Still, it is also evident that it has no choice but to end, or at least reduce, its aggressive propaganda, and that it has no choice but to make a statement or pass a resolution which, in the absence of the Hungarian delegates, it would not have done.

I do not want to exaggerate the role of the delegation of Hungarian Jews in the World Congress. Clearly, the concessions made by Nachum Goldmann towards the Hungarian delegation may simply be bait for the Jewish bodies in the other Socialist countries.

The participation of the Hungarian Jewish denomination in the World Jewish Congress is an attempt – a test of whether, in the current situation, we can influence the positions taken on specific international issues and, in the more distant future, we can even change the balance of power within the World Congress.

If the attempt fails, the Hungarian Jewish denomination can leave the World Congress at any point in time, doing so in such a manner that we draw political benefit.

Budapest, 3 February 1959
(Imre Miklós)

2 Proposal for the Exit of the Hungarian Jewish Denomination from the World Jewish Congress

15 June 1960

National Archives of Hungary, XIX-A-21-d (9.d.)
Collection: State Office for Religious Affairs [Állami Egyházügyi Hivatal, ÁEH]

Proposal

For the exit of the Hungarian Jewish Denomination from the World Jewish Congress

The Hungarian Jewish Denomination has been a member of the World Jewish Congress since July 1957. Participation in this world organisation was an attempt to use this forum to propagate the peace policy of the Socialist countries, to unveil the actions of imperialism in the religious field, to refute the defamations being made against the Socialist countries, and to seek to influence the positions of the World Jewish Congress in concrete international issues, such as the neutrality of the State of Israel. The delegates of the Hungarian Jewish denomination represented our objectives in an adequate fashion and achieved certain successes when they took part in the various meetings of the World Jewish Congress. For instance, at the meeting of the Executive Committee in Amsterdam in March 1958, a pre-elaborated draft resolution slandering the Soviet Union was withdrawn by the chairman following a statement by the Hungarian delegate. At Geneva, in the summer of 1958, based on a peace decree submitted by the Hungarian delegation, the World Jewish Congress condemned the atomic-weapon experiments and demanded their termination.

The conduct of the World Jewish Congress seen in 1957–58 has recently taken a negative turn. The more moderate stance has been replaced by the most extreme and reactionary politicising, made particularly manifest in the resolutions of the Stockholm meeting of 19 August 1959.

According to one of the resolutions, freedom of worship for Jews is being prevented in the Soviet Union, and they protest against this. Another resolution expresses gratitude to the West-German government for giving reparations to Jews and its disappointment with the German Democratic Republic for failing to pay reparations to Jews, etc.

The same meeting rejected the Polish proposal for the Congress to condemn West-German rearmament and the supply of weapons by Israel, etc.

Under the present circumstances, the participation of the Hungarian Jewish Denomination in the World Jewish Congress is creating confusion, particularly as the Jewish communities of other Socialist countries are not officially members of the World Jewish Congress. The situation causes problems, in particular, for the Israeli Communist Party. For this reason, the Hungarian Jewish Denomination has not been attending the meetings of the World Jewish Congress for more than a year now. On multiple occasions it has protested against the current stance of the World Jewish Congress, doing so, however, in vain.

Based on the above, I propose that in the course of July 1960 the Hungarian Jewish Denomination should officially leave the World Jewish Congress.

The Ministry of Foreign Affairs agrees with the proposal, as does the Ministry of Interior.

The text is authentic: Károly Olt, manu propria

Attachment

State Office for Church Affairs

Memorandum

to Comrade Gyula Rapai

The State Office for Church Affairs has submitted a proposal to the Political Committee, in which it proposed that the Jewish Denomination should leave the World Jewish Congress in July 1960. Concerning the proposal made in the submission, Comrade Rapai instructed me by telephone to request Comrade János Péter, the Deputy Foreign Minister, to consult – prior to the exit from the World Jewish Congress – with the Soviet and Czechoslovak comrades, because it is possible that there is a politically beneficial side to the Hungarian Jewish denomination remaining a member of the World Jewish Congress. In line with the instruction, I made the request to Comrade János Péter, who, on 30 June informed me of the following:

He discussed the matter with the leaders of the Ministry of Foreign Affairs, and the view was formed that it would be necessary to ask once again for the opinions of the Soviet and Czech comrades, because it was absolutely clear from the consultations of last year that the Socialist camp does not have an interest in the participation in the Jewish World Congress of the Hungarian Jewish Denomination, indeed whether, from this perspective, an exit would even be desirable.

Comrade János Péter mentioned how the Ministry of Foreign Affairs had taken into consideration the previous consultation when expressing its agreement with the Hungarian Jewish Denomination leaving the World Jewish Congress.

Budapest, 2 July 1960

3 The Aims of the World Jewish Congress with Regard to the Hungarian Jewish Denomination

27 July 1962

Historical Archives of the Hungarian State Security 3.1.5. O-17169

From: Ministry of Interior
II, Sub-department 5-c

Subject: The aims of the World Jewish Congress with regard to the Hungarian Jewish denomination

Report

Budapest, 27 July 1962

At the beginning of this month the leaders of the National Representation of Hungarian Israelites received a message from Dr SIGRID RÓTH [sic! – AK] secretary of the European section of the World Jewish Congress. The essence of the message was that Dr Nachum Goldmann, President of the World Jewish Congress and the World Zionist Organisation, is to visit Romania in September, where he will view the denominational institutions there and hold talks with Romanian official circles. Dr Nachum Goldmann would like to come to Budapest prior to his visit to Romania and discuss with the leaders of Hungarian Jewry and perhaps with representatives of the state organs the matter of the compensation claimed from the West Germans by Hungarian Jewry. (The verified damages claim is 60 million marks = 15 million dollars.)

In the message the leaders of the NRHI are asked to seek out information from the state organs concerning the matter of the invitation of Nachum Goldmann. The message emphasises that the probing should not take place on behalf of Goldmann, but rather as the forwarding of Sigfrid Róth's idea.

This wish is essentially a response to a motion from the leaders of the denomination concerning the desire to hold a meeting with Nachum Goldmann somewhere abroad for the purpose of discussing matter of the compensation claims of Hungarian Jewry.

The speedy and audacious reaction to the proposal is linked with the desire on the part of Dr Nachum Goldmann, which he has had for some time, for representatives of the Jews in the Eastern-European countries and the Soviet Union to take part in the World Jewish Congress. Now that they have turned to him, he considers the time is ripe for a return to this issue.

At the end of May a leader of the NRHI held talks in Vienna with Dr Sigfrid Róth on the matter of compensation. On behalf of the World Jewish Congress and Nachum

Goldmann, Sigfrid Róth set out the prospect of their full support for the matter of the compensation claims, and yet, as a kind of condition for this, he wanted Jews in Hungary to show some kind of movement towards the Congress.

Sigfrid Róth stated that as a condition of membership they do not want Hungarian Jewry to abandon its political position. If they do not agree with something, they can say this in an open forum or vote against it, but it would be better to be there. In response to the claim of the Congress being anti-Soviet, Sigfrid Róth stated the following on behalf of Nachum Goldmann:

- They do not consider the detention of denominational leaders in the Soviet Union to be "official antisemitism", but a criminal matter. These persons have committed crimes for which they would be punished in any country.
- Since the World Jewish Congress represents the interests of world Jewry, they therefore exercise criticism of the Soviet Union with regard to the situation of Soviet Jewry. Thus, for instance, they had complained about the lack of a united organisation for the Soviet Union's Jews.
- More than 500,000 Soviet Jews had identified Yiddish as their native language; thus, a Soviet Jewry does exist. Even so, they do not have the same cultural opportunities as other nationalities. (Schools, theatres, newspapers.)
- They complained about the religious inequality that exists in the Soviet Union. The Russian Orthodox, Roman Catholic and other churches in the Soviet Union have united organisations and can participate in various international conferences; indeed, the Russian Orthodox Church had even become a member of the World Council of Churches. Why is it not possible for the Jews to enjoy the same rights?

Sigfrid Róth stated that what they are complaining about with regard to the situation of Soviet Jewry does not exceed legitimate criticism, but that they – as Jewry's advocacy body – were obliged to do this. After raising these points, Sigfrid Róth spoke once again in favour of Hungarian Jewry's joining the Congress.

In order to make the Congress attractive and membership of the body acceptable, he then noted the following:

- He emphatically stated that the Congress does not intend to criticise the Soviet Union.
- He explained that the Congress supports peace, and that there is a basis for co-operation on this issue.
- The Congress is the international body of various shades of Jewry, but it is not a Zionist organisation. In theory, an anti-Zionist organisation could be a member. As an example, he mentioned the organisation of Swiss Jewish communities.
- In his view, the Congress supports neutrality. As he said, Nachum Goldmann also wants to achieve Israel's neutrality, but considers this to be almost impossible to implement.

- Even though he said it incidentally, his main point was that the Congress could offer more effective support on the matter of compensation if Hungarian Jewry had membership of the Congress.

The above topics are raised at almost every meeting abroad.

[...]

As a result of the machinations of visitors from abroad and the [*Israeli* – AK] Embassy, a situation has arisen in which even among the official denominational leaders the focus is increasingly on the person of Nachum Goldmann and on the necessity of German reparations, and they place all their attention on the World Zionist Organisation, ignoring the political danger of doing so.

Completed in 3 copies

Record no. 38
Distr.   1 copy to Comrade Geréb
         1 copy to the advisor Comrade [*Soviet advisor* – AK]
         I copy for information

4 On the Foreign Relations of the Hungarian Jewish Religious Denomination

16 May 1966

National Archives of Hungary, XIX-A-21-d (34.d.)
Collection: State Office for Religious Affairs [Állami Egyházügyi Hivatal, ÁEH]

Completed in 3 copies
Copy no. 1

Report

on the foreign relations of the Hungarian Jewish Religious Denomination

In the past two-three years, there has been a revival of interest in the societal and social situation of Hungarian Jewry and their religious circumstances on the part of the Western Jewish organisations, private individuals and Jewish emigrants.

Over the past year, around 1,200 Jewish tourists have visited – either in groups or as individuals – the various Jewish religious, cultural and social institutions.

Interest has spiked since the election of the new leadership [*in January and March 1966, see Document 10 in Chapter 5* – AK] of the National Representation of Hungarian Israelites (NRHI), particularly on the part of the Western international Jewish organisations and institutions.

The increased international interest has necessitated the appraisal and co-ordination of the international relations of the Jewish religious denomination.

I.
The relationship towards the international Jewish organisations and institutions

[…]

a./ In the first instance, after Liberation, the relationship developed in such a manner that an office of the WJC operated – under the name "Hungarian Section of the WJC" – as an independent organisation alongside the NRHI. At the time, the organisation was concerned with appraising the wartime damages of Hungarian Jewry, searching for lost and missing family members, offering social assistance to a certain extent, and gathering together Hungarian-Jewish related documents on Fascism.

Over the years, the activities of the WJC's Office gradually became dominated by efforts to realise the political demands of the various Western imperialist powers and capitalist groups, and so, by 1950, the dissolution of the Hungarian Section of the WJC, or rather its assimilation into the NRHI framework, had become necessary.

In this way, the WJC's Office functioned, with three officials and reduced competences, until 1953, whereupon all contact with the WJC was broken off.

b./ In the second instance, in 1957 contact was established between Hungarian Jewry and the WJC. At that time, the NRHI officially joined the WJC, as a consequence of which Hungarian Jewry received two places in the European executive. Contemporaneously, the Hungarian Committee of the WJC was established in Hungary, whose office operated within the NRHI framework.

In the summer of 1960, relations between Hungarian Jewry and the WJC were severed once more.

There were basically two causes of the split:

1./ In early 1958, a nascent Jewish organ convened in Rome, in which the WJC also represented itself. This Rome meeting wanted to declare that Jews living in the Soviet Union could not freely manifest their religion and culture.

This meeting was led by Nahum Goldmann.

2./ In 1959, the WJC expressed "its grateful thanks" to the West-German government for paying out reparations to Jews. At the same time, however, the Jews of many countries – including Hungarian Jewry – were excluded from such reparations for political reasons.

Last month <u>the leadership of the World Jewish Congress restored</u> relations with representatives of Hungarian Jewry <u>with a view to the NRHI participating in the work of the WJC as a full member</u>.

The WJC's representative Armand Kaplan, the secretary-general, stated that the WJC would hold its fifth plenary world conference in Brussels on 31 July of this year.

The leadership of the WJC considers it extremely important that representatives of Hungarian Jewry attend the world conference and join the WJC.

He mentioned that prior to his arrival in Hungary he had visited Romania and Czechoslovakia. Romania had agreed to take part in the work of the WJC once again, while Czechoslovakia was considering the issue and would give a definite answer later on.

According to Secretary-General Kaplan, the leadership of the WJC had accepted that in future, the Congress must pursue a policy of realism.

[...]

Another matter raised during the talks was the WJC's relationship with the Soviet Union and with respect to the situation of Soviet Jewry.

The secretary-general stated that within the WJC, and with Nahum Goldmann at the fore there was an increasingly strong group who had accepted that the "tone" and methods employed by them against the Soviet Union were not correct, and that it was not possible to negotiate with the Soviet Union in such a tone.

There was a great desire on their part for representatives of Jewry in the Soviet Union to take part in the work of the WJC.

It was unambiguously clear from the talks that the leadership of the WJC would consider the participation of the Socialist countries' Jews in the work of the Congress to be extremely important. As they explained: in place of the present monologue, they would like, in the future, to hold a dialogue on the great and all-embracing problems affecting humanity and Jewry.

The WJC secretary-general laid out the prospect of significant financial support for Hungarian Jewry if representatives of Hungarian Jewry were to agree to participate in the work of the WJC as a full member.

[...]

IV.
Proposals

1./ Our relations with the World Jewish Congress must be discussed in advance with the Ministry of Foreign Affairs and with the Offices for Church Affairs of the Socialist countries affected, in particular the Soviet Union and Czechoslovakia.

For the time being and subject to approval from above, Hungary should merely send observers to the World Conference, which is to be held in Brussels from 31 July, while a final decision on participation in the work of the WJC should be made once we have acquired some experience.

2./ The representatives of Hungarian Jewry should not rule out making contact with the more loyal and influential leadership members of the World Federation of Hungarian Jews, and fostering and enhancing the existing contacts.

[...]

3./ The board of the NRHI should further expand its relations with the associations of Hungarian Jews in various capitalist countries, above all the associations of Hungarian Jews in Canada and Uruguay.

[...]

4./ It must be ensured that relations between the Israeli Embassy and the religious denomination are of a religious nature.

At the same time, in their official and private relations – similarly to other foreign representations – they must adhere to the rules of protocol.

The newly elected leaderships of the NRHI and the BJC are suitable for establishing relations with the State of Israel and its Embassy in Budapest that are more beneficial than before and more appropriate to the interests of our state and our society.

[...]

6./ The recent attempts by the State of Israel to establish relations in the religious-cultural, cultural, literary and artistic fields by way of the Hungarian Jewish Religious Denomination or utilising the denomination must be warded off in future. Judgement on the appropriateness of such relations lies within the competence of the appropriate Hungarian state or societal cultural organs.

5 On the Fifth Conference of the World Jewish Congress in Brussels

20 September 1966

National Archives of Hungary, XIX-A-21-d (34.d.)
Collection: State Office for Religious Affairs [Állami Egyházügyi Hivatal, ÁEH]

Completed in 3 copies

Copy no. 1: Ministry of Culture, Comrade P. Ilku
Copy no. 2: HSWP CC, Comrade L. Orbán
Copy no. 3: State Office for Church Affairs

Copy no. 3

Report

on the fifth conference of the World Jewish Congress in Brussels

The 5th plenary conference of the World Jewish Congress (WJC) was held in Brussels from 31 July until 9 August. The conference was attended by the Jewish religious and political organisations of 57 countries as well as several international organisations (UN, UNESCO, etc.). From the Socialist countries, representatives of the Yugoslav, Romanian and Hungarian religious denominations were present – the Hungarians as observers.

Most of the comments and statements made at the assembly, as well as the resolutions adopted, support our earlier assessment that nothing has changed in the basic political stance of the World Jewish Congress over the past eight to ten years.

As before, the Congress is still characterised by strong Zionism, maximum subservience to imperialist interests and hostility towards the Soviet Union.

Experience has shown that the representatives of a policy of realism constitute a significantly smaller force than in other world religious organisations. This is presumably a consequence of the direct – without transference – political and economic relations of the World Jewish Congress with the United States.

Certain changes could be perceived in the tone and negotiating methods of the official leaders of the WJC. This, however, is merely a tactical change and the clever division – or redistribution – of roles, as several of N. Goldmann's statements also prove.

- The unchanging Zionist stance of the Congress is reflected, apart from in the various resolutions and reports, mainly in the speeches of Goldmann. For the chairman spoke emphatically and in every case of the "Jewish people", which has, in his view, a real state: Israel, to which, as the "centre of collective Jewish life", Jews belong wherever they are living in the world, and which, for this very reason, it is obligatory to support.

- The anti-Soviet stance of the WJC is exhibited most graphically in the resolution on the situation of Soviet Jewry. The resolution calls on the Soviet authorities to guarantee in full and without hindrance the practice of religion by the Jewish religious communities in the country, the establishment of a national Jewish representative body and the realisation of the national and cultural rights of Jews. It requests the Soviet government to enable the unification of Jewish families that have been separated "in Israel or elsewhere". The conference also took a position on keeping the situation of Soviet Jewry on the agenda of world public opinion. To this end, "the friends of the Soviet Union, including the major Communist groups, must be won over for the cause", the resolution states. A tactical change in their stance is shown in the following statement by Goldmann: "On this issue, many sought a tougher stance than mine, but I hold the flute in higher esteem than the drum".
- The resolution concerning the relationship between Jewry and West Germany – despite protests from some of the delegates – defended the diplomatic and other relations that have arisen between Israel and West Germany as something that serves to strengthen Israel. All signs indicate that the WJC seeks a compromise with neo-Nazism, and the only brake on this endeavour for the time being are the Jewish masses who find it more difficult to forget.
- At the proposal of the Hungarian observers, the resolution adopted on the issue of "German reparation" also mentions the necessity of making amends to the Jews living in the Eastern-European countries. What this stance by the World Jewish Congress really means in practice is shown by the response given to the Hungarian observers by Rieger [sic! – AK], the secretary-general: "With this resolution alone, you will not get far. What is also needed is for the Hungarian Minister of Foreign Affairs to turn to the West-German government with a similar request".
- An "internal" resolution of the conference deals with relations between Christianity and the Jews. It determines that it will organise in the future a permanent committee, which will maintain more intensive relations between the WJC and various Christian churches, and above all with The Vatican, the World Council of Churches and the Anglican Church. There is no doubt that the WJC is willing to accept the ecumenical invitation of the Christian churches, thereby forgetting all the humiliation and persecution of 2,000 years – presumably because this "religious ecumene" has been, for some time now, anti-Communist rather than religious – in line with American instructions.
- The resolution on human rights urges the ratification of the concept of human rights and the establishment of the office of a human rights commissioner, because, as it argues, "in all parts of the world, reactionary and extreme nationalist movements have raised their heads". The aim of this nebulous generalisation

is clearly to disguise the increasingly nationalist, revisionist and racist endeavours in certain capitalist countries – above all in America and West Germany.

[…]

- The leadership of the WJC dealt with the representatives of the religious denominations of the Socialist countries "with particular attentiveness". N. Goldmann held a special reception for them, where he laid emphasis on his desire for the Socialist countries to form a so-called "Eastern bloc" so that they could represent their interests in the most appropriate manner at the Congress. The formation of an "Eastern bloc" would be the first step towards the martyr celebration to be held in Sarajevo in October of this year, to which, in addition to religious denominational representatives of the Socialist countries, the leaders of the WJC, including N. Goldmann, had also been invited. At the Brussels meeting of the WJC, it became clear that "their particular loyalty" shown towards the Socialist countries, together with the criticism of conditions in the Soviet Union and efforts to form an "Eastern bloc" constitute integral parts of the endeavours of imperialism to loosen and to penetrate [*the bloc of Socialist countries* – AK]. To this end, they are, of course, willing to make financial sacrifices. In this respect, Secretary-General Kaplan made the following comment to the Hungarian observers: "We are even willing [to give] financial support, but it all depends on you".
- The Hungarian observers – according to our information – consistently emphasised in their anti-Fascist speeches that Jewry should serve social progress and peace. They highlighted that Hungarian Jews too had been liberated by the Soviet army and that, together with their compatriots of other religions and worldviews, they are building a new and just society.

Chairman Géza Seifert, as well as Chief Rabbi Beneschofszky [*sic!* – AK], were interviewed by several Western newspaper and radio reporters. They became acquainted with many distinguished foreign Jewish figures, all of whom showed great interest in the People's Republic of Hungary and the life of Hungarian Jewry. Several of them promised to visit our country soon. Thus, among others, Nahum Goldmann also announced that he wishes to visit Hungary in the spring of next year. He has not yet received a response to his announcement.

Tasks:

1./ The content of our report on the WJC's Brussels meeting and the assessment must be made known to the offices for church affairs in other Socialist countries, in particular those of the Soviet Union, the GDR, Czechoslovakia and Yugoslavia. Where possible, there must be direct consultations with them on the issue.

2./ Concerning further relations with the WJC, the current observer status should be maintained and we should fight consistently from this position against the reactionary endeavours of the Congress.

3./ The efforts of Goldmann and his associates to develop an "Eastern Jewish bloc" should be monitored and studied in relation to all of the Socialist countries, which, from this aspect, requires that our relations become more intensive.

4./ The planned visit to Hungary of N. Goldmann and the other WJC leaders should be made the subject of an inquiry, whereby any further positions and statements by them should be monitored. We should not give space in the future to efforts on their part to influence the Hungarian religious denomination by holding out the prospect of greater financial assistance.

5./ Regarding the official relations with the world conference, it may be far more beneficial to make correct use of the wide-ranging personal acquaintances made by the Hungarian observers in Brussels. The leaders of the National Representation of Hungarian Israelites, above all, the observers who participated in the WJC, should elaborate a proposal concerning the identity of those conference acquaintances with which they wish to maintain contact in the future, and how they can do so.

(József Prantner)

6 The Fifth Conference of the World Jewish Congress

Brussels, 31 July – 9 August 1966

National Archives of Hungary, XIX-A-21-c (83.d).
Collection: State Office for Religious Affairs [Állami Egyházügyi Hivatal, ÁEH]

Memorandum

on the fifth conference of the World Jewish Congress (Brussels, 31 July – 9 August 1966)

[…]

IV.
The participation of the Hungarian delegation

1/ Preliminary conceptions
    a/ The Hungarian delegates take part only as observers, given that Hungarian Jewry left the World Congress earlier on (due to its anti-Soviet stance and because it did not take a stand against West Germany's discriminatory policy on the matter of compensation).
    b/ The Hungarian delegation does not negotiate during the conference on joining the World Congress,
    c/ or on financial aid.
    d/ The Hungarian delegation demands an end to discrimination in the field of compensation and persuades, if possible, the World Congress to take the same position.
    e/ Members of the delegation can speak in their capacity as observers, particularly on the burning issues affecting humanity.
    f/ In cases of crude anti-Sovietism, the Hungarian delegation will protest.

2/ It can be concluded that these conceptions were <u>satisfactorily implemented</u> by the Hungarian delegation.

V.
Evaluation, proposals

1/ Compared with the position in the past, there has appeared, in the work of the World Congress, <u>a new kind of tone</u>, but without one being able to perceive any significant changes of substance. There are tactical reasons for the change in tone.

2/ The duality of the new tone and the unchanged substance is manifest above all in the stance taken in relation to the Soviet Union. The tone has become a little smoother in a formal sense and the tactics have also been refined, but the basic hostility towards the Soviet Union has remained the same as it was before.

3/ A main objective of the World Congress is to win over the Jews of the Socialist countries, to achieve their membership and – to a certain extent – their cohesion. At the same time, the symptoms of the policy of division are also manifest (creating a rift between the Soviet Union and the other Socialist countries).

4/ The Zionist stance was perceptible throughout the conference, although from place to place the points of non-Israeli Jews were also made.

5/ The documents address, in several points, international and world political issues. The statements made on peace and disarmament contain numerous positives. One should not forget, however, that the decisive groups openly expressed the tactical tone and background of such resolutions.

On the Vietnam issue, the statements show nothing particularly positive. Here, too, an American effort to avoid the Vietnam issue being addressed became clear, and if this effort failed, then they would seek by all means to achieve the taking of weakened positions on the matter.

6/ There were several tangible signs of an increase in American influence.

7/ The leaders of the World Congress seek the friendship of the FRG. They do so mainly in order to secure the reparation sums and in support of the State of Israel's foreign-policy objectives. It is clear, however, that this position still encounters emotionally justified opposition among broad Jewish circles.

8/ On several points the consequence can be drawn that the World Congress is, tactically speaking and on an on-going basis, employing the prior division of roles (The French leader Kaplan's forming a friendship with the Hungarian delegation, the debate concerning the Soviet Union and then concerning Germany).

9/ The Hungarian proposal concerning compensation was included in the conference document. This is positive even if they tried by all means to counter the proposal. (The call for the GDR to provide compensation was an attempt to divide.) The issue now is the extent to which they try to ensure the application in practice of the resolution.

10/ Thus, there are some changes in the course taken by the World Congress and in its operation. Most of these are tactically motivated. Experience has shown, however, that among the members of the World Congress there is a significant number of groups and leading figures with attitudes reflecting a policy of realism. From the Hungarian side, it may be useful to maintain contact in the future with these groups and figures.

11/ There were positive results of the Hungarian delegation's participation (the compensation resolution, the propagandising opportunities). Accession to, or retraction from, the World Congress, however, could only be considered if

a/ the anti-Soviet tendency would end for good;

b/ the Zionist approach would end or at least be given less prominence;

c/ there would be more positive and forceful resolutions on issues affecting humanity;

d/ and, finally, if the compensation of Hungarian Jewry were to be realised in practice.

7 The Foreign Relations of the Jewish Religious Denomination

19 November 1966

National Archives of Hungary, XIX-A-21-d (34.d.)
Collection: State Office for Religious Affairs [Állami Egyházügyi Hivatal, ÁEH]

Memorandum

on the foreign relations of the Jewish Religious Denomination

Concerning the foreign activities of the Jewish Religious Denomination, several issues arise where a final position must be formed.

These are the following:

I The NRHI's relations in the future with the World Jewish Congress

[…]

Regarding the future relations with the WJC, there are two options:
 a./ Continue to maintain relations at their current level – observer status;
 b./ Join the WJC as a member.

In terms of making a decision, the following phenomena should be considered:

1./ The Brussels conference of the WJC has proven that the WJC is – despite some forced tactical prevarication – a loyal servant of the political line taken by the United States.

[…]

2./ The WJC exhibits a strongly anti-Soviet stance

[…]

3./ The WJC is under the management of international Zionist forces:

[…]

4./ A majority of the leaders of Hungarian Jewry – explicitly or in an implicit, reasoning manner – are sympathetic to the idea of joining the WJC.
 Among these those with more progressive political attitudes support membership primarily in the hope of financial support, while those who are more negative do so in the spirit of international Jewish cohesion/solidarity as well as for financial reasons.

It may be argued that in the event of membership the NRHI would receive more significant and regular financial support by way of the WJC, which would undeniably resolve for a temporary period the threat of succumbing to its regular annual losses of several million forints.

Proposal:

- According to the opinion of the department, a more correct solution is for the NRHI not to become a member of the WJC for the time being, but rather, by maintaining its current status, to take part as an observer in the various manifestations of the WJC.
- The NRHI representatives should utilise the position as observer to draw the WJC's attention to the reactionary endeavours with which Hungarian Jewry cannot agree and which isolate the Congress and prevent if from forming the broadest international relations.
- On the occasion of our upcoming talks with representatives of the Soviet Union's Council for Church Affairs, there must be consultation on the issue of our relationship with the WJC.

[...]

III./ The visit to Hungary of Jack Weiler, Vice-Chairman of the Joint

[...]

J. Weiler pledged to arrange for the Joint to transfer a one-time grant of 150,000 dollars for use by the Jewish social institutions in Hungary. This event is significant because since the break with the Joint, that is to say, since 1953, this is the first instance on their part when they seek to directly support Hungarian Jewry.

According to the opinion of the department, the dollar grant that has been offered will be acceptable if no political conditions are attached to it.

To date, we have not observed such an endeavour.

IV./ The issue of West-German reparations

As is known, the proposal of the WJC leaders on this issue was that the Hungarian Ministry of Foreign Affairs should turn to the West-German government with a request for payment of the reparations.

In Sarajevo, Secretary-General Rigner [sic! – AK] suggested to Seifert that he, as chairman of the NRHI, should write a letter directly to Gerstenmöyer [sic! – AK] with a view to the payment of reparations. Rieger [sic! – AK] referred to the fact that Kadelburg, the Yugoslav chairman, had written a similar letter to Gertonmöyer [sic! – AK], and so they can rightly expect the payment of reparations.

Concerning this issue, our suggestion is that Chairman Seifert should not write a letter on this matter to Gerstenmaier.

According to the opinion of the WJC leaders at the time, Gertenmayer [sic! – AK] is the candidate with the greatest chances for the position of chancellor, and this is why they invited him rather than anyone else to the Brussels conference of the WJC.

V./ <u>Organising the Eastern-European Jewish Bloc</u>

At the Brussels meeting of the WJC, N. Goldmann stated his desire for the establishment of an Eastern-European Jewish bloc. Its aim, in his view, would be for Eastern-European Jewry to represent a unanimous position in the WJC.

The main organiser and patron of the establishment of the bloc was the Chief Rabbi of Romania, Mózes Rósen [sic! – AK].

Our supposition that the WJC leaders and Rózen [sic! – AK] wanted to use the martyr celebrations in Yugoslavia to organise the creation of the bloc, proved correct.

The Hungarian delegation attending the celebrations played a decisive part in preventing the realisation of the creation of the Eastern-European Jewish bloc, by emphasising that they had come to Yugoslavia to celebrate rather than organise [a bloc].

In our opinion, such attempts at unification must to be prevented in the future too, because they reflect in part an anti-Soviet tendency, and in part a Zionist tendency.

8 On the Visit to Hungary of Dr Nahum Goldmann and his Colleagues

18 April 1967

National Archives of Hungary, XIX-A-21-d (37.d.)
Collection: State Office for Religious Affairs [Állami Egyházügyi Hivatal, ÁEH]

Completed in 5 copies

Copy no. 1: HSWP CC, Comrade Á. Pullai
Copy no. 2: Ministry of Culture, Comrade P. Ilku
Copy no. 3: Ministry of Foreign Affairs, Comrade J. Péter
Copy no. 4: HSWP CC, Comrade I. Darvasi
Copy no. 5: State Office for Church Affairs

Copy no. 5

Report

on the visit to Hungary of Dr Nahum Goldmann and his colleagues

Dr Nahum GOLDMANN, Chairman of the World Jewish Congress (WJC), and his colleagues – Dr Gergart [sic! – AK] Riegner, Secretary-General of the WJC, Dr Armand Kaplan, Deputy Director of the Foreign Affairs Committee of the WJC and Dr Stephen Róth [sic! – AK], Secretary-General of the European Section of the WJC – visited Budapest from 3 April until 7 April as the guests of the National Representation of Hungarian Israelites.

The visit to Hungary of the leading functionaries of the WJC was part of an information-gathering tour, in the course of which they also visited Czechoslovakia, Romania, Yugoslavia and Poland.

During their stay, Goldmann and his associates visited several Jewish religious, cultural and social institutions, they met with representatives of Hungarian Jewish religious life, they held talks with the leaders of the religious denomination, and they also paid a courtesy visit to the head of the State Office for Church Affairs.

– They made statements expressing sincere admiration for the situation and activities of the Jewish religious, cultural and social institutions. At the same time, they did not fail to note that "they would be happier if, in other Socialist countries too, Jewry would receive similar esteem and would have similar rights to those in Hungary".
– Goldmann and his group had two opportunities to meet with the wider plenum of Hungarian religious Jews – at the religious denomination's liberation celebra-

tions and a reception held at the Hotel Gellért, which was attended by a broader circle. Goldmann utilised both occasions to speak in public. In the introduction to his speeches, he spoke positively of the Soviet Union, which in the 1930s had been the first and only country to recognise the danger of Fascism and had called on the peoples to take a common stand against Fascism. He praised the Soviet Union's role as liberator, a factor to which the remnant Hungarian Jewry owed their lives. In the other parts of his speech, Zionist ideas were predominant. He explained at length the significance of the State of Israel, as the homeland of Jews wherever they are living in the world. Citing Heine, he stated that, ultimately, every Jewish person "carries his homeland on his shoulders, in the Torah scrolls". He also mentioned neo-Nazism and the antisemitism that is awakening once again in certain countries as a factor that should be watched. But for Goldmann, this is not the main danger to Jewry; rather, in his view, it lies in the assimilation of Jewry. In being sucked away into the nation and the society as a whole and ceasing to exist as a "separate people". Goldmann's speeches were not an undivided success, and this was especially true of his second speech, which was received by rather sporadic and "polite" applause.

The following issues arose during the visit by Goldmann and his colleagues to the State Office for Church Affairs and during their talks with the leaders of the religious denomination:
- They portrayed the WJC in the most positive terms, as an international organisation that was fighting against Fascism and on behalf of human progress. Their goal is that the Jewry of every country should take part in the work of the Congress.
- They announced their intention to give financial support to the Hungarian Jewish Religious Denomination, the means of which were soon to be discussed with the Denomination.
- They stated their willingness to support the payment of reparations to Hungarian Jewry by West Germany in the event of diplomatic relations being established between Hungary and West Germany. They suggested that the Hungarian State raise, at governmental level, the reparation issue with the West Germans.

To the questions raised, Goldmann and his group essentially received the following answers:
- We emphasised that Hungarian Jewry has only one homeland: the People's Republic of Hungary, where the majority of citizens of Jewish religion had found their place, felt themselves comfortable and as citizens with full rights. This is also the basis for relations between the Religious Denomination and the various international Jewish organs.
- We pointed out that the WJC had, for some years, been openly supporting the Cold-War policies of imperialism and even today had failed to take a clear stance

on such important issues as the U.S. aggression in Vietnam and the persecution of black people.
- On the issue of reparations, we criticised the discriminatory stance of the West-German government and, irrespective of diplomatic relations, we continue to view Hungarian Jewry's demands for reparations as legitimate.
- We do not exclude the possibility of Hungarian Jewry receiving financial support from the WJC, subject to it not being tied – either overtly or covertly – to political conditions.

Goldmann agreed in general with the responses we gave, seeking merely to prove that the WJC had spoken out several times against the Vietnam War and the persecution of black people.

[...]

Goldmann's visit to Hungary did not make a particularly great effect at the rabbinical faculty or within the religious Jewish population. His haughty and condescending manner created a distance between him and many people who had previously nurtured illusions about him. The leaders of the denomination – above all Dr Géza Seifert, the chairman – treated Goldmann and his associates as equals and held their ground in every respect.

Based on the experiences made in the course of the visit, one may conclude that the religious policy line followed with respect to the Hungarian Jewish Religious Denomination is the correct one and corresponds with the goal. The relationship between the religious denomination and the WJC must be kept at the current level, and for the time being there is no need to change this.

(József Prantner)

9 Conversation with Dr Philip Klutznick, President of the World Jewish Congress

25 January 1978

National Archives of Hungary, XIX-A-21-01-d (101.d.)
Collection: State Office for Religious Affairs [Állami Egyházügyi Hivatal, ÁEH]

Completed in 6 copies

Copy no. 1: Ministerial Council, Comrade G. Aczél
Copy no. 2: HSWP, Comrade I. Győri
Copy no. 3: HSWP CC, Comrade Dr G. Móna
Copy no. 4: Ministry of Foreign Affairs, Comrade F. Puja
Copy no. 5: Ministry of Interior, Comrade L. Karasz
Copy no. 6: State Office for Church Affairs

Memorandum

on a conversation with Dr Philip Klutznyck [*sic!* – AK] President of the World Jewish Congress

At the invitation of the National Representation of Hungarian Israelites, Dr Philip Klutznyck, President of the World Jewish Congress (WJC), visited Budapest from 15–19 January 1978. Before his departure, he paid a visit to the State Office for Church Affairs, accompanied by Armand Kaplan, Head of the International Department of the WJC; Imre Héber, Chairman of the National Representation of Hungarian Israelites; and Mr Dr Géza Seifert, General Secretary of the NRHI.

During the conversation, Philip Klutznyck posed two issues:

1./ The possibility of the participation of Hungarian Jewry with full rights in the work of the World Jewish Congress, where at present the denomination takes part merely as an observer.

2./ The support to be offered by the JOINT to the Hungarian Jewish denomination.

He mentioned that he had also consulted with the U.S. ambassador in Budapest, who had encouraged him to raise these issues during the discussion with the chairman of the State Office for Church Affairs. (According to our information, he had been prepared preliminarily to speak of the possibility of the granting of most-favoured nation status, but he and Ambassador Kaiser had agreed that he would not speak of this issue.)

– Concerning the first issue, he pointed out that the conditions were ripe for the Hungarian Jewish denomination to participate as a full member in the work of the WJC. While observer status enables them to be present at the meetings and to make their voice heard, they cannot take part in adopting concrete resolutions. He referred to the fact that, among the Socialist countries, both Romania and Yugoslavia were participating as full members in the work of the world organisation. In his view, the WJC evaluates the situation of Jewry in an objective and realistic fashion and does not undertake any activities that would offend the Socialist countries.

- Concerning aid provided by the JOINT, he stated that in his opinion an unjust situation had arisen. For instance, Jewry in Romania are receiving an annual sum of 3.5 million dollars, even though the number of Jews there is significantly smaller than the number living in Hungary, who receive only around a fifth of the above sum. While the division of aid does not fall under the competence of the WJC, on his return to the United States he will use his influence to ensure that Hungarian Jewry receive greater support for their social institutions.

I made known our position as follows: I am pleased about the meeting with the new president of the WJC, because in this way I have an opportunity to explain in person what I earlier told Nahum Goldmann and other leaders of the WJC. I consider it natural that he consulted with the ambassador of the United States of America. And I consider it understandable that he also sought out a representative of the Hungarian government.

- Concerning the participation of the Hungarian Jewish Denomination in the work of the World Jewish Congress, the leadership of the denomination has the authority to take a position. It depends primarily on them; do they want to change their status or not. Of course, the National Representation of Hungarian Israelites, like any other denomination, cannot keep itself removed from politics, and just as he too consulted with the U.S. ambassador in Budapest on the issue, so the leaders of the denomination also ask us about our opinion.
- To Nahum Goldmann too, I stated that it depended primarily on the WJC and its leaders as to how the leadership of the Hungarian denomination would decide on the issue of further participation in the work of the WJC. If the favourable trends continue, which contributed to the Hungarian Jewish Denomination participating as an observer in the recent congress of the WJC, then clearly additional options will also be examined. If, however, there is a strengthening of the anti-Soviet and anti-Communist wing, this will exclude the possibility of further participation. For us and for the Jewish denomination, the relationship to the Soviet Union is also an issue of principle. The Hungarian people, including those of Jewish religion, can thank the Soviet Union for freedom and life, and so we naturally keep our distance from any organisation that undertakes anti-Soviet activity.
- Concerning aid provided by the JOINT, I pointed out that it is up to the leadership of the JOINT to decide whether or not to support the Hungarian denomination. We shall not beg for such aid, and we will not allow the provision of aid to the denomination to be tied to any political or economic conditions. There is a need

for the JOINT to elaborate its proposal, which we are ready to examine. The Hungarian state has done its utmost to mitigate the burdens faced by Jewish people left on their own and to assist in resolving their problems. In the future too, we will support the denomination in line with our capacities. This will make it possible for members of the denomination to reach the standard of living available to other citizens in our country.

Philip Klutznyck sought to provide an apology for the activities of the WJC. He referred to the fact that an anti-Soviet stance and anti-Communism were not characteristic of the whole of the WJC, but only of the opinions and positions of certain participating individuals. He is decisively against all such manifestations, but we have to understand that not everyone can be prevented from expressing an opinion. Their resolutions were, so to say, never anti-Soviet; rather, they merely called on the Socialist countries to be in harmony with their own principles. He agreed with the points made by the Hungarian denomination in connection with the aid to be provided by the JOINT. He promised to make use of what had been said at the February meeting of the Executive Committee of the JOINT.

He also mentioned how he had made some very good experiences and received very good impressions in Hungary, and that he was particularly pleased to have had the opportunity to exchange opinions on these issues.

In the concluding part of our conversation, I emphasised our openness to every religious world organisation and that our relations with several major religious world organisations had improved in the past year. It was up to the WJC as to whether the obstacles to the Jewish denomination participating in future in the work of the World Congress – perhaps in another status – could be averted.

The meeting, which lasted an hour and a half, was conducted in an open and constructive spirit throughout.

(Imre Miklós)

10 Negotiations Held with the Leaders of the World Jewish Congress

28 November 1986

National Archives of Hungary, XIX-A-21-d (146.d.)
Collection: State Office for Religious Affairs [Állami Egyházügyi Hivatal, ÁEH]

Completed in 2 copies

Copy no. 1: Czechoslovak State Office for Church Affairs – Hungarian Embassy in Prague
Copy no. 2: State Office for Church Affairs

Ministry of Foreign Affairs has no purview.
Dr István Szatmári

Memorandum

on negotiations held with the leaders of the World Jewish Congress

In the summer of this year, the leaders of the World Jewish Congress (WJC) turned to the Board of the National Representation of Hungarian Israelites (NRHI) and to our Office with the request that the WJC be permitted to hold one of its meetings in 1987 in our country, in Budapest.

In preliminary discussions we made known to the representatives of the WJC that it is theoretically possible for a meeting to be held in our country in 1987, but before final approval is given, we must receive an appropriate guarantee that the interests of the Soviet Union and the Socialist countries will not be damaged at their meeting. They must take into consideration that our country is a member of an alliance, of the system of the Socialist countries; we do not have diplomatic relations with Israel and the interests of the Jewish denominations of the European Socialist countries include primarily peace, the issues of European security and co-operation, as well as the fight against all forms of antisemitism and neo-Fascism.

After the negotiations, a circular letter from Theo Klein, the French chairman of the EJC [European Jewish Congress], appeared, in which the matter of Jewry in the Soviet Union and enhanced assistance for the State of Israel featured as the central topics of next year's meeting.

A delegation of the Board of the NRHI took part in a meeting of the EJC in Paris in November 1986 and firmly protested against the programme suggested by Theo Klein. They stated that if they wanted to discuss such issues at next year's meeting, then there was no way Budapest could be the venue.

Of particularly useful help to the NRHI delegation was a letter sent to Theo Klein by Bohumil Heller, Chairman of the Council of Jewish Religious Communities of the ČSSR, in which Heller specifically and firmly protested against the ridiculous programme. The Board of the NRHI agrees in full with the contents of Chairman Bohumil Heller's letter and expressed this in the talks held with the WJC leaders.

Also in attendance at the EJC meeting in Paris was Dr Israel Singer, the Secretary-General of the WJC. Referring to the lack of agreement, they arranged for Theo Klein to officially withdraw the ominous circular letter, and they gave a pledge to elaborate a new programme that would give the fullest consideration to the interests of Jewry in the Socialist countries.

On 12 November, Comrade Imre Miklós held talks in Budapest with Dr Israel Singer, the secretary-general, who confirmed that the requested guarantees would be upheld by the WJC and that, together with President Edgar Bronfman, they undertook to ensure that the Budapest meeting will feature only such topics that do not violate the interests of the Soviet Union and the European Socialist countries. They also undertook that when elaborating the topics, they will consult with the Board of the NRHI, present in advance the lectures to be given, and will also ask for our opinion on persons coming as "observers" [to the conference].

Our experiences to date suggest that the WJC leaders consider it an important issue to represent their world-organisation status and the international nature of the Congress by holding a meeting in a Socialist country. To this end, they are willing to make compromises that are favourable to us. In view of the circumstances and the guarantees received, we have made a proposal concerning authorisation for the holding of the planned meeting in Budapest.

If the meeting is indeed held in Budapest, it is desirable that Czechoslovakian and Hungarian Jewry take part in it while continuing to co-operate well.

11 On the Suggestion to Hold in Budapest the 1987 Annual Assembly of EJC

November 1986

National Archives of Hungary, XIX-A-21-d (146.d.)
Collection: State Office for Religious Affairs [Állami Egyházügyi Hivatal, ÁEH]

From: Ministry of Interior

Report

The senior management of the World Jewish Congress (WJC) has taken steps to approach the board of the National Representation of Hungarian Israelites (NRHI) and the State Office for Church Affairs with a view to the holding in Budapest of the 1987 annual assembly of the European Jewish Congress (EJC).

In doing so, they are seeking to realise their endeavour going back several years. To this end, at the EJC held in Geneva in 1986, Dr Israel Singer, the Secretary-General of the EJC, asked Dr András Losonci, the Chairman of the NRHI, to pass on their suggestion to the Hungarian state organs.

The State Office for Church Affairs gave its preliminary consent to the commencement of talks, and it requested assurances from the management of the WJC that they would not give space for anti-Soviet, anti-Socialist and Zionist propaganda at the planned event in Budapest.

There was no common position in the management of the WJC on the subject of assurances. At the talks held with the board of the NRHI, they sought to portray the holding of the EJC event in Budapest as something that would be primarily in the interest of the NRHI and the Hungarian government, meaning that the EJC is not obliged to give assurances.

Over the past half-year, there have been significant personnel changes at the EJC; Theo Klein, the French Jewish leader known for his Zionist attitudes, became the chairman of the EJC.

In his inaugural circular letter, he spoke out "in defence of the human rights of Soviet Jewry" and for a broadening of relations with the State of Israel. An essential point in Klein's letter is that he announces the WJC as a political movement with a different line from the previous one, in the tone of which the extreme Zionist style reappeared for the first time in many years.

In the situation described above, at the plenary meeting of the EJC held in Paris in November 1986, the delegation of the NRHI called on the WJC management to return to the principles of Nahum Goldmann and to clarify the problems raised. In his response, Dr Israel Singer assured the NRHI delegation of his full agreement, with regard to both the Klein letter and the need for guarantees. Various different explanations were heard of how the cited letter had come into being, but irrespective of such explanations, there was full agreement concerning its damaging and erroneous nature. Theo Klein himself apologised for the ideas found in the letter, which could be misunderstood.

Dr Israel Singer held discussions with the leaders of the NRHI in Budapest on 10–12 November. In the course of the talks, he stated that the board of the WJC is currently planning, in order to raise the prestige of the annual general assembly of the EJC, for the office of chairman to be occupied by Edgar Bronfman, the chairman of the WJC. The narrow circle of invitees would be determined in consultation with the Hungarian side. The selection of the participants in this manner would represent, according to Singer, the guarantee demanded by the Hungarian government for filtering out extremist elements. At the same time, such an event would provide an opportunity for the important economic experts and the persons with capital-investment potential who are active in the management bodies of the World Jewish Congress to travel to Hungary, which might also promote a strengthening of economic relations.

As an additional argument, Dr Singer set out the prospect of the Joint contributing, with the provision of a substantial sum, to the renovation of the dilapidated religious buildings and historical monuments of the NRHI. A guarantee for this is the current chairman of the WJC – Bronfman – who is one of the main sponsors of the aid organisation.

According to the assessment of the NRHI, the WJC continues to have a significant political interest in the holding in Budapest of the EJC event. To this end, they utilise, as an argument, political and economic blackmail, doing so in unbridled fashion. The realisation of such an idea, even leaving aside the statements made and the closing documents, would be a great political and moral achievement for the WJC. They regard as a step forward a further improvement of relations with the state bodies, with a view to achieving recognition of the State of Israel.

Recipients:
    1./ Comrade István Horváth
    2./ Comrade János Berecz
    3./ Comrade Judit Csehák
    4./ Comrade Ernő Lakatos
    5./ <u>Comrade Imre Miklós</u>

12 Comments of the Secretary-General of the WJC

17 February 1987

National Archives of Hungary, XIX-A-21-d (151.d.)
Collection: State Office for Religious Affairs [Állami Egyházügyi Hivatal, ÁEH]

From: MINISTRY OF FOREIGN AFFAIRS

Recipients: Comrade Ernő Lakatos
Comrade Imre Miklós

Comments of the Secretary-General of the World Jewish Congress

Israel Singer, the Secretary-General of the World Jewish Congress, and Elen [sic! – AK] Steinberg, the Executive Director of the organisation, said the following to our consul general to New York who was paying them an inaugural visit:

The meeting in Budapest in May of the leadership of the World Jewish Congress will positively impact on the image of Hungary in America and internationally. The effect will be favourable in an East-West sense too, because it will dispel the prejudice of many participants that in Socialism there can only be religious repression.

They appreciate the flexibility of the Hungarian political leadership. They will not cause any unpleasantness for the hosts. In the field of information and propaganda, they will only do what we wish them to. If we want, they will keep completely quiet about the event, but if we want them to present Hungary's results, its open policy to both East and West, and everything that the opportunity to hold the meeting in Budapest symbolises – that, too, will be possible:
- They will arrange for a reporter from the New York Times and a TV crew to accompany them, who will report in a guaranteed positive tone.
- There could be a joint propaganda campaign too. For instance, prior to the meeting we could hold a joint press conference in Budapest or New York (with the participation of our consul general).
- If we give our consent, they will also invite Elie Wiesel, the Nobel Prize-winning writer, with Wiesel's Hungarian ancestry providing a good reason to do so. In case of our agreement, he would give a talk in a lecture or theatre hall. He would speak only about the Nazi years, emphasise the importance of peace and avoid any unpleasant reference for us.

They do not regard as a significant problem the minor antisemitic incidents that have occurred in Hungary in recent times (e.g. a football match) [*antisemitic slurs at a football match on 29 November 1986* – AK]. They know and appreciate the Hungarian government's position. They do observe, however, how some people – partly in Jewish circles and partly in right-wing and presumably opposition Hungarian émigré circles – are not pleased about the "rapprochement between Jews and Hungary" and magnify such incidents.

For this reason they hope that Bronfman, the WJC president, will meet with Comrade Kádár. For them it would be a help and a referential point if a half-sentence reference would be made to how "in our country, too, there have been one or two minor problems, which occur everywhere, but we will resolve them".

It would be satisfactory if this were to be said by Comrade Miklós too.

Concerning the position of Waldheim, the Austrian president, they stated that according to a copy of the minutes of the UN War Crimes Commission, dated 19 February 1948, Yugoslavia accused Waldheim of murder and the killing of hostages. New documents prove that Waldheim also committed war crimes on the territory of Hungary, near the Yugoslav border. In the near future, they will hand over the documentation to the Hungarian government.

Bronfman and Singer will travel next week to the Soviet Union with an important message from the Israeli government that "will be a significant advance on an earlier letter from Peres to Gorbachev. They are counting on Comrade Gorbachev receiving Bronfman too.

In approx. two weeks' time, Singer will host our consul general at a lunch.

13 The Meeting in Budapest of the Executive Committee of the WJC

15 April 1987

National Archives of Hungary, XIX-A-21-d (151.d.)
Collection: State Office for Religious Affairs [Állami Egyházügyi Hivatal, ÁEH]

From: MINISTRY OF FOREIGN AFFAIRS
7th Regional Department
Dr Vilmos Kopányi

Memorandum

Subject: the meeting in Budapest of the Executive Committee of the World Jewish Congress

At the request of the Syrian ambassador, together with Comrade Zoltán Pereszlényi, we received the five members of the Council of Arab Ambassadors accredited to Budapest: Syrian Ambassador Masharika, Iraqi Ambassador Al-Rawi, Algerian Ambassador Boutaieb, as well as Ghadban, the temporary chargé d'affaires of the Libyan People's Bureau, and Dweik, the deputy head of the PLO's representation in Budapest.

The Syrian ambassador emphasised that they had asked for the visit as the representatives of Arab states with friendly relations with the People's Republic of Hungary. Several months ago they had read in the Western-European press that the Executive Committee of the World Jewish Congress was to hold its next meeting in Budapest. They had sought to check the validity of the report in the Hungarian press, but they had found no trace of it there. They thought that the publication of such a report in the Western-European press was designed to undermine Hungarian–Arab friendly relations. They had grown accustomed to this on the part of the Western-European press, and so initially they had not attributed significance to the matter.

Thereafter they had received various answers to their questions from Hungarian figures. Some knew nothing about it, while others had responded that the WJC's Executive Committee meeting would be held in Budapest, but that it would not address political issues. According to others, the People's Republic of Hungary had an interest in developing tourism, and so it was willing to serve as a venue for the events of various international organisations. The answers received had not been satisfactory for them.

The aim of their visit to the Ministry of Foreign Affairs was, in addition to fostering Hungarian–Arab friendly relations, to voice their disquiet at the holding in Budapest of the meeting of the WJC's Executive Committee and to receive information from the Hungarian side.

The Syrian ambassador submitted, on behalf of the Council of Arab Ambassadors, a note (attached), in which they express "their profound concern and disappointment" that the People's Republic of Hungary "has shown itself willing to hold the meeting of the WJC's Executive Committee". According to the note, the basis of the WJC's operation is "interference in the domestic affairs of other states, in places where people of Jewish religion are living, and to undertake activities against the Socialist community". The Arab states are afraid that "the WJC will understand this step by Hungary as a kind of expression of support".

In my response, I made known our opinion on the meeting in Budapest of the WJC, which Comrade Pereszlényi then expanded. The main elements of the stated points are:

- the Budapest meeting is to be examined, not in the Arab–Israeli context
- nor in the regional aspects of the foreign policy of the People's Republic of Hungary
- but within the relationship between the Hungarian state and the churches.
- We understand and respect their reservations concerning the WJC. They too should understand that they should also respect our approach.
- The balanced and internationally recognised relationship between state and Church is a significant achievement of our social development. We cannot discriminate among the recognised churches in Hungary. The NRHI is a regular member of the WJC, in which it seeks to strengthen the positive trends, which, however, also serve the interests of the Arab countries. The holding of the WJC meeting in Budapest will promote this anticipated role.
- We handle Hungarian–Israeli relations in separation from this. Our theoretical position has not changed since 1967. It did not even change when certain Arab countries established diplomatic or other relations with Israel.
- The Budapest meeting of the WJC is not an extraordinary event, it is not linked with Hungarian–Arab relations, and we have no greater interest in holding it than do the Arab countries themselves.
- We are striving for the uninterrupted development of our relations with the Arab countries, we would like to establish diplomatic relations with those Arab countries which have so far declined [such a move].
- We strive for balanced relations with every church in the world. We are ready in the future to give space in Budapest to other churches. At present, we are in discussions with the Islamic world organisation about the establishment of an Islamic centre in Budapest. (This announcement – and the letter about it in the Arab language – met with great interest on the part of the Arab ambassadors in attendance.)

In the course of the conversation that ensued, the Syrian and Iraqi ambassadors and the PLO representative emphasised the secular political nature of the WJC. They referred to the earlier activities and resolutions of the organisation, concerning which they submitted an information brochure, identifying the WJC with the World Zionist Organization. (For our part, we pointed out that the WJC is not the same as that organisation!)

The Arab heads of mission confirmed once again that they attribute great significance to the matter of the holding in Budapest of the meeting of the WJC's Executive Committee, and, for this reason, they wished to meet with our Minister of Foreign Affairs. They expressed their hope that their position would be made known to him. In the view of the PLO's representative, one cannot evaluate on the same basis the WJC holding its meeting in Vienna or in Budapest. This explains why news of the meeting being held in Budapest gave rise to particular attention in those Arab states enjoying friendly relations with the People's Republic of Hungary.

During the conversation we pointed out the role played by the NRHI, as well as the pledge made by WJC leaders that opinions would not be voiced infringing on the foreign-policy principles of the People's Republic of Hungary, nurtures the hope that the holding of the meeting of the WJC's Executive Committee in a Socialist country might strengthen positive trends within the organisation and this could indirectly serve the cause of the Arab countries. In this connection the Iraqi ambassador inquired what the Hungarian side would do if the WJC leaders failed to keep their promise.

The Syrian ambassador expressed thanks for the information received and, on behalf of his associates, he promised to forward it. He expressed hope that our information would be convincing for their governments. He added that they would continue to monitor the matter of the meeting in Budapest of the WJC and that they wish for it to end with good results.

The conversation, which lasted for about 100 minutes with the Arabic interpretation, became more and more relaxed, and while the heads of the Arab missions did not revoke their opinion, one could feel the effect of our argument as food for thought and its favourable reception on the part of the individuals.

V **Mechanisms of Repression and the Jews**

Introduction

The documents in this next chapter reveal the means by which the Communist Party-state obtained information about the internal affairs of the Jewish religious community and, more generally, about Jewish people living in the country. The documents also show how such information was then used to realise the regime's political goals concerning Hungary's Jewish population and its Jewish institutions.

In each of the East-Central European Communist countries, the political supervision of Jews as a religious denomination was the task of the state organs for church and religious affairs. To this end, such organs made use of data from the secret services as well as information obtained during on-going consultations with religious community leaders. The manipulative and repressive policies employed by the Party-state against the Jewish denomination were no different from those pursued against other religious denominations. However, Jews were affected by additional forms of repression, inflicted on real or perceived manifestations of secular, non-religious Jewish identities and activities.

Sometimes, these activities occurred within the framework of the legal Jewish institutional system, but when Jews appeared to be transgressing the borders of these institutions, or freeing themselves from institutional control, they were soon subjected to the repressive mechanisms of the system. The perennial question of the time was where these boundaries actually lay.

As the documents in Chapter 5 demonstrate, the boundaries not only changed over time but were drawn, even within the same period, at different points by the state apparatus and the state security organs. The differences and changes reflected, on the one hand, changes in the international political context; at the same time, they were also symptomatic of policy conflicts arising within the individual Communist leaderships and/or between the various elements and levels of the each country's institutional structures.[1] It should also be noted, however, that conflicts of opinion or interest among the various sub-systems of the Party-state provided the Jewish institutions with some leeway for action, and thus they could seek out supporters or allies within the institutional system when seeking to increase their autonomy.

---

[1] Chapters 1, 3 and 4 of this volume cover conflicts in this field in Hungary between the various departments of the Ministry of Foreign Affairs, between the Ministry of Foreign Affairs and the Foreign Affairs Department of the Party, and between the economic and political leadership. For differences of view and conflicts between religious policy makers and the secret services, see Labendz, Renegotiating Czechoslovakia, 439–440; on the fractious struggle within the Polish United Workers' Party and the role of antisemitism therein, see Schatz, *The Generation*, 276, 281, 293; Dariusz Stola, Anti-Zionism as a Multipurpose Policy Instrument: The Anti-Semitic Campaign in Poland, 1967–1968. In *Anti-Semitism and Anti-Zionism in Historical Perspective*, ed. Jeffrey Herf (New York: Routledge, 2007), 159–184; and Szaynok, *Poland–Israel 1944–1968*, 398–399; on differences between the foreign and domestic affairs apparatus in Poland, see ibid, 375, 398–399.

In the post-Stalinist era, each East-Central European Communist Party-state had similar frameworks for managing the secret service organs responsible for religious and Jewish affairs. State control of churches and religious affairs was undertaken either by way of an independent quasi-ministry, as in Hungary, or via the independent units of other state organisations, as in Czechoslovakia and Poland.[2] In the case of the secret services, Jewish matters were handled by the intelligence and counter-intelligence bodies, and by departments monitoring "domestic reactionary forces". All these bodies closely co-operated with Soviet intelligence and counter-intelligence,[3] but departments responsible for specific issues or matters changed from time to time. The issues they investigated – "the struggle against religious reaction", "clandestine Zionist plotting", "hostile diversions by Israeli bodies" – appear in contexts that partly differ and partly overlap, depending on the period in which the documents were created. In all countries and throughout the period, there was a steady exchange of information between the secret services and the state organs responsible for church and religious affairs. Moreover, when they deemed it necessary, both these institutional structures would make direct contact through their own channels with the competent Party bodies and government ministries, for the purpose of forwarding information or requesting instructions.

The documents on "Jewish affairs" reveal the blurred and transient definitions of the group targeted for repressive measures: "Jews", "Jewry", and "Zionists". Evidently, the targeted group included members, dignitaries and employees of the Jewish religious denomination, and, in Poland, members of a legalised secular organization, the Social and Cultural Association of Jews in Poland. Even so, it was never clarified which individuals among the secular Jewish population or among people of Jewish ancestry were to be included in the potential target group for the state organs dealing with "Jewish affairs". This uncertainty may well have given rise to a phenomenon – the "listing" of Jews in Communist countries – that has been interpreted in so many different ways by historians.[4]

---

2 Labendz, op. cit., 499–500.
3 Such cooperation is best documented by the papers in the Stasi archives. See BStU, *MfS HA XX/4 2157*, Berichte über Beratungen mit den Sicherheitsorganen Ungarns in Berlin und Budapest, Dez. 1982, Nov. 1986, Juli 1987, Nov. 1988; BStU, *MfS HA XX/4 144*, Entwurf einer Arbeitsvereinigung zwischen der V. Verwaltung der polnischen GD und der HA XX, Apr. 1977; BStU, *MfS HA XX/4 2158*, Berichte über die Beratungen mit den Sicherheitsorganen der ČSSR, 1977–1988; BStU, *MfS HA XX/4 235*, Zusammenarbeit mit den Sicherheitsorganen der UdSSR, 1971–1972, 1974–1979. Cf. Szaynok, *Poland–Israel*, 325, 331–332. Material documenting the international relations of the Hungarian secret service has not been transferred to the archive containing documents that are available for public research (Állambiztonsági Szolgálatok Történeti Levéltára, ÁBTL – Historical Archives of the Hungarian State Security).
4 Michael Checinski, *Poland: Communism, Nationalism, Antisemitism* (New York: Karz-Cohl, 1982), 239–240; Kovács, Antisemitic Elements in Communist Discourse; Labendz, op. cit., 106, 439–446, 473–490; Szaynok, *Poland–Israel 1944–1968*, 422–423.

The sources researched to date indicate that "lists of Jews" were drawn up by the secret services in Czechoslovakia, East Germany, Hungary, and Poland. Assumptions about the existence of these lists had already arisen after the Polish antisemitic campaigns of 1967 and 1968. This suspicion was fostered primarily by the authorities' surprisingly fast and effective identification during the "anti-Zionist" campaigns of people of (often partly) Jewish ancestry in various institutions in order to later force them to emigrate. This included those who, until they received the order to emigrate, did not know that they had Jewish ancestry.[5] The documents made public since that time reveal that after the Six-Day War, the Polish secret services did indeed create a database containing the data details of persons of Jewish ancestry, and, it would seem, of people who had close contacts with them.[6] Among the papers of the East German State Security Service, the Stasi, we also find, for some years, detailed lists with the names and personal data of members of the Jewish congregations in East Germany. The first such list stems from 1953 and mentions 1,200 individuals, while the final list was drawn up in 1988 and contains the details of approximately 300 persons. An executive order issued in East Germany on 27 July 1967 (that is, around the time of the drafting of the Polish list) expressly instructed the compilation of a full list of members of the Jewish congregations in the country "in view of the situation in the Middle East". In the end, the list, which was completed by the deadline of 17 August 1967, contained almost 600 names.[7]

In Hungary, we have also found lists of names among the state security papers. Compiled in the period 1965–1977, the lists relate mainly to the teachers and pupils of the Jewish grammar school and members of certain Budapest congregations.[8] The documents created by the secret police in Czechoslovakia provide the deepest insights into the practice of drawing up "lists of Jews". The infamous "Action Spider", which aimed at creating a full list of Czechoslovak Jews, is the subject of on-going academic debate.[9] This campaign, which began in the 1950s, was temporarily halted in 1961 and recommenced in 1972, several years after the suppression of the Prague Spring. The list was still being compiled in the late 1980s. Indeed, the number of registered names in the 1988 list was close to 10,000.

A document drawn up in March 1987 frankly states the purpose of the campaign: "The decision to map and register all persons of Jewish denomination and descent was undertaken in July 1972, with the aim of learning about the distribution and concentration of these persons in the highest spheres of our society".[10]

---

5 See Checinski, op. cit., 239–240.
6 Szaynok, *Poland–Israel 1944–1968*, 422–424.
7 BStU, *MfS XX* 4 754, Jüdische Gemeinde DDR, 1953–1968, 3. 203–221.
8 Historical Archives of the Hungarian State Security 3.1.5. O-17169/5, Folder: "Zionists undertaking hostile activities" ["Ellenséges tevékenységet kifejtő cionisták"], vol. 6.
9 For a summary of the debates, see Labendz, op. cit., 439–443.
10 "Akce PAVAOUK. Informace pro 1. NMV ČSSR." Archive of the Ministry of the Interior, Prague, carton F-16S/93. Cited by Heitlinger, *In the Shadow of the Holocaust and Communism*, 34.

Opinions are divided on the function of such lists. In Czechoslovakia, it was claimed that the lists contained the potential targets of Arab terrorists residing in the country.[11] Others were of the view that the lists formed part of preparations ordered by the Soviet leadership in the aftermath of the suppression of the Prague Spring for an anti-Zionist trial similar to the earlier Slánský trial. (In post-1968 propaganda, anti-Zionist rhetoric did, indeed, become a feature of the attacks levelled at leading Communist reformers of Jewish descent such as Eduard Goldstücker, Frantisek Kriegel and Ota Šik.)[12] For Alena Heitlinger, the main goal of the programme was to intimidate ordinary Jews, as Jewish ancestry offered sufficient grounds to harass them at any point in time.[13] Jacob Ari Labendz, on the other hand, has claimed that in the post-1967 period and particularly after the suppression of the Prague Spring, the campaign was recommenced by antisemitic functionaries working for the security services. These functionaries exploited favourable political conditions to incorporate the campaign into their activities targeting the "enemies of Socialism".[14]

We cannot exclude the possibility that the "listing" of Jews was undertaken in a co-ordinated manner in the Soviet bloc countries under Soviet instruction, but nevertheless carried out differently in each country. To date, this supposition could not be proved on the basis of the archival sources, as researchers have found no such Soviet instructions or direct references thereto. Nevertheless, arguments in favour of the supposition can be made based on the documents. Indeed, we know from the documents at our disposal – some of which have already been cited – that Soviet intelligence and counter-intelligence organs were in regular contact with their counterparts in the "fraternal countries", and that "Zionist activity" was one of the fields regularly surveyed. A Stasi document compiled from Soviet sources summarising the nature of "Zionist diversion" includes the assertion that the agents and potential agents of the Israeli secret services were to be found among the Jewish population in every country.[15] This conviction may have been perceived – especially in critical political circumstances – as sufficient grounds to compile a list of "potential spies". A degree of co-ordination may also be inferred from the fact that the campaigns in the various Communist countries of East-Central Europe coincided with each other: all such campaigns took place after the 1967 war. Another sign of some kind of co-ordination might be the appearance of several random lists of Jews in Hungary during this period. The sheer size of the country's Jewish community meant that exhaustive lists

---

[11] Peter S. Green, Czechs Seek to Indict Officials Who Assembled Lists of Jews, *International Herald Tribune*, 27 November 2003.
[12] Prague Daily Warns of Mounting Anti-Semitism in Czechoslovakia, Asks Ban. *Jewish Telegraph Agency*, 10 April 1969. Accessed on 27 September 2016 at http://www.jta.org/1969/04/10/archive/prague-daily-warns-of-mounting-anti-semitism-in-czechoslovakia-asks-ban.
[13] Heitlinger, op. cit., 35.
[14] Labendz, op. cit., 473–490.
[15] BStU, *MfS HA II Nr. 24003*, February 25, 1985. Informationen über Erkenntnisse zur Arbeitsweise des israelischen Geheimdienstes gegen die UdSSR und die soz. Staatengemeinschaft, S. 5–12.

could never be completed. It may be that on realising the impossibility of the task, the Hungarian authorities decided to draw up the lists as a kind of alibi, and merely with a view to meeting Soviet expectations in a formal sense.

The appendix to Chapter 5 includes a document created in the course of Action Spider,[16] and which provides an unambiguous answer as to whom Communist officials regarded as Jews when discussing Jewish matters. The document states the following:

> To ensure consistency when registering people of Jewish origin, it is necessary to introduce these terms:
> — a person of Jewish faith: a person who is active in the JRC (or a Synagogue Congregation) and features on the list of its members or a person who, although not participating in the activities of the JRC (or a Synagogue Congregation), is registered on the list of members.
> — a person of Jewish origin: a person who does not profess Jewish faith and does not feature on the register of the JRC (or a Synagogue Congregation) but who has at least one parent who is/was of Jewish faith or who, before 1948, declared Jewish nationality or was a member of the Zionist organisation Hashomer Hacair, which worked legally in the ČSSR until 1948, or of any other Zionist or Jewish organisation [...].

As is clear from the text, the political police employed, for operational aims, what is clearly a Nuremberg-style racial definition of Jews. This shows that in certain situations (e.g. when the Communist leadership felt that "Jewish affairs" necessitated institutional intervention), the racist foundations of their image of the Jew surfaced. In public and within the broader Communist Party context, discourses concerning Jewish affairs took place in mostly codified form, so that the word "Jew" rarely appeared. In this way, discourses conformed to the norms of official ideology. Within the narrower Party context, however, they did not automatically retain the use of codified language, and it is here that we see the overt use of a racial definition of Jews and traditional anti-Jewish stereotypes.[17] Ultimately, at the level where, due to institutional pressures, the meaning of the word 'Jewish' had to be operationalised, racist speech appeared openly.

The Party and state bodies – and the secret services that worked in co-operation with them – wanted first and foremost to bring Jewish denominational institutions and other associated bodies under their control. The primary means of control was the system of the Party-state nomenklatura, which functioned in each of the Communist countries and which, in Hungary, was regulated with respect to the Jewish denomination by Law-Decree No. 22 of 1957. Under the provisions of this legislation, the prior consent of the Presidential Council of the People's Republic of Hungary was required when appointing (or dismissing) the Chairman, Deputy Chairman and General Secretary of the National Representation of Hungarian Israelites, the Presi-

---

[16] See attachment to Chapter 5.
[17] See Kovács, Antisemitic Elements in Communist Discourse.

dent and Vice-President of the Budapest Israelite Congregation, and the Chairmen of the Neolog and Orthodox rabbinical councils. Furthermore, the consent of the head of the State Office for Church Affairs was required when appointing (or dismissing) the director of the Rabbinical Seminary, and the principal of the Jewish Grammar School.

Religious denominations in Hungary were financially dependent on the state. Indeed, state funding accounted for almost their entire budgets, and thus the state had further opportunities to control and interfere. In Hungary, the annual sum granted to the Jewish denomination was regulated by an agreement signed in 1948, which stated that the amount of funding would be reduced by 25 per cent every five years for the next two decades, and that funding would cease completely from 1968.[18] This agreement, which resembled agreements signed with the major churches in Hungary, was unsustainable, given the absence of other sources of income. For this reason, in 1957, the Party leadership agreed to implement the reduction in state funding foreseen in the earlier agreement in such a way that the reductions would be offset by equivalent amounts of "extraordinary state aid" for the denominations. However, the "political justification" for this latter type of funding was to be reviewed annually. This new framework remained in force during the subsequent period. In effect, it made the religious denominations even more dependent on the whims of the Communist state.[19] Nevertheless, even the control exercised by state authorities via legal provisions manipulating leadership elections and governing the use of state funding was no guarantee that these authorities would be able to influence everyday events to the extent desired by the Party-state leadership.

In the post-Stalinist era, the regime sought to maintain the impression of legality. So, for instance, it was reluctant to make use of its right of appointment under the nomenklatura system, doing so only when all else failed. Instead, the organs of the Party-state were inclined to maintain democratic appearances, and to assist individuals loyal to (and dependent upon) the state in achieving leading positions by means of manipulating religious denominations' election processes.[20] Additionally, in order to ensure a constant presence in the everyday workings of these denominations, the state authorities made efforts to place reliable cadres even in posts where interventions could not be made legally under the nomenklatura system. In addition to the manipulation of elections, and the prevention or management of conflicts regarded as indicative of political "deviations" or as otherwise politically or ideologically sensitive, the main aim of such surveillance and interference was to prevent the development of groups that might gain some form of autonomy. In each country, the secret services and religious affairs organs paid particular attention to younger age groups, to youth groups operating (often informally) within the denomination, to individuals inside or outside the denomination who were in contact with the Israeli Embassy and

---

18 Hungarian Jewish Archives, XXXIII-5-a-19, 7 December 1948.
19 National Archives of Hungary, XIX-A-21-d 6.d. 0047/1959 (16 October 1959).
20 On this practice, see Documents 1 and 10; Labendz, op. cit., 397, 504–505; Heitlinger, op. cit., 36.

Israeli institutions, and to individuals and groups who sought regular contact with Jewish émigrés.[21]

The authorities called such groups and the individuals who comprised them "Zionists", thereby legitimising, in the context of official ideology, their control and harassment by the state. Attention was focused on "foreign agents of Zionist subversion": foreign institutions who might provide financial or other support to small groups and personal networks wishing to escape state control as much as possible. Such institutions were foreign Jewish organisations, Israeli diplomatic representations and their members, and Jewish personalities who came to the country seeking contact with domestic Jewry.[22] Information was gathered mainly by the secret services, while the combatting of "Zionism" – that is, dealing with Jewish affairs – was the task of both counter-intelligence and the domestic security organs. Most of the information collected and evaluated by the secret services was placed at the disposal of the religious affairs organs, and decisions on the required measures and on the bodies responsible for their implementation were then taken in line with these organs. The senior Party leadership would also be informed directly about matters considered particularly important. The documents published below from the Hungarian archives give detailed insights into how such mechanisms worked.

Some of the documents below were created by the State Office for Church Affairs but the majority stem from the various departments of the domestic secret services. The Hungarian state security organs regularly compiled an annual report on Jewish issues. Examining them, we find that the organs did not deal systematically with Jewish issues between the 1956 Revolution and 1961.[23] The need to reorganise the apparatus tasked with fighting "Zionism" and hostile elements in the Jewish community and the network of secret informers within Jewish institutions, appeared for the first time in a report of September 1961.[24]

In August 1962, the Hungarian secret services were restructured. Out of the Department for Political Investigations (Department No. II), which had elaborated the above-mentioned working plan to "fight Zionism", was formed a new top secret services organisation, the Interior Ministry's State Security Directorate No. III, which comprised five departments (III/I – intelligence; III/II – counterintelligence; III/III – counter domestic reaction; III/IV – military intelligence; III/5 – operational technol-

---

21 See Heitlinger, op. cit., 105–125; Labendz, op. cit., 430; Szaynok, *Poland–Israel 1944–1968*, 377, 380–381.
22 Szaynok, *Poland–Israel 1944–1968*, 325–330, 381–383.
23 According to the report, surveillance of "Zionism" was suspended after 1956, but reintroduced in December 1961 on the basis of a working plan drafted by the II/2 and II/3 departments. As the report states, the work had to be started anew, as much of the prior operative material had been destroyed in 1956. (This statement contradicts the fact that quite a few pre-1956 folders on "Zionist issues" are to be found among the folders stored in the ÁBTL). On the reintroduction of regular surveillance, 127 former Zionists were found to feature in the operative records (see Document 4, 12 April 1962).
24 See Document 3 (4 September 1961).

ogy). Until 1974, counterintelligence, which included "Zionist issues", was handled by Department III/II, whereby operational work was considered to be one aspect of counter-espionage (see Document 16). After 1974 however, it was rather the organs dealing with "domestic reaction" which dealt with "Zionist issues" and other "domestic enemies", particularly Department III/III-1, which specialised in church and religious issues; Department III/III-2 which targeted hostile elements among young people; Department III/III-3 which organised the control of people placed under observation; and Department III/III-4 which targeted hostile persons working in culture.[25] Consequently, most of the post-1974 documents were created by these departments, which did not work in strict separation. Rather, they co-operated on a mutual basis, sharing both information and informers.

At the time of the "reopening" of the "Jewish line", five years after the 1956 Revolution, no Zionist organisation had been operating in Hungary for long time. The vast majority of former Zionists had either left the country or renounced their former views. Not surprisingly, those at the political police responsible for the issue thought that the time was ripe to redefine groups to be targeted by units dealing with "Zionist affairs", and to determine why the surveillance and harassment of "Zionists undertaking hostile activities" should extend to the Jewish denomination and individuals with rather loose connections to it. This is addressed in Document 4, dated 3 April 1962. What was asserted at that time went on to determine, for the following decades, the work of the secret service units dealing with domestic Jewish affairs:

> It has become clear to the Zionists that they cannot appear openly, and that their practical methods applied in the past are not applicable under the present conditions. For this reason, they have started spreading the nationalist and Zionist propaganda by legal means and utilising, for this purpose, the religious institutions and religious education. They do not undertake overt Zionist propaganda, but through the teachings of the Talmud and the Torah they seek to keep alive "spiritual cohesion" in the Zionist sense, while also encouraging a "love of the Holy Land".

In the language of this document – and in that of Document 3 created a few months later – we find the Communist-era stereotypes that only surfaced in the wider public domain during major antisemitic campaigns: the anti-national cosmopolitanism of Jews; their occupation of elite positions in society; Jewish oversensitivity; and clannish Jewish cohesion and solidarity supported by international conspiratorial networks. It would seem that similar organs in the "fraternal countries" used the same language, a good example of which is provided in a document created by the Czechoslovak secret service, according to which the solidarity of persons of a pro-Zionist orientation in Czechoslovakia:

---

25 A Belügyminisztérium III/III. Csoportfőnökség ügyrendje [Standing Orders of the Ministry of Interior III/III Head of Department]. Accessed on 3 October 2016 at http://www.abtl.hu/sites/default/files/forrasok/ugyrend_3.pdf.

[I]s founded on the basis of common ethnic ancestry and religion [...]. [They] are bearers of the ideology of bourgeois nationalism. These persons come largely from the ranks of former bourgeoisie and intellectuals. They have a bond of cosmopolitan solidarity, their relation to the Czech and Slovak nation is rather tepid, and they are completely indifferent to the development of our society. It has been noted that these persons are mutually promoting each other at the expense of other intellectuals, and that they are trying to gain positions in the most important spheres of our society with the goal of influencing public opinion.[26]

The shared attitudes and language which formed the basis of co-operation between the "fraternal" secret services is manifest in several of the documents. Such co-operation meant not only the exchange of information, but also participation in joint actions, including the transfer of agents, as in the case of Jewish immigrants from the Soviet Union[27] (see Documents 13 and 16).

Several documents provide insights into the secret services' activities, modus operandi and targets (groups and individuals), as well as their relations with various other institutions. It is the secret services' annual reports, however, that enable us to reconstruct how these organisations operated in the field of "Jewish affairs" (see Documents 14 and 16). We learn that information was gathered partly by technical means such as bugging,[28] with such methods proving increasingly effective. For instance, the entire conversation (in Yiddish) between a group of Soviet Jewish leaders and WJC leaders during the Budapest conference was secretly recorded. The tape recording was then attached to a document summarising the contents of the conversation (see Document 16).

Informers within religious institutions and various Jewish groups (including secret informers, agents and social contacts) represented a further resource for gathering information and manipulating events. Between 1961 and 1978, there were between four and 11 such informers in Hungary.[29] The secret service heads considered this to be insufficient (see Documents 4 and 14), despite the fact that the informers included senior religious officials and rabbis. As Documents 7 and 8 demonstrate, from the secret service's perspective, a spectacular failure of its network of informers occurred in 1965, when an instruction was given for a specific political action

---

26 "Akce PAVAOUK", 34.
27 See footnote 3.
28 The meanings of code-words used in the documents to signify various technical means of surveillance are as follows: K-check = mail checks, 3/a measure = telephone bugging, 3/e measure = room bugging. K-apartment, T-apartment: apartments used by the secret service for conspiratorial purposes.
29 In the secret service documents, *secret informers* were those individuals who cooperated with the secret service out of conviction, while the *secret agents* were those who had been blackmailed to cooperate by the secret services who possessed some kind of incriminating or compromising information about them; and/or who had received certain benefits, such as a passport, payments, hard currency, or promotion at work. *Social contacts* were those individuals who provided information on an irregular basis, and without formalizing their cooperation in a signed agreement.

but subsequent events unfolded differently. In this specific case, and with a view to ultimately reducing the influence of the Israeli Embassy in Budapest over Hungary's Jewish community, the secret service sought in vain for its informers within various Jewish institutions to take the stance that Hungary's Jews opposed the establishment of diplomatic relations between Israel and West Germany, on the pretext that such a move would be a betrayal of the Jewish issue.

Information relating to "Jewish affairs" was placed in various types of files and folders. Most of the documents published here originate from a six-volume "object file" entitled "Zionists undertaking hostile activities", but the secret services also maintained so-called group and personal files on related matters under various cover names.[30] The tasks of counter-intelligence organs targeting "internal enemies" and dealing with "Jewish affairs" were summarised most succinctly in a memorandum on activities between 1974 and 1978, and which also contained a retrospect of earlier years (see Document 16). Here we read that the main task "was to acquire, on a continuous basis, information of operational value and of assistance to [the formulation of] religious policy on domestic and foreign hostile endeavours, objectives and methods. We then have to draft appropriate information material on these for the leadership and, if necessary, for the state security bodies of friendly countries, etc."

A secondary task was summarised as follows: "We had to organise the investigation and control of the Jewish national groupings that had come into being and of the persons involved in such activities, thereafter taking proper measures to disrupt such groups and suppress and terminate their detrimental activities".

Between 1956 and 1988, Party-state documents on Jewish issues estimated that there were 75–100,000 Jews living in Hungary, around 65,000 of whom lived in Budapest. According to data contained in the documents, 20,000 Jews paid "church tax" in 1962, which evidently referred to the number of people who paid the annual voluntary denominational donation. In the early 1960s, it was reported that there were in total 30 active rabbis in Hungary, with 18 Jewish congregational districts in Budapest, and four congregational districts in other parts of the country. A document dating from 1975 mentions 76 Jewish congregations, 105 functioning synagogues, and 26 rabbis.[31] In the 1960s, the Jewish denomination was reported to have 500–600 employees. Although this number was falling, the state's religious affairs authorities

---

[30] In the object folders, information was gathered on certain institutions or subject matters (in this case, Jewry in general). In the group folders, information was gathered on groups of individuals under surveillance, and the personal folders contained information gathered on individuals under surveillance. The "work folders" contained the informers' written reports. The folder with the codename "Ellenséges tevékenységet kifejtő cionisták" ["Zionists Undertaking Hostile Activities"] comprises six volumes and contains a total of more than 2,000 pages of documents. In the documents published here, mention is made of the group folders codenamed "Együttműködők" [Co-operators], "Túristák" [Tourists] (Document 6) and "Salom" [Shalom] (Document 11), as well as the personal folders with the codenames "Direktor" [Director] and "Milliomos" [Millionaire].
[31] National Archives of Hungary, XIX-A-21-d 84.d. 0020-1/1975 (21 June 1975).

applied pressure to bring about a more rapid decline. In addition to providing the institutional background for religious activities, the denomination also maintained a substantial network of social institutions, with assistance being offered to several thousand individuals (10,000 in 1961). It also ran a nursing home and a hospital, as well as the Anne Frank Grammar School and the Budapest Rabbinical Seminary. In this period, the Jewish weekly newspaper *Új Élet* [*New Life*] had a print run of 6–7,000 (see Documents 2, 4 and 9).

While such data may not have been entirely accurate, the figures clearly show that in the field of "Jewish affairs", the organs of the Party-state in Hungary, including the secret police, were required to employ methods that differed substantially from those used by similar bodies in Czechoslovakia and Poland, whose Jewish communities were so much smaller. As mentioned above, the numbers in Hungary precluded, for instance, the drawing up of exhaustive lists of Jewish individuals, even if there had been a Soviet directive to this effect. In line with Party directives, the secret services, when reinstituting the systematic surveillance of Jewish organisations, groups and individuals, designated areas that required on-going monitoring (see Documents 3 and 4). Targets included groups attending religious classes at the synagogue (mostly children of school age and their parents), Jewish educational institutions (the grammar school and the Rabbinical Seminary headed by Sándor Scheiber), the Central Social Committee (headed by Mihály Borsa, and which distributed most of the social assistance), and the Israeli Embassy in Budapest (with its array of contacts among the local Jewish population).

These institutions and their staff were not the only subjects of surveillance, for the monitoring also extended, on occasion, to individuals with rather tenuous links to Jewry. The logic behind the designation of targets was clear: the aim was to constantly monitor those institutions, informal networks and personalities suspected of being potentially able to extricate themselves from the tight control of the denomination, and to obtain funding from outside sources. Throughout the entire period, the logic of the disruptive and often repressive measures, as well as the identity of the targeted groups and individuals, remained essentially unchanged. A 1967 document drafted during the intensification of "anti-Zionist" efforts following the Six-Day War restates the designated aims, employing the customary rhetoric to do so:

> Zionist manifestations occur principally among young rabbis, theology students and Jewish youths, and they mainly affect those individuals who have come into close contact with the Israeli Embassy. Zionism's main base was the Israeli Embassy. [...] In recent years, the activity level of international and denominational reaction has increased. [...] Zionism is characterised by anti-Communism – hostility to the Soviet Union, subservience to international imperialism, the praising of capitalist Israel, an emphasis on Jewish superiority, and the enticement of Jews to Israel. [...] Our political work relating to the Jewish denomination is made more difficult by the circumstance that they are receiving significant amounts of Western aid. Such aid influences even the most progressive [*meaning: supporters of the Party* – AK] Jewish leaders, especially in

regard to their positions on the WJC and on Western Jewry. [*The designated goals ... – AK*] a./ The NRHI should dispose of the foreign aid sent to the denomination. Irregularities that have surfaced in the field of the organisation and distribution of foreign aid must be resolved. [...] The training of rabbis should be made more democratic in spirit. The system of rotation of deans should be introduced to rabbi training, and the teaching staff should be refreshed with the addition of several progressive rabbis.[32]

A report from 1977 summarised the targets of surveillance from the 1960s onwards as follows: "1. The role and activities of the Israeli Embassy until 1967; 2. After 1967, the National Rabbinical Seminary, private apartments and public places; 3. From 1972–73, the influence of Western Jewish organisations and the involvement of Hungarian Jewry in international work".[33]

In many ways, the goals and activities of the Hungarian secret police with respect to Jewish young people, Jewish youth groups and the Israeli Embassy resemble those of their counterparts in Czechoslovakia and Poland. In Hungary, however, there were two institutions that managed to preserve a degree of autonomy, even in the most difficult periods, largely as a consequence of the indomitability and successful tactical manoeuvring of their leaders, but also thanks to their relations with organisations abroad. It comes as no surprise that both institutions received the particular attention of religious affairs organs and the secret service throughout the period. The first such institution was the Central Social Committee, headed by Mihály Borsa, which distributed funds received from Jewish organisations abroad (principally the Joint) with little input from the denomination's leadership, a situation that severely limited the state's capacity to control and monitor. Borsa had been under surveillance since the early 1960s. His correspondence was monitored, his telephone tapped, and he had been declared a suspected spy on several occasions. On this basis, from 1966 until 1974, documents about him were stored in a file code-named "Milliomos" [Millionaire].[34]

The second institution with a degree of autonomy and independence was the Budapest Rabbinical Seminary, headed by the world-famous scholar of Judaism Sándor Scheiber. In the manner of a case study, the documents relating to Scheiber and the Rabbinical Seminary serve to provide insights into the workings of the entire regime. Concerning the Rabbinical Seminary, the aims of the state and state security organs were manifold. First of all, they strove to subordinate the Seminary to the community leadership which was ready to collaborate in every case, and without any conditions. The first step in this direction took place in August 1960 when the State

---

[32] National Archives of Hungary, XIX-A-21-d 37.d. 002-a-3/d/1967 (2 November 1967).
[33] Historical Archives of the Hungarian State Security 3.1.5. O-17169/5, Folder: "Zionists undertaking hostile activities" ["Ellenséges tevékenységet kifejtő cionisták"], vol. 6. (31 October 1977). Document 16 is a later version of this report.
[34] Historical Archives of the Hungarian State Security 3.1.5. O-13558/1, Personal folder: "Milliomos" [Millionaire], Nr.: Sz-7088, opened 27 July 1966.

Office for Church Affairs arranged new elections for the Board of the Seminary. Scheiber protested in vain against the list of candidates which had been put together by the head of the Community, who was a secret informer. A new Board was elected, two of its members functioned as secret informers and a third was known as the most reliable supporter of the Party in the Rabbinate.[35]

The following year, the secret service placed Scheiber and the students of the seminary under systematic surveillance. They bugged his office and apartment, and intercepted his mail; these measures were repeated regularly in subsequent years. The results of such surveillance and all connected materials were stored in a file under the name "Direktor", which was not available at the time of writing.[36] The authorities noted with regret that Scheiber had been elected to the Board of the World Jewish Congress, and had received the authority to distribute Claims Conference funds in Hungary (see Document 4). Scheiber neglected the bureaucratic rules for spending these funds, using them instead for both academic and social purposes. This was a recurrent subject in the reports by agent "Xavér", the director of the Jewish Museum in Budapest, a person close to Scheiber. And it was this little freedom that was exactly what the authorities wanted to hinder: uncontrolled research activities and publications under the aegis of the Seminary, interpreted as a cover for a "Zionist conspiracy". Having realised that Scheiber was not seeking to leave the country – he refused to accept a leading academic position in Britain – the authorities tried to cut him off from the broader Jewish community.[37]

In February 1964, the rabbi mentioned above as a Party line representative submitted a resolution to the Rabbinate to prohibit all non-Rabbinate members – including Scheiber – from rabbinical practice. The resolution was passed, but the Rabbinate was later unable to enforce it.[38] A report sent to the Agitation and Propaganda Department of the HSWP by the State Office for Church Affairs stressed that: "The Rabbinical

---

35 Historical Archives of the Hungarian State Security 3.1.5. M-37478; vol. 2. Work folder: "Xavér", file: Jelentés a Rabbiképző Intézőbizottságának újraválasztásáról, 1960. augusztus 12. [Report on the Re-election of the Rabbinical Board, 12 August 1960].
36 The surveillance of Scheiber and the Seminary is already mentioned in a report drafted in the immediate aftermath of the elaboration of a systematic surveillance plan (1961). See, for instance, Historical Archives of the Hungarian State Security 3.1.5. O-17169/0, Folder: "Zionists undertaking hostile activities" ["Ellenséges tevékenységet kifejtő cionisták"], vol. 1. (14 March 1962). Many subsequent reports also contain notes on the continuous surveillance and bugging, as well as the folder with the codename "Direktor". See, for instance, the following files in the above folder: 17169/4, vol. 5. (20 October 1976); 17169/5, vol. 6. (23 November 1974); 17169/5, vol. 6. (26 November 1976).
37 Historical Archives of the Hungarian State Security 3.1.5. M-37809; vol. 1. Work folder: "Sárvári György", file: Jelentés Scheiber amerikai útjáról. 1964. január 17. [Report on Scheiber's Visit to America. 17 January 1964]. According to the report, Scheiber was offered a leading position at the London Seminary, an offer he declined. The evaluating officer expressed surprise at Scheiber's decision.
38 While the vote was taken in secret, the agent reporting on the decision knew who had voted and how. The report evaluated the vote as "a victory for the loyal group that we also support." See Historical Archives of the Hungarian State Security 3.1.5. O-17169/1, Folder: "Zionists undertaking hostile

Seminary is a hotbed of Zionism, and we have recently examined its activities and have begun to implement the required political measures".³⁹

In 1968, having organised a trial of students accused of "Zionist activities" and incitement against the state,⁴⁰ and with a view to forcing Scheiber out, the Rabbinate decided to introduce a rotational system for the position of Seminary director. It also prescribed additional mandatory classes on Marxist philosophy and social science (see Document 11).⁴¹ These efforts also proved unsuccessful. Scheiber's popularity grew, and in the 1970s many young people regularly attended his Friday evening *Kiddush*, before continuing their debates and conversations in coffee-houses and apartments. Although the Friday evening lectures adhered strictly to religious themes, hundreds of pages were filled with agents' reports about the "Zionist-suspect" activities that were taking place in and around the Rabbinical Seminary. In 1977, a summary report mentioned with boastful pride how the state authorities had successfully prevented the public circulation of Scheiber's monumental work *Folklore and Material Culture*, leading him to attempt to circulate it through private channels.⁴²

Yet in the late 1970s, the reports became more resigned in tone: they recorded how the professor's "hostile activities" were continuing, how his "Zionist-nationalist views" had received strong support from foreign Jewish organisations, how his scholarly achievements in the field of Hungarian-Jewish literature were widely acknowledged and, consequently, how his international reputation was on the rise. The cited report concludes, however, that while it might have been possible to put Scheiber on trial for non-political criminal offences (for example financial irregularities), the presentation of evidence might have uncovered the informers in his circle. Moreover, in view of Scheiber's domestic and international reputation, a legal procedure might have produced a serious backlash. The final decision was to continue surveillance, to seek to intensify the conflict between Scheiber and the community leadership, and to recruit further informers from Scheiber's circle.⁴³ Indeed, in a document entitled *Proposal for operational measures related to the centenary of the Rabbinical Seminary*,

---

activities" ["Ellenséges tevékenységet kifejtő cionisták"], vol. 2. (18 February 1964), file: "Sárosi" tmb. jelentése [Report submitted by Secret Informer "Sárosi"].
39 National Archives of Hungary, XIX-A-21-d, 37.d 002-2/1967 (21 February 1967).
40 This was the so-called "realization" of the "Shalom" case, which meant that the secret investigation codenamed "Shalom" was turned into a court case. Finally, on 9 October 1968, two members of the youth group were sentenced to four months imprisonment. See Historical Archives of the Hungarian State Security 3.1.5. O-13772; vol. 1–3, Group folder: "Salom".
41 Historical Archives of the Hungarian State Security 3.1.5. O-17169/2, Folder: "Zionists undertaking hostile activities" ["Ellenséges tevékenységet kifejtő cionisták"], vol. 3. (18 May 1968).
42 Historical Archives of the Hungarian State Security 3.1.5. O-17169/5, Folder: "Zionists undertaking hostile activities" ["Ellenséges tevékenységet kifejtő cionisták"], vol. 6. (25 April 1975 and September 1975]. The memoranda reveal how the sale of the book by state-owned book distributors was prevented as it might "incite Zionist sentiments."
43 Historical Archives of the Hungarian State Security 3.1.5. O-17169/4, Folder: "Zionists Undertaking Hostile Activities" ["Ellenséges tevékenységet kifejtő cionisták"], vol. 5. (20 October 1976).

and in another document in which the officer responsible for the operation evaluates the work of the agent network, 11 secret informers and agents involved in an action are mentioned, among them the head and financial director of the community, the chief rabbi of the Dohány Street Synagogue, and some students of the Seminary.[44]

Several factors explain Borsa and Scheiber's relative success in maintaining their relative independence. The principal factors were their contacts abroad and, in Scheiber's case, an international reputation. A second factor was the ability of both men to exploit conflicts arising within the religious community and the State Office for Church Affairs and, between these two institutions. They regularly used these conflicts to win supporters for their cause. Borsa and Scheiber had a fine sense of how far they could go, and where the boundaries lay. They proved adept at striking a balance between co-operation and resistance. Borsa made effective use of his good contacts among former Smallholder Party politicians who had been co-opted into the senior Communist political hierarchy, for whom he obtained various financial advantages bordering on bribery (e.g. funding for trips abroad, importing cars free from custom tax), and to whom he often referred in the course of meetings held with denominational leaders or the functionaries of the State Office for Church Affairs. Scheiber's political capital was his international reputation as a scholar: the authorities had to reckon with the fact that any measure taken against him would be widely reported in the Western media to the detriment of Hungary's international reputation. Micro-historical analyses of these two men and their institutions would greatly contribute to a better understanding of the functioning of the post-Stalinist regimes.

From the latter third of the 1970s, we do not find any secret service documents relating to "Jewish affairs" in the public archives. The few documents to which we do have access provide a picture that resembles the one that may be formed from documents relating to contacts with international Jewish organisations: while the institutions of state control and interference continued to operate in an unchanged fashion, the Jewish institutions' scope for action increased after the signing of the Helsinki Accords. Even so, the customary policies of control and manipulation successfully prevented the development of movements seeking significant institutional autonomy within the existing system of Jewish institutions.

In the late 1970s and early 1980s, a few informal groups were established outside the official Jewish institutional system in Hungary, although they never attained the degree of institutionalisation as part of the oppositional counter-culture that was characteristic of contemporary informal Jewish educational groups in the Soviet Union, Poland and – in the late 1980s – Czechoslovakia.[45] Only in the mid-1980s did there appear – in the illegal press of the semi-clandestine democratic opposition – a

---

[44] Historical Archives of the Hungarian State Security 3.1.5. O-17169/5, Folder: "Zionists undertaking hostile activities" ["Ellenséges tevékenységet kifejtő cionisták"], vol. 6. (7 December 1976 and 14 November 1977).
[45] For a detailed analysis of Jewish youth groups in Czechoslovakia, see Heitlinger, op. cit.

political programme that formulated both the demand for sovereign Jewish politics, and the possible principles of such politics in the name of a clandestine Jewish oppositional group, Shalom.[46]

The Hungarian secret service's final campaign in the field of Jewish affairs for which we have documentary evidence relates to the informal Jewish groups in Budapest. It took place in 1985–86, by which time the fledgling Jewish network of mostly young people had been under surveillance for some time, as evidenced by a report written for the East-German secret service preserved in the Stasi archives[47], and by subsequently published memoirs.[48] Once again, the tactics of intimidation and disruption were successfully employed first to manipulate and then, in 1986, to break up these groups.

Shortly before the collapse of the regime, the State Office for Church Affairs made a number of rather desperate attempts to restrict the ground for emerging Jewish initiatives outside the religious community. It suddenly proposed, for instance, the establishment of a secular Jewish cultural magazine and a secular cultural association, suggesting that the latter be run under the auspices of the religious community.[49] However, all such endeavours – together with the State Office for Church Affairs – were soon swept away by the tide of change.

---

46 Nyílt levél a magyar társadalomhoz és a magyar zsidósághoz [An Open Letter to Hungarian Society and Hungarian Jews] in *AB Hírmondó* 6–7, May–June 1984, 23–37. For *Shalom*'s open letter, see Kovács, Hungarian Jewish Politics, 124–156.
47 "Auf das Bestreben der Zionisten, dass auf die Erhöhung des Einflusses der Juden in Ungarn gerichtet ist, verweist auch, dass verschiedene Personen in ihrer eigenen Wohnungen systematisch Versammlungen für jüdische Jugendgruppen veranstalten. Sie wurden von Personen geleitet, die sich bewusst als gegen die sozialistische Gesellschaftsordnung auftretende Personen vorstellen und sich in der Konspiration auskennen. Ihre Zusammenkünfte legalisieren sie mit jüdischer religiöser Tätigkeit. Zur Organisierung ihrer Tätigkeit erhalten sie systematisch über verschiedene Kanäle materielle Hilfe, Instruktionen und Popagandamaterial von ihrer Verbindungen." BStU, *MfS HA XXII, Nr. 1767*, Information der Sicherheitsdienste Ungarns über die subversive Tätigkeit der israelischen Geheimdienste und der zionistischen Organisationen (21 February 1985).
48 "Szóval azt mondja, aki zsidó, tartsa magát zsidónak?" Mihancsik Zsófia interjúja Rácz Andrással ["So whoever is Jewish should regard themselves as a Jew?" Zsófia Mihancsik interviews András Rácz]. *Budapesti Negyed* 8 (1995), 227–259.
49 National Archives of Hungary, XIX-A-21-d 159.d. 0017/6-4/1988 (1 August 1988), and 164.d. 0017/4/1989 (23 February 1989).

Documents

1 The Current Situation of the Jewish Denomination

13 May 1957

National Archives of Hungary, XIX-A-21-d-0029-1/1957 (2.d.)
Collection: State Office for Religious Affairs [Állami Egyházügyi Hivatal, ÁEH]

On 18 April 1957, based on a preliminary discussion with the State Office for Church Affairs, we arranged for Dr Lajos Heves, Chairman of the National Office of Hungarian Jews and the Budapest Israelite Congregation, to resign [from his posts]. The reason for his resignation was in part a consideration of the operational aspects [*aspects essential for the security organs* – AK] and in part the fact that as the leader of Hungarian Jewry he has been pursuing a denominational policy in opposition to the government.

From 1954 onwards, he established, as chairman, close relations with the Israeli Embassy in Budapest, falling completely under its control. He took his measures – in relation to Hungarian Jewry – having first discussed them with the Embassy and with its approval. He ignored or applied only in an ostensible manner the criteria received from the State Office for Church Affairs. He did not support wholeheartedly the correct measures arising from the political and economic situation. For a lengthy period he gave his full support to Jewish nationalist ideology and he performed his tasks as chairman in this spirit. This explains why, after the October events [*the 1956 anti-Communist Revolution in* Hungary – AK], he was unwilling to make a statement on the revolutionary or counter-revolutionary nature of the events in Hungary. According to our concrete data, on this issue too, he represented the view of the Israeli Embassy in Budapest. With his Jewish nationalist views and through the concrete application of this ideology, he promoted the large-scale illegal wave of emigration. Exaggerating some of the antisemitic outbursts manifested at the time of the October counter-revolution, he utilised them to increase Jewish nationalism. He continued this activity throughout his time as chairman, and even after his dismissal he still represents this position, seeking to achieve – and the attempt could be successful under current circumstances – the "liquidation" of the religious leaders of Jewry from Hungary.

His listed actions have compelled a significant proportion of denominational persons to emigrate, thereby causing panic among Hungarian Jewry, who are now leaving or seeking to leave the country in large numbers. He took his Jewish nationalist propaganda to such a level that, in several instances, he spoke in front of leading Jewish persons of the coming pogroms, thereby making their emigration even more likely.

Many leading functionaries in the denomination disagreed with the Jewish nationalist line taken by Dr Lajos Heves and with his close contact with the Embassy.

These persons even voiced their opinion, whereupon Dr Lajos Heves had them removed from the leadership, forcing his arbitrary rule on a part of the prefecture.

He developed around his person a narrow group of those in agreement with his leadership line; however, these persons, together with Dr Lajos Heves, are fully opposed, in a political sense, to the people's democracy system.

[...]

Naturally, these persons seek the same Jewish nationalist line and to maintain the close relations with the Israeli Embassy in Budapest.

This clique has fully subordinated the denomination to the Embassy and they consider the Israeli Embassy rather than the Hungarian government as their highest organ, whose guidance they view as obligatory.

A group of those who support the other line, whom Dr Lajos Heves had removed from the leadership by exploiting the October events, display a loyal attitude to the government and they fully agree with and support its policies. They oppose the denomination's tutelage to the Israeli Embassy in Budapest and they consider the Hungarian government rather than the Israeli Embassy to be their superior organ. In their view, for as long as the Jews in Hungary are living here, it is their obligation to support the policy of the Hungarian government, and they view the principles laid down in the Constitution of the People's Republic as compulsory. This opposition force seeks the unification of Jewry, its education in an anti-Zionist spirit, and the establishment of trust towards the government.

Dr Lajos Heves disagreed with these principles and did his utmost to discredit these persons, so that he could continue, in an undisturbed fashion, his Jewish nationalist denominational policy.

Summarising the current situation of the denomination, it can be stated that, since his resignation, he has sought to influence the present leadership and promote his Jewish nationalist denominational policy. Through his reactionary friends in the leadership, he hinders the advance of the opposition camp – that is, those that seek to realise the correct line of leadership, and, in doing so, he seeks to increase the authority of his own person towards Israel.

This dubious situation exerts a grave influence on Jewry and on the life of the denomination. A significant part of Jewry wants, in view of these circumstances, to emigrate, because they do not see the practice of the life of the denomination assured amid all the rivalry. A majority of Hungarian Jews supports the loyal policy of the opposition, agree with its denominational policy, and make this policy their own.

Based on the foregoing, we propose:

1./ To hold a discussion with the State Office for Church Affairs concerning the taking of effective measures to put a stop to the Jewish nationalist line of leadership. This can be accomplished by the State Office for Church Affairs calling upon Dr László Fleischmann, deputy chairman, to reinstate to their original posts the persons who have been deprived of their functions, who can then bring an end to the Jewish nationalist line of leadership. The return of these persons to the leadership of the denomination is vital on operational grounds.

2./ For a temporary period, the denomination should be led by the two deputy chairmen in co-operation, whereby a loyal denominational policy can be realised free of external influence.

3./ Constant contact with the State Office for Church Affairs is necessary to ensure that when certain persons are placed in functions ,we can also take the operational criteria into account.

4./ The State Office for Church Affairs should invite the deputy chairmen Dr László Fleischmann and Dr Géza Seifert for a discussion, informing them of the State Office's position that they disapprove of the continuation of the Jewish nationalist line of leadership.

2 The Jewish Denomination

13 May 1963

National Archives of Hungary, XIX-A-21-d (20.d.)
Collection: State Office for Religious Affairs [Állami Egyházügyi Hivatal, ÁEH]

The Jewish Denomination

I.

The supreme religious, social and cultural administrative body of the 80,000 Hungarian Jews who remain out of the 500,000 Jews of the pre-WWII era is the National Representation of Hungarian Israelites: NRHI. The leadership of the NRHI, which comprises a president, a general secretary and 5 deputy chairmen, is elected at a national conference for a period of four years by the leaders of congregations in the provinces based on the five geographical regions in the country and of the Budapest Israelite Congregation, which includes approx. 65,000 members.

The task of the NRHI is to operate the Nursing Hospital, the Boys' and Girls' Orphanages, the Jewish Seminary [*the Rabbinical Seminary of Budapest* – AK], the five nursing homes and the six soup kitchens (which distribute 2,500 lunches per day). But it is also to care for the cemeteries, synagogues, prayer houses etc., as well as to operate the industrial and commercial units relating to ritual life (butchers, kosher wine-handling, matzah production, etc.)

Relations among the secular and religious leaders of Hungary Jewry are characterised by permanent discord of an open or implicit nature. This is caused in part by the [*fight for the* – AK] acquiring of power, which is accompanied by financial advantages, and in part by the attraction to the rich Jewish population in the West and the maintenance of overt and hidden relations with the State of Israel. Among the disruptive methods utilised by the leaders, one finds all kinds of means from idle gossiping to anonymous letter campaigns.

[…]

In the Jewish denomination, the reactionary group is manifest in two forms. First, it criticises those members of the central leadership who co-operate with the state. It always undertakes such attacks, however, in the disguise of defending the truth, as if it were defending the true interests of Jewry, whereas in reality it seeks merely to discredit and topple those leaders who are ready to work with the state. The intellectual leader of this movement is Sándor Scheiber, who has succeeded, by means of offering financial assistance – given that he manages the funds of the Claims Conference – in winning over the disaffected. Included in that group is Mihály Borsa, who seeks popularity in his endeavour to occupy the seat of chairman.

The other type of the manifestation of reactionary forces is the active, illegal propaganda work, which is pursued among Hungarian Jewry – above all using financial means – by the Israeli Embassy to promote Zionism and emigration. Given that Zionism is thriving among the religious functionaries and the Orthodox Jews, they are sympathetic to, and in contact with, the Embassy. In the past year, János Péter and Károly Szarka spoke with the Israeli chargé d'affaires about the propaganda activity, who sought to evade the accusations and has since proceeded with his illegal work in a more cautious fashion.

It is to be noted that the two forms of the reaction overlap to a certain degree, just as the intellectual motor behind each school of thought is Sándor Scheiber.

For our part, we regularly inform the Ministry of Foreign Affairs about the activities of the Embassy that have come to our knowledge. Even so, there is a need for the Ministry to re-examine this problem. Another requirement would be for the leaders of the Jewish denomination to meet with the head of the Office, in order to exchange views on the above problems.

II.

Other than the congregations in Debrecen, Pécs, Szeged and Kaposvár, regular denominational life is seen only in the 18 Budapest congregations. In the smaller places, noteworthy religious activity occurs only at the time of major festivals, occasional celebrations and events. The rituals are performed nationally by 31 rabbis (15 Neolog and 16 Orthodox rabbis) and 18 cantors. In addition, there are numerous occasional hazzans and Torah readers, particularly in the remote places. (With a view to mitigating the lack of rabbis, there are currently 10 [*handwritten correction on the document: 8 – AK*] students studying at the Rabbinical Seminary. The Luach (or denominational calendar), published in 10,000 copies each year, promotes the religious life of the diaspora populations.

A bigoted religious life is lived only by the small number of Orthodox Jews, who live in separation [*from the majority of Jews – AK*]. Other than this, only the elderly Neolog Jews attend synagogue regularly. Among those who attend synagogue now, one cannot expect their numbers to decrease in the Orthodox branch, while in the Neolog congregations only a very slow decline in numbers is anticipated. Most Jews, however, feel themselves as belonging to the community, which, however, is expressed only on certain occasions (major festivals, bar mitzvah, weddings, funerals, etc.).

Official religious instruction for youths is undertaken only in the yeshiva or at the Jewish Grammar School. Still, various other means (Talmud lessons, Torah readings, etc.) are used to get acquainted with the basic tenets of the religion.

Recently – since there has been the in-fighting at the NRHI – the centre has lost control and direction of religious life in areas outside Budapest. This does not mean that activities relating to religious life have declined in such country areas. Rather, we do not know their activity and their attitudes. In any case, we intend to use the rabbi candidates and activate some members of the NRHI in order to enable us to follow what happens in the religious life of Jews outside Budapest.

III.

The international relations of the leaders of Hungarian Jewry are lively and developing. In the recent past, delegations have visited Paris, Brussels and London. Now the initial steps have been taken towards the Jewish community in Austria.

Among the People's democracies, their relations with the GDR are the most intensive, and they provide regular political, denominational, cultural and moral support to German Jews. Unfortunately, to date it is only with Polish Jewry that healthy relations have not been established.

For those religious and secular leaders of the denomination who are deserving in a political sense, we are gradually enabling them to speak personally about the domestic life of Hungarian Jewry in the capitalist states.

Hungarian Jewry maintains contact with family members who have, in many cases, emigrated, and with the various international organisations, which are observing attentively the integration of Hungarian Jewry into Socialist society. In 1962, almost a hundred foreign (above all American and British) religious and secular denominational leaders visited Hungary, viewing the Jewish religious institutions and events either as guests of the NRHI or as private individuals. Extensive reports and articles were published in Western Jewish magazines and in Western newspapers about their realistic and positive experiences. On the occasion of the [Jewish] New Year of 5723, 75 foreign Jewish leaders or organisations sent their good wishes to the NRHI, compared with 50 such greetings in the preceding year.

In 1962, interest in the current situation of Hungarian Jewry was expressed for the first time from the Latin-American states. We are only beginning to appreciate the advantageous side of Hungarian Jewry's foreign contacts, and to date such contacts have been of an accidental or desultory nature. The time has now come for us to focus – in harmony with the competent organs – on building and consolidating international relations, doing so in a planned and future-oriented manner.

At present, around 20,000 Jews pay the religious tax levy, but this number is continuously, albeit slowly, decreasing. The main additional sources of revenue are the fees levied on kosher products. (Owing to a decrease in the number of veal calves slaughtered, there is currently a large decline in this area.) The denomination has many other minor sources of revenue (CHEVRA, donations, etc.), but these too are slowly decreasing.

The cost of wages for the more 500 workers employed in the field of the NRHI is not decreasing – albeit most of them receive low wages. And so the deficit is covered from the sale of disused synagogues. Initially, the response to the sales was great. Today, however, the problem is finding buyers, because there is now an awareness of the extent of the financial problem presented by the upkeep of the disused buildings. Of course, the property sales must be monitored to prevent the possibility of mutual speculation or the speedy liquidation of synagogues.

The main funding source for the social expenditures is the 25 million forints provided by the SSE on an annual basis. Meanwhile, the Claims Conference provides 40,000 dollars annually in financial aid for the cultural purposes of Hungarian Jewry, which covers book publications and research on the Jewish past.

The state provides the denomination with an annual sum of .... forints congrua [*sum is missing; state contribution to salaries of rabbis* – AK], pensions, maintenance of buildings, etc.

It is extraordinarily important that, as revenues slowly fall, the expenditure of the denominational institutions should also decrease. However, rationalisation can only be achieved by way of considered and circumspect measures, lest it cause panic and the competent organs use the declining costs for the purpose of propaganda concerning the liquidation of the denomination.

Proposal

1./ For the sake of expanding foreign relations, to consolidate existing relations and seek contact with Jewish populations in additional countries (Ministry of Foreign Affairs).

a./ Based on the good relationship that arose out of the journey to England, enhancing relations in the religious and cultural fields and inviting progressive British religious Jewish leaders.

b./ Making contact with progressive Jewish communities in the South-American states.

c./ Contacting Hungarian Jewish communities abroad (World Federation of Hungarians).

d./ Clarify with the Polish comrades whether or not it is still necessary to isolate Polish and Hungarian Jews from each other.

2./ Restricting the propaganda activity of the Israeli Embassy (Ministry of Foreign Affairs).

3./ Timely discussions by the Office [*State Office for Religious Affairs* – AK] with the secular and religious leaders of the Jewish denomination.

4./ To reduce costs, compel the NRHI to make the savings necessary in every field.

3 Operational Situation of the Jewish Denomination

4 September 1961

Historical Archives of the Hungarian State Security 3.1.5. O-17169
Folder: "Zionists undertaking hostile activities" ["Ellenséges tevékenységet kifejtő cionisták"], vol. 1.

Ministry of Interior
II, Sub-department 5-C.

Subject: operational situation of the Jewish denomination

Report

Budapest, 4 September 1961

Since 1958 and the dismissal of the Denomination's president, Dr Lajos Heves, the activities of the leaders of the Jewish Denomination in Hungary have been characterised by an attempt to establish better co-operation between the new leadership and the state bodies. Proof of this are the positive sounding articles published in Új Élet [*New Life*], as well as statements made at various events – which call for integration within the system.

We have no knowledge of the influence of the Israeli Embassy exerting a greater effect on the religious denomination than in earlier years. By way of agents, we have managed to ensure that staff members of the Embassy attend events held by the religious denomination only to a minimum extent. We also have no knowledge of the Embassy continuing to provide illegal aid.

I.

The number of Jews in Hungary can be put at around 75,000, although the leaders of the religious denomination speak of 100,000. In doing so, however, their aim is clearly to ensure that they keep receiving the same amount of foreign aid. (Nearly 90 per cent of Jews live in Budapest.) Religious life in the community is in constant decline, which has spurred the leaders of the religious denomination to raise the number of taxpayers (by way of agents we managed to put an end to this). The necessity of this is justified by the fact that, despite the sharp decline in numbers, an apparatus of 600, appropriate for the pre-war community of 700,000, is still maintained. There are two shades of the Jewish religion in Hungary, and in line with this there are Neolog headquarters and Orthodox headquarters, both having an adequate number of staff. The number of Orthodox Jews is not so high, approx. 5,000 people. Apart from Budapest, only Debrecen has an Orthodox congregation. Despite the small numbers, the Orthodox community is the more dangerous, in view of it being more organised and more influential. Their integration into the system of a People's democracy is unlikely, and they do not take part in productive work. In Budapest they have one operating synagogue, which has a lively religious life. In addition, they also have a working Yeshiva, providing religious instruction throughout the day.

The Neolog branch is less unified and not so well organised, but also much richer than the Orthodox one. It has a rabbinical seminary with 4 students, a hospital with 200 beds and a network of nursing homes throughout the country, including two in Budapest. Incidentally, the congregation provides financial assistance to almost 10,000 persons, while 2,300 individuals receive meals at a soup kitchen, and this is not to mention the assistance given in the form of clothing, medicines and food. The division of such assistance is the task of the "Central Social Committee" [*Központi Szociális Bizottság, KSZB*], which is independent of the congregation. The employees and senior managers of the Committee have no links with denominational life and are increasingly distant from the correct religious denominational policy. Illustrative of their independence is that they do not allow the leaders of the congregation to examine their affairs, even rejecting the very idea of this. Also in operation is a fairly well respected <u>museum</u>. The Budapest Israelite Congregation is divided into 18 districts, and there are almost 30 synagogues in operation. In terms of the denomination, the country is divided into 6 parts, known as denominational districts.

<u>These are:</u>

1./ Budapest
2./ Northern Transdanubia (Győr)
3./ Southern Transdanubia (Pécs)
4./ Great Plain (Szeged)
5./ Transtisza (Debrecen)
6./ Northern Hungary (Miskolc)

A characteristic development is the flow of provincial Jews to Budapest and to the major cities from villages and minor towns. Accordingly, large congregations are to be found only in the seats of the denominational districts. Over the past two years, a development related to this migration flow to the cities has been the sale of 15 synagogues (mostly in areas outside Budapest) to the state – to be used as cultural centres, stores or for some other purpose. At present, negotiations are underway concerning the sale of several synagogues – including two in Budapest. The sale of the synagogues in Budapest is justified by the downturn in religious life and low attendance.

The leadership and priesthood of the denomination are far from united. From time to time, groups or tiny groups arise with the aim of defeating the present leadership. To date, such endeavours have been successfully countered. Such groups are not long-lived, because they usually break up in consequence of other disputes or they do not continue their activities for fear of being suspected of forming a movement. Of course, a major factor in this is fear of losing one's position. The wave of emigration can now be regarded as concluded, whereby reports of Israel's difficult economic situation have been a contributory factor. The number of people who would leave the country for Israel can be estimated at 3,000. The number of returning emigrants is substantially larger. The leaders of the denomination estimate that there are 20,000 who would return if this were a possibility.

News reports from Romania – the on-going "deportation" of Romanian Jewry – cause some agitation from time to time. (This was confirmed by Agent "Doktor" [Doctor] who visited Romania.) Some Hungarian Jews think that the same thing will happen in Hungary one day.

The leadership of the denomination has, officially, no links with the Israeli Embassy. However, from time to time, staff members of the Embassy visit the synagogues in a district and converse there with people. We do not know of any assistance given or of permanent contacts. There are only several persons concerning whom we have signs of indirect contact.

We have data indicating that the Embassy is inviting an increasingly large circle of Jewish intellectuals to its events, especially people from the scientific and artistic fields. A great amount of interest is shown by Jewish intellectuals in the events held by the Israeli Embassy.

The Embassy conducts active propaganda. It sends its bulletins – mostly by post – to a broad range of Jewry, and it also undertakes propaganda work by way of official distributors or other distributors. The bulletin is published in approx. 3,000 copies at irregular intervals, from once to three times a month. With reference to the Eichmann trial, the number of copies has been increased recently.

Since the counter-revolution, there has been a gradual expansion of the international contacts of the Budapest Israelite Congregation – and today the network is a substantial one. Indeed, they are in contact with the Swiss Societe Secour [sic! – AK] (Joint) Jewish assistance organisation, with the Claims Conference (a body dealing with the distribution of funds originating from German reparation and compensation payments). But they also have good relations with Jewish bodies in almost all the Western-European countries. The only body with which there is no contact is the World Jewish Congress. However, the possibility of restoring contact has been raised.

There has been a huge increase in the number of foreign visitors to the Jewish denomination. Some of these come on a permanent basis as merchants and seek out contact with the congregation primarily in a private capacity. The "core" of such visitors come to the country as tourists, and they establish a wide range of contacts. In many cases it was only after their departure from the country that it became clear they were in the country on a commission for a Jewish body. There are also some individuals who arrive for the purpose of conducting official talks with the Budapest Israelite Congregation, but they are in a minority.

In the case of each of the three forms of visiting, it can be observed that the visitor first makes some private visits – as if for the purpose of orientation – and then the official contacts are made. Such visits bring no benefits, but we are not in a position to prevent them.

II.

A peculiarity of the field is that almost all the persons belonging here have wide-ranging relations with the West, in view of the fact that Jews who left or emigrated from Hungary have spread all around the West.

The second peculiarity is the strong nationalism seen in the categories [*of persons belonging to the field* – AK]. In case of a real or perceived grievance, they feel themselves to have been offended in terms of their Jewish identity. They are very sensitive to any manifestation of antisemitism.

The third peculiarity is that almost all of them work in intellectual professions – medical doctors, journalists, officials. A favoured field is a career in commerce.

The fourth peculiarity is that many of them have experience in conspiracy; even the cleanest of business deals are made in secret. The custom that is seen in retailing has become their practice in everything they do.

The fifth peculiarity is that, unless absolutely necessary, they avoid all contact with Christian persons. This is linked with the fact that they live in compact areas.

All of these peculiarities make their presence felt in operational work.

At present, in the religious sphere, we have no knowledge of specific hostile activities. However, we have inadequate data suggesting that three areas deserve particular attention:

1./ The rabbinical seminary and its director Sándor Scheiber. We do not know exactly what activities are underway here. But the fact that Scheiber was, from 1953–58, one of the main actors in the illegal assistance programme run by the Embassy and that in 1955 he received the assignment to collect data for the Israeli Documentation Center, and that Scheiber is a nationalist – he educates the seminary students in a Zionist spirit and stands in opposition to our system – which his statements prove, means it is justified to concern ourselves with this field and with the persons involved. All the distinguished visitors [from Israel] seek out Scheiber. As the representative of the Claims Conference, he disposes of an annual sum of one million forints. Although the money serves scientific and cultural goals, nevertheless several hostile persons receive monthly amounts of 1,000 forints from this sum.

[...]

He also has influence over the grammar school. Scheiber has influence over some of the rabbis from Budapest and the provinces. Typically, such persons oppose the people's democracy system.

We have only limited opportunities of controlling Scheiber's hostile activities by means of agents. Scheiber is compatible with no-one and sees an agent in everyone – he himself was an agent – [*this statement of the author, an anonymous secret-service official, is without any documentary proof* – AK] and these factors make an approach more difficult.

2./ The other area is the Central Social Committee. By means of this body, Hungarian Jewry receives an annual sum of a million dollars in assistance from the Joint and through the mediation of the Societe Secour. This is the equivalent, together with the supplement of the State Office for Church Affairs, of 30 million forints. The official purpose of the funding is to assist the elderly and people who cannot work.

[…]

We do not know the extent or objective of the assistance provided in this area. The persons receiving assistance are not known to us, and we have no data concerning the criteria for offering assistance. According to the information we have received, the Central Social Committee also deals with studying individuals in whom the foreign centre has expressed an interest.

[…]

It may be supposed, albeit we have no data for this, that the assistance conceals hostile activities. This suspicion is supported by the fact that the assistance is made in semi-legal circumstances, and the means used resemble those of the Embassy's assistance campaign. Mihály Borsa, head of the Central Social Committee, travels abroad 4–5 times a year to attend talks with the centre [*of the hostile agency* – AK]. We do not know the extent to which such travel is justified or the nature of the talks held. Borsa has wide-ranging contacts in Jewish religious intellectual circles.

[…]

4 Operational Work against the Zionist Movement

3 April 1962

Historical Archives of the Hungarian State Security 3.1.5. O-17169
Folder: "Zionists undertaking hostile activities" ["Ellenséges tevékenységet kifejtő cionisták"], vol. 1.

Ministry of Interior
II. Sub-department 5-c

<u>Report</u>

on the results of our operational work against the Zionist movement and further tasks

The resolution of the Political Committee of the Hungarian Socialist Workers' Party, dated 21 July 1961, declares that currently the most organised opposition force in our country is the clerical reaction. Reflecting this resolution, we consider it necessary to examine the signals coming from the Jewish denominations. Based on the operational data at our disposal, we wish to report on the following:

The representatives of Zionism – as a political movement – conduct their activities in relation to Hungary in a complex and multi-faceted manner. Regarding their political goals, relative to the position in earlier years, there have been some changes. The conclusion they have drawn from the 1956 counter-revolutionary events and the development of the international situation is that the bourgeois democratic regime for which they had hoped cannot be realised under the given conditions in Hungary. Having recognised this state of affairs, they have directed all their efforts towards the support of Israel, viewing this as the central issue. Their endeavours seeking to broaden their mass influence also serve this goal. It is with this goal as a point of departure that they organise the foreign assistance dispatched to the Jewish denominations. They have also taken steps to draw the leadership of the congregations under their influence. They organise attacks against leaders that display loyal attitudes towards the state. According to our data, in such actions one can find indirectly the activity of the Israeli Embassy.

[…]

II.

At present, we know of approx. 250 Zionist activists or former leaders in Hungary. Among them, 127 feature on the operational records. To date, we have examined the situation of 150 former Zionists.

The occupational breakdown of the 130 persons is as follows:

Physician	5 persons
Engineer	23
Official	46
Worker	30
Artisan	10
Merchant	25
Univ. student	2
Housewife	8
Rabbi	1

The Zionist persons examined do not take part – apart from several exceptions – in the life of the denominations. However, their influence on the middle management of the denominations and, through them, on the religious masses is great and steadily increasing. Alongside the increase in their influence, one can also observe an attempt to undermine the leadership and alienate the leaders from the religious masses. It is this goal that is served by the anonymous letters and, in general, by the attempts to undermine the leadership. Influential persons distance themselves from a loyal stance towards the state, which further increases the distance between the leadership and the masses. In consequence, the districts seek independence and the Zionist tendencies come to the fore. Despite the leadership having prohibited it, they are in permanent contact with the Israeli Embassy; they invite them to their events, and they view the Embassy as their interest representation body.

Currently, the securing of the above category by means of agents is not assured to a satisfactory extent. We employ four agents on the Zionist line.

[...]

It has become clear to the Zionists that they cannot appear openly, and that their practical methods applied in the past are not applicable under the present conditions. For this reason, they have started spreading the nationalist and Zionist propaganda by legal means and utilising, for this purpose, the religious institutions and religious education. They do not undertake overt Zionist propaganda, but through the teachings of the Talmud and the Torah they seek to keep alive "spiritual cohesion" in the Zionist sense, while also encouraging a "love of the Holy Land". The greatest activity in this area is directed towards the youth. Their main endeavour is to develop, by means of religious education, separation trends in the youth while they are in their childhood, which can then be increased and strengthened. This objective is served by book publishing, the holding of cultural events and tea parties, as well as by group excursions. They always explain such separation from the others around as a response to antisemitism. The aim of the concept of separation and introversion, which is funded and directed from abroad, is to remove the youth from Marxist-Leninist influence, so that they can "always be counted upon as Jews".

It is for this purpose that they maintain, alongside the synagogue districts, the so-called Talmud-Torah circles, to be attended by children of school age. The number of persons in the circles in a particular district is 80–120. Considering the 18 synagogue districts in Budapest, the total number attending can be estimated at 7–800. It is noteworthy that the reactionary Zionist rabbis have groups with the largest numbers. For example, the group run by Chief Rabbi Dr L. S. [*László Salgó* – AK] has in excess of 150 persons.

So-called religious-cultural lectures are held for secondary-school pupils, university students and youths who have outgrown school.

Recently, the Israeli Embassy in Budapest has been extraordinarily active with regard to the denomination. Their legal efforts are clearly of a propaganda nature towards the districts and their events. Their goal is to be visible and that they too should get to know as many people as possible. On the occasion of a festival, they visit 8–10 synagogues, where they disperse donations. In general the districts are pleased to see staff members of the Embassy, and give them prominent seats. There was even a case when the Hatikvah – the Israeli national anthem – was sung in their honour.

We have few data concerning the Embassy's illegal activities and the nature of such activities. It is a fact, however, that several Zionists among the leadership of the Jewish denomination have a conspiratorial relationship with the Embassy.

Dr S.S. [*Sándor Scheiber* – AK], the director of the rabbinical seminary and a person of hostile Zionist attitudes, was the main organiser of the assistance dispersed by the Embassy. According to our data, Dr S.S. is in contact with the Embassy at the present time, too.

[…]

It has come to our knowledge that Dr S.S. has been elected as a member of the five-member board of the World Jewish Congress, whose task in theory is to elaborate the cultural and educational programme. He has wide-ranging contacts with officials of various ranks working at the international Zionist organisations and institutions, and those coming to Hungary often visit him.

Dr S.S. has great influence over the members and leadership of the denomination and particularly over the youth.

[…]

He has succeeded in bringing under his influence the principal of the Jewish grammar school as well as several teachers, and, by way of them, he also exerts influence on the pupils' education. J. Z. [*Jenő Zsoldos* – AK], the principal of the grammar school, stated with regard to the objectives of the teaching work:

"Modern ideas are not worthy of Jewish schools, because they speed up and facilitate assimilation. The youth have to be educated in such a way that they would feel remorse if they were unable to keep a festival or a dietary or other law".

[...]

The authority and influence enjoyed by him [*Sándor Scheiber* – AK] among the adults stem from the fact that, like the director of the seminary, they are reputed as "great academics", and this is an important factor particularly among elderly religious people. They have wide-ranging contacts with such people and can influence them on any issue.

[...]

The financial basis for the Zionist activity comprises funds originating abroad that arrive in the country in a legal fashion. The Central Social Committee, functioning under the auspices of the National Office of Hungarian Jews, receives an annual sum of USD 1 million (= 30 million forints) from one of the Joint's mediatory bodies for the purpose of assistance. Under an agreement with the state, no-one – other than the foreign bodies – has the right to check how the above amount is used. The head of the Central Social Committee, Dr M. B. [*Mihály Borsa* – AK] is a former state secretary of the Smallholders Party [*the leading centre-right party of the post-war governing coalition* – AK], who has been mentioned in the field of counter-espionage as a suspected spy in several respects. Putting all this together, such an enormous sum in the hands of a person in leading position could be a means for financing hostile activities. It does not seem likely that the Joint would transfer the above sum without getting something in return or some visible benefit.

[...]

Other than the Zionists, no other category disposes, in a legal fashion, of such a large sum for the financing of their activities. The international Zionist organisations evidently place great weight on ensuring that these funds continue to come to Hungary. Clearly, they consider the use of the sum to be satisfactory and they are also content with the outcomes of its use. The influence gained from the submission of the above amounts by the international Zionist organisations is significant.

The political and operational experiences made on the Zionist issue can be summarised as follows:
- The current objective of Zionist activities is to influence the masses and to win over the youth. The development of a public mood in which the process of assimilation is slowed down and there is increased isolation and introversion.

- Surround the Embassy with Israel sympathisers, from whose circles intelligence can get its cadres
- The illegal Zionist activities are being conducted – according to the indications we are receiving – under central control. The control takes place firstly from abroad and secondly by means of the Israeli Embassy in Budapest.
- They have the necessary number of cadres and the financial resources to continue the illegal activity. Their cadres are embedded, in a legal fashion, in the life of the denomination. Replacement forces are recruited mainly from the institutions of the denomination.

Based on experiences to date, we suggest that the main directions of counter-intelligence should be determined as follows:

1./ In order to uncover the illegal Zionist activity in its breadth and depth, there should be a much more audacious policy of recruiting informers among senior leaders and the youth.
- There has to be more co-ordinated processing work by agents, using the II/2 and II/3 departments. We must endeavour to get hold of as much data as possible in order to compromise the staff members of the Israeli Embassy.

2./ Working with the II/2 and II/3 departments and using more forceful measures, we should bring under control the financial basis for Zionist activities. We must ensure that we receive reports about the use of the sums in time.

3./ We must uncover and then document the Zionists' illegal contacts with the controlling centres – the Israeli Embassy and the international Zionist organisations.

4./ Technical infiltration [*bugging* – AK] must be implemented in the case of several major figures and secret house searches must be undertaken in their homes for the purpose of acquiring documentation.

5./ Differences of views among the members of various groups that have arisen within the Jewish congregation should be strengthened on the level of the individuals too. These differences should be utilised in accordance with our operational objectives. Support should be given to persons suitable for leadership in such a manner that they gradually obtain the major posts.

6./ By means of processing the youth groups, we should seek to discover who the theoretical leaders are. These persons should then be brought under active processing. At the same time, we should ensure that, among the youth, wide-ranging illegal organisations and movements cannot be established.

7./ In the course of the processing work, draft proposals should be prepared concerning which form of administrative measures should be used to terminate these groups.

At the same time, within such circles, we should undertake disruptive activities on a continuous basis with a view to preventing their re-emergence.

8./ To promote the political struggle against the Zionist movement, we will suggest that the names of some of the misled adults and young people who have fallen under Zionist influence, should be passed on to the competent Party and Alliance of Young Communist organisations so that they deal with these persons through re-education.

Completed in 5 copies, 12 pages

5 Conditions for the Indemnification of the Hungarian Jews

9 March 1964

Historical Archives of the Hungarian State Security 3.1.5. O-17169/1
Folder: "Zionists undertaking hostile activities" ["Ellenséges tevékenységet kifejtő cionisták"], vol. 2.

Ministry of Interior
Directorate III/I

Information Report

Conditions for the indemnification of Hungarian Jews

The American journalist Carl Fell who, in August 1962, spent time in Hungary at the expense of the Press Department of the Ministry of Foreign Affairs, told a member of our UN mission in New York about the possibilities of indemnifying Hungary's Jews as well as a proposal concerning the "benefits" of such for the Hungarian state "that cannot be ignored".

Fell, in his offer – which was made in all likelihood at the behest of the Zionist movement and of Goldman [sic! – AK], leader of the World Jewish Congress, related that Erhard had promised Goldman a payment of 100 million dollars for the indemnification of Hungarian Jews. Under the terms of Fell's proposal, Goldman would submit the amount to the Hungarian state subject to the fulfilment of the following conditions:

- The Hungarian government authorises the official celebration of the birthday of – or the anniversary of the death of – Dr Theodore Herzel [sic! – AK], the Hungarian-born Jew and world founder of Zionism, and then invites Goldman to Hungary for this occasion. Fell makes no secret of the fact that – in their opinion – the significance of the celebration would reach beyond Hungary's borders, and so representatives from Israel and of the Jews of other countries could also be invited.

Note:

1. The "confidential messages" given by Carl Fell are evidently part of the Zionist campaign against the countries of the Socialist camp. It can be stated that Goldman's group seek to link the long-running issue of indemnification with political conditions, and that, in doing so, they are seeking to make political capital not only against the People's Republic of Hungary.
2. Fell made a similar "proposal" already in January 1963, but at that time the amount mentioned was 50 million dollars, and, as it transpired, it was conditional on the Hungarian government receiving the amount in goods, from the sale

of which the compensation claims could then have been settled. At that time too, Fell urged the acceptance of his "proposal", referring to the need to wrap it up before Adenauer's retirement, since, as an exceptional opportunity, it was thanks only to the good personal relationship existing between Adenauer and Goldman.

Completed: in 6 copies
             Info.
             Directorate III/III,
             Sub-department 1
             Records.

6 On Zionist Issues

27 April 1964

Historical Archives of the Hungarian State Security 3.1.5. O-17169/1
Folder: "Zionists undertaking hostile activities" ["Ellenséges tevékenységet kifejtő cionisták"], vol. 2.

MINISTRY OF INTERIOR
III/III, Sub-department 2-a.

Subject: on Zionist issues

Report

1./ In the matter of the "Együttműködők" [Co-operators] code-named group folder for preliminary observation, which we opened in May 1963, we have determined, in the course of the processing work carried out so far, that the decision to open the folder was the right one.

The persons involved in the matter have generally pro-Western views, represent – within the Jewish denomination – the Zionist wing, and are in contact with other Zionist persons, directing their activities towards undermining the loyal leaders and members of the congregation and bagging for themselves the leadership posts. These persons have close relations with the Western Zionist bodies and their leaders, and they also hold conspiratorial meetings with members of staff of the Israeli Embassy in Budapest, whom they inform about the internal situation in the Jewish denomination and about issues relating to various persons.

Based on the above, we can see that the direction of the processing work is correct. Concerning the continuity, speed and effectiveness of the processing work, there are inadequacies, particularly because, although additional informers have been recruited, we do not have the appropriate network for the matter, a network that would be capable of radical exploratory work.

2./ In the matter of the "Tanulók" [Students] code-named group folder for preliminary observation, which we opened in January 1964, we have determined that the young people involved in the matter come together on a regular basis, learn Hebrew, and read and study newspapers and other Zionist propaganda materials, which stem from the Embassy. The leaders of the group and some of its members are in regular contact with the Israeli Embassy. The content of their activities: Zionist education; assisting young people to emigrate to Israel, etc. The above is supported by the fact that the family of someone attending the group has already migrated to Israel, while another family is in the process of emigrating. The above activities hinder the integration of the Jewish population in our Socialist system, and so, here too, we are talking about activities that are dangerous for society.

Based on the above, it may be stated that the launch and direction of the processing work were correct.

The existing network is capable of exploratory work principally in an indirect fashion. Here, too, there is a need for further and deeper network infiltration.

3./ Based on indicators in addition to the above (we have not opened case-folders in these instances, because, beyond the primary indicator of the activities of persons featuring in the indicators, we dispose of no other data), we took control operational measures in the matter of two groups of young intellectuals.

[...]

II.

Regarding the operational and technical means applied in the processing work, we endeavoured to make full use of the old, existing network in the aforementioned matters and indications, and we also recruited additional informers (4 agents in total). The recruitment was realised either by way of compromising material or through an appeal to patriotic sentiment – or through a combination of the two. In essence, the recruitment was carried out gradually everywhere. Seven agents and two social contacts are participating in the processing work. Concerning the effectiveness of their work, it can be stated that they are generally working well and submitting reports that have an operational value and are informative in nature. Even so, some of them are incapable of undertaking in-depth exploratory work, while the others constitute a new network and require considerable attention before they can become functional and qualified agents in both a political and a professional sense.

Thus, the conclusion may be drawn that we require further network people who are suitable for more in-depth work. The recruitment of such persons needs to be thoroughly prepared. However, it should be noted at this point that, in providing materials, the existing network and the new one have assisted significantly the process of studying new candidates to be recruited as informers.

The techniques used in the course of the processing work – the application of measure 3/a in particular – have proved extraordinarily beneficial. We received many valuable insights that facilitated the implementation of the planned recruitment drive and other operational tasks. It is crucial to state that in the case of some persons under processing, results could be achieved only through multiple or continuous and long-term checks and controls, yielding specific data on contacts of a conspiratorial nature with the Israeli Embassy. At present, we have at our disposal measure 2 pieces of 3/a. There is a half 3/e line, whose material we are only now beginning to receive.

III.

1./ One of the biggest deficiencies is that the existing network obtains the information we need by indirect means and is not properly involved in the matters.

[...]

3./ On several occasions we tried to introduce agents to observe the persons under processing (speaking here of our own agency and the agencies of related departments). However, these attempts were either unsuccessful or brought minimal results. This also shows the high qualifications of the persons under processing (e.g. in the case of Mihály B.).

[...]

7./ It is important to point out that the persons under processing in the matter of the "Együttműködők" are assessed according to different criteria by us and by the state and societal organs, which makes the processing work much more difficult and has a disruptive effect both on the agency and on loyal persons in the denomination.

[...]

Police Major Ferenc Mélykuti
Completed in 2 copies
Recipients: 1 copy to Sub-department Management
                1 copy CD-2381

7 On the Israeli Embassy

17 March 1965

Historical Archives of the Hungarian State Security 3.1.5. O-17169/1
Folder: "Zionists undertaking hostile activities" ["Ellenséges tevékenységet kifejtő cionisták"] vol. 2.

MINISTRY OF INTERIOR
Directorate III/II, Sub-department 5-a.

Subject: Reducing the influence of the Israeli Embassy

I authorise:
Lajos Tóth
[*Handwritten note of L.T: in the margin* – AK]: We should be vigilant and not to assign tasks to agents who are double-dealer or disloyal, because the whole action will lose its effects.

Proposal

Abusing the correct measures of our Party and government, which are aimed at the democratisation of public life, the Israeli Embassy accredited to Budapest has, in the course of recent years, expanded significantly the range of its relations with society and has substantially increased its influence in several directions, including in the direction of the Hungarian Jewish religious community. The above influence has been manifested in pro-Israel propaganda and in increasing people's love of the State of Israel.

To date, no measures have been taken to reduce the growing influence of the Israeli Embassy. On several occasions in recent years, however, we have seen dissatisfaction with Israel's policies on the part of ordinary sensible people and loyal leaders in several districts of the denomination. For instance, the news that Israel supplies armaments to West Germany was met by widespread indignation.

At present, the governments of West Germany and Israel are striving for closer bilateral co-operation. On the radio this morning, it was reported that Israel's parliament has approved the establishment of diplomatic relations with West Germany.

The aforementioned foreign policy events are disquieting for some Hungarian Jews. Yesterday we encountered cases of some Jewish religious persons expressing their dissatisfaction and indignation concerning Israel's foreign policy, which they made known to the Israeli Embassy in letters or by telephone.

Sensible and loyally thinking Jews consider it a betrayal for the Israeli government to befriend that Germany which is the legal successor of Hitler's Germany, where Nazi mass murderers are hiding and occupying top positions.

Given the proper operational measures, we can utilise the rightful indignation of the masses belonging to the Hungarian Jewish denomination to suppress the propaganda activities of the Israeli Embassy and reduce their contacts in society. In so doing, we can reduce in an effective manner the Embassy's propaganda work among the masses.

In the implementation of this campaign, we will involve those members of our network who are known for their loyal behaviour and those agents that are reliable but who are no longer capable of in-depth exploratory work in hostile milieus.

In order to reduce the influence of the Israeli Embassy, we shall implement the following measures:

The tasks of Agent "Sárosi":

1./ Organising six or seven people among the district chairmen and leadership members to write letters of protest, on an individual basis, to the Embassy. In addition, they should contact the chairman of the National Representation of Hungarian Israelites and the editorial board of Új Élet [*New Life*] asking them to protest.

2./ Members of the district leaderships in their circle of friends should arrange for three to four people in their milieu to write letters of protest to the Embassy.

3./ The chief rabbis István Dér, Miklós Máté and Artur Geyer should protest individually by letter and each of them should also arrange for four to five people to protest in individual or family letters addressed to the Embassy.

4./ Around six persons from among the family or close relatives or friends of Agent "Sárosi" should protest, on an individual basis, in letters addressed to the Embassy, while they should also ask the chairman of the National Representation of Hungarian Israelites to express their protest.

5./ Chief Rabbi Henrik Fisch should arrange for eight to ten of the faithful to write similar letters of protest to the Embassy.

6./ János Hartmann, director of Chevra, should arrange for four to five people from his milieu to write similar letters to the Embassy.

7./ The wife of Agent "Sárosi" and the wife of János Hartmann, who are functionaries in the women's section of the congregation, should also organise six to eight people for a similar purpose.

8./ From their pulpits, loyal rabbis should express their indignation in front of the faithful.

9./ At any district meetings that take place, they should arrange for one or two people to speak, who then express their indignation at Israel's policies.

The task of Agent "Xavér":

1./ Persuade his elder brother, who is national chief rabbi, to express his indignation in a letter to the Embassy.

2./ In addition, arrange for two to four more people to do something similar.

3./ "Xavér" herself should express her indignation to diplomats working at the Embassy.

The task of Social Contact "Tanító" [Teacher]:

1./ Protest himself in a letter to the Embassy and arrange for six people in the two cities outside Budapest in his area to protest in letters addressed to the Embassy, who should also call upon the chairman of the National Representation of Hungarian Israelites and the editorial board of Új Élet to protest.

The task of Social Contact "Sipos":

1./ Inform about the wave of protest by means of the letters sent to him, and himself express his indignation, as a senior leader, to the Embassy.

2./ Arrange for four to five people among his intellectual contacts for a similar purpose.

3./ Express public indignation in the columns of Új Élet.

Agent "Pesti Péter":

1./ Inform about the indignation by means of the letters sent to Új Élet and write an article in the newspaper. Then arrange for three to four people to write letters as individuals.

2./ Speak with the editor György Kecskeméti and ask him as the trade union leader to arrange for letters of protest to be written by trade union members (eight-ten persons).

Rabbinical Council:

The above matter must be placed on the agenda of the next rabbinical meeting and a resolution of protest adopted, with copies being sent to the leaders of the National Representation of Hungarian Israelites, the Embassy, the chief rabbi of Israel, and the editorial board of Új Élet.

Committee of the Victims of Nazism:

Here, by way of the reliable contacts of Comrade Police Captain István Dékány, letters of protest should be arranged, to be sent by several people.

In addition to the above, our agents "Sárosi", "Xavér", "Pesti Péter" as well as the social contacts "Sipos" and "Tanító," should write individually to their contacts in Israel and the West expressing their indignation. Their reliable friends and relatives should also write to people abroad.

The timing of the above action for the next few days is good because this is a favourable moment in a psychological sense and the necessary spontaneity is also assured. Thus, there is no need to employ various political and administrative measures and Socialist slogans. Rather, the departure point is the offended and ignored "Jewish emotions", which simply has to be pushed in the right direction, whereby we can reduce the range of the influence exerted by the Israeli Embassy.

On commencement of the campaign, we will increase the frequency of meetings with our network persons and increase the scope of control by means of various measures, with a view to keeping the campaign on its proper course and ensuring its success.

Based on the above, we request authorisation for implementation of the campaign.

Police Captain István Lukács, head of sub-department
Police Major Ferenc Mélykuti
Police Major László Katona, head of department

Completed in 1 copy

8 Campaign to Reduce the Influence of the Israeli Embassy

17 May 1965

Historical Archives of the Hungarian State Security 3.1.5. O-17169/1
Folder: "Zionists undertaking hostile activities" ["Ellenséges tevékenységet kifejtő cionisták"], vol. 2.

MINISTRY OF INTERIOR
Directorate III/II, Sub-department 5-a.

Subject: implemented campaign to reduce the influence of the Israeli Embassy

Report

Budapest, 17 May 1965

On 17 March 1965, we drafted a proposal for a campaign to partially reduce the influence of the Israeli Embassy. As the basis for the campaign, we took the increasing co-operation between West Germany and Israel and the disquiet among some Hungarian Jews about this.
   In brief: the main features of the campaign were as follows:

1./ A letter campaign targeting the Embassy and the leading bodies of the Jewish congregation.

2./ Sermons from the pulpit in the synagogues.

3./ A well-edited political article in Új Élet [*New Life*], the Jewish bi-weekly paper.

The campaign could be realised successfully only in part. Concerning the dispatch of the letters, we fathomed out the Committee for the Victims of Nazism through a reliable contact. The leaders of the Committee were dismissive of the idea and stated that co-operation between Israel and West Germany was, exclusively, a domestic matter for Israel and that we Hungarian Jews have nothing to say on this issue, and anyway they are preoccupied with the struggle against expiry [*of the right to make a claim for reparations* – AK].
   The publication of an article on the relationship between West Germany and Israel through reliable social contacts was aborted at the State Office for Church Affairs, where they were unable to give a clear answer as to whether it was correct or incorrect to publish an article of such nature.
   Having regard for the above negative developments, we aborted the letter campaign.
   We achieved some success in terms of the synagogue pulpit sermons. In Budapest's largest and best-attended synagogue (the Dohány Street synagogue) and in a

major synagogue outside Budapest, sessions condemning Israeli–West German relations were held.

In addition, entitled "A strange pairing", a politically well-edited and well-timed article was published in the Jewish newspaper Új Élet, together with several articles arguing against West Germany's policies.

The above writings were well received by patriotic and loyal Hungarian Jews, who agreed with them and condemned Israel.

According to multilateral network reports, around 50 per cent of Hungarian Jews were positive about the campaign. The other 50 per cent showed either indifference or hostility – about half and half – towards the campaign.

This is also supported by a report drafted by a deeper agent, who reported that the pro-Western and reactionary wing of the Hungarian Jewish religious community – with Marcell Steiner, vice chairman of the National Representation of Hungarian Israelites, and Sándor Scheiber, director of the rabbinical seminary, at the fore – consider the above article to be damaging from the vantage point of Israel.

The positive accomplishments of the campaign are particularly well illustrated by the words spoken by the diplomats David Ilan and Nachmann Ran on this subject, who, in an upset manner, scolded the article and its writer, stating "... this article has turned the Jews away from Israel and has greatly harmed us".

Thus, based on the foregoing, we can state that the campaign – despite setbacks – was correct and successful.

Police Captain Ferenc Mélykuti

Completed in 1 copy

9 The Economic Situation of the National Representation of Hungarian Israelites and the Budapest Israelite Congregation

11 August 1965

National Archives of Hungary, XIX-A-21-d (29.d.)
Collection: State Office for Religious Affairs [Állami Egyházügyi Hivatal, ÁEH]

[...]

2./ <u>The economic situation of the National Representation of Hungarian Israelites and the Budapest Israelite Congregation</u>

It is a known fact that, for some years now, economic management at the NRHI and the BIC has failed to meet the basic requirements of economic efficiency; economic management has been loss-making.

In many instances, our office has drawn this to the attention of the board of chairmen, requesting them to elaborate suitable proposals and sensible solutions for proper economic management.

While the board has made certain attempts to make savings in recent years, it has been fundamentally unable to resolve the problems, owing to an unwillingness to address the root of the problems.

There was no understanding for our warning that it is not possible to speak of efficient economic management as long as the denomination seeks to maintain such a large administrative and unproductive apparatus – together with its institutions and premises – which was oversized even in relation to the pre-war denomination with more than half a million members. Without solving this problem, an advance in the economic field is unlikely in the future.

The board of the NRHI – or at least some of its members – expected that our office would elaborate the reorganisation programme, its principles and topics, so that it could once again be a point of reference for "the board [to say it] is only implementing the will of the state".

Our office will not elaborate such a programme, [neither now] nor in the future, but it will fully support the newly elected board of chairmen, as they finally dismantle the superfluous and costly apparatus.

Nor has the significant sum arising from the sale of synagogues and other premises – about 6.5 forints [*sic! – probably 6.5 million forints* – AK] over the past five years – resolved the loss-making economic management.

The new leadership has to face up to an even greater responsibility, because there are not an infinite number of disused premises and selling them is becoming increasingly difficult. Thus, while it is correct to count on this source of income, the sales cannot be regarded as "a bottomless sack of money".

In a financial sense too, our state has fulfilled, or even exceeded, the pertinent part of the agreement with respect to the Jewish denomination [*See Introduction to Chapter 5* – AK].

In past two years alone, they have received around 850,000 forints in excess of the budget, to make up for the lack of funds.

One has to reckon with the fact that public finance, which has recently been tightened up, will not be in a position to make the extraordinary financial contributions in the future.

The task now faced by the Jewish denomination is to radically reduce the size of the apparatus and then introduce a system of planned economic management accompanied by financial discipline.

3./ <u>Jewish educational institutions</u>

a./ A significant change took place at the Jewish grammar school over the summer, as the principal, Mr Zsoldos, resigned from his post and went into retirement.

His deputy and Sándor Scheiber, the Religious Instruction teacher, showed solidarity with Zsoldos, and they too left the grammar school. László Davidovics, a member of our Party and an old Party worker, was appointed as the new principal. [...]

b./ We must address the situation of the Rabbinical Seminary in more detail, because that institution is headed by Dr Sándor Scheiber and because the composition of the teaching staff is not comforting from a political standpoint. It is an undeniable fact that the Rabbinical Seminary is now subject to Scheiber's monocracy and omnipotence. The management of the seminary should be the task of a so-called Executive Committee. Included among the members of the Executive Committee are several members of the boards of the NRHI and the BIC, including Endre Sós, the chairman. However, this committee is not operational, and it has allowed management to be in Scheiber's hands.

Another fact is that the students graduating from the seminary in the past 1–2 years cannot be called progressives in terms of their politics; indeed, they sympathise with Zionism.

[...]

Dr Scheiber has also played a significant role in spreading this political attitude. He is respected by theologians for his outstanding knowledge and bigoted religiosity, and because he is a talented speaker and a good teacher.

All of these features and his comfortable financial situation (Clems monies) [*sic!* – AK] have encouraged Scheiber to have his students or an even wider milieu accept his indifferent political views [*meaning: not supporting the existing political system* – AK].

Should Dr Sándor Scheiber be regarded as clearly a reactionary? If the question could only be answered with a yes, then our task would be easier – he must be dismissed, various means must be used to suppress him, etc. While Scheiber is not a friend of our People's democracy system, the fact that someone is not our friend does not necessarily mean that he is our enemy; nor can one exclude the possibility that someone who is not yet our friend, will not become one later on.

In Scheiber's case this will not be easy, but it cannot be ruled out. He is an Orthodox Jew dressed in the skin of a Neolog, who takes his religion seriously, has more than the average amount of nostalgia for the ancient homeland, Israel. And – and this is not rare among academic people – he is extremely foppish to science and above all to what is valued in "Western" Jewish circles.

We should not give up on Scheiber, even in the future. At the same time, in view of his current political and human conduct and attitudes, we cannot accept him as he is.

He needs to be dealt with in a multifaceted and differentiated fashion.

To recognise his knowledge and his abilities and to esteem him on the basis of his actions, and then express our trust in him accordingly. (In essence this aim is served by the authorisation of his current trip to England.) When he deserves it, we should express our recognition of him – for he is a vain man.

At the same time, we must criticise him; indeed, we should even "put him in his place" by taking the right measures, in all cases where this is necessary, for otherwise he will run away and go off the rails.

We must make it clear to him, applying correctly selected and alternate methods, that a love of one's religious denomination is only realisable, both in Hungary and abroad, in conjunction with a love of one's homeland, and that for him too this is the only way to get on.

[...]

In the meantime, however, certain measures must be taken to break his over-developed "self-confidence" and "self-esteem".

To this end, I propose the following:
- His closest associates and supporters must be separated from him in a methodical manner. [...] And this task can be performed gradually and methodically.
- The monocracy of Scheiber at the Rabbinical Seminary must be broken, and his perceived monopolistic position shaken up. To this end, we need to arrange for the new board to reintroduce the earlier practice whereby the rector of the seminary could be replaced every year, based on a proposal by the Executive Committee and a nomination by the NRHI. The resigning rector could then serve as vice rector in the new academic year. Similarly to the theologies of other churches, we could manage to ensure that a suitable rector might keep the official position for 2–3 academic years. [...]

- We need to ensure that the Seminary Executive Committee meets the standards of the vocation and refuses to let the theoretical and political management be snatched out of its hands.
- We should take action to ensure that theology teachers who are too old or indifferent are steadily replaced by suitable rabbis.

[...]

Financial aid from abroad and its management.

The accounting of the social assistance managed by the KSZB [*Central Social Committee*] is in order, has been checked by our office, and use of the sums is expedient: (e.g. soup kitchen, orphanage, hospital, nursing home, personal assistance etc.).

This cannot be said about the management and "expedient" use of funds provided by the Claims Conference – originally for cultural purposes.

This situation arose because the so-called Claims Committee, which was established for the use of cultural assistance, did not meet the standards of its vocation; it let the financial management be taken over by Dr Sándor Scheiber, who was then able, in view of the lack of proper controls, to distribute the sum as if it were "pocket money" – often for objectives that did not best serve Jewish culture.

At the same time, institutions such as the Jewish museum, which do really serve and preserve the Jewish past and Jewish culture, are still struggling with unresolved financial problems, owing to the pettiest of personal differences.

[...]

(Sándor Telepó)

10 Chairmanship Elections at the National Representation of Hungarian Israelites and the Budapest Israelite Congregation

21 December 1965

Historical Archives of the Hungarian State Security 3.1.5. O-17169/1
Folder: "Zionists undertaking hostile activities" ["Ellenséges tevékenységet kifejtő cionisták"], vol. 2.

MINISTRY OF INTERIOR
Directorate III/II, Sub-department 5-a.

Subject: On the status of the chairmanship elections at the National Representation of Hungarian Israelites and the Budapest Israelite Congregation

Memorandum

In January 1966, and in March, elections for the position of chairman will be held at the Budapest Israelite Congregation and the National Representation of Hungarian Israelites.

With a view to suppressing the reactionary elements and guiding the elections in the right direction, we have pushed out several Israel-centric persons from the leadership through the use of network and operational means and with the collaboration of the State Office for Church Affairs. Some of these people were replaced by reliable and loyal persons, but also the number of members of the board was reduced, which will make it easier to direct the life of the Jewish denomination, and there will be a reduction in unnecessary expenditures, etc.

Using various pretexts we initiated conversations with several important persons of the religious life. The conversations and hearings held with persons who have been compromised to a greater or lesser extent resulted in a reduction in the level of activity of members of the reactionary wing and helped to steer the elections in the right direction.

We undertook several measures by way of the operational network, by means of which we sought to ensure that our candidate will receive the majority of votes in the upcoming elections. The indications we have received to date, show that the overt and secret measures were successful in terms of their overall effect.

As we had indicated previously to our leaders, the leaders of the State Office for Church Affairs have decided on the holding of open elections. The competent forums of our Party have also accepted the principle of free elections.

This principle means that the chairmen of the Budapest Israelite Congregation and the National Representation of Hungarian Israelites can be chosen from two candidates.

[...]

About a week ago, Comrade József Prantner, chairman of the State Office for Church Affairs, announced – after the Presidential Council of the People's Republic of Hungary had approved the above list – the approved list of persons for election as the competent leaders of the Jewish religious community, and he emphasised that two candidates for the chairmanship would run in the elections, whereby the chairman would be the one whom the Jewish denomination chooses. This marked the beginning of the election campaign within the Jewish denomination.

III.

For our part, we have accepted the principle of free elections, and – as we mentioned already in the first part – we have prepared and launched a series of measures, through the application of which we hope to ensure the election of Dr Géza Seifert.

Concerning the elections, we have held talks on two occasions with Comrade Imre Miklós, the vice chairman, and with his colleagues. During the negotiations, we agreed upon the following:

1./ Endre Sós, the current chairman, cannot stay any longer at the National Representation of Hungarian Israelites, and together we support the election of Dr Géza Seifert.

The issue is such that the leaders of the State Office for Church Affairs are agreed on the candidature of Dr Géza Seifert and the support given to him, but externally the free election principle will be upheld. The task has fallen to us to influence the election campaign by directing the public mood in the right way, so that, as the end result, Endre Sós is removed from the leadership and Dr Géza Seifert is placed at the head of the National Representation of Hungarian Israelites.

2./ The removal of Endre Sós, who, as we have jointly determined, has not been a success as chairman of the National Representation of Hungarian Israelites, should occur using the most peaceful of means. (To this end, utilising the mood that has arisen among the rabbis and in agreement with the State Office for Church Affairs, we provided an opportunity, by means of the influence won through network operational means, for the Rabbinical Council to convene and adopt a resolution on the most peaceful administration of the chairmanship elections. The Rabbinical Council has convened, and at the meeting the unanimous decision was taken to offer clear support, within their districts, for the candidature of Dr Géza Seifert, and to request Sós resign from the post of chairman for the sake of the community.

[...]

5./ On the issue of the vice chairmanship of Dr Mihály Borsa, we agreed that Comrade Imre Miklós would speak with him in person and make clear to him that the Central Social Committee is an integral part of the National Representation of Hungarian Israelites and that if he decides against taking on the denominational role that goes with the vice chairmanship, then there would be no obstacle to him resigning from the post of chairman of the Central Social Committee, etc.

6./ Finally, we agreed – at the wish and to the satisfaction of both sides – that we would co-ordinate more closely the relations on issues of religious policy between the two bodies, especially during the period of the elections.

At present, there is no crucial issue concerning which there is disagreement between the State Office for Church Affairs and our opinion. We have debated all the problems arising in a comradely atmosphere and in agreement.

This is how the current situation relating to the chairmanship elections at the National Representation of Hungarian Israelites can be summarized in brief.

Police Major Ferenc Mélykuti

Completed in 1 copy

11 Policy Measures in the Field of the Jewish Religious Community

18 May 1968

Historical Archives of the Hungarian State Security 3.1.5. O-17169/2
Folder: "Zionists undertaking hostile activities" ["Ellenséges tevékenységet kifejtő cionisták"], vol. 3.

MINISTRY OF INTERIOR
Directorate III/II, Sub-department 4-A.

Subject: Implementation of church policy measures undertaken and in progress in the field of the Jewish religious community

Memorandum

Budapest, 18 May 1968

Based on the proposal approved by the Head of the Ministry of Interior's Directorate III, in the course of 1967 we realised [*handing over secretly gathered information to the juridical authorities* – AK] the Zionist grouping code-named "SHALOM". With the ending of the investigation and in the spirit of the additional measures that were approved in our proposal, we informed, by way of the Ministry of Interior's Investigative Department, the leaders of the State Office for Church Affairs of the content and nature of the case. In doing so, our purpose was that, having received the information, they should be able to take appropriate church policy measures in the field of the Jewish religious community.

With our agreement, the leadership of the State Office for Church Affairs summoned to its offices the senior secular and religious leaders of the Jewish denomination and told them about the aforementioned matter. The State Office for Church Affairs explained the position of the Hungarian state and requested those present to express their opinions on the matter.

In essence the leaders of the denomination distanced themselves unanimously from the activities of the Zionist groups and offered assurances concerning their loyalty to the People's Republic of Hungary.

Having received the information at the State Office for Church Affairs and after a discussion of the questions arising, Dr Imre Benoschofszky, the chairman of the rabbinical council, took the matter before the rabbinical meeting with a view to informing the rabbis of the events and of further church policy measures, as well as the position of the state on this issue. The rabbis and the secular leaders made statements condemning the harmful Zionist activities, and then they distanced themselves in a memorandum from such harmful activities.

[...]

II.

Since it has been established, based on data obtained in the "Shalom" case and in the course of a network operational investigation of the National Rabbinical Seminary, that negative and damaging influences prevail at the Rabbinical Seminary (whereby, in consequence of Zionist propaganda, several students have left the country illegally, have emigrated or have taken part in education for young people in a Zionist spirit), we agreed with the State Office for Church Affairs on the elaboration and implementation of the following personnel and religious policy measures:

1./ With the active collaboration of the State Office for Church Affairs, we shall introduce the rotation in the position of the director of the National Rabbinical Seminary. In this way, we can exert adequate pressure on Dr Sándor Scheiber, director of the Rabbinical Seminary, for the purpose of persuading him to move the education of the rabbinical students in a positive direction. If he fails to do so, with reference to the rotation system, a more loyal and politically appropriate person can be appointed as director at any time.
    The introduction of the new system is now in progress.

2./ Based on consultations with us, the State Office for Church Affairs shall take steps to ensure the introduction of instruction in the social sciences, with the aim of developing correct political education and shaping a world view. For this purpose, a reliable and politically well-trained teacher will be appointed at the Rabbinical Seminary. The measure is already underway.

3./ At our proposal, the State Office for Church Affairs will, in future, give greater attention, by way of the competent desk officer, to more intensively concerning itself with the teachers and students of the Rabbinical Seminary, doing so on an individual basis.

[...]

4./ We proposed to the competent staff members of the State Office for Church Affairs that, for the sake of educating in the right direction those Jewish youths who are drawn to the religious community, a special programme must be elaborated with the involvement of loyal religious and secular leaders.
    The leaders of the State Office for Church Affairs agree with our proposal and will take steps themselves to this end.

Note: Based on the conclusions drawn from the methods and nature of the Zionist endeavours and groups arising within the ranks of the denomination, we see that young people are demanding actions and events organised by the institutions that are closer to their circle of interests and are more flexible. Here we are thinking of the on-going imperative of organising – at the time of the minor and major Jewish festivals – positive events of a religious, political, social and cultural nature that also include dancing, whereby the objective would be to gradually eradicate Zionism from the thinking of Jewish youths.

The aim of the measures that have been briefly outlined is to sow the seeds of Socialism and internationalism among these circles, with the anti-Fascist soil as a departure point and with the help of more flexible methods. We need to make them understand that the survival of Jewry is only possible in Socialism, and then gradually turn them into people who are loyal to Socialism and to the People's Republic of Hungary.

We have supported the implementation of the above measures by way of the network persons and we shall support it even more forcefully in the future.

I have attached to this memorandum a copy of the minutes of the meeting of the Budapest Israelite Congregation rabbis of 24 January 1968.

Lieutenant-Colonel Ferenc Mélykuti

Completed in 1 copy / 4 pages

12 Reports on the World Federation of Hungarian Jews and the Meeting of the Former Pupils of the Jewish Grammar School

2 October 1973

Historical Archives of the Hungarian State Security 3.1.5. O-17169/3
Folder: "Zionists undertaking hostile activities" ["Ellenséges tevékenységet kifejtő cionisták"], vol. 4.

MINISTRY OF INTERIOR
Directorate III/II.

Copy no. 2

[*Handwritten note by L. Karasz in the margin – AK*]: Comrade Ambrus, The nature of the topic and the danger it means for the People's Republic of Hungary is a matter of course, therefore it was unnecessary to add the remark about whether the Israeli intelligence had or did not have a role in it.

Information report

Reports concerning the World Federation of Hungarian Jews and the meeting of September 2, 1973 of the former pupils of the Jewish Grammar School in Budapest
(Only for members of the Political Committee)

The 28th Zionist World Congress, held in Jerusalem in January 1972, adopted a resolution for the cohesion and unity of Jews living outside Israel – principally in the Socialist countries, among them the People's Republic of Hungary – and for the launch of their emigration to Israel or the acceleration of such emigration. The principles and practical realisation of this resolution were debated and approved at a conference of the World Federation of Hungarian Jews, held in Tel Aviv on 8–11 May 1973. At the conference, the WFHJ elected – on account of various considerations – a new leadership. The U.S. citizen Tibor J. WALDMAN, president of the American branch of the WFHJ, was elected as overall chairman, while Dr KAUDERS BEN CION, president of the Israeli branch, was elected as co-chairman. An objective of the new leadership is the more intense propagation and realization of the resolutions of the Zionist World Congress. Extremist views such as this were heard: "It is time for the emigration of the entire Jewish population in Hungary, to which end a consistent struggle must be launched". In their view, "Hungarian Jewry has to be awoken to the need to consider not only what it can expect from Israel but also what it can give Israel". They also want to raise awareness that "they are awaited in Israel and will be welcomed there".

In certain Western – above all American, Canadian and Israeli – newspapers, a propaganda campaign for the popularisation of the resolutions has already begun. György EGRI, chief editor of "MENORA," a Zionist magazine published in Canada, called attention to the fact that "Hungary is the only country behind the Iron Curtain with a significant Jewish population, from which there has been no emigration in recent years". In his view, "it is a false notion that Hungarian Jewry does not want to emigrate because it is doing well. There is an intent – particularly among young people – and the only thing lacking is encouragement and assistance". In Egri's view, preparations for a wave of emigration from Hungary should be made both in Israel and in America.

The organisation of a meeting of students who had graduated from the Jewish Grammar School in the 1930s, at the Radnóti Miklós Grammar School on 2 September and then at the Gellért Hotel [*after 1961 the original building of the JGS served as the building of the grammar school named after the poet Miklós Radnóti – AK*], may be viewed as part of the announced propaganda campaign. (We provided information about preparations for this meeting on 29 August 1973.) The fraternity of former pupils of the Jewish Grammar School was established in 1969 at the initiative and with the financial support of the U.S. citizen Dr László TAUBER, a professor of surgery, and a meeting was held first in New York and thereafter every year in a different city (Toronto, Washington, Montreal). Key roles in organising the meeting in Budapest have been played by László GEIGER, the co-president of the American branch of the WFHJ, by the U.S. citizen Pál ELEK and by several Hungarian citizens. The meeting held at Radnóti Grammar School was attended by approximately 130 persons, while 188 attended the event at the Hotel Gellért. Eighteen of those in attendance arrived from the American continent. Some of them also attended the Debrecen congress of physicians, held in late August 1973. Among the Hungarian citizens in attendance there were several persons in senior positions (e.g. members of staff from the National Planning Office, the Ministry for Foreign Trade, the Hungarian Academy of Sciences, the Karl Marx University of Economics and the State Book Distribution Enterprise etc.). They also invited representatives of the Fencing and Athletics Club [*Vívó és Atlétikai Club, VAC, a Zionist sports club founded in 1906 – AK*], a sport club that was officially closed down in 1952 on account of its overt Zionist activities. In addition to people of various age groups, several youths were also in attendance.

At the meeting, both the foreign and the Hungarian speakers praised the "vibrant Jewish life" which had characterised the grammar school. The glory of the grammar school had been spread, in their view, by the fact that it had completed many eminences and several of its teachers had undertaken recognised scientific work, thereby developing further Jewish science and old literary traditions. Still, its greatest merit was that the Jewish spirit is still alive even today, even if "the stone that was thrown had broken the surface of the water, and the water is glistening again, the stone is still down there in the riverbed". In his speech, Dr László Tauber stated that they were seeking to spread everywhere the sense of Jewishness and Jewish cohesion that had been drummed into them at the grammar school, and for as long as even a single Jewish grammar school pupil remained alive, these teachings would be upheld. In his view, the large numbers in attendance at the meeting demonstrate that "the spirit of the Jewish Grammar School has forged us together and is keeping us together". He also recalled the close relationship that had existed between the former Jewish Grammar School and the Fencing and

Athletics Club. He emphasised the role played by various sportsmen who, in the competitions, had "represented the entire Jewish people".

One of the speakers said – among other things – that "we shall live forever, because it is our calling to uphold the humane spirit, philanthropy and a humanity that faces extinction".

According to unverified information, the organisers of the meeting wish to create a "Hungarian group in the fraternity of former Jewish grammar school pupils" from among former pupils of the school who are still living in Hungary. The plan is to hold the next meeting – scheduled for 1974 – in Israel.

According to our information, further objectives of the World Federation of Hungarian Jews are as follows:
- the realisation of the old plan for the National Representation of Hungarian Israelites to become a member of the WFHJ;
- education and influence of Jewish youth in a nationalist spirit;
- within the framework of the organisation "AMERICAN JEWISH CONGRESS", the provision of support and assistance to the activities of the WFHJ for the purpose of establishing closer relations between foreign and domestic Jewry – between 18 May and 19 October 1974, they plan to send, on 11 occasions, groups of 40 people to the People's Republic of Hungary;
- in both Europe and the United States of America, they will establish emigration offices for the purpose of launching a wave of emigration from Hungary;
- to achieve a situation in which the position of the leadership of the WFHJ is realised – namely that the WFHJ – as the central body of Hungarian Jewry – is called to proceed "in the matter of the universal problems facing Hungarian Jewry" vis-à-vis the government of the United States of America and the governments of other countries, as well as the diplomatic representations.

Note: Concerning the meeting of the former pupils of the Budapest Jewish Grammar School, no data arose that would suggest that Israeli intelligence lay behind it. To detect and prevent this and other similar meetings, our organs will implement active measures.

(The information stems from reliable and verified sources.)

Police Lieutenant-Colonel Sándor Ambrus
Deputy Head of the Directorate

Completed in 4 copies
SUBMITTED TO:
Copy no. 1: Police Maj.-Gen. P. Rácz
Copy no. 2: Police Maj.-Gen. L. Karasz
Copy no. 3: Inform. Processing and Supervisory group directorate
Copy no. 4: Deposited

13 On the Activities of Domestic and Foreign Zionists

6 February 1975

Historical Archives of the Hungarian State Security 3.1.5. O-17169/5
Folder: "Zionists undertaking hostile activities" ["Ellenséges tevékenységet kifejtő cionisták"], vol. 6.

Memorandum

on experiences of the activities of domestic and foreign Zionists

Our operational experiences show that the main direction of hostile activities of a Zionist nature corresponds with activities of this nature undertaken by international reactionary forces. They consider their main task to be sustaining and fostering the Jewish spirit as well as preventing assimilation. To this end, they organise group meetings, with the involvement principally of young people, and then they seek to influence them in this spirit.

Another attribute of their activities is popularising Israel and supporting its policies, while also taking a stand against the policies of, and being hostile towards, the Soviet Union. We have one-sided indications that, alongside the propaganda work in support of Israel's policies, they are also supporting Israel financially and organising collections. (To date, we have not been able to document such a case or check it from various sides.)

There are a significant number of people who maintain active correspondence and personal contact with their relations and acquaintances living in Israel or in other Western countries. Several have requested passports for travel to the FRG, whence they travel on to Israel without the knowledge of the Hungarian authorities. Sometimes Hungarian citizens meet in Romania with their relatives from Israel, arranging such meetings by letter.

Experiences of the activities of foreign Zionist individuals and organisations directed at Hungarian Jews:

The World Federation of Hungarian Jews, which is a member of the "World Zionist Organization", is making efforts to involve the National Representation of Hungarian Israelites (NRHI) in the activities of the international organisations, with a view to strengthening their influence over the NRHI.

The NRHI regularly receives from the Joint annual assistance worth 750,000 dollars. At present, talks are under way concerning the granting of an additional and extraordinary sum of 600–800,000 dollars to the NRHI over a period of several years.

They regularly check how the sums are used, and so they often have an opportunity to come to Hungary. They use such visits to collect various reports and to survey the situation, etc.

For instance, in December 1974, Dr Israel MOWSHOVITZ, president of the Rabbinical Council of New York, arrived in the country. He visited the various institutions of the NRHI, and then, in the course of discussions, expressed an interest in the following questions:
- Is there antisemitism in Hungary?
- Do Jewish youth organisations exist?
- Do people want to emigrate to Israel?
- Does the Jewish religious community have contacts with other religious denominations?

He called on the leaders of the denomination to urgently begin a dialogue above all with the Protestant churches and win them over for the "cause of Israel".

Concerning the treasurer of the World Federation of Hungarian Jews, László Keller, we have data showing that he organises and supports the emigration of Hungarian persons.

Counter-intelligence is currently undertaking operational processing and investigative work in 4 cases with opened operational folders and 2 preliminary investigations.

In their nature, these are primarily groups of young people. At their meetings the main aim is establishing group cohesion among the young people and fostering the Jewish spirit.

In these cases, we have around 100–120 persons under processing or control as part of the preliminary investigations.

Among these, the following are particularly noteworthy:
- "Direktor" code-named case, approx. 30–40 persons meet regularly
- "Jubilálók" [Jubilants] code-named case, approx. 15–20 persons
- "Segélyezők" [Supporters] code-named case, approx. 12–15 persons
- 2 groups among people who resettled in Hungary from Carpatho-Ukraine, approx. 15+15 persons
- 10 additional persons from Carpatho-Ukraine are under surveillance, who are forwarding letters between their acquaintances living in the Soviet Union and in Israel.

Among the Socialist countries, there are – in view of the people who resettled in Hungary from Carpatho-Ukraine – direct points of contact in terms of counter-intelligence with the Soviet Union.

During the past two years, 1,130 people received permission to resettle in Hungary. It would seem that, by means of such resettlement, they hope to facilitate their joining their relatives in Israel or the West. Our data suggest, however, that so far only a few people have moved on to the West.

At present, we are aware of two groups among those who resettled in Hungary. Each of these groups comprises approx. 15 persons. In terms of their attitudes, they are strongly pro-Israel and anti-Soviet.

[...]

Agent "Gromov" of the Soviet state security organs has also reported on the Grünzweig group [*a group of Carpatho-Ukrainian Jews around the physicist Miklós Grünzweig living in Hungary* – AK]. The comrades have suggested that we should elaborate a plan for the agent to come to Hungary and for the joint processing of the group. A response is currently being elaborated.

Agent "Zóla" of the Soviet state security organs resettled in Hungary from Ungvár [*Uzhhorod* – AK] and is currently living in Budapest. The comrades have offered to transfer him, but this has not occurred so far. "Zóla" has a good opportunity to obtain intelligence in the grouping run by Mrs Szanka [*an other group of Carpatho-Ukrainian Jews around Mrs. Szanka living in Hungary* – AK] and so his transfer as soon as possible is a necessity.

14 On the Operations in the Jewish Religious Community in 1977

16 November 1977

Historical Archives of the Hungarian State Security 3.1.5. O-17169/5
Folder: "Zionists undertaking hostile activities" ["Ellenséges tevékenységet kifejtő cionisták"], vol. 6.

MINISTRY OF INTERIOR
III/III, Sub-department 1-c.

Subject: work in 1977

Summary report

The operational status of reactionary forces in the Jewish religious community in 1977 was as follows:

In the preceding years, we registered a great deal of interest as well as intensive information gathering activity on the part of various Zionist and Jewish nationalist organisations with regard to the situation of Hungarian Jews, their life circumstances, religious life and position in society. We attributed all of this to the fact that there is minimal demand for emigration amongst Hungarian Jews, who are generally satisfied with their life and the other circumstances that socialist society assures them.

In addition, we also discovered attempts to involve and activate the leaders of the Hungarian [Jewish] denomination in various Jewish organisations. In this field, the leaders of the World Jewish Congress were particularly active. At the same time, they sought to show a loyal face to the Soviet Union and the Socialist countries and – emphasising the necessity of the universality of the WJC – to strengthen contacts with Jewish leaders in the Soviet Union and the other Socialist countries.

The data gathering and data evaluation activities of earlier years continued in 1977. We acquired knowledge of a number of individual and group visits to Hungary, in the course of which data were gathered on Hungarian Jewry.

Based on the results obtained in the course of the evaluation of data, WJC leaders have concluded that Hungarian Jews are living under proper circumstances and, moreover, that similar circumstances should be provided to Jews living in the other Socialist countries. In essence, they speak of a Hungarian model, which could serve as an example to the other Socialist countries. Several leaders specifically stated this.

A fundamental change has occurred in the attitude of WJC leaders to Hungarian Jewry. They are giving particular attention to the Hungarian Jewish leaders, and NAHUM GOLDMANN and several WJC leaders wish to travel to Hungary in December 1977, while the new president of the WJC, P. KLUTZNIK [sic! – AK], also wishes to come in January 1978.

This heightened interest, apart from giving emphasis to the role of Hungarian Jewry, can also be attributed – according to operational data – to an intent to request the Hungarian Jewish and state leaders to act as mediators in the establishment of contacts between the WJC and Soviet Jewry.

[...]

The old situation still prevails in relation to the National Representation of Hungarian Israelites and the World Federation of Hungarian Jews. The leaders of the WFHJ seek to strengthen their influence over Hungarian Jewish leaders. They regularly travel to Hungary, establishing contacts and offering financial support of an insignificant amount to the National Representation of Hungarian Israelites. To strengthen their positions here, they seek to develop good relations with members of the Hungarian diplomatic representations in Washington and at the UN as well as with the World Federation of Hungarians.

We have also experienced attempts by other Zionist and non-Zionist organisations to build relations, but these have not yet come to fruition, and so we do not know in detail their true aims and objectives.

The postal dispatch to Hungary of hostile propaganda material by various organisations and private individuals has continued. In particular, one should highlight the activities in this field of the BIRD information agency (Jerusalem). The BIRD agency regularly sends – to various Hungarian bodies, organisations and private individuals – summary information material on events in the Middle East and Africa, which are primarily anti-Soviet in content. Most of the material has been removed from circulation and destroyed by Department III/3.

In the first half of 1977, private individuals often sent newspaper articles of hostile content in their letters to relatives and acquaintances. Most of these were – at our behest – removed by Department III/3 from the post and destroyed. This activity has exhibited a declining trend in the second half of the year; the amount is significantly less than in the preceding period.

[...]

Group and individual Jewish travel to Hungary has continued – from the U.S., the UK, the FRG and Israel. The travellers usually visit the Jewish institutions and take part in various events and meetings where, in statements or simply through their presence, they bear witness to a conduct that is nationalist and popularises Israel and the associated U.S. policies and which also emphasises the worldwide cohesion of Jews. They are careful, however, not to go beyond the limits of the law. Of particular significance in this regard was the 25-member Israeli delegation that appeared at the FIJET congress in October; the delegation was led by Dan Ofry, who works for Israeli radio and has extreme Zionist views.

The effect of such endeavours manifests itself in various forms in the domestic aspect of counter-intelligence.

In earlier periods, the leaders of the National Representation of Hungarian Israelites undertook a policy that was consistent and in line with religious policy. Under the influence of the above, this has changed as follows.

Even today they still completely accept the direction set by the State Office for Church Affairs and they represent this position in their statements at international forums.

At the same time, in terms of their actions and their statements to one another, one can experience a degree of Western orientation or one might also say a Jewish nationalist orientation. Perhaps this was already present earlier on, but it has certainly grown stronger this year.

This is best reflected in the tone whereby before they take a position on any issue, in almost every case they ask what the West will say or what will the leaders of the WJC, the WFHJ and the Joint say. Or, for instance, a completely unknown journalist happens to arrive, let's say, from Canada. They give him priority attention and deal with him at the chairmanship level, lest he should write something "disparaging" about them in his article, and so forth.

Or the chairman and the secretary-general took part, on several occasions, in meetings of a Jewish nationalist nature organised by the targeted person "DIREKTOR" [Sándor Scheiber – AK], emphasising and approving of – through their presence – the spirit prevailing there.

The spiritual/intellectual centre of the Zionist and Jewish nationalist activity continues to be the targeted person "DIREKTOR" and his milieu. It can be clearly concluded that a Jewish elite is being trained at the Friday evening meetings held at the Rabbinical Seminary. Similarly to earlier periods, these meetings are attended by 100–150 people. Jewish leaders, journalists and other people in intellectual occupations regularly attend the meetings, occasionally even giving talks whose main message is often the necessity of worldwide Jewish unity and the importance of Israel's role.

With a view to reducing assimilation, various marriage agencies continue to mediate in terms of the Soviet–Hungarian and Hungarian–Western relations. The organiser of this continues to be the targeted person "DIREKTOR".

During the year, by way of measure 3/e, we made certain of the extremely hostile attitudes of "DIREKTOR". He made strongly hostile and anti-Soviet outbursts in connection with the Moscow conference of World Religions. Or, while preparing a speech for the centenary anniversary of the Rabbinical Seminary, one of his closest friends sought to persuade him to include in the speech the terms "liberation," [by the Soviet Union – AK], "socialism," and the "People's state" but he strongly rejected this, saying that he was not a prostitute.

Despite all this, thanks to the aforementioned new orientation of the leaders of the National Representation of Hungarian Israelites, it can be stated that the status of the targeted person has become even firmer, and so he is even more audaciously carrying out his detrimental activities and also openly expressing his hostile views.

The groupings of a Jewish nationalist nature that we observed in earlier periods continue to exist. However, owing to the operational disruptive measures carried out under various covers, the holding of meetings in public places – e.g. in the Dunapark and Európa restaurants – has largely ceased. Many people have left the groups, but those who remain, having been atomised, continue to meet in smaller groups in private apartments. Next year, one of our tasks will be to obtain specific data about such groups and then take further disruptive measures.

The operational status of those people who resettled in Hungary from the Soviet Union has not essentially changed during the year. There continues to be lively contact between them and, on the one hand, their relatives and acquaintances who are still in the Soviet Union and, on the other, persons who emigrated to Israel or to other Western countries. It often happens that they simultaneously invite persons living in the Soviet Union and those who have emigrated to the West, and these persons then meet with each other here, but we have not observed specific hostile actions and activities in this context.

The contacts of resettled persons continue to be dominated by material interests and trafficking; they undertake such activities in a wide-ranging manner.

During the year, we did not receive data of specific hostile activity in this category.

II.

1./ The number of pieces of information that came into our possession in 1977: 496
    a./ Their sources:

a./ Network (persons)	153
b./ Technical	145
c./ Official contact	3
d./ From a co-organisation	44
e./ Operative analysis	32
f./ Reported	-
g./ other means	119
b./ Secret investigation:	54
c./ Preliminary checks:	11
d./ Required taking of measure:	69

2./ Evaluation of secret investigations and preliminary checks:

[...]

"DIREKTOR" code-named case 13-Cs-759 and 11-SZ-8983/.

The group folder was opened by the Interior Ministry's III/II-4 Department on 20 May 1971. According to the basic information, the director of the National Rabbinical Seminary and three of his associates exploited legal loopholes to undertake wide-ranging illegal organising activities among Jewish youths.

We employed several network persons in the case, and we also applied the 3/e and "K" checks.

The data and information arising in the course of the checks clearly proved that in recent years the National Rabbinical Seminary has become the site of widespread illegal Jewish nationalist organising activities, directed by the head of the Seminary.

Exploiting the legal loopholes to the fullest extent, they organise and hold Friday evening meetings, at which Jewish nationalist speeches and talks are given.

On a regular basis, foreign persons are invited to the meetings, who are then given a chance to speak there. The targeted person is in close contact with several foreign international Zionist organisations and individuals.

The information arising in the course of the checks prove that the hostile activities are centred on one person.

Based on the above, we suggest the closure of this group folder and the continuation of the matter in a personal folder.

We opened the "SZ" folder [*personal folder* – AK] code-named "DIREKTOR", Nr. 11-SZ-8983 on 9 May 1977.

In the course of processing, we concluded that the targeted person, as the head of the National Rabbinical Seminary, is seeking, by way of his domestic and foreign contacts, to establish an operational situation which enables him to get rid of the control of the leadership and direction of the National Representation of Hungarian Israelites.

He undertakes wide-ranging organising activities at the international level with a view to gaining recognition for his person and his "scientific" activities. He actively searches for contacts and opportunities at home and abroad on the basis of which he would be recognised at the state level too.

Based on his hostile and reactionary attitudes and his boundless drive for positions, he opposes the denominational leaders that are loyal to the state.

On occasion he criticises them and seeks to discredit them. Under the legal auspices of the institute he runs, he has gathered around him those Zionist and Jewish nationalist intellectuals who take a reactionary and oppositional stance against our society.

We have concluded that the targeted person has extremely hostile views and regularly makes anti-Soviet and anti-Communist statements among his narrow circle of friends, abusing the Soviet Union. Despite the greatest efforts of the competent leaders, he firmly refuses to even mention in his speeches "liberation", "Socialism", "People's state" or other such similar terms.

In the matter, we applied several network persons as well as the measures 3/e and 3/a. We gave signals to the heads of the State Office for Church Affairs.

"FŐMÉRNÖK" [Chief engineer] preliminary checks

From 18 May 1977, we have held under a preliminary check FERENC LOVÁSZ (b. 1929). […]

According to the basic information, illegal Jewish religious services and religious instruction sessions were held for youths in the apartment of Ferenc Lovász. In the course of the preliminary checks, we found that from time to time a loose-knit group of youths would meet at Ferenc Lovász's apartment. Ferenc Lovász plays a role as initiator, intermediary and organiser in the arrangement of the meetings. In terms of those attending and its activities, the youth group is closely linked with the Friday evening meetings at the National Rabbinical Seminary.

The head of the grouping and most of the young people are under the spiritual/intellectual direction of Dr Sándor Scheiber.

We prolonged the preliminary checks on one occasion. We employed two network persons in the investigation, and we applied measure 3/a for a period of 30 days.

[…]

3./ Measures of a preventive nature:

In addition to the secret investigations and preliminary checks, we have also implemented several measures with a view to preventing various hostile objectives and steps of such nature. The most important of these were as follows:
- We took several measures concerning the filling of the chairmanship and other senior posts at the National Representation of Hungarian Israelites, the purpose of which was to prevent persons with hostile attitudes from occupying such positions.
- We checked continuously – by way of the "K" check – postal dispatches to or from Israel. At our behest, much material of hostile content was seized and destroyed.
- We continuously monitor the visa applications of persons seeking to travel to Hungary from Israel, and at our suggestion the applications of several persons with hostile attitudes who wished to come to the country, were turned down.
- Regarding travel to and from Hungary, we prevented the departure of several people and one person was put on the list of persons prohibited to enter Hungary.
- Utilising passport applications and other legal opportunities, we had conversations with several people, who then assisted in the disruption of various groups or we prevented the formation of a group.

In general we can state that our measures were successful. It is necessary, however, to apply similar methods to a greater extent in the future.

4./ Network measures:

[...]

Numbers in the network:

On 1 January 1977:	Secret informers:	9 persons
	Agent:	1 person
	"K" apartment:	1
	"T" apartment:	1
	Total:	12 persons

[...]

In the annual plan, we anticipated employing more informers, but we did not implement the plan owing to the unsuitability of the persons, avoidance of the field and for other objective reasons. Nor did we manage to recruit among people who resettled in Hungary from the Soviet Union.

[...]

5./ Use of operational means:

During the year, we used operational technical means in secret investigations, in preliminary checks, for checking network persons and for goals of a preventive nature.

In numbers:

3/e   in 1 instance
3/a   in 7 instances
"K" checks were used on 20 people (based on the list)

Measure 3/e was used in the secret investigation "DIREKTOR.". The bugging was undertaken in July, in two official rooms [...]. The period since then has provided very valuable data from an operational and political perspective about the hostile foreign contacts of the targeted person, his hostile attitudes, activities, and objectives.

Use of measure 3/a was successful in each case. It greatly assisted our operational work. In every case we drafted evaluative reports.

The "K" checks were successful principally in an Israeli aspect. A lot of material of hostile content had to be seized and destroyed. We received valuable data about various leaders of the World Federation of Hungarian Jews and their contacts in Hungary.

6./ Persons affected by the measures:

During the year we took measures against a total of 9 persons. These were:

- Pre-trial detention: 1 person
- House search: 3 persons
- Police warning: 1 person
- Inclusion on list of banned persons
  [*not allowed to enter Hungary* – AK]: 1 person
- Prevention of entry to Hungary: 2 persons
- Prevention of departure from Hungary: 1 person

In all cases, the measures accorded with the requirements of legality.

[…]

11./ International relations:

In 1977, we had common actions with the Soviet, Czechoslovak, and GDR state security organs.

We had several common initiatives with the Soviet state security organs, which related to the implementation of tasks by agents.

In two instances we took part in personal discussions. We offered them written information on five occasions concerning information of an international nature acquired by way of the network.

We turned to the Czechoslovak state security organs with one request for information, to which we received an answer. Similarly, we too provided one piece of information.

At the request of the GDR state security organs, we checked a group that arrived in Hungary from the FRG. We then provided information on what we had learned.

Police Lieutentant-Colonel József Fülöp

15 The Centenary of the National Rabbinical Seminary

16 December 1977

Historical Archives of the Hungarian State Security 3.1.5. O-17169/5
Folder: "Zionists undertaking hostile activities" ["Ellenséges tevékenységet kifejtő cionisták"], vol. 6.

MINISTRY OF INTERIOR

Report

Celebrations to mark the centenary of the National Rabbinical Seminary (Budapest) were held in Budapest on 5–6 December 1977.

In addition to the Hungarian guests, 34 people from the Western countries and 17 representatives of Jewish organisations in the European Socialist countries took part.

For the first time ever, 4 leaders of the World Jewish Congress attended the event in Hungary.
– Dr Nahum Goldmann, founding president
– Armand Kaplan, director of the international department
– Dr Siegfried Roth, director of the European Section
– Gerhard M. Riegner, secretary-general of the WJC

Other participants included:
– Three leaders of the World Federation of Hungarian Jews – Miklós Nánási, László Keller, Arthur Schneier – persons living in the United States.
– The vice chairman and a member of staff of the American Jewish Committee (JOINT) [*sic!* – AK]
– The vice chairman and secretary of Societé de Secours, the Swiss aid organisation.
– The director of the Memorial Foundation, a cultural organisation.

In the course of their official statements and private conversations, the leaders of the WJC and several delegates noted how they considered the event to be of major significance, because they could obtain personal experience of the life of Hungarian Jewry. They assessed this experience as positive and as better than expected.

All of them also emphasised the significance of the event in terms of providing an opportunity for an international meeting at which the leaders of the WJC and other organisations could hold direct discussions with the leaders of the Jewish communities in the Socialist countries.

Speakers at the event addressed the past, present and future of world Jewry. They spoke in a loyal tone and extremist expressions were not heard. They consciously avoided mentioning Israel and the Middle-East problem.

The central theme of Dr Nahum Goldman's [sic! – AK] speech was the current situation of Jewry. He explained how Jews needed to struggle on two fronts, first externally against antisemitism and neo-Fascism and for the implementation of human rights, and so forth. Secondly, they must struggle – and this is the main issue – for order in their own ranks. In his judgement, Jewry is threatened by the danger of assimilation. The most valuable elements of Jewish youth are being swallowed up by society; the intellectual and spiritual values of Jewry are being lost. The principal task is to prevent this from happening.

One could observe how the leaders of the WJC acted in line with a pre-determined division of roles.

Dr Goldman held talks with state and religious leaders. His schedule was organised and administered by Armand Kaplan. Dr Siegfried Roth dealt with the Soviet delegates and was in close contact with Dr Sándor Scheiber, the director of the seminary. Gerhard Riegner sought to establish close relations with the Czechoslovak and Polish delegates and then hold discussions with them.

Their opinions and ambitions, as expressed in the course of their activities, can be summarised as follows:

Subjects at the focus of discussions with the various leaders of the National Representation of Hungarian Israelites were a revival of Hungarian Jewish cultural life and the issue of cohesion and activation among Jewish youth. WJC leaders stated that they were satisfied with the religious life of Hungary Jewry and the conditions provided for it, but that greater efforts should be made to propagate and revive Jewish culture.

A pledge was made concerning the intent of the Memorial Foundation to provide more funding for Hungarian Jewry, subject to the National Representation of Hungarian Israelites issuing an assurance that the sum would be used for cultural rather than social purposes. Based on this, press and book publications should be increased, and the launch of a Hebrew language course would perhaps be necessary, concluded by the issuing of a certificate.

In the course of the negotiations, WJC leaders mentioned to the leaders of the National Representation of Hungarian Israelites that they would like for the representative of Hungarian Jewry – similarly to Yugoslavia and Romania – to move from observer status to permanent membership of the WJC. In this way, they could be elected to the Advisory Council, thereby making the work more successful.

They asked whether, if the situation in the Middle East were to be resolved, there might be a possibility of holding a meeting of the European Section of the WJC in Budapest. The leaders of the National Representation of Hungarian Israelites did not give a concrete response.

They announced the intention to establish, in 1978, a commission in Paris or Vienna which would comprise various Jewish scientists and public figures with the task of working on a Jewish-Arab rapprochement. They expressed their wish that a representative of Hungarian Jewry should take part in the commission, and they would like Dr Sándor Scheiber to be this person. As they did not receive a clear answer concerning Dr Sándor Scheiber, the writer György Száraz was mentioned at Scheiber's proposal, and Dr Siegfried Roth then contacted him.

Dr Siegfried Roth held discussions with Dr Sándor Scheiber, who informed him in detail of the internal situation and leaders of the National Representation of Hungarian Israelites. During this conversation, Scheiber vilified those leaders who support the official religious policy, accusing them of being informers [*of the secret services* – AK].

He stated that Imre Héber, the chairman of the National Representation of Hungarian Israelites, who had been elected eight months earlier, was an honest Jew of goodwill, whom, however, the aforementioned persons were misleading. He advised Roth that both in the West and in Hungary, efforts were required to strengthen Imre Héber's position vis-à-vis "these people". The means of strengthening him were to provide proper press coverage and to make him popular in this way, and that Héber should be made aware of this. [Scheiber] recommended to Roth that Héber be given their confidence in the West and that they should do their utmost to ensure he prevails.

WJC leaders and the leaders of the National Representation of Hungarian Israelites discussed the visit to Hungary of the new president of the WJC, P. Klutznyk [*sic!* – AK]. They agreed on the visit taking place on 15–18 January 1978.

WJC leaders stated their demand that Klutznyk be received by the state at the same level as had been Goldman. They also requested the leaders of the National Representation of Hungarian Israelites to convene a meeting and make it possible for Klutznyk to speak before a larger audience.

They noted that this would be Klutznyk's first visit to a Socialist country, and that he also planned to make such visits to Czechoslovakia and Poland in 1978.

It was their wish that he should receive a reception in these countries too – one that would be similar to his reception in Hungary.

On 5 December, WJC leaders visited the representatives of Soviet Jewry at their hotel and held a long a discussion with them.

They did not mention the issue of emigration in the course of this discussion, which addressed three main issues:
- Shortcomings of religious freedom and in fostering Jewish culture. In this respect, they stated that they were willing to send appropriate press material and books, but that the leaders of Soviet Jewry had to give an assurance that the material would then be distributed and disseminated. The Soviet delegates stated that they had no need for such material.
- A primary problem, in their view, is Soviet Jewry's lack of a unified organisation whose leaders could then represent Soviet Jews abroad. They consider the establishment of such an organisation to be necessary. The opinion of the Soviet Jews on this issue was that such an organisation could not be established in the form

presented, because Soviet Jews live in several Soviet republics, scattered around [the Soviet Union].
- Dr Goldman mentioned that he would like to visit the Soviet Union. He said that he is waiting to receive an official invitation and that he hopes to be received at the proper state level. The Soviet delegates avoided giving a concrete answer, citing the absence of their chairman, without whom a decision on the matter could not be taken.

During his stay in Budapest, Dr Nahum Goldman held, on several occasions, conversations with the other WJC leaders and other foreigners that were noteworthy in terms of the international political and economic issues covered.

From these conversations we can conclude that the WJC leaders have close relations with leading circles in the FRG – with government and Party leaders there – and with Austrian government leaders.

In the course of one conversation, Goldman told his partner in conversation that two days before his arrival in Budapest he had talked with Willy Brandt for several hours. Brandt had informed him that a visit to Bonn by Comrade Brezhnev could not be arranged before February 1978. This was – allegedly – because of the position of the leaders of the United States, who wanted Comrade Brezhnev to visit the United States first, and only thereafter travel to Bonn. They knew, however, that the visit to America could not take place sooner – i.e., before February.

Goldman told several persons that he plays a mediatory role between the leaders of the FRG's three political parties – the SPD, CDU and CSU. The aim of such mediation is to smooth over differences of view between the Party leaders or at least to bring their respective positions closer. To this end he has held talks with Brandt, Schmidt, Kohl and Strauss. He has successfully brought together Kohl and the two Social Democratic leaders, but there are still difficulties with Strauss.

The good relations between the government of the FRG and the WJC leader are also manifested in the substantial funding provided by the government of the FRG. In the near future, a sum equivalent to 180 million dollars will be made available for the assistance of Jews who have emigrated from the Soviet Union. This amount would be granted not to Israel but to the WJC. According to Goldman, the Jewish emigrants from the Soviet Union will go not to Israel but primarily to America, where, however, there is no need for such support. For this reason, the money will be used for some other purpose.

His idea is to divide up a part of the sum among various foundations. The other part would be used to create a secret fund to finance initiatives and campaigns that serve the new policy of the WJC.

A committee comprising a narrow circle would be established to oversee the use of the secret fund thus established. In a legal sense, the committee would operate as a body directing the struggle against antisemitism and neo-Nazism. Members of the committee will be selected soon.

Goldman also spoke of his intent to organise a conference in Vienna in early 1978, which would be attended by various Jewish and Arab academics and public figures. In organising this conference, he is receiving assistance from the leaders of the FRG. Willy Brandt had spoken of approx. 20 persons who could be invited to the conference from Egypt, Lebanon and Morocco. Goldman himself has a similar list of 11 persons, whose invitation to the conference is being organised. They did not mention in person who will attend; nor did they speak of the concrete programme.

NOTE

Contents of the 5 tape recordings in the envelope:

4–8 December 1977, in the room in the Grand Hotel Margitsziget (Budapest) in which JAKOV FISHMAN, the chief rabbi of Moscow, and JAKOV MICKENBERG, vice chairman of the Moscow Jewish Congregation have stayed.

On 5 December, they were visited by World Jewish Congress leaders DR NAHUM GOLDMANN, founding chairman, ARMAND KAPLAN, director of foreign affairs, and DR SIEGFRIED ROTH, director of the European Section of the WJC, and a conversation lasting 2.5 hours was held in Mickenberg's room.

The conversation – which was held in Yiddish – was recorded <u>by secret means</u>, and the attached tapes contain it.

16 The Jewish Clerical Reaction in the Past 3 Years

[*Undated, probably 1978 – AK*]

Historical Archives of the Hungarian State Security 3.1.5. O-17169/5
Folder: "Zionists undertaking hostile activities" ["Ellenséges tevékenységet kifejtő cionisták"], vol. 6.

MINISTRY OF INTERIOR
III/III, Sub-department 1-c.

Memorandum

Our experiences of the activities of Jewish clerical reaction in the past 3 years can be summarised as follows:

I.
Operational situation of the topic area.

Concerning the nature, forms and methods of the hostile Zionist and Jewish nationalist activities in the topic area, three periods can be identified beginning in the early 1960s:
- Until 1967, the Israeli Embassy in Budapest was active and, in essence, they played the main role; foreign influence was predominant.
- After 1967, the foreign influence and orientation declined significantly. The centre of activities switched to the National Rabbinical Seminary. Instead of large-scale public events organised in the congregations, the focus switched to loose-knit groups of people coming together in public places, restaurants and private apartments.
- The third period dates to 1972–73, at which time Western Jewish organisations – with Israel remaining in the background – launched a large-scale campaign to integrate Hungarian Jewry in the work and sphere of communication of the international Jewish organisations.

The goals in each of the periods were essentially the same: to uphold and strengthen the Jewish spirit principally among young people, to emphasise the worldwide cohesion/solidarity of Jews, and the necessity of supporting Israel, and making its role popular. After 1967, these ambitions were coupled with anti-Soviet and anti-Communist agitation and propaganda.

The past five years have seen the gradual and large-scale activation of hostile Zionist forces. The activation has proceeded in two directions. On the one hand, regular relations have been established with Hungarian Jewish leaders. To this end, visits to Hungary have become a regular occurrence; various Western Jewish leaders and the leaders of the World Federation of Hungarian Jews have visited the country every one or two months to strengthen and foster their relations with Hungarian Jewish leaders.

To render relations even closer, they make use of the financial possibilities provided by the Joint. The discussion of financial problems, as well as the checks on the use of the funding granted, provide additional opportunities for them to maintain contact on an on-going basis and – furthermore – to influence and, on occasion, to blackmail.

In recent years, the activists of various Jewish organisations, as well as persons and groups of the most varied social status, have visited the country for the purpose of gathering data and appraising the situation and life circumstances of Hungarian Jewry. Such efforts have ranged from broad social assessments to the recording of the tiniest of details.

Such include, for instance:
- The number of Hungarian Jews, their organisational life, their institutions.
- Media, newspapers, book publication, cultural life, opportunities for fostering Jewish culture.
- Possibilities for sustaining religious life, providing the conditions for such.
- The situation and position in society of Hungarian Jews. Are there Jewish university professors? Are Jewish youths discriminated against when applying for college or university?
- Do Jews want to emigrate? The position of the state on emigration matters, possible discrimination as a consequence of this factor.
- The situation of Jewish young people, do they have organisations etc.?

Such assessments have been made by hundreds of people, from the vice chairman of the World Federation of Hungarian Jews, to a journalist from South America, to the mayor of a city in the FRG.

In 1975–76, the U.S. Embassy in Budapest also became active in this field. Embassy officials of various ranks – sometimes acting on a pretext – have visited the offices of the National Representation of Hungarian Israelites. In 1977, following the appointment of Kaiser as ambassador, such activity increased further. The ambassador makes a show of going to the Dohány Street Synagogue, and he has invited the leaders of the National Representation of Hungarian Israelites to his apartment on several occasions, and so forth.

The process will peak in December 1977 with the visit to Budapest of Dr Nahum Goldmann, chairman of the WJC, who seeks to hold talks with the leaders of the National Representation of Hungarian Israelites and with our senior government leaders.

Another form of hostile activity consists of various Western Jewish information centres – e.g. the BIRD information centre in Jerusalem – sending to the country, on a regular basis, propaganda material which is addressed to various government and non-government organisations, to other organisations and to private individuals. In such material, they provide information on political problems and areas of tension in the Middle East, Africa and South America. The main topic is the Soviet Union's policy in these regions, which is evaluated, in the main, from a hostile perspective, and so the material is suitable for inciting an anti-Soviet mood.

Among the material sent to Hungary a noteworthy element are various cut-out newspaper articles, mostly from "ÚJ KELET," [*New East, Hungarian-language newspaper published in Israel from 1948 until 2016* – AK] which also contain Hungarian-related information of a hostile content.

Here we should also mention our experiences regarding persons who have resettled in Hungary from the Soviet Union. At present, approx. 10,000 such persons are living in Hungary. Most of them are in close contact with their relatives who moved to Israel or to another Western country and with similar persons who stayed in the Soviet Union. They receive some of them as visitors, and in many cases persons still living in the Soviet Union and others who migrated to the West meet up in Hungary. Many of the persons living in Hungary serve as intermediaries between people in the Soviet Union and others who migrated to the West. They forward letters, official documents, and messages; indeed, they even undertake the forwarding of hostile, anti-Soviet publications. For instance, anti-Soviet works by Solzhenitsyn and published in the West were sent to the address of a Budapest resident, who then forwarded them to given addresses in the Soviet Union.

All these efforts had an activating effect on the domestic elements of the category.

Further loose-knit groupings came into being with the involvement of Jewish youths, and the groupings are larger in size than were the previous ones. We know of 4–5 restaurants and public places of entertainment where such meetings are held regularly.

There are even more groupings that come together in private homes. We have data on approx. 8–10 such groupings.

The main aim at such meetings still corresponds with the aims and ambitions of Zionism. Their main objective is to foster the Jewish spirit, to acquire knowledge of Jewish history, to create cohesion among youths, and to hinder assimilation by promoting "clean" marriages. (Jew with Jew.)

From time to time, they also address, in an indirect fashion, political issues. By learning about the situation of their relatives and acquaintances in Israel or the West, they popularise Israel and the Western lifestyle, keeping people's interest in Israel on the surface.

Other persons disseminate Zionist and anti-Soviet material received by post or brought into the country by visitors. In one case, a person sold for money to his acquaintances copies of "ÚJ KELET" that had been brought into the country. We even initiated criminal proceedings concerning the dissemination of such material. Jewish persons also sold such books in second-hand bookshops.

Various persons have organised Hebrew language lessons for groups of 6–8 people in their apartments. They receive the necessary materials and language books from their Western contacts.

There is even one person who holds group discussions with young graduates about the relationship of various social scientific and religious issues. The intellectual centre for such activities remains the National Rabbinical Seminary.

Every Friday evening, 100–150 people come together at the Seminary, where they can hear lectures on Jewish history and culture. The leaders and activists of Western Jewish organisations take part in these meetings, in many cases giving lectures of a Jewish nationalist nature and content.

At these meetings, marriages are mediated not only between domestic Jewish youths but also in a Hungarian–Soviet and Hungarian–Western relation. We can evaluate this as a method of resettlement to Hungary from the Soviet Union or of emigration from Hungary to the West.

The central role played by the Rabbinical Seminary is also indicated by the fact that students from the Seminary are present at most of the aforementioned meetings held in public places and in private apartments, and these students have a leading role.

These activities and the role of the Rabbinical Seminary have become "official" in the recent period. Firstly, because they take place with the knowledge of the State Office for Church Affairs and, secondly, because the leaders of the National Representation of Hungarian Israelites have recently attended, on several occasions, the Friday evening meetings and have participated in the meetings.

From the operational situation portrayed, it can be concluded that Zionism and Jewish nationalism have strengthened their positions in our country in recent years. They are using our country as a base against the other Socialist countries, in particular the Soviet Union. Meanwhile, according to the latest data, the leaders of the Western Jewish organisations seek to utilise the Hungarian Jewish leaders to establish contact with the leaders of Soviet Jewry and, perhaps, with state leaders too.

It is expected that, in consequence of the high-level visits that are to take place soon, Jewish nationalist activity will increase and become even more manifest.

In the counter-intelligence field, we must mention two things in terms of our operational positions. One of them is that, in the leadership of the National Representation of Hungarian Israelites, we have satisfactory positions in both network and technical terms. Using these positions we are able to survey the field and obtain data of operational value about foreign hostile efforts.

The other side is that in relation to various groupings, we do not have an appropriate information base; what we do have is good, but it is not enough. In this field, we must establish new information sources based on additional network and technical capacities.

II.
Operational measures.

Until 1974, the counter-intelligence field belonged to Department III/II-4, where the operational work was performed on the basis of the particular aspects of counter-espionage.

After the transfer of responsibilities we had to realise the following main tasks:
- The material received and the operational equipment had to be re-categorised and re-evaluated in accordance with the criteria of domestic counter-intelligence, and we had to establish the bases and information sources necessary for successful work.
- The main task was to acquire, on a continuous basis, information of operational value and of assistance to [the formulation of] religious policy on domestic and foreign hostile endeavours, objectives and methods. We then have to draft appropriate information material on these for the leadership and, if necessary, for the state security bodies of friendly countries, etc.
- We had to organise the investigation and control of the Jewish national groupings that had come into being and of the persons involved in such activities, thereafter taking proper measures to disrupt such groups and suppress and terminate their detrimental activities.

After the transfer of responsibilities we continuously restructured and elaborated the employment line of network persons. Using the existing materials we selected those persons that were suspected of pursuing hostile propaganda work and anti-Soviet activities or who had such contacts, and we began to check them and continuously process them.

We determined that the decisive majority of such persons were aged 70–80 or were even older, and so there was no possibility of taking overt measures against them. By means of various operational combinations, however, we were able to reduce their harmful activities. Such measures were, for instance: we seized and destroyed hostile or Jewish nationalist material sent to them. Or: we asked people who knew them to answer questions about them, which they clearly told them or their family members, etc.

It is a fact that the activity of such persons declined significantly in 1977.

There were, however, persons in a younger age group among them. For instance, the targeted person codenamed "LEVELEZŐ" [Pen friend] regularly received material of hostile content from Israel and from the FRG, which he then passed on to his circle of acquaintances and he also undertook hostile agitation by word of mouth. We processed the case within the framework of a secret investigation and then passed the case on to Department III/1 for the purpose of an inquiry. In the course of the inquiry, several witnesses were heard and a house search was held. The targeted person was convicted by the court and several police authority warnings [*verdict issued by a police court against persons who were under investigation for committing political offences –* AK] were issued.

All of this became widely known in the category, and we observed a significant deterrent effect.

[...]

In the course of the processing work, several Jewish nationalistic groups were uncovered. Having identified the members of the groupings, we took measures to disrupt and disorganise them. Such measures were, for instance:
- We made signals to various state organs and to the work bosses of the persons participating in the groupings.
- Based on command 04/1963 of the Ministry of Interior, we summoned several persons to the Passport Department, and in the course of the discussion, we asked about the activities undertaken by the grouping and its membership, etc. We made it clear during such conversations that we had received the information from a leading figure in the grouping.
- We sought then to strengthen this by network means [*by informers* – AK]. All these measures led to an atmosphere of distrust; they searched for "infiltrators" etc.

In consequence of these measures, many people left the groups. Some groups broke up, while others became atomised and their numbers declined.

[...]

In addition, we also took – and continue to take – several measures of a preventive nature to reduce the effect of hostile materials flowing in from abroad and of the harmful activities of visitors, for instance:
- We continuously keep under the "K" checks "K" materials arriving from Israel and from the Western Jewish organisations and known persons. We are continuously seizing materials of hostile content.
- We are regularly monitoring [...] persons arriving from Israel. We do not allow into the country those Israelis who have hostile attitudes or who are suspected of conducting such activities.
- We also constantly check up on persons from Israel and other Western countries who come to visit persons who have resettled in Hungary from the Soviet Union. Here too, we have prevented several persons from entering the country.
- We have implemented several network members' journeys to various Western Jewish organisations and to their leaders, from which we obtained valuable information. In case of need, we have forwarded such information to the state security organs of the friendly countries.

IN SUMMARY: Based on the information obtained, it can be stated that international Zionism is making efforts to influence Hungarian Jewry and to acquire positions among them for the purpose of strengthening its influence. This influence and its effect have grown perceptibly in the past 1–2 years, and this serves to encourage domestic reactionary elements.

In consequence of our measures, we managed, from time to time, to disrupt the domestic hostile elements, to provoke distrust among them, and to hinder to a certain extent the realisation of their hostile activities.

It must also be acknowledged, however, that, in view of the substantial increase in hostile endeavours, the previous extent of measures is proving to be insufficient to suppress the hostile endeavours.

For this reason, new intelligence sources, the more intense and combined use of operational means, and more effective measures, will be required.

Police Lieutenant-Colonel József Fülöp

17 Appendix. Orientation for a Systematic Register of the People of Jewish Origin

1985

Archival Collection of the Ministry of the Interior, Prague, collection A 34/1, Folder 451[50]

10th Administration of the Corps of National Security
1985

Orientation for a Systematic Register of the People of Jewish Origin active in objects monitored by counter-intelligence sections of the 2nd, 3rd, 4th, 10th, 11th and 12th Administration of the Corps of National Security

Within the problematic of the fight against Zionism in a non-Judaic sphere, under the nationwide project SPIDER, we have conducted a consistent record of the people of Jewish origin, who can be bearers of pro-Zionist ideas and can be exploited for a hostile activity against the Czechoslovak Socialist Republic, finding out and unfolding hostile activities of people of Jewish origin, particularly demonstrations of Zionism and Jewish bourgeois nationalism, illegal groupings of people of Jewish origin dealing with hostile activity against the ČSSR and other Socialist countries, and groupings of people of Jewish origin related to foreign Jewish and Zionist organisations. A permanent attention is given to the most important spheres of social activity, in which, according to the latest findings, have arisen conditions for a spread of Zionism and Jewish bourgeois nationalism, and those spheres of social activities, in which the concentration of people of Jewish origin occurs. At present these spheres seem to be the following:
a) media
b) culture
c) science and education
d) health service
e) domestic and foreign commerce

Given the elaboration of the specifics of the problematic of the fight against Zionism in the non-Judaic sphere, in which the people of Jewish origin are dispersed, working in varied areas of social activities, the operations themselves are conducted in objects that are selected for elaboration within the relevant Administrations and Sections of the State Security. To secure a systematic registration of the people of Jewish origin,

---

50 This document was attached to the informative report on "Countrywide Project Spider", written by the head of the Organizational and Operational Section of the Second Administration of CNS (counter-intelligence dealing with external enemy) in June 1987. First published in Marie Crhová, Jews under the Communist regime in Czechoslovakia. In *Jewish Studies at the CEU. III. Yearbook 2002–2003*, ed. András Kovács (Budapest: Central European University, 2004), 290–294.

a comprehensive survey of the spheres of their activity, tracing and unfolding their hostile activity, and paralysing the negative influence of the foreign Zionist and Jewish organisations on the activity of the Czechoslovak Jewish religious community, the elaboration itself must be conducted in a close co-operation with the relevant Sections of the 2nd, 3rd, 4th, 10th, 11th, and 12th ACNS, which will secure a complete and integrated information flow on the people of Jewish origin. The information is being collected at the 1st Department of the 4th Section at the 10th ACNS, which is the guarantor of the nation-wide project SPIDER.

The Tasks For the Operation Sections of the 10th Administration of the CNS and the 2nd Section of the Administration of the State Security

- determine the employment (at the army administration and retirement fund) of the people registered in the nation-wide project SPIDER. People working in selected objects will be suggested for control to relevant units.
- find out adult children of the people registered in the nation-wide project SPIDER, others – see parents.
- request from other relevant units data of people suspected of a relation to Jewishness and Zionism, inspect them in the archives, and suggest their control retrospectively (people that work in selected objects).

To secure a consistent course when registering the people of Jewish origin, it is necessary to introduce these terms:

1) person of Jewish faith – is a person, who is active at the JRC (or a Synagogue Congregation) and is kept on the list of its members or a person, who, although not participating in the JRC's (Synagogue Congregation's) activities, is registered on the list of members.

2) person of Jewish origin – is a person, who does not profess Jewish faith and is not kept in the JRC's (Synagogue Congregation's) register, but at least one of the parents is/was of Jewish faith, or, before 1948, declared Jewish nationality, or was a member of the Zionist organisation Hashomer Hacair, which worked legally in the ČSSR till 1948, or any other Zionist or Jewish organisation.

Information Collected at 4th Section of the 10th ACNS

1. Information about the work of the people of Jewish origin/faith in individual subjects and about their work categories.
2. Information containing state-security findings about the activities of the people of Jewish origin/faith, particularly:
   a) dissemination of Zionist ideas and ideas of Jewish bourgeois nationalism

b) contacts with foreign Zionist and Jewish organisations
c) activity in one of the JRC or Synagogue Congregations in the Czech Socialist Republic or Slovak Socialist Republic
d) previous activity in Zionist organisations operating on the territory of the ČSSR till 1948
e) propagation of Jewish religion
f) keeping any sort of contacts with people of Jewish origin abroad
g) frequent departures for capitalist countries, both business and private trips
h) illegal groupings of people of Jewish origin, e.g. Yiddish classes, various cultural or literary clubs, choirs and the like, formed by the people of Jewish origin
i) other state-security findings about a negative activity of people of Jewish origin

3. Information about people of Jewish origin – foreigners – that come to the ČSSR for various purposes – tourism, business and the like, and information containing state-security findings about their activities.
4. Information about the leading officials and members of the foreign Zionist and Jewish organisations.
5. Information about the activities of the foreign Zionist and Jewish organisations in respect of the USSR.
6. Information about the activities of the employees of capitalist states' embassies in the ČSSR in respect of the Jewish Religious Community in the ČSSR.

Information-sending to the 4th Section of the 10th ACNS

1. When information about an activity of a person of Jewish origin, Czechoslovak citizen, is traced in an object selected for elaboration at the 2nd, 3rd, 4th, 10th, 11th, 12th ACNS, such information must be sent in a form of a register card.
2. In case any state-security findings are traced about such a person, this information must be elaborated in "AZ" form and sent together with the register card.
3. When tracing information about foreigners, people of Jewish origin, leading officials and members of the foreign Zionist and Jewish organisations, the activities of these organisations as well as about illegal groupings of people of Jewish origin on the territory of the ČSSR, such information must be sent in "AZ" form.

Processing Register Cards

On the register card of the Ministry of the Interior, store number 27, the following data will be:
a) code name SPIDER in the right upper corner
b) family name and first name, including the former ones, academic degree

c) date and place of birth
d) the way Jewish origin/faith of the person was authenticated (Jewish registries, membership at JRC and the like)
e) residence
f) occupation, profession, social status and positions held
g) membership in political and social organisations of the National Front
h) parents of the registered person (personal data)
i) siblings of the registered person (date and place of birth, employment)
j) wife/husband of the registered person (date and place of birth, employment, and her/his parents with personal data)
k) children of the registered person up from the age of 15 (date and place of birth, residence, employment, their wives'/husbands' – date and place of birth, employment)
l) a picture of the registered person <u>will possibly be attached</u>

To the Interior Ministry Register Card – store number 27 will be clipped an Interior Ministry Register Card – store number 29, which will include following findings about the particular person:
a) indications and findings about a pro-Zionist activity (if the person in question has been reported upon before, penalised)
b) contacts with and important departures for foreign countries
c) other important state-security information

One of the parents of the particular person must always be of Jewish origin. In case the family members, who are cited on the register card, have been found to be of Jewish origin, an individual card must be issued. The cards will be made only for people permanently residing in the ČSSR. When processing information for the 2nd, 3rd, 4th, 10th, 11th and 12th Sections of the ACNS, it is possible to make use of the existing central register of the people of Jewish origin/faith at the 1st Department of the 4th Section at the 10th ACNS.

Biographical Notes

Aczél, György – Hungarian Deputy Minister of Culture and Education 1957–1967; secretary of the Central Committee of the HSWP 1967–1974; Deputy Chairman of the Council of Ministers (deputy prime minister) 1974–1982.

Antos, István – Hungarian Deputy Minister of Finance 1951–1954; Minister of Finance, member of the Central Committee of the HSWP 1957–1960.

Arif, Abdul Rahman (see also Aref) – Iraqi general, third President of Iraq 1966–1968; Prime Minister in 1967.

Baczoni, Jenő – Hungarian Deputy Minister of Foreign Trade 1954–1968; first Deputy Minister, later Under-Secretary 1968–1975.

Becher, Kurt – SS Untersturmbannführer, Chief of the Economic Department of the SS Command in Hungary in 1944. Becher represented the SS in negotiations with the Relief and Rescue Committee of Budapest headed by Rezső Kasztner; as a result of a statement provided on his behalf by Rudolf Kasztner, he was not prosecuted as a war criminal.

Beck, István – Hungarian diplomat, head of department at the Ministry of Foreign Affairs in 1967.

Beck, Tamás – Head of the Hungarian Chamber of Commerce 1982–1988; Minister of Trade 1988–1990.

Benoschofsky, Imre (see also Benesofszky, Beneschovszky, Benoschofszky) – Rabbi, chief rabbi of Hungary 1960–1970.

Berecz, János – Hungarian party functionary, head of the Foreign Policy Department of the HSWP 1974–1982; member of the Central Committee of the HSWP 1980–1989; secretary of the CC HSWP 1985–1989; member of the Political Committee of the HSWP 1987–1989.

Biszku, Béla – Hungarian Minister of Interior 1957–1961; Deputy Chairman of the Council of Ministers (deputy prime minister), 1962; member of the Political Committee of the HSWP 1957–1980; secretary of the Central Committee 1962–1978.

Borsa, Mihály – Hungarian politician and Jewish official; Member of Parliament for the Independent Smallholders Party 1946–1949; Chairman of the Central Social Committee (Központi Szociális Bizottság) 1959–1974, the social welfare organization of the National Representation of Hungarian Israelites.

Boumediène, Houari (see also Bumedian) – Chairman of the Revolutionary Council of Algeria 1965–1976; second President of Algeria 1976–1978.

Brand, Joel – Leading member of the Aid and Rescue Committee in 1944 in Budapest, and one of Rudolf Kasztner's closest colleagues. Gave evidence for the defence in the Eichmann trial.

Bronfman, Edgar – Canadian-American businessman and philanthropist, President of the World Jewish Congress 1981–2007.

Csécsei, Kálmán – Deputy Head of Department II/3 of the Hungarian intelligence service until 1962; Resident of the Hungarian intelligence service in Tel-Aviv as Chargé d'affaires ad interim at the Legation of Hungary in Israel 1965–1967.

Darvasi, István – Deputy Head of the Agitation and Propaganda Department of the HSWP Central Committee 1958–1968.

Domán, Ernő – Rabbi, Professor of Talmud at the Rabbinical Seminary in Budapest until his death in 1976.

Egri, György – Journalist who emigrated in 1956 from Hungary; thereafter publisher and editor-in-chief of *Menora*, the Canadian Hungarian-language Jewish magazine.

Erdélyi, Károly – Hungarian functionary; János Kádár's secretary in 1957; Deputy Minister of Foreign Affairs 1962–1970; member of the Central Committee of the HSWP 1966–1971; head of the Foreign Policy Department of the HSWP 1970–1971.

Eshkol, Levi – Third Prime Minister of Israel 1963–1969; Minister of Defence 1963–1967.

Fedorenko, Nikolai Trofimovich – Soviet Deputy Minister of Foreign Affairs 1955–1958; thereafter Soviet ambassador to Japan. Appointed as Permanent Representative of the USSR to the United Nations, and Soviet representative at the Security Council of the UN in 1963.

Fekete, János – Deputy President of the National Bank of Hungary from 1968; first Deputy President of the NBH 1980–1988.

Fisch, Henrik – Rabbi of the Dohány Street Synagogue in Budapest 1959–1971.

Fishman, Jakov – Chief Rabbi of Moscow's Choral Synagogue 1971–1983.

Fock, Jenő – Secretary of the Central Committee of the HSWP 1957–1961; Deputy Chairman of the Council of Ministers 1961–1967; Chairman (prime minister) 1967–1975.

Foertsch, Friedrich Albert – Lieutenant General of the Wehrmacht; prisoner of war in the Soviet Union 1945–1955, where he was sentenced to 25 years of forced labour. After his release, he joined the Bundeswehr of the FRG. Inspector General of the Bundeswehr 1961–1963.

Fuchs, Frantisek – Head of the Council of Jewish Communities in Czechoslovakia 1966–1974.

Garai, Róbert – Hungarian diplomat, served at the Legacy of Hungary in Tel Aviv 1955–1959; Ambassador in Djakarta 1962–1964; Deputy Minister of Foreign Affairs 1972–1985.

Geréb, Sándor – High-ranking officer in the Department for Political Investigations of the Hungarian intelligence service; later at the State Security Directorate of the Hungarian Ministry of Interior; head of department responsible for church affairs 1966–1971.

Gerstenmaier, Eugen (see also Gerstenmöyer, Gertonmöyer, Gertenmayer) – Member of the German anti-Nazi resistance in the Third Reich; politician of the Christian Democratic Union of Germany after 1945; member of the Bundestag 1949–1969; President of the Bundestag 1954–1969.

Globke, Hans – Official at the Ministry of Interior in Nazi Germany, participated in drafting several anti-Jewish laws. Director of the Federal Chancellery of the FRG under Konrad Adenauer 1953–1963. Sentenced to life imprisonment *in absentia* in the GDR in 1963.

Goldman, Ralph I. – American Zionist activist, a confidant and advisor of David Ben-Gurion. Associate Director of the Israel operation of the Joint in 1968; Chief Executive of the Joint 1976–1985 and 1986–1988.

Goldmann, Nahum (see also Nachum Goldmann, Goldman) – Founder and President of the World Jewish Congress 1948–1977; President of the World Zionist Organization 1956–1968.

Goldstücker, Eduard – Czechoslovak literary historian, journalist and diplomat; first Ambassador of Czechoslovakia in Israel 1948–1951; political prisoner 1951–1955; one of the leaders of the reform movement from the early 1960s and later the Prague Spring.

Gomułka, Władysław – Polish Communist Party leader, First Secretary of the Polish Workers' Party 1943–1948; First Secretary of the Polish United Workers' Party 1956–1970.

Görög, János – Hungarian lawyer and later diplomat; head of the Department of International Law at the Ministry of Foreign Affairs 1983–1989; first Hungarian Ambassador to Israel 1989–1994.

Grechko, Andrei – Soviet general, Marshal of the Soviet Union; Minister of Defence 1963–1976; Commander of the Unified Armed Forces of Warsaw Pact 1961–1967.

Hazai, Jenő – Hungarian Communist functionary; Deputy Minister of Defence until 1956; head of the counter-intelligence department at the Ministry of Interior 1957–1962.

Hayman, Erwin – Swiss attorney; worked for the American Jewish Joint Distribution Committee after World War II; represented the Joint on behalf of the Swiss-based Société de Sécours et d'Entraide (SSE) in Eastern Europe in the 1960s.

Házi, Vencel – Official at the Ministry of Foreign Affairs in Hungary from 1957; Ambassador in Iraq and Greece; head of department at the Ministry of Foreign Affairs 1964–1968; Deputy Foreign Minister 1968–1970 and 1976–1983.

Héber, Imre – Chairman of the National Representation of Hungarian Israelites (MIOK) and the Budapest Israelite Congregation (BIH) 1977–1985.

Heller, Bohumil – President of the Council of Jewish Religious Communities in Bohemia and Moravia 1985–1989.
Heves, Lajos – Lawyer; Chairman of the MIOI (National Bureau of Hungarian Israelites) and the Budapest Israelite Congregation (BIH) 1953–1957.
Hoettl, Georg Wilhelm – Austrian Nazi and SS officer; worked for the German central intelligence and security agency, the Reichssicherheitshauptamt (RSHA) 1939–1945. After the German invasion of Hungary in March 1944, he participated in organizing the deportation of Hungarian Jews.
Hollai, Imre – Hungarian functionary; head of the Foreign Policy Department of the HSWP 1960–1963; Ambassador in Greece 1964–1970; Deputy Minister of Foreign Affairs 1970–1974 and 1980–1984; head of the Hungarian UN delegation 1974–1980.
Horowitz, Louis D. (see also Luis Horovitz) – American Jewish official; representative of the Joint in Tunisia in the early 1950s; Director General of the Israeli services of the Joint 1958–1962; held leading positions in the European branch of the Joint in the 1960s and 1970s.
Horváth, Imre – Minister of Foreign Affairs in Hungary and member of the Central Committee of the HSWP 1956–1958.
Horváth, István – Hungarian Minister of Interior 1980–1985 and 1987–1989; Secretary of the Central Committee of the HSWP 1985–1987.
Horváth, János – President of the State Office for Church Affairs (ÁEH) in Hungary 1952–1959.
Ilku, Pál – Hungarian Minister of Culture 1961–1973.
Illyés, Gyula – Hungarian writer and public intellectual, leading representative of the interwar "populist" group of writers.
Juhár, Zoltán – Hungarian Deputy Minister of Interior Trade 1969–1982; Minister of Interior Trade 1982–1987; Ambassador in Australia and New-Zealand 1988–1990.
Kádár, János – General Secretary of the Hungarian Socialist Worker's Party 1956–1988; Chairman of the Council of Minister (Prime Minister) 1956–1958.
Kadelburg, Lavoslav – President of the Federation of Jewish Communities in Belgrade 1964–1991; member of the Executive of the World Jewish Congress.
Kaiser, Philip Mayer – United States Ambassador in Budapest 1977–1980.
Kállai, Gyula – Hungarian Minister of Culture from 1957; Deputy Chairman of the Council of Ministers 1960–1965; Chairman of the Council of Ministers (Prime Minister) 1965–1967; Chairman of the Parliament 1967–1971.
Kálló, Iván – Hungarian Ambassador in Italy 1951–1956; Minister at the Legation of Hungary in Israel 1957–1959.
Kaltenbrunner, Ernst – SS Obergruppenführer and head of the German central intelligence and security agency, the Reichssicherheitshauptamt (RSHA); sentenced to death in Nuremberg, 1946.
Kaplan, Armand – Secretary General of the French Section of the WJC from 1950; Deputy Director of the Foreign Affairs Committee, and Head of the International Department of the WJC in 1969.
Karasz, Lajos – Hungarian state security official; held various leading positions at the state security organs 1962–1973; Deputy Minister of Interior and Head of the III. General Directorate (intelligence and counter-intelligence) 1973–1982.
Karádi, Gyula – Deputy Minister at the Ministry of Foreign Trade in Hungary 1957–1967; Deputy Chairman of the National Office for Economic Planning 1967–1973.
Kardos, Géza – Hungarian Deputy Minister of Finance 1957–1968.
Kasztner, Rudolf (see also Kastner, Rudolf and Kasztner, Rezső) – Head of Vaad, the Rescue and Relief Committee during the Nazi occupation of Hungary of 1944. Conducted the "blood for goods" negotiations with Eichmann. After the war, he moved to Israel, where he was accused of collaboration. Assassinated in Tel Aviv in March 1953.

Kauders, Ben-Zion (see also Ben Cion Kauders) – Director of the legal department of the Hungarian National Association to Assist Jews (OMZSA) in 1943. Elected as Co-chairman of World Federation of Hungarian Jews in 1978.

Keller, László – One of the leaders of the New York-based World Federation of Hungarian Jews from the early 1960s until 2003, and the World Jewish Congress.

Klein, Theo – President of the Conseil représentatif des institutions juives de France (CRIF) 1983–1989; French Chairman of the European Jewish Congress in 1986.

Klutznick, Philip (see also Klutznyck, Klutznik, Klutznyk) – President of the World Jewish Congress 1977–1979.

Komócsin, Zoltán – Hungarian party functionary; member of the Central Committee and the Political Committee of the HSWP 1957–1974; secretary of the Central Committee, responsible for foreign affairs 1965–1974.

Kós, Péter – Diplomat; Hungarian Ambassador in the USA and head of the Hungarian mission at the UN 1956–1957; head of a department at the Ministry of Foreign Affairs 1957–1961; Hungarian Ambassador in various countries (Ghana, India, Japan) from 1961.

Koucký, Vladimir – Secretary of the Central Committee of the Communist Party of Czechoslovakia, responsible for foreign affairs 1958–1968.

Kriegel, Frantisek – Doctor, Czechoslovak politician, member of the Communist Party reform wing before 1968; as Chairman of the Central Committee of the National Front, and member of Presidium of the Central Committee of CPCz, one of the leaders of the Prague Spring.

Kubowitzki, Leon – Secretary General of the World Jewish Congress 1945–1948.

Lahav, Yehuda (Weiszlovits, Istvan) – Israeli journalist of Hungarian origin; banned from entering Hungary and Czechoslovakia 1969–1981.

Lakatos, Ernő – Deputy President of the Information Office of the Council of Ministers of Hungary 1969–1977; President of the Hungarian Telegraphic Agency 1980–1982; head of the Agitation and Propaganda Department of the HSWP Central Committee 1982–1988.

Lévai, Jenő – Hungarian writer, editor and journalist, first historian of the Holocaust in Hungary.

Losonci, András – Hungarian medical doctor; Chairman of the National Representation of Hungarian Israelites and the Budapest Israelite Congregation 1985–1989.

Losonczi, Pál – Hungarian politician; Member of the HSWP Central Committee from 1957; Minister of Agriculture 1960–1967; President of the Council of Presidents (Head of State) 1967–1987.

Máté, Miklós – Hungarian rabbi, teacher and headmaster of the Secondary School of the Jewish Congregation of Budapest 1967–1979.

Mere, Ain-Ervin – Estonian military officer; Obersturmbannführer in the Waffen SS and head of the *Sicherheitspolizei* in Estonia. After the war, he was accused of arresting and killing Estonian Jews during the Holocaust.

Mélykuti, Ferenc – Lieutenant-Colonel of the Hungarian security services; responsible for Jewish issues 1965–1973.

Mód, Péter – Diplomat; Ambassador and Head of the Permanent Representation of Hungary at the UN 1957–1962; First Deputy Minister of Foreign Affairs 1962–1968; Ambassador in France 1968–1974.

Miklós, Imre – Leading official of the State Office for Church Affairs (ÁEH) 1951–1989; Deputy President 1956–1970; President, State Secretary 1971–1989.

Mikunis, Shmuel (Samuel) – Secretary of the Central Committee of the Palestine Communist Party in 1939. General Secretary of the Communist Party of Israel 1948–1974.

Mowshovitz, Israel – President of the New York Board of Rabbis in the 1960s. Member of the rabbis' delegations to the Soviet Union to investigate the conditions of Soviet Jewry in 1956. He also traveled to Poland, Romania, and other countries on similar missions.

Nagy, János – Hungarian diplomat; Ambassador in various countries 1957–1971; Deputy Minister of Foreign Affairs 1971–1980; State Secretary of the Ministry of Foreign Affairs 1980–1985.

Németh, Miklós – Hungarian politician; held leading positions at the Department of Economic Policy at the Central Committee of the HSWP 1983–1987; Chairman of the Council of Ministers (Prime Minister) 1988–1990.

Norden, Albert – East-German Communist politician, member of the Central Committee of the Socialist Unity Party of Germany from 1955. Head of the Agitation Committee 1955–1967; member of the Political Committee from 1958; responsible for propaganda and foreign policy until 1979.

Novotný, Antonín Josef – General Secretary of the Communist Party of Czechoslovakia 1953–1968; President of Czechoslovakia 1957–1968.

Nyerki, Gyula – Chargé d'affaires ad interim at the Legation of Hungary in Israel 1959–1965.

Oberländer, Theodor (see also Oberlaender) – Officer of the Wehrmacht; Minister for Expellees (Bundesvertriebenenminister) in the FRG 1953–1960. Accused of participating in the killing of Jews in Lviv in 1941, tried in absentia in the GDR in April 1960, resigned his post.

Olt, Károly – Hungarian Minister of Finance 1950–1956; head of János Kádár's secretariat 1956–1959; President of the State Office for Church Affairs 1959–1961.

Orbán, László – Head of the Agitation and Propaganda Department of the HSWP 1959–1967; Deputy Minister of Culture 1967–1974; Minister of Culture 1974–1976; Member of the HSWP Central Committee 1957–1978.

Pereszlényi, Zoltán – Diplomat, official of the Hungarian Ministry of Foreign Affairs from 1966; served at the department of Arab and African states; Ambassador in various Arab states 1981–1986 and 1989–1993.

Péter, János – Hungarian delegate at the peace talks after the Second World War; Reformed Church bishop 1949–1956; Head of the Institute of Cultural Relations 1956–1958; Deputy Minister of Foreign Affairs 1958–1961; Minister of Foreign Affairs 1961–1973; member of the Central Committee of the HSWP 1966–1988.

Podgorny, Nikolai Viktorovich – Soviet politician; First Secretary of the Central Committee of the Communist Party of Ukraine 1957–1963; Chairman of the Presidium of the Supreme Soviet 1965–1977.

Prantner, József – Official holding various positions at the State Office for Church Affairs 1951–1961; President of the State Office for Church Affairs 1961–1971.

Pudlák, Ján – Deputy Foreign Minister of ČSSR in 1967.

Puja, Frigyes – Deputy Minister of Foreign Affairs in Hungary 1959–1973; head of the Department of Foreign Policy of the Central Committee of the HSWP 1963–1968; First Deputy Minister of Foreign Affairs 1963–1973; Minister of Foreign Affairs 1973–1983; member of the Central Committee of the HSWP 1966–1989.

Pullai, Árpád – Hungarian functionary, member of the HSWP Central Committee 1962–1985; Head of Party and Mass Organisations Department 1966–1976; in charge of foreign affairs 1973–1975.

Rapai, Gyula – Deputy Head of the HSWP Department for Agitation and Propaganda 1958–1961; Ambassador in Moscow 1970–1976.

Ránki, György (see also George Ranski) – Hungarian historian of economic history and World War II; Deputy Director, and later Director of the Institute of History at the Hungarian Academy of Sciences 1962–1986.

Riegner, Gerhart Moritz (see also Gergart, Gerhard, Rieger, Rigner) – Secretary General of the World Jewish Congress 1965–1983.

Robinson, Donald M. – Leading official of the Joint in the United States 1970–1985.

Rosen, Moses (see also Mózes Rósen, Rózen) – Chief Rabbi of Romanian Jewry 1948–1994; President of the Federation of Jewish Communities of Romania 1964–1994.

Roth, Siegfried later **Roth, Stephen** (see also Sigrid Róth, Sigfrid Róth, Stephen Róth) – Jewish politician born in Hungary. First post-World War II Director of the World Jewish Congress (WJC) office in Budapest; moved to the United Kingdom in 1947, where he became general secretary of the WJC British Section, then the WJC European Director; director of the WJC's Institute of Jewish Affairs in London from 1966; Chairman of the Foreign Affairs Committee of the Board of Deputies of British Jews 1979–1985; Chairman of the UK Zionist Federation 1985–1990.

Rusakov, Konstantin Viktorovich – Soviet politician, official in the Ministry of Foreign Affairs 1964; head of a department of the Central Committee and assistant to the General Secretary, Leonid Brezhnev 1968–1977.

Sauckel, Fritz – German Nazi politician, Gauleiter of Thuringia. Sentenced to death in 1946.

Scheiber, Sándor – Hungarian rabbi and Jewish scholar; Director of the Rabbinical Seminary in Budapest 1950–1985.

Schneier, Arthur – Viennese-born rabbi, human right activist; survived Nazi occupation in Budapest and emigrated to the United States in 1947; Senior Rabbi at Park East Synagogue in New York City 1962–2012; member of the U.S. Delegation for Return of the St. Steven Crown to Hungary in 1979.

Schön, Dezső (see also Schőn) – Journalist, worked for the Zionist newspaper *Új Kelet* [New East] in Transylvania; left for Israel in 1948; editor-in-chief of *Új Kelet* 1975–1986.

Sebes, István – Hungarian Deputy Minister of Foreign Affairs 1956–1959; Ambassador in Austria 1959–1964.

Seifert, Géza – Hungarian lawyer; Deputy Chairman of the Budapest Israelite Congregation (BIH) from 1957; Chairman of the National Representation of Hungarian Israelites (MIOK) and the Budapest Israelite Congregation 1966–1976.

Sík, Endre (see also Sik) – Member of the Hungarian Communist emigration in Moscow before World War II; Minister of Foreign Affairs 1958–1961; member of the Central Committee of the HSWP 1959–1970.

Šik, Ota – Czech economist and politician, one of the key figures of the Communist reform movement and the Prague Spring; Deputy Prime Minister of Czechoslovakia April–September 1968; fled to Switzerland after the Soviet invasion.

Singer, Israel – American Jewish official, Secretary General of the World Jewish Congress 1986–2001.

Slánský, Rudolf – Czech Communist politician; General Secretary of the Communist party 1946–1952; arrested, sentenced to death in a show trial and executed in 1952.

Słowikowski, Jan – Polish diplomat; Polish Charge d'Affaires in Israel 1954–1958.

Sobolev, Arkady – Soviet diplomat; Soviet Ambassador to the United Nations 1955–1960.

Sós, Endre – Journalist; Chairman of the National Representation of Hungarian Israelites (MIOK) and the Budapest Israelite Congregation (BIH) 1957–1965, editor-in-chief of the Jewish newspaper *Új Élet* [New Life].

Steinberg, Elan (see also Elen) – Leading functionary of the WJC; Executive Director of the WJC 1986–2004.

Szántó, Dénes – President of the National Bank of Hungary 1956–1960.

Szarka, Károly – Hungarian diplomat and politician; Deputy Minister of Foreign Affairs 1956–1968, Ambassador in Egypt 1968–1970; Hungarian Ambassador to the UN 1970–1974; Deputy Minister of Foreign Affairs 1974–1983; Ambassador in Japan 1983–1987.

Száraz, György – Hungarian journalist, writer, author of *Egy előítélet nyomában* [In the Wake of a Prejudice] (Budapest, 1976), the first essay published on antisemitism in Hungary after the 1956 Revolution.

Szilágyi, Béla – Hungarian politician and diplomat; head of a department at the Ministry of Foreign Trade until 1958; Hungarian Ambassador in Great Britain 1959–1963; Deputy Minister of Foreign Affairs 1963–1970; Ambassador in Greece 1970–1975.

Szirmai, István – Hungarian functionary; Zionist activist in Transylvania in his youth; functionary of the Romanian Communist Party from 1931, and later of the Hungarian Communist Party; held various senior posts after 1945; arrested and accused of Zionist conspiracy in 1953, released in 1954. Secretary of the Central Committee of the HSWP responsible for ideological issues 1959–1966; member of the Political Committee of the HSWP 1962–1969.

Szűrös, Mátyás – Hungarian functionary, diplomat; Ambassador in the GDR 1975–1978; Ambassador in the Soviet Union 1978–1982; member of the Central Committee 1978–1988; Secretary of the Central Committee of the HSWP responsible for foreign affairs 1983–1988; provisional President of State 1989–1990.

Tauber, László – Doctor; head surgeon at the Jewish hospital of Budapest 1940–1945; practiced medicine in the US from 1947; founder of the Tauber Institute for the Study of European Jewry at Brandeis University.

Telepó, Sándor – Functionary of the State Office for Religious Affairs (ÁEH) in Hungary in the late 1960s, responsible for Jewish affairs.

Tuval (Touval), Meir – Israeli lawyer, diplomat; Minister at the Israeli Legation in Hungary 1956–1959.

Ulbricht, Walter – East German Communist politician; Secretary General of the Socialist Unity Party in GDR 1950–1971; Head of State 1960–1973.

Várkonyi, Péter – Hungarian politician and diplomat; head of János Kádár's secretariat 1961–1965; Deputy Head of the Foreign Policy Department of the Central Committee of the HSWP 1968–1969; member of the Central Committee 1975–1989; Secretary of the Central Committee responsible for foreign affairs 1982–1983; Minister of Foreign Affairs 1983–1989; Hungarian ambassador in the Unites States 1989–1990.

Vilner, Meir – Israeli Communist politician, leader of the Communist Party of Israel; member of the Knesset 1949–1990, representing various pro-Soviet Party factions.

Weiler, Jack D. – American businessman; held a number of positions in the Joint, including Vice Chairman 1958–1973, Chairman of the National Council 1966–1973, Chairman 1975–1977, and Honorary President 1978–1995.

Winkelmann, Otto – SS Gruppenführer, Chief SS and Police Commandant in Hungary during the German occupation; witness in the Eichmann trial.

Wisliceny, Dieter (see also Wisliczeny) – SS Hauptsturmführer, a member of Adolf Eichmann's commando organizing the ghettoization and liquidation of Jewish communities of Greece, Hungary and Slovakia; executed in 1948.

Yahil, Chaim – Director General of Ministry of Foreign Affairs of Israel 1960–1964.

Yaron, Yerahmiel Ram – Israeli diplomat; Minister at the Embassy of Israel in Hungary 1958–1962.

Zhivkov, Todor – First Secretary of the Bulgarian Communist Party and the head of state of the People's Republic of Bulgaria 1954–1989.

Bibliography

Archival sources

National Archives of Hungary [Magyar Nemzeti Levéltár, Országos Levéltár, MNL OL]
Collection: Ministry of Foreign Affairs [Külügyminisztérium, KÜM]
  MOL XIX-J-1-j (Israel)

Collection: State Office for Religious Affairs [Állami Egyházügyi Hivatal, ÁEH]
  MOL XIX-A-21-a – Elnöki iratok [Papers of the President]
  MOL XIX-A-21-c – Adattár [Data collection]
  MOL XIX-A-21-d – Titkosan Ügykezelt Iratok [Confidential papers]

Collection: Papers of the Central Bodies of the Hungarian Socialist Workers Party, HSWP [MSZMP Központi Szervei]
  MOL M-KS 288/5 – Politikai Bizottság [Political Committee]
  MOL M-KS 288/22 – Agitációs és Propaganda Osztály [Agitation and Propaganda Department]
  MOL M-KS 288/32 – Külügyi Osztály [Foreign Affairs Department]
  MOL M-KS 288/36 – Tudományos, Közoktatási és Kulturális Osztály [Science, Education and Culture Department]
  MOL M-KS 288/47 – Kádár János Titkársága [János Kádár's Secretariat]

Hungarian Jewish Archives [Magyar Zsidó Múzeum és Levéltár, MILEV]
  MILEV XXXIII – Letétek [Deposits]

Historical Archives of Hungarian State Security [Állambiztonsági Szolgálatok Történeti Levéltára, ÁBTL],
  3.1.5. O-17169; vol. 0–5, Object folder: "Ellenséges tevékenységet kifejtő cionisták" [Zionists undertaking hostile activities]
  3.1.5. M-37478; vol. 1–4., Work folder: "Xavér"
  3.1.5. M-37809; vol. 1–3. Work folder: "Sárvári György"
  3.1.5. O-13558/1, Personal folder: "Milliomos" [Millionaire], Nr.: Sz–7088
  3.1.5. O-13772; vol. 1–3, Group folder: "Salom"

Stasi Records Agency [Die Behörde des Bundesbeauftragten für die Stasi-Unterlagen, BStU]
  BStU MfS XX 4 754, Jüdische Gemeinde DDR [The Jewish Community of the GDR], 1953–1968
  BStU MfS HA XX/4 235, Zusammenarbeit mit den Sicherheitsorganen der UdSSR [Co-operation with the security organs of the USSR], 1971–1972, 1974–1979
  BStU MfS HA XX /4 2158, Berichte über die Beratungen mit den Sicherheitsorganen der ČSSR [Reports on deliberations with the security organs of the ČSSR], 1977–1988
  BStU MfS HA XX/4 144, Entwurf einer Arbeitsvereinigung zwischen der V. Verwaltung der polnischen GD und der HA XX [Draft work association between the 5th administration of the Polish secret service and Main Department XX]

BStU MfS, *HA XXII, Nr. 1767,* Information der Sicherheitsdienste Ungarns über die subversive Tätigkeit der israelischen Geheimdienste und der zionistischen Organisationen [Information from the Hungarian Security Services on the subversive activities of the Israeli Secret Service and Zionist organizations]

BStU *MfS HA XX/4 2157,* Berichte über Beratungen mit den Sicherheitsorganen Ungarns in Berlin und Budapest [Reports on deliberations with the Hungarian security organs in Berlin and Budapest]

BStU *MfS HA II Nr. 24003,* Informationen über Erkenntnisse zur Arbeitsweise des israelischen Geheimdienstes gegen die UdSSR und die soz. Staatengemeinschaft [Information on the findings into Israeli Secret Services operations against the USSR and the socialist states]

National Archives of the Czech Republic

Archive of the Central Committee of the Communist Party of Czechoslovakia (Národní Archiv, Ústřední Výbor Komunistické Strany Československa)

Collection: Antonín Novotný II
Collection: Central Committee of the Communist Party, Presidium

Archival sources online

Foreign Relations of the United States, 1964–1968, Volume XVIII, Arab–Israeli Dispute, 1964–67, *Office of the Historian.* Accessed on 27 September 2016 at
https://history.state.gov/historicaldocuments/frus1964–68v18/comp1.

Lyndon Johnson Administration: State Department Documents from the 1967 War, *Jewish Virtual Library.* Accessed on 27 September 2016 at
https://www.jewishvirtuallibrary.org/jsource/US-Israel/1967war7.html.

Cold War International History Project (CWIHP)

Wilson Center Digital Archive, History and Public Policy Program.

Accessed on 28 September 2016 at http://digitalarchive.wilsoncenter.org/.

Historical Archives of Hungarian State Security [Állambiztonsági Szolgálatok Történeti Levéltára, ÁBTL]. Accessed on 6 November 2016 at
http://www.abtl.hu/iratok/segedletek/digitalizalt_forrasok.

Monographs and articles

Baev, Jordan. Eastern Europe and the Six-Day War: The Case of Bulgaria. In *The Soviet Union and the June 1967 Six-Day War,* Yaacov and Morozov (eds.), 172-196. Stanford, CA: Woodrow Wilson Center Press, Stanford University Press, 2008.

Bar-Noi, Uri. The Soviet Union and the Six-Day War: Revelations from the Polish Archives. *Cold War International History Project,* e-Dossier No. 8. Woodrow Wilson Center. Accessed on 28 September 2016 at https://www.wilsoncenter.org/publication/the-soviet-union-and-the-six-day-war-revelations-the-polish-archives

Beizer, Michael. 'I Don't Know Whom to Thank': The American Jewish Joint Distribution Committee's Secret Aid to Soviet Jewry. *Jewish Social Studies: History, Culture, Society* 15 (2009): 111–136.

— American Joint Distribution Committee. *YIVO Encyclopedia of Jews in Eastern Europe*. Accessed on 27 September 2016 at http://www.yivoencyclopedia.org/article.aspx/American_Jewish_Joint_Distribution_Committee#id0evlag

Bibó, István. Zsidókérdés Magyarországon 1944 után [The Jewish Question in Hungary after 1944]. In *Válogatott tanulmányok* [Selected Studies], István Bibó, 621–798. Budapest: Magvető, 1986.

Birn, Ruth Bettina. Fifty Years After: A Critical Look at the Eichmann Trial. *Case Western Reserve Journal of International Law*, 22 March 2011. Accessed on 10 April 2015 at http://www.thefreelibrary.com/Fifty+years+after%3a+a+critical+look+at+the+Eichmann+trial.-a0296255592

Bohus, Kata. Jews, Israelites, Zionists: The Hungarian State's Policies on Jewish Issues in a Comparative Perspective (1956–1968). PhD thesis, Central European University, 2013.

— Not a Jewish question? The Holocaust in Hungary in the Kádár regime's propaganda during Adolf Eichmann's trial. In *The Holocaust in Central and Eastern Europe: New Perspectives and Research Results*, a special issue of the *Hungarian Historical Review* 4:3 (2015): 737–772.

Bulínová, Marie (ed.). *Československo a Izrael v letech 1945–1956. Dokumenty, Ústav pro soudobé dejiny* [Czechoslovakia and Israel in the Years 1945–1956. Documents at the Institute for Contemporary History]. Prague: AV CR, 1993.

Cała, Alina. *The Image of the Jew in Polish Folk Culture*. Jerusalem: Magnes, 1995.

Cała, Alina, Helena Datner-Spiewak (eds.). *Dzieje Żydów w Polsce 1944–1968* [History of the Jews in Poland 1944–1968]. Warsaw: Teksty zdrólowe, 1997.

Cantorovich, Nati. Soviet Reactions to the Eichmann Trial: A Preliminary Investigation 1960–1965. *Yad Vashem Studies* 35:2 (2007): 103–141.

Checinski, Michael. *Poland. Communism, Nationalism, Antisemitism*. New York: Karz-Cohl, 1982.

Crhová, Marie. Jews under the Communist regime in Czechoslovakia. In *Jewish Studies at the CEU. III. Yearbook 2002–2003*, András Kovács (ed.), 290–294. Budapest: Central European University, 2004.

Darvas, József. Őszinte szót a zsidókérdésben! [An Honest Word on the Jewish Question!]. *Szabad Nép*, 25 March 1945.

Dénes, Béla. *Ávós világ Magyarországon. Egy cionista orvos emlékiratai* [The World of State Security in Hungary. Memoirs of a Zionist Doctor]. Budapest: Kossuth, 1991.

Duschinsky, Eugene, Peter Meyer, Bernard D. Weinryb, Nicolas Sylvain (eds). *The Jews in the Soviet Satellites*. Ithaca, NY: Syracuse University Press, 1953.

Engel, Pál. Úrigyerekek tévúton [Young Ladies and Gentlemen on the Wrong Path]. *Népszabadság*, 12 May 2001.

Frojimovics, Kinga. The Role of the World Jewish Congress in the Reestablishment of Jewish Communal Life in Hungary after the Holocaust (1945/1953). In *The Holocaust in Hungary. A European Perspective*, Judit Molnár (ed.), 300–315. Budapest: Balassi, 2015.

Golan, Galia. The Soviet Union and the Six-Day War in Light of Archival Materials. *Journal of Cold War Studies* 8:1 (2006): 3–19.

Green, Peter S. Czechs Seek to Indict Officials Who Assembled Lists of Jews. *International Herald Tribune*, 27 November 2003.

Gross, Jan T. *Fear. Antisemitism in Poland after Auschwitz: An Essay in Historical Interpretation*. Princeton, NJ: Princeton University Press, 2006.

Heitlinger, Alena. *In the Shadow of the Holocaust and Communism. Czech and Slovak Jews since 1945*. New Jersey and London: Transaction, 2006.

Herf, Jeffrey. East German Communists and the Jewish Question: The Case of Paul Merker. *Journal of Contemporary History* 29 (1994): 627–661.

— (ed.). *Anti-Semitism and Anti-Zionism in Historical Perspective*. New York: Routledge, 2007.

Hershberg, James G. The Soviet Bloc and the Aftermath of the 1967 War. *Cold War International History Project*, e-Dossier No. 13. Woodrow Wilson Center. Accessed on 26 September 2016 at https://www.wilsoncenter.org/publication/the-soviet-bloc-and-the-aftermath-the-june-1967-war

The Jewish Situation in Czechoslovakia after Dubcek. Background paper no. 13. London: Institute of Jewish Affairs in association with the World Jewish Congress 1969.

Karády, Viktor. Zsidóság és modenizáció a történelmi Magyarországon [Jewry and modernization in historical Hungary]. In *Zsidóság és társadalmi egyenlőtlenségek (1867–1945)* [Jewry and Social Inequalities (1867–1954)], Viktor Karády, 7–40. Budapest: Replika, 2000.

— *Túlélők és újrakezdők* [Survivors and Re-beginners]. Budapest: Múlt és Jövő, 2002.

Kovács, András. Hungarian Jewish Politics from the End of the Second World War until the Collapse of Communism. In *Jews and the State. Dangerous Alliances and the Perils of Privilege. Studies in Contemporary Jewry, XIX,* Ezra Mendelsohn (ed.), 124–156. Oxford: Oxford University Press, 2004.

— A zsidókérdés a mai magyar társadalomban [The Jewish Question in Hungarian Society Today]. In *A Másik szeme. Zsidók és antiszemiták a háború utáni Magyarországon* [The Eye of the Other. Jews and Antisemites in Post–War Hungary], András Kovács, 19–51. Budapest: Gondolat, 2008.

— *The Stranger at Hand. Antisemitic Prejudices in Post–Communist Hungary*. Leiden and Boston, MA: Brill, 2011.

— Antisemitic Elements in Communist Discourse. A Continuity Factor in Post–War Hungarian Antisemitism. In *Antisemitism in an Era of Transition. Continuities and Impact in Post–Communist Poland and Hungary*, François Guesnet, Gwen Jones (eds.), 135–147. Frankfurt am Main: Peter Lang, 2014.

Krajewski, Stanislaw. Jews, Communism, and the Jewish Communists. In *Jewish Studies at the CEU. I. Yearbook 1996–1999*, András Kovács (ed.), 115–130. Budapest: Central European University, 2000.

Labendz, Jacob Ari. Lectures, Murder, and a Phony Terrorist: Managing "Jewish Power and Danger" in 1960s Communist Czechoslovakia. *East European Jewish Affairs* 44:1 (2014): 84–108.

— Renegotiating Czechoslovakia. The State and the Jews in Communist Central Europe: The Czech Lands, 1945–1990. PhD thesis, Graduate School of Arts and Sciences of Washington University, 2014.

Lánicek, Jan. *Czechs, Slovaks and the Jews, 1938–48. Beyond Idealization and Condemnation*. New York: Palgrave Macmillan, 2013.

Losonczy Géza levele Révai Józsefnek, 1949. július 14-én [Géza Losonczy's Letter to József Révai, 14 July 1949]. *Budapesti Negyed* 8, András Kovács (ed.) (1995): 209–227. Letter published by Éva Standeisky.

Mastny, Vojtech and Malcolm Byrne (eds.). *A Cardboard Castle? An Inside History of the Warsaw Pact, 1955–1991*. Budapest: Central European University Press, 2005.

Margolius-Kovály, Heda. *Under a Cruel Star: A Life in Prague, 1941–1968*. Teaneck, NJ: Holmes and Meier, 1997.

Meining, Stefan. *Kommunistische Judenpolitik. Die DDR, die Juden und Israel*. Münster, Hamburg, London: LIT Verlag, 2002.

Mendelsohn, Ezra (ed.). *Jews and the State. Dangerous Alliances and the Perils of Privilege*. Studies in Contemporary Jewry XIX. Oxford: Oxford University Press, 2004.

Ministerstvo spravedlnosti. *Proces s vedením protistátního spikleneckého centra v čele s Rudolfem Slánským* [Ministry of Justice. The Trial against the Leadership of the Conspiratorial Center of Traitors Headed by Rudolf Slánský]. Prague: Orbis, 1953.

Molnár, Adrienne (ed.). *A „hatvanas évek" emlékezete* [The Memory of "the Sixties"]. Budapest: 1956-os Intézet, 2004.

Molnár, Erik. Zsidókérdés Magyarországon [The Jewish Question in Hungary]. *Társadalmi Szemle* 5 (1946): 326–333.

Nagy, Imre. *Snagovi jegyzetek. Gondolatok, emlékezések 1956–1957* [Snagov Notes. Thoughts and Recollections 1956–1957], István Vida (ed.). Budapest: Gondolat, 2006.

Nyílt levél a magyar társadalomhoz és a magyar zsidósághoz [An Open Letter to Hungarian Society and Hungarian Jews]. *AB Hírmondó* 6–7, May–June 1984: 23–37.

Pelle, János. *Az utolsó vérvádak* [The Last Blood Libels]. Budapest: Pelikán, 1995.

Prague Daily Warns of Mounting Anti-Semitism in Czechoslovakia, Asks Ban. *Jewish Telegraph Agency*, 10 April 1969. Accessed on 27 September 2016 at http://www.jta.org/1969/04/10/archive/prague-daily-warns-of-mounting-anti-semitism-in-czechoslovakia-asks-ban

Rácz, András. "Szóval azt mondja, aki zsidó, tartsa magát zsidónak?" Mihancsik Zsófia interjúja Rácz Andrással ["So Whoever is Jewish Should Regard Themselves as a Jew?" Zsófia Mihancsik Interviews András Rácz]. *Budapesti Negyed* 8 (1995): 227–259.

Rajk László és társai a népbíróság előtt [László Rajk and his Associates at the People's Tribunal]. Budapest: Szikra, 1949.

Ramet, Sabrina P. (ed.). *Religion and Nationalism in Soviet and East European Politics*. Durham, NC: Duke University Press, 1989.

— (ed.) *Catholicism and Politics in Communist Societies*. Durham, NC: Duke University Press, 1990.

Ro'i, Yaacov and Boris Morozov (eds.). *The Soviet Union and the June 1967 Six-Day War*. Washington, DC and Stanford, CA: Woodrow Wilson Center Press and Stanford University Press, 2008.

Rudnicki, Szyman and Marcos Silber (eds.). *Stosunki Polsko–Izraelskie (1945–1967). Wybór Dokumentów, Nczelna Dyrekcja Archiwów Panstwowych* [Polish–Israeli Relations (1945–1967). Selection of Documents, Head Office of State Archives]. Warsaw: Archiwum Panstwowe Izraela, 2009.

Schatz, Jeff. *The Generation. The Rise and Fall of the Jewish Communists of Poland*. Berkeley, CA: University of California Press, 1991.

Šmok, Martin. "Every Jew is a Zionist, and Every Zionist is a Spy!" The Story of Jewish Social Assistance Networks in Communist Czechoslovakia. *East European Jewish Affairs* 44 (2014): 70–83.

Smolar, Aleksander. Les Juifs dans la mémoire polonaise [Jews in Polish Memory]. *Esprit*, June 1987: 1–31.

Standeisky, Éva. A kommunista zsidóellenesség [Communist Antisemitism]. *Budapesti Negyed* 8 (1995): 209–227.

— *Antiszemitizmusok* [Antisemitisms]. Budapest: Argument, 2007.

Svéd, László. Dokumentumok. A magyar zsidóság és a hatalom 1945–1955 [Documents. Hungarian Jewry and the Authorities 1945–1955]. *Múltunk* 2–3 (1993): 248–298.

Szalai, Ágnes. A magyarországi kommunista diktatúra zsidóáldozatai (1949–1954) [Jewish Victims of the Communist Dictatorship in Hungary (1949–1954)]. In *Tanulmányok a holokausztról, 4. kötet* [Studies on the Holocaust, vol. 4], Randolph L. Braham (ed.), 217–268. Budapest: Presscon, 2006.

Szaynok, Bożena. *Poland–Israel 1944–1968. In the Shadow of the Past and of the Soviet Union*. Warsaw: Institute of National Remembrance, 2012.

— The Kielce Pogrom (July 4, 1946). Accessed on 27 August 2016 at http://www.jewishvirtuallibrary.org/the-kielce-pogrom

Titkos kiegyezés a padlásszobában. Interjú Görög János volt izraeli magyar nagykövettel [A Secret Compromise in the Attic Room: An Interview with János Görög, Former Hungarian Ambassador to Israel], *Hetek* 4 (2000): 2–3.

Tolts, Mark. Population and Migration. Migration since World War I. *The YIVO Encyclopedia of Jews in Eastern Europe*. Accessed on 28 September 2016 at http://www.yivoencyclopedia.org/article.aspx/Population_and_Migration/Migration_since_World_War_I#id0emxbi

Ungváry, Krisztián. *A Horthy-rendszer mérlege* [The Balance-Sheet of the Horthy Regime]. Budapest and Pécs: Jelenkor and OSZK, 2012.

Węgrzyn, Ewa. L'émigration des Juifs de Pologne en Israël dans les années 1956–1959, *Bulletin du Centre de recherche français à Jérusalem* [En ligne], 22 | 2011, mis en ligne le 25 mars 2012, accessed on 24 November 2016 at http://bcrfj.revues.org/6531

Yaacov, Ro'i and Dima P. Adamsky. Conclusion. In *The Soviet Union and the June 1967 Six-Day War*, Yaacov Ro'i and Boris Morozov (eds.), 268–280. Washington, DC and Stanford, CA: Woodrow Wilson Center Press and Stanford University Press, 2008.

Index of Persons

Aczél, György 255, 354
Adamovicz, Magda 18
Adenauer, Konrad 78, 113, 118, 121–2, 126, 304
Ajtai, Miklós 225
Alexandrov, Andrei 145
Ambrus, Sándor 324, 326
Amer, Abdel Hakim 141, 146, 150, 160, 166
Amir, Rehavam 77
Andrzejewski, Piotr 18
Antos, István 44, 354
Arafat, Yasser 212
Arif, Abdul Rahman (in the text: Aref) 180, 354
Aubert, Pierre 199
Baczoni, Jenő 22, 26, 39, 354
Balló, István 223
Barity, Miklós 198
Bar-Noi, Uri 129
Barta Mrs [?] 180
Bebők, Gábor 53, 55
Becher, Kurt 81, 110, 354
Beck, István 55, 62, 354
Beck, Tamás 213, 354
Beizer, Michael 225
Ben-Gurion, David 49, 78, 85, 110, 112–3, 115, 119, 121
Benoschofsky, Imre (also as Beneschofszky, Benesovszky, Benoschofszky) 191, 231, 244, 321, 354
Bibó, István 3–4
Bényi, József 198
Berecz, János 55, 62, 261, 354
Bergmann, Werner 18
Birn, Ruth Bettina 78
Biszku, Béla 170, 354
Bohus, Kata 18, 82
Bojti, János 62
Bormann, Martin 116
Borsa, Mihály 226–7, 279–80, 283, 289, 296, 300, 320, 354
Boumediène, Houari (also as Bumedian) 133, 136, 157, 180, 183, 188, 354
Boutaieb, Mustapha 264
Brand, Joel 108, 354
Brandt, Willy 341, 342
Brauch, Julia 18

Brezhnev, Leonid Ilyich 130–4, 136–7, 140, 142–3, 145, 148, 149, 156, 157, 163–4, 178, 179, 180, 341, 359
Bronfman, Edgar 223–4, 259, 261, 263, 354
Bulínová, Marie 16
Byrne, Malcolm 129
Cała, Alina 2, 16
Cantorovich, Nati 77, 81
Ceaușescu, Nicolae (also as Ceausescu) 132, 142–3, 148, 153–4, 163, 168
Checinski, Michael 270–1
Crhová, Marie 18, 350
Csécsei, Kálmán 55–6, 61, 354
Csehák, Judit 261
Dan, Joshua 44–9, 52
Darvas, József 7
Darvasi, István 252, 354
Datner-Spiewak, Helena 16
David, Václav 171
Davidovics, László 315
De Gaulle, Charles 130, 141, 144, 145, 146–7
Dékány, István 311
DellaPergola, Sergio 18
Demus, László 198
Dénes, Béla 7
Dér, István 309
Domán, Ernő 354
Dulles, Allen 120
Duschinsky, Eugene 4, 6
Egri, György 324–5, 354
Eichmann, Adolf 11, 14, 15, 17, 77–82, 84–6, 87–8, 89–91, 92–4, 95–6, 97–101, 102–5, 106, 108, 110–1, 112–26, 294, 354, 356, 360
Elek, Pál 325
Engel, Pál 3
Erdélyi, Károly 55, 62, 149, 354
Erhard, Ludwig 303
Ernest [?] 23, 28, 44–6, 48–9
Ertsams, [?] 126
Eshel, Arieh 37
Eshkol, Levi 150, 354
Esztergályos, Ferenc 106
Farkas, Mihály 225
Fedorenko, Nikolai Trofimovich 150, 355
Fekete, János 27–8, 31, 44, 74, 355
Fell, Carl 303–4

Fisch, Henrik 309, 355
Fishman, Jakov 342, 355
Fleischmann, László 286
Fock, Jenő 136, 183–4, 355
Foertsch, Friedrich Albert 114–5, 355
Fóti, Tamás 18
Frojimovics, Kinga 219
Fuad, Ahmed 174
Fuchs, Frantisek 355
Fülöp, József 337, 349
Gandhi, Indira 59
Gane, Andrew 18
Garai, Róbert 33, 230, 355
Geiger, László 325
Geréb Sándor 237, 355
Gerstenmaier, Eugen (also as Gerstenmöyer, Gertonmöyer, Gertenmayer) 250–1, 355
Geyer, Artur 309
Globke, Hans 114–19, 121–23, 126, 355
Golan, Galia 129
Goldman, Ralph I. 228, 355
Goldmann, Nahum (also as Nachum Goldmann, Goldman) 221–2, 230–2, 235–7, 239, 242–5, 251, 252–4, 256, 260, 303–4, 330, 338–42, 344, 355
Goldstücker, Eduard 272, 355
Gomułka, Władysław (also as Gomulka) 11, 131, 154, 157, 166, 355
Gorbachev, Mikhail 137, 263
Görög, János 138–9, 355
Grechko, Andrei 151, 355
Green, Peter S. 272
Gross, Jan T. 4, 6
Grünwald, Malchiel 108
Grünzweig, Miklós 329
Grygar, Antonín 101
Guesnet, François 2
Guevara, Ernesto 133
Győri, Imre 255
Györke, József 202, 211
Haasz, Károly 188
Halevy, Benjamin (in the text: Hahlevi) 108
Hartmann, János 309
Hayman, Erwin (in the text: Haymann) 226, 355
Hazai, Jenő 41, 355
Házi, Vencel 30, 74, 355
Héber, Imre 255, 340, 355
Heine, Heinrich 253
Heitlinger, Alena 10, 12, 271–2, 274–5, 283

Heller, Bohumil 259, 356
Helli, Imre 66
Herf, Jeffrey 7, 269
Hershberg, James G. 129, 136,
Herzl, Theodor (in the text: Herzel) 303
Heves, Lajos 285–6, 292, 356
Himmler, Heinrich 113
Hirsch, Pál 188
Hitler, Adolf 112–3, 117–8, 122, 187–8
Hochberger, László 191
Hoettl, Georg Wilhelm 120, 356
Hollai, Imre 85, 356
Horn, Gyula 198
Horowitz, Louis D. (in the text: Luis Horovitz) 227, 356
Horváth, Imre 34, 37, 356
Horváth, István 261, 356
Horváth, János 219, 225, 356
Höss, Rudolf Franz Ferdinand 90
Ilan, David 313
Ilku, Pál 190, 242, 252, 356
Illyés, Gyula 170, 356
Ilyés, András 55
Jones, Gwen 2, 18
Johnson, Lyndon B. 140, 141, 142, 144, 145, 146–7
Juhár, Zoltán 212, 356
Kádár, János 10, 79, 82, 85, 130, 132, 134–6, 140, 141, 142, 145, 146, 148, 149, 155, 157, 158, 178, 179, 180, 181, 184, 199, 202, 224, 263, 354, 356
Kadelburg, Lavoslav 251, 356
Kaiser, Philip Mayer 255, 344, 356
Kállai, Gyula 57, 356
Klló, Iván 24–5, 36, 38, 356
Kaltenbrunner, Ernst 113, 356
Kaplan, Armand 222, 239, 244, 247, 252, 255, 338–9, 342, 356
Karádi, Gyula 43, 356
Karády, Viktor 2, 4, 21
Karasz, Lajos 255, 324, 326, 356
Kardos, Géza 44, 356
Kasztner, Rudolf (also as Kastner) 80–1, 106, 108–9, 110, 354, 356
Katona, László 106, 311
Kauders, Ben-Zion (in the text: Ben Cion Kauders) 324, 357
Kaul, Friedrich 119
Kecskeméti, György 310

Keller, László 328, 338, 357
Khrushchev, Nikita 169
Kishon, Ephraim (in the text: Kishont) 201
Klacsmann, Borbála 18
Klein, Theo 258–9, 260–1, 357
Klutznick, Philip (also as Klutznyck, Klutznik, Klutznyk) 227–8, 255, 330, 340, 357
Kohl, Helmut 341
Komócsin, Zoltán 144, 158–9, 187, 189, 357
Kopányi, Vilmos 264
Korem, [?] 34–6, 37
Kós, Péter 24–5, 219, 357
Kosygin, Alexei Nikolayevich 140, 147, 157, 178
Koucký, Vladimír 101, 357
Kovács, András 1–4, 7, 12, 14, 270, 273, 283, 350
Kovács, László 198
Kővári, Péter 198
Krajewski, Stanislaw 4
Kriegel, Frantisek 272, 357
Krzyzanowska, Zofia 117
Kubica, Alexandra 18
Kubowitzki, Leon 357
Kudryashov, [?] 179
Labendz, Jacob Ari 7–8, 10, 13–6, 21, 135, 221–3, 225, 269–72, 274–5
Lahav, Yehuda 202, 357
Lakatos, Ernő 261, 262, 357
Lánicek, Jan 3–4, 6
Lévai, Jenő 81, 106, 357
Lőrincz, N. János 55
Losonci, András 260, 357
Losonczi, Pál 199, 203, 357
Losonczy, Géza 8
Lovász, Ferenc 335
Lukács, István 311
Malik, Yakov Alexandrovich 183
Margolius-Kovály, Heda 3
Mastny, Vojtech 129, 134
Máté, Miklós 309, 357
Meining, Stefan 8, 11, 78
Meir, Golda 25, 28, 34–6, 37, 52, 113,
Mélykuti, Ferenc 307, 311, 313, 320, 323, 357
Mendelsohn, Ezra 4
Mengele, Joseph 116
Mere, Ain-Ervin 126, 357
Merker, Paul 7
Meyer, Peter 4
Mickenberg, Jakov 342

Miklós, Imre 223, 226–8, 232, 257, 259, 261, 262–3, 319–20, 357
Mikunis, Shmuel 80, 110–1, 357
Miller, Michael L. 18
Mód, Péter 55, 62, 357
Molnár, Adrienne 83
Molnár, Erik 7
Mona, Gyula (in the text: Móna) 255
Morozov, Boris 129–31, 33–4
Mowshovitz, Israel 328, 357
Nagy, Imre 9
Nagy, János 198, 358
Nánási, Miklós 338
Nasser, Gamal Abdel (also as Nasir) 59, 130–2, 140, 141, 142, 145, 149–56, 161, 166–7, 174, 178, 179, 182, 187–9
Nemes, János 188
Németh, Miklós 228, 358
Norden, Albert 78, 358
Novotný, Antonín Josef (also as Novotny) 97–8, 131, 152, 161, 171, 358
Nyerki, Gyula 108, 358
Oberländer, Theodor (also as Oberlaender) 93, 115, 121, 358
Ofry, Dan 331
Oistrakh, David 60
Olt, Károly 234, 358
Orbán, László 242, 358
Pachta, [?] 23, 27, 45
Palos, Krzysztof 18
Pashkavichius [?] 126
Pécsi, Vera 18
Pekárková, Eliška 18
Pelle, János 6
Peres, Shimon 138, 199, 204, 213, 263
Pereszlényi, Zoltán 264–5, 358
Péter, János 55, 62, 86, 89,106, 190, 234, 252, 289 358
Podgorny, Nikolai Viktorovich 131, 178, 179, 358
Prantner, József 221, 245, 254, 319, 358
Pudlák, Jan 171, 358
Puja, Frigyes 358
Pullai, Árpád (also as Pulai) 170, 190, 252, 358
Rácz, András 284
Rácz, Pál 326
Rajk, László 7
Ramet, Sabrina P. 5
Rákosi, Mátyás 8–9

Ran, Nachmann 313
Ránki, György (in the text: George Ranski) 120, 358
Rapai, Gyula 234, 358
Rappaport, Ottó 202
Révai, József 8
Riegner, Gerhart Moritz (also as Gergart, Rieger, Rigner) 243, 250–1, 252, 338–9, 358
Robinson, Donald M. 228, 358
Rónai, András 202
Rosen, Moses (in the text: Mózes Rósen, Rózen) 251, 358
Roth, Siegfried (also as Sigrid Róth, Sigfrid Róth, Stephen Róth) 220, 235–6, 252, 338–40, 342 359
Ro'i, Yaakov 129–31, 33–4
Rudnicki, Szyman 16, 77–8, 81
Rusakov, Konstantin Viktorovich 148, 178, 359
Ruzsa, Ágnes 18
Sadat, Anwar 212
Salgó, László 299
Sanbar, Moshe 202
Sattath, Dow 36
Sauckel, Fritz 115, 359
Schatz, Jeff 4, 9, 269
Scheiber, Sándor 191–2, 227, 279–83, 288–9, 295–6, 299–300, 313, 315–7, 322, 332, 335, 339–40, 359
Schmidt, Helmut 341
Schneier, Arthur 338, 359
Schoeps, Julius H. 18
Schön, Dezső (in the text: Schőn) 57, 359
Schroeder, Gerhard 115
Schüler-Springorum, Stephanie 18
Sebes, István 40, 359
Seifert, Géza 191–2, 223, 227, 244, 250–1, 254, 255, 287, 319, 359
Servatius, Robert 110, 115, 119, 122–3
Shamir, Yitzhak 199
Sík, Endre 27, 51–2, 89
Šik, Ota 272, 359
Sikachev, Nikolai 179
Silber, Marcos 16, 77–8, 81
Simonov, Konstantin 60
Singer, Israel 259, 260–1, 262–3, 359
Slánský, Rudolf 7, 272, 359
Slowikowski, Jan (in the text: Slovikovski) 32, 359
Šmok, Martin 225

Smolar, Aleksander 3–4
Sobolev, Arkady 86, 359
Solzhenitsyn, Aleksandr 345
Sós, Endre 231, 315, 319, 359
Speidel, Hans 115
Stalin, Joseph 9
Standeisky, Éva 2–3, 6, 8
Steinberg, Elan (in the text: Elen Steinberg) 272, 359
Steiner, Marcell 313
Strauss, Franz Joseph 115, 341
Studený, Luboš 18
Svéd, László 225
Sylvain, Nicolas 4
Szalai, Ágnes 7, 18
Szanka, Tibor Mrs. 329
Szántó, Dénes 45, 359
Száraz, György 340, 359
Szarka, Károly 22, 42, 44, 51–2, 55, 62, 89, 289, 359
Szatmári, István 258
Szaynok, Bożena 2, 6–7, 10–1, 13–4, 16, 21, 81–2, 134–5, 269–71, 275
Szendrő, [?] 42, 44–5, 49
Széphelyi, Zoltán 89
Szilágyi, Béla 39, 55–6, 62, 69, 221, 360
Szirmai, István 80, 83, 84, 169, 360
Szűrös, Mátyás 202, 360
Tauber, László 325, 360
Telepó, Sándor 317, 360
Tischler, János 18
Tito, Josip Broz 59, 132–4, 136, 148, 152–4, 159, 162, 164, 166, 178, 222
Titov, Fyodor Yegorovich 130, 141, 144, 146, 180
Tolts, Mark 23
Tömpe, István Mrs. 62
Topolevsky, Gregorio 116
Tóth, Elek 55, 62
Tóth, Lajos 308
Treß, Werner 18
Tuval, Meir 25, 34, 36, 37–8, 45, 360
Ungváry, Krisztián 2, 18
U Thant 188
Ulbricht, Walter 78, 131–2, 155, 360
Varga, István 89, 198
Várkonyi, Péter 106, 198–9, 360
Veress, Péter (also as Veres) 26, 31, 74
Vilner, Meir 171, 202, 220, 229, 360
Waldheim, Kurt 263

Waldman, Tibor J. 324
Weiler, Jack 250, 360
Weinryb, Bernard D. 4
Wiesel, Elie 262
Wilson, Harold 144, 145, 146–7
Winkelmann, Otto 120, 360
Wisliceny, Dieter (in the text: Wisliczeny) 89, 360

Wolniak, Zygfryd 77
Yahil, Meir 82, 360
Yaron, Yerahmiel Ram 52, 360
Zádor, Tibor 55
Zagyi, János 69
Zhivkov, Todor 131, 133, 153, 360
Zsoldos, Jenő 299, 315

www.ingramcontent.com/pod-product-compliance
Lightning Source LLC
Chambersburg PA
CBHW080117020526
44112CB00037B/2765